The Age of Spectacle

Tom Dyckhoff is one of Britain's best-known commentators on architecture and urbanism. He is the presenter of *The Great Interior Design Challenge* and the Radio 4 series *The Design Dimension*. He was previously architecture and design critic for BBC2's flagship arts programme *The Culture Show* and architecture critic for *The Times*. He presented *The Secret Life of Buildings* for Channel 4, and his seven-part BBC2 series, *Saving Britain's Past*, examined Britain's obsession with heritage. An Honorary Fellow of the Royal Institute of British Architects, Dyckhoff has written widely for publications including the *Guardian*, *GQ*, *Wallpaper*, and the *New Statesman*. He lives in London.

The Age of Spectacle

The Rise and Fall of Iconic Architecture

TOM DYCKHOFF

To my wife and children. This is what I've been doing in the study with the door shut. Well, this and checking Twitter.

1 3 5 7 9 10 8 6 4 2

Windmill Books
20 Vauxhall Bridge Road
London SW1V 2SA

Windmill Books is part of the Penguin Random House group of companies
whose addresses can be found at global.penguinrandomhouse.com.

Penguin
Random House
UK

First published by Random House Books in 2017
First published in paperback by Windmill Books in 2018

www.penguin.co.uk

A CIP catalogue record for this book is available from the British Library.

ISBN 9780099538233

Typeset in 10.12/13.65 pt Bembo by Jouve (UK), Milton Keynes
Printed and bound in Great Britain by Clays Ltd, St Ives Plc

CONTENTS

'Spaces sometimes lie.'

Henri Lefebvre[1]

'It is only shallow people who do not judge by appearances. The true mystery of the world is the visible, not the invisible.'

Oscar Wilde[2]

PROLOGUE

THE BUILDING THAT LOOKS LIKE
A PAIR OF UNDERPANTS

What did it? What was it that tipped me over the edge? It was 4 September 2012, and a headline popped into my Twitter feed. 'British-Designed Skyscraper Resembles Big Pants, Say Angry Chinese.'[1] That's right – pants. Big pants. I clicked on the headline, and there it was on the screen in front of me: a building that looked like a pair of underpants. A 74-storey pair of underpants, to be precise. More long johns, I'd say, than Y-fronts or boxer shorts, but pants nonetheless.

In my time, I'd seen buildings that looked like all sorts of things. A gigantic pineapple? The 'Dunmore Pineapple' in Scotland was crafted out of stone in the eighteenth century for a greenhouse growing – what else? – pineapples. A pair of binoculars? Claes Oldenburg, Coosje van Bruggen and Frank Gehry's Binoculars Building in Venice Beach, Los Angeles, is a little unconventional, I'll grant you, even for a city built around ego and showbiz. But as an office for a firm in advertising, an industry in the business of attention-seeking, a pair of gigantic binoculars seemed almost appropriate. Underpants, though. This was something else.

The Gate to the East, as the giant pants are more formally known, had been built in Suzhou, one of those ever-proliferating Chinese megacities. Given its name, the building's design was presumably intended to resemble a gateway or triumphal arch. Indeed, Chinese journalists initially welcomed the building warmly, dubbing it the 'Arc de Triomphe of the East', as if obediently reciting the phrase from its accompanying press release. Soon after, though, opinions cooled. 'Is it an arch or just plain pants?' asked *Shanghai Daily.* Pants, appeared to be the consensus of China's blogging community. 'Some were more risqué with their critiques,' reported the *Daily Telegraph*, 'pointing out that London's phallic "Little Cucumber" – Norman Foster's 30 St Mary Axe or Gherkin project – would fit snuggly inside Suzhou's Gate to the East. "Together, together!" cooed one of the raunchier posts.'

The building's architects were the British firm, RMJM, founded in the 1950s, and, back then, the epitome of serious, even dour, modernism, the kind of architects whose bread and butter was designing the schools, universities and hospitals that underpinned Britain's postwar welfare state.

Sixty years later, though, RMJM appeared to have had a change of direction. It was designing serious, dour modernism no more. It was designing clickbait. The Age of Spectacle had definitely arrived.

INTRODUCTION

'The (hi)stories we tell of cities are also (hi)stories of ourselves.'

Jane Rendell[1]

'The progressive Westerner is determined always to better his lot. From candle to oil lamp, oil lamp to gaslight, gaslight to electric light – his quest for a brighter light never ceases, he spares no pains to eradicate even the minutest shadow.'

Junichiro Tanazaki[2]

The folly of youth

For my eighteenth birthday, my godfather took me to the Lloyd's Building in London. Not just *to* the Lloyd's Building, but *inside* it. Inside it! Being without my parents in London was excitement enough for a teenager from a small, provincial city in the Midlands. But to actually get past the commissionaires in their uniforms, *into* the building! I was, I realise with hindsight, a slightly odd teenager. Definitely a geek, but an odd geek at that. Geeks are at least meant to obsess, collectively, over computers or comic books, but, alone among my friends, I obsessed over buildings, bollards and town planning. And while eighteen-year-olds in more fashionable parts were discovering MDMA and acid house, I was high on Zaha Hadid. I got my thrills from the *Architectural Review*. I was the only teenage architecture geek in Worcester.

And I was born at the right time. Because architecture was about to take a turn for the spectacular. My pin-ups were Daniel Libeskind and

Frank Gehry, not superheroes or pop stars, and to eighteen-year-old me, the Lloyd's Building was the Spider-Man, the Stone Roses, the Jesus and Mary Chain of buildings, all rolled into one. And here I was, inside it.

In 1989, three years after it opened, Lloyd's was still the most famous building in Britain. I'd only ever seen it in photographs, in the newspapers whose architecture pages I cut out each week and filed neatly away, and in the architectural magazines I stuffed under my bed to read at night. Its curled spirals of shining metal seemed so perfect in photographs, so alluring on magazine covers, so odd. At the time, its only rival for fame was Stuttgart's Neue Staatsgalerie, star of a popular 1980s British television advert for Rover, in which a car's German occupants, after driving slinkily along its slopes, are shocked by the revelation at the end that this elegant building was designed by a 'Britisch Architekt', James Stirling. The shock being, presumably, that after the savage deindustrialisation of the 1970s and 1980s, Britain was still actually capable of crafting, engineering and making something sizeable, stylish and modern without going on strike.

Lloyd's, though, was more than a star; it was a symbol. In the architectural magazines I so loved, it represented the final, belated triumph of modernism. British architecture in the 1980s was entirely dominated by tit-for-tat 'style wars' between Prince Charles and the modernists. There was no middle ground. It was trench warfare. You were either with us, or against us. For most of the decade, the traditionalists had gained ground. So powerful was the influence of Prince Charles in the planning committees of Little Britain, scant significant contemporary architecture had been built for years. I grew up during a nadir in British architecture.

Until Lloyd's. All around it were the sites of battles lost by the modernists – Paternoster Square to the west, further east the Lord Mayor of London's Mansion House, where the prince had delivered a famous speech; and across the street the site where property magnate Peter Palumbo had hoped to resurrect a long-dead design by arch-modernist Mies van der Rohe opposite the Bank of England, until

Charles had his way. I was a modernist. Of course I was. I was a teenager. It was my own, geeky version of teenage rebellion. And, best of
all, Lloyd's was designed by my leader, King of the Modernists, Richard Rogers, Prince Charles's nemesis to this day.

For some, though, like my sixty-something godfather, Lloyd's was a
symbol of unwelcome change. Vic had been an insurance underwriter in
the City, London's financial district, since the days of bowler hats, black
brollies and a *Financial Times* under the arm. There were thousands more
like him. However, since the Big Bang in 1986 had deregulated how the
City made its money and opened it up to powerful, lightning-quick
international flows of capital, a new, more aggressive, more showy
breed had arrived in his patch. These were the twin bogeymen of British
1980s popular culture: red-braces-wearing, slick-haired 'yuppies' and
working-class, Essex Boy 'Loadsamoneys' hollering on mobile phones
across new, computerised trading floors. Vic's new boss was a yuppy, and
they had a very strained relationship.

For my godfather, the Lloyd's Building represented this sudden
transformation of his life, manifest in the once-sedate and really rather
pleasant place in which he'd spent his entire life slowly but surely
working his way up. As Vic showed me around inside I got the impression that, three years on, he wasn't overly impressed by his cavernous
new workplace. 'I always get lost finding the toilets,' he confessed,
rather mournfully. He didn't even like the killer stack of see-through
escalators rising through that new-fangled thing, an atrium, their
inner workings on display for all to see. How cool was that?

I couldn't get enough of the place. It was brash, it was sleek, it was
romantic. It didn't fit in, no matter how hard Richard Rogers claimed
it respected the City's medieval streetscape, or how creatively critics
suggested it was a modern interpretation of pinnacled gothic architecture. The broadsheets called it 'the espresso machine'. I had no idea
what espresso was. We didn't have it in Worcester. Who cared? Lloyd's
felt like nothing I'd ever experienced before. A castle of steel. A cathedral of glass. Just the sight of the outside was thrilling enough, the
dizzying spirals of its staircase towers delivering a rush to the head,

whirling to the skies up from the sensible streets of the City, its turrets
ripping past church steeples.

What its critics hated – its novelty, its strange shape, its difference –
I loved. I liked the fact that it *didn't* fit in. To me it was science fiction.
It was *Metropolis*. It was the spaceship in *Alien*. It was Los Angeles in
Blade Runner. Its great glass elevators were pure Roald Dahl. Vic,
meanwhile, was trying to tell me about his job. But it's hard to get a
teenager, even a geeky one, interested in insurance underwriting. Not
when they're in a spaceship.

A few months later, I took a girlfriend to gaze at it on a date one
night, lit up romantically (or so I thought) in blue. It looked more like
a spaceship than ever. 'Isn't that the most amazing thing you've ever
seen?' It wasn't. A few days later she dumped me. Can you blame her?

But I didn't care. *This* was the future.

The Wowhaus

Fifteen years later, as architecture critic for *The Times*, I am in The
Admiralty, a government ministry on Whitehall, London, sitting
opposite John Prescott, then British deputy prime minister under
Tony Blair, and – as the politician responsible for urban planning – the
most influential man in British architecture. 'People ask me, "What is
wow?"' he says, staring intently into my eyes, while shaking a dossier
above his head. 'Look. There. We've defined it. "By getting architects,
town planners and developers to work *together*,"' he reads, emphatic-
ally, '"we have created *a new 'wow' factor*."' He pauses to deliver his
finale: 'That's WHAT IT IS! It's buildings that strike you and you say,
"*Bloody 'ell*."' It seemed I wasn't the only one who loved the sugar rush
of modern architecture. This geek had found a soulmate.

'The DPM's thoughts right now are very much with the vernacular,' explains the press officer, as if reading his great leader's mind.
With the fresh-faced enthusiasm of one new to the subject, Prescott
tells me about his favourite architects, whom, he hopes, he will attract

to daub the then economically vibrant UK in what he calls the 'wow factor'. True to his reputation for spoonerisms, he has a tendency to get the odd name wrong. 'Whatsisname? Calvatrari,' he says. '[Santiago] Calatrava?' suggests his adviser. Prescott – not, generally, a smiler – chucks him a scowl.

He reels off a list of his 'wow' buildings: Herzog & de Meuron's Laban Centre in south-east London ('Hell, that's an experience . . .'); Terry Farrell's The Deep in Hull; Norman Foster's Sage Music Centre, Gateshead; Future Systems' Selfridges, Birmingham. ('It's got the bulge factor . . . It's biowhatdyoucallit? Biosomething.' 'Biomorphic,' suggests noises off.) 'These were cities with no bloody heart whatsoever,' he thunders, red-faced and getting into his stride. 'Now they've got a heart!' Indeed, my childhood hero, Richard Rogers, had become Prescott's advisor, nudging the government through his Urban Task Force to instigate a cities-first policy, putting the brakes on building in the suburbs in favour of focusing construction in the centre of towns and cities. 'We've stopped all them malls now outside towns. This is the first year we've done more building inside towns than outside. Even though I get a lot of pressure about it, I think it's right. We want people back into our cities.' Prescott is quite the evangelist. One wag wondered if he was about to found a Wowhaus.

Now this is unexpected. John Prescott is not a man generally remembered for aesthetic theorising. And yet here he is giving me a lecture John Ruskin would be proud of. Just a few minutes earlier he was leading me through his newly decorated and extended ministry like a TV makeover host, rhapsodising about colour tones and the pros and cons of carpet or wood floors. 'Look at that! Eh? Isn't that . . .' A staircase renders him momentarily speechless. 'Christ, that's something, isn't it?' Then the *pièce de resistance*: a glass-and-metal atrium linking two old buildings. 'The way they've married it together. And the press just say, "How much did that cost?" Such space and light. Spectacular, eh?'

John Prescott knew which way the wind was blowing all right. The wow factor. The bulge factor. Buildings that strike you and you say, "Bloody 'ell." What I experienced at the Lloyd's Building – the thrill of the odd, the pulse-racing peculiarity of dazzling new architecture – had, fifteen years later, not only become commonplace; it had become government policy.

In the past two decades something very unusual has happened to our towns and cities, and the buildings inside them. It's crept up on us, but in recent years it has become ubiquitous. Buildings that are strange, flamboyant and spectacular-looking are now the norm, rather than the exception. The kind of architecture I fell in love with as a kid is now all around us. Lloyd's was an omen, a herald of what was to come: the age of the superstar building, the age of 'iconic' architecture, designed to thrill – the age of the Wowhaus, perhaps.

When I was a child in the 1970s, modern architecture was rarely flashy. The kind I grew up with housed libraries, schools, town halls, hospital wards and, occasionally, offices. It was built to fulfill sober and serious needs such as welfare, housing people or treating the sick, by sober and serious architects. It had a clear moral purpose, which it wore earnestly on its sleeve not in gold lamé or glitzy shapes but in grey straight lines and chiselled concrete – well-meaning, but a little dour, like my 1950s primary school. At its most functional, indeed, modernist architecture was, in theory at least, not meant to symbolise or be decorative; 'the architect,' wrote historian Nikolaus Pevsner in the 1930s, 'to represent this century of ours, must be . . . cold'.[3] You might or might not have liked its appearance, but at least you knew it served its purpose.

Forty years on, though, a new architectural age has dawned – one whose buildings look radically different from what has gone before. This is architecture specifically designed to dazzle us, to impress us – just like gothic cathedrals and Renaissance palaces before them.

There are the famous so-called 'iconic' buildings of course, the ones that appear on the adverts and travel posters, the ones everybody knows – Frank Gehry's Bilbao Guggenheim, Norman Foster's Gherkin, Daniel Libeskind's Berlin Jewish Museum. But what is astonishing about the spread of this new attitude in architecture is its reach and ubiquity. In London, self-styled world city, buildings routinely rise designed to resemble helter-skelters, mobile phones, shards of glass, quills, cucumbers, cheesegraters. But you find similarly iconic, more bargain-basement architecture far outside London's centre, too, on average high streets where, these days, it is unremarkable for an ordinary block of apartments to be shaped as two interlocking giant spheres, like beer bellies, or, in my part of town, for a new sports centre to be wrapped in a patchwork facade of harlequin primary colours, that, at night, backlit, flashes in sparkling twinkles.

Wowhaus architecture has spread far, far beyond the capital, too. You'll find it on average streets in ordinary towns. Few places have escaped a proliferation of strange shapes, shards, wedges and bulges in recent years. Buildings have been designed in Britain that resemble a giant harp, a deodorant bottle, a crumpled packet of cigarettes, or, as one proposal by architect Frank Gehry was described, 'four transvestites caught in a gale'. In Edinburgh a building has been designed that spirals up like a golden meringue. In 2002, Sky Vault – a vast structure of illuminated netting shaped like a lobster pot – was proposed to cloak a stretch of the M1, Britain's busiest motorway, as a 'gateway' to draw attention to the East Midlands, a region that required a little more profile on the world stage. The net of lights was meant to symbolise not, through its lobster pot-ness, the sea (the East Midlands is as far from the coast as it is possible to be on this island), but 'the diverse parts of the East Midlands'. 'It will be like having our own little Eiffel Tower' said Martin Freeman, chair of the Great East Midlands Campaign.[4] Mercifully, perhaps, it came to nothing.

Yet lobster-pot structures outside Northampton are but small fry compared to what spectacles are being built in richer parts of the planet. I have a recent copy of *Mark* magazine. At £14, it is the nearest architectural magazines get to pornography, its expensive pages slick with this new breed of cavorting, shapely buildings in every corner of the world. Whatever your architectural fantasy, it's within these pages: in Istanbul a disaster-prevention centre shaped like angular rolling hills; in Wujiang, China, an impossibly shiny, shrink-wrapped sky-scraper tower like a giant electric razor stabbed into the earth; in Hong Kong, a 'car park tower' like a series of stacked, teetering plates poised to collapse. Anything goes.

Indeed, buildings today can be any shape or colour you want them to be. They don't necessarily have to have dependable rectilinear walls and ceilings and roofs like they used to. The tyranny of the right angle has long been vanquished. The freedom afforded to architects by their magical new tool, the computer, has transformed what they are able to design. A building of luxury apartments was proposed for Dubai, for instance, in the shape of an iPod. You'd expect that in Dubai, land of consumer excess, where such architectural spectacle is now ubiquitous, and its aesthetics are limitless. *Mark* magazine once featured a particularly remarkable skyscraper design: twin towers, linked, two-thirds up, by two explosive bulges. No form of expression seems to be out of bounds, these days, even a homage to 9/11.

Not everyone, of course, appreciates this new fashion. Architects of a less flamboyant hue decry the culture of the 'icon'. Even the president of China, Xi Jinping, is not a fan. In 2016, in a bout of aesthetic protectionism, the Chinese State Council issued a directive banning 'bizarre', 'oversized, xenocentric, weird' architecture, the kind that had been increasingly built since economic liberalisation began in the country in the 1990s – like those giant underpants, perhaps, or the Guangzhou Circle, at 138 metres high the world's tallest circle-shaped building. Such architecture is now thought to clash with Chinese traditions. New architecture, the Council's decree stated, must be 'suitable, economic, green and pleasing to the eye', though whose eye and what kind of pleasure was not firmly defined.

We have built spectacular buildings throughout our history, of course, just never in such numbers. For as long as humans have had egos and money they have employed architects to impress and celebrate themselves or their gods with wild, often strange-shaped monuments. What are the pyramids, the Palace of Versailles or St Peter's in Rome if not iconic? What is baroque or Victorian neo-gothic architecture if not flamboyant? Even in the decades of cool, sober, supposedly 'style-less' international-style, the 1950s and 1960s, there was visual extravagance – Frank Lloyd Wright's Guggenheim Museum in New York, say, or Eero Saarinen's TWA Terminal at John F. Kennedy Airport. And even LeCorbusier – capable of continual reinvention – shocked the ascetic modernist establishment with his 1955 chapel at Ronchamp, eastern France. Its bulging, blowsy sides featured on French stamps and tourist advertisements and became, among architects at least, the most famous building of the 1950s.

However, while such flamboyance was once the exception, not the rule, and reserved for special buildings, today the exceptional has become the norm. These days such buildings are called 'icons', spectacular structures that we visit in droves, expecting to be transformed by the experience, to leave us seeing the world a little differently. They are designed not just to house us, or school us, or heal us, but to impress us. Form does not ever follow function any more. Form *is* the function.

Chinese whispers

Architecture is just another method humans use to communicate with one another, like writing or painting a picture. In fact, it's one of the oldest forms of communication. It predates writing, though not quite painting. The oldest surviving structures in the world – the tombs, tumuli and temples constructed in those regions first settled after the last ice age – are less than 10,000–12,000 years old, while the proliferation of figurative cave paintings dates from 30,000 to 40,000 years ago. At some point, though, after the thawing of the ice, tribes in the fertile crescent of Mesopotamia and Anatolia gave up being nomadic hunter gatherers. They stopped using caves – nature's ready-made architecture, with their cathedral halls and stalactite columns – as special places for ritual, celebration and expression, and created their own structures. In doing so, architecture was invented.

Admittedly, as a form of communication, architecture is a little less immediate than writing or painting. Heaving massive stones across the landscape or digging foundations is not as easy as wielding a stick. Architecture requires collective organisation and project management. It requires a massive investment of time and effort. It is generally done, therefore, by organised societies when there is a desire to create something more important, more meaningful than mere shelter. There is no architecture without organised society, and vice versa. Stone-age architecture, from the mysterious carved pillars of Göbekli Tepe in Turkey to the astonishing neolithic monuments of Ireland, Britain and France, was an attempt to express some kind of meaning about the society that created it, its belief system, its hierarchies, its experiences, its view of the cosmos – though what that meaning is, a few thousand years on and without any written records, is today devilishly hard to fathom.

For, compared with writing or painting, architecture is a far more imprecise form of expression. It doesn't have at its disposal hundreds of thousands of complex words or nimble grammatical constructs. The bond between an architectural shape and the meaning connected to it is far vaguer than that between a word and *its* meaning. Classical architecture, for instance, can, with similar columns and pediments, represent ancient Greek democracy, Renaissance harmony or Stalinist totalitarianism, depending upon where you are in history and geography. This is what Roland Barthes called 'the terror of uncertain signs',[5] whose fluid meanings keep slipping and sliding – the more so in our age of dizzying global communications – despite our vain efforts to fix them.

The enormous collective effort required to build architecture also hinders its ability to communicate clearly, compared with writing, music or painting. It is harder for a vast group to speak as one than for an individual to do the same. Buildings are created by committee. The way in which we build architecture today, too, and the kinds of complicated buildings we create, such as airports and skyscrapers, also disturb its clarity of expression; because today 'we' do not build architecture at all. It is built for us, in ever more complex ways. We outsource architecture to groups employed on our behalf of whom we are only dimly aware: contractors, builders, quantity surveyors, town planners, developers, consultants, plumbers and, on occasion, architectural firms. For most of these groups, creating an architecture that expresses society's view of the cosmos is not top of their list. Buildings are, after all, a business.

And the more complex our architecture becomes, the more distant it seems from us, the ones who inhabit it. We have less and less control over what gets built, even in our own backyard. Others are employed to create environments that don't just house us and give us places in which to work, but which at the same time are meant to speak to us. But how do these others *know us*, we who live in their buildings, go to work in them, shop in them, eat in them, laugh in them, love in them, get drunk in them, argue in them, make up in them, get bored in them, get inspired in them, raise children in them, grow old in them? How do they know what we want our buildings to be like? These others rarely talk to us. Perhaps they don't want to. Perhaps there are other reasons for building architecture.

It always amazes me that, like the pharoahs or Louis XIV before them, these others still lavish wealth on architecture that does more than offer shelter. Today we have far faster, nimbler, more subtle forms of communication and expression than architecture. We have the internet. We have mobile phones, Snapchat and Skype. And yet we still build architecture, despite it being, apart from war and space programmes, the most expensive activity human beings have ever devised. Oligarchs build lavish homes designed to impress. Blue-chip companies spend millions – billions – on astonishing HQs. Terrorists destroy ancient temples or mid-century skyscrapers because of what they represent. Architecture still matters. The physical persists in an age of the virtual and the digital. The power of architecture perhaps lies precisely *in* its sheer heft, its solidity, its physicality, its ubiquity, its ability to surround us and encase our lives. Not even the internet is *quite* everywhere you look, not yet. Architecture, on the other hand, is impossible to avoid. It is always there, saying something to you, even if it's the plainest shack in the back of beyond.

But *what* is architecture saying? That's the question. What is this new breed of flamboyant, iconic architecture trying to say? What are its strange shapes, its shards, blobs and cheesegraters – each shouting ever louder than its neighbour – telling us? What does the 'Wowhaus' mean?

The bottom line

Architecture in an advanced capitalist society, being rather an expensive pastime, cannot exist without a business plan. Someone has to stump up the cash. The German philosopher Georg Hegel thought architecture the basest of the arts for this very reason, the purity of aesthetics dirtied by the grubby compromises of acquiring land and installing plumbing.[6] Yet architecture can only come into being if there is a demand for it and someone to pay the bills. And architecture is expensive. It needs land to exist; it also needs a great deal of materials. And if it needs land and materials, it needs money. And if it requires money, land and materials, it cannot avoid politics.

In the past, the grandest, and, therefore, most expensive architecture was always created by the most powerful and rich: Roman senators, Ottoman sultans, medieval monks, French kings, or, for most of the twentieth century, the state – whether the gentle modernism of Roosevelt's New Deal in America, and Clement Attlee's British welfare state, or the more aggressive architectural campaigns of Adolf Hitler, Joseph Stalin or Saddam Hussein. But in the capitalist West since the 1970s, in the absence of any other unifying faith or ideology, architecture, inevitably, pragmatically, has come to serve what has filled the void: the free market. In doing so, the practice and purpose of architecture have been transformed. Just as the patronage of the monasteries fuelled the spread of medieval gothic, and that of the Catholic church let baroque flourish after the late sixteenth century as

a mammoth campaign against the Reformation, so the rise and domin-
ance of free-market economics since the late 1970s has created its own
architectural movement: the Wowhaus. Architecture always reflects
the conditions of its creation, its political and economic context. Flamboyance and spectacle is the inevitable result of a political-economic
system that encourages individualism and competition.

Since the high tide of modernist architecture in the 1960s, thousands of new building styles have bloomed. Many have called this
postmodernism. But it has come in all sorts of shapes and sizes and
'isms', as architects and others criticised the modernist buildings that
dominated the previous half-century for, in part, their alleged failures
to fulfill the impossible brief their architects set for themselves: to
create buildings that not only helped in those great twentieth-century
missions, eradicating ignorance and sickness, poverty and the slums,
but to do so with a global architectural language of honesty, universal
quality and meaning for rich and poor alike. In its stead, postmodern
architects have sought languages more tailored to individual places
and peoples. Countless attempts have been made since the 1970s to
surround us with buildings of a shape and style, with metaphors, similes and symbolism that better express us and our tribes than modernism
did, that communicate with us, *mean* something to us in all our diversity, whether through neoclassical columns, smooth cool glass or gold
lamé drums.

Some languages were very popular, for a while: the ironic columns,
pediments and DayGlo colours of the 'Po-Mo' architecture of Michael
Graves and Venturi Scott Brown fulfilled our desire for an architecture of understandable meaning and nostalgia, but, quite intentionally,
lacked depth and staying power; its polar opposite, the 'deconstructivism' and strange new shapes created in the 1970s by architects like
Bernard Tschumi and Peter Eisenman might have been high falutin
and intellectual, but they lacked mass appeal, or at least a shape that
we, the ones who actually have to inhabit the buildings, could vaguely
make head or tail of.

Instead, in the postmodern battle of architectural styles since the

1960s, a peculiar hybrid of both Po-Mo and deconstructivism has surged ahead – strange new shapes that appeal to our love of novelty, but which don't require a PhD to decipher. It is an architecture of weightless sheen and spectacular, contorting visual imagery that encapsulates perfectly our postmodern age of nomadism, globalisation, individual freedom, short-term employment contracts, digital information, corporate power and fast-flowing streams of international finance through which our lives are now ruled. In the twentieth century, as pioneering academics such as Jean Baudrillard, Frederic Jameson and Beatriz Colomina have proposed, architecture became just another form of media, the building 'a mechanism of representation'.[7] The postmodern battle of architectural styles has been won by the architecture best able to communicate in this age of instantaneous global communication, the one that is the most visible, the most thrilling, the most profitable. Welcome to the Wowhaus.

The confessions of an architecture critic

It is no accident that the rise of the Wowhaus in the past twenty years has come at *exactly* the same time as the internet has transformed the media. Both have fed off each other, and propelled the other forward. A media industry and an audience ever hungrier for imagery ever more incredible; a building industry that can create that imagery ever faster and in more flamboyant, spectacular form; and a means of communicating both globally and instantly. A perfect storm.

Like most writers, I have felt the creeping, invidious force of this change: the request by an editor for an 'exciting' story, with 'good images'; the continual rejection of suggestions for articles on 'serious' (for which read 'worthy') topics; the star-studded architectural prize (an easy way of generating readership and, therefore, advertising revenue) judged through photos emailed to you, because it is too expensive to actually send you to see the physical object; the gradual reduction in word counts for articles, and the simultaneous increase in

space for alluring images that will slow down the promiscuous attention span of the reader; the demand from on high for bullet-pointed
articles on the 'top ten' this or that ('The top ten seaside buildings',
'Frank Gehry's top global buildings', 'The hottest architects in the
world right now'); the reduction in and eventual disappearence of
travel budgets, forcing the writer to become reliant upon the PR
agencies of developers and architects to pay for their travel to look at
the building about which they are meant to be writing impartially;
the subtle rise in power of such PRs, who become gatekeepers for
access to celebrity buildings and architects, and who now pay for your
travel and accommodation, too – 'You were a little bit naughty in
your last article, Tom.'

Judged individually, these are small, insignificant anecdotes. But,
en masse, experienced by thousands of other writers, or editors trying
to make going concerns of independent writing, magazines and websites, they add up to a huge shift, one repeated in other worlds – the
Hollywood press junket ruled over by viper-like PRs, say, or pop stars
distanced onstage from their fans by a gaggle of suited corporate VIPs
at the front.

Within architecture the consequence has been a culture, or cult, of
the image. We look at dazzling new architecture, but we don't see it.
With a few exceptions, impartial criticism has shrivelled away, and, in
its place has come partial celebration. Architecture and its media are
locked in a dizzying embrace of superlatives: the wow factor. Writers,
those that are left, are often too obsessed by what a building looks like,
by 'style wars' or the biographical details of its famous architect. Few
look left or right, because there isn't time or money to do so, and the
publisher is often breathing down the writer's neck. Read much writing about buildings today and it is as if architecture, the form of culture
most influenced by politics and economics, were created in a vacuum,
with just the genius and creativity of the architect to explain it. The
global financial crisis since 2008 has, perhaps, allowed some to take
stock, and focused attention a little more on, say, the gang labour of
immigrants employed to build landmark architecture in less democratic

corners of the world. But, by and large, the conditions under which our new pleasuredomes are created remain obscured by the dazzle and spectacle.

The myth persists, therefore, of the heroic genius in architecture, so forcefully explored in Ayn Rand's novel *The Fountainhead*, and the 1949 Hollywood version starring Gary Cooper as Howard Roark, the uncompromising loner who will stop at nothing to see his edifice erected. It is a strange myth, because more than any other form of culture, architecture requires a vast team to will it into being, not a single individual. In part it's explained by society's perpetual love of the stoic outsider. But it is a myth perpetuated by many architects themselves who, with occasional ambivalence, play public roles that conform to the various stereotypes demanded of them by society, or at least the media: the naive architect whose beautiful building turns out to be impractical in use, or which falls to bits; the uncompromising dictator who treats their staff like battery hens; the erudite intellectual, hopelessly outmanouevered by wily property developers.

All of which would be 'so what?', were architecture not so important. You can turn off a film or a pop song, close your laptop. You can never switch off architecture, unless, of course, you strap your eyes into your virtual reality headgear and warp speed yourself into the digital world.

A sightseer's guide to the city of spectacle

An architecture critic is not much more than a sightseer. We go around as if on holiday, and look at the sights. We take photos. We write in our journals. We might be expected to form a critical opinion, but we are basically professional tourists. Nice work if you can get it.

So this book is *my* journal, an account of what I have seen, and who I have spoken to, as a professional tourist wandering around the monuments and cities built for us in this age of spectacle, on my 21st-century grand tour of the Wowhaus. Like any good tourist, though, I'm curious. I try not only to look, but to see, and to ask questions about what I see. Simple questions. Why has architecture become so strange-looking? How does it work? How do you explain architecture like this? Why does that building look like a pair of underpants?

I have written down the answers in this book. It is not *the* history of contemporary architecture. It is *a* history of contemporary architecture. A history of a particular kind and culture of contemporary architecture. There are many others, many tales, many architects, cities and buildings both good and bad that I have left out. This one, though, is simply *my* history of contemporary architecture.

In this book I will tell two stories. The first recounts how a shift in the shape of architecture and a shift in the nature of where it gets built – cities – coincided, and fuelled one another. As the West changed its economy from industrial to post-industrial, and as cities declined as a result, so architecture, increasingly part of our burgeoning consumer culture and so-called 'leisure industry', metamorphosed from being a jester or sideshow of the economy, to the main event. You simply cannot explain, I think, why our buildings are like they are today without connecting them to the context in which they came to be: namely, the rise of a neoliberal global economy and the cities it produced. These cities, like the buildings inside them, have also changed shape. When I was growing up were dying. Newspapers and television bulletins told countless stories about the riot-torn 'inner city', the decline of downtown, how everyone was moving to the suburbs. Now, in the most financially successful cities and towns, the opposite is true. The richest live in the centre, while in many places the poor have been displaced to the suburbs. Cities have been born again. Cities have been gentrified.

The second story is about how architects, with something of an image problem following the collapse of their reputations after the savaging of modernist architecture in the 1960s and 1970s, reinvented themselves, as their business shifted sharply from the public to the private sector; and, dusting themselves down after this collapse in postwar idealism, how these same architects, with new purpose, new designs and a new tool – the computer – unleashed a radical new architectural language. Radical in form, perhaps, but not in politics. This language, born in the 1970s, took twenty years to take root. But when the time was right, this rather apolitical generation of architects – obsessed, mostly, with the form of their buildings rather than their political or ethical content, in striking contrast to the modernist architects before them – became stars and celebrities.

The book looks first at how cities changed as a consequence of these huge shifts in world economics and politics; then how architects, in order to survive, had to alter how they operated; and, finally, how the architecture they designed changed shape. Economy, politics, cities, architects, architecture: like the cogs of an immense machine, each one connects with the other, each one drives the other onwards.

Contained within are two calls to arms. First, a demand for a kind of architecture that truly engages with you and me not just through what it looks like, or how spectacular it is, but how it is made – one that actively encourages us all to help make it. Secondly, a call for a kind of architecture that engages with the politics and economics and circumstances in which it finds itself, that is at least truthful about its artifice, even when it is busy pulling the wool over our eyes.

So, in the cause of honesty, it only seems right that I am truthful about my own artifice. We all have our particular ways of seeing the world. This is mine. I like to write stories about the landscapes we live in. In doing so, I can't help but be influenced by those who have done so before me.

First, cultural geographers and historians. I have long been indebted to John Berger's approach to culture, and that of countless other British writers about landscape over the past half-century – people such as Raymond Williams, Denis Cosgrove, Richard Mabey, Stephen Daniels and David Matless – who see the landscape, including the seemingly artificial landscape of towns and cities, as the consequence of the interaction of human beings and nature. It seems a simple, obvious point, but, I think, it is one worth repeating.

My second set of influences: the academics Henri Lefebvre and David Harvey. Architecture is a vital part of this artificial landscape;

through its very size and ubiquity and stubborn longevity it dominates every patch of earth beyond wilderness. Its expense means that, of course, it is inevitably most controlled by those with most power, although as Lefebvre and Harvey contend, the spaces around us are also created and influenced by those with less or no power. The built landscape is not some abstract, innocent or passive thing we look at, or visit as tourists with our packed lunches and smartphones, or, as Lefebvre put it, a 'mere "frame" . . . a form or container of a virtually neutral kind, designed simply to receive whatever is poured into it'.[8] It is instead something that we all viscerally inhabit every minute of the day, that we experience with all our senses, and help create, no matter how poor or powerless we are. We are all architects, of a kind. Architecture goes on being made and remade, argued over, ploughed over long after it is supposedly 'completed'. The spaces around us are constantly seething with excitement, expression, contradictions and conflict.

Thirdly, a particular kind of architectural history taught to me by the historian Adrian Forty. 'Dismayed', Forty once wrote, 'by the failure of architectural history to throw any light on architecture's relationship to the rest of the world', he set up a pioneering course at University College London with Mark Swenarton that 'approached architecture not as a series of monuments, but as a process – a process in which the monuments themselves were just one stage'.[9] We studied not only how buildings are made, 'how a plot of land', wrote Forty, 'could be the vessel into which money, labour, political concerns, social values and artistic ideas could flow', but also how they go on being made and remade. The story of a building does not end when its final brick is laid. The story is only just beginning. As architecture becomes inhabited by us, adapted, photographed, filmed, knocked about, written about, walked past, neglected and rediscovered, millions of stories are told about it, as various and diverse as the people that tell them.

Sometimes, though, these stories do not get told. 'Sometimes,' writes John Berger, 'a landscape seems to be less a setting for the life

of its inhabitants than a curtain behind which their struggles, achieve-
ments and accidents take place.'[10] It is a truism that people with power
often use architecture to seek immortality, no matter how often the
obvious opposite is pointed out to them: being made of ordinary matter, architecture has a habit of decaying. But while we wait for it to
decay, architecture is also startlingly good at obliterating what was
there before it. When a building is demolished and replaced, how
easily we forget what was there before. That is why its construction and
its destruction is such a political act. That is why it is always important
to remember, and to reveal, *all* the stories behind a landscape. It is the
job of the writer about such things to draw back the curtain, to expose
what is or was or will be there.

In this book, I'm less interested in why this or that architect designed
this or that building in this or that way – the subject of much, if not
most, writing about architecture – than in connecting why and what
they did to the wider context. I am more interested, say, in why a
wealthy client or city mayor *paid* for a particular kind of building – what
were they hoping to achieve? – than in the idealised theories of beauty
lurking in an architect's imagination. To really understand architecture,
you must understand the power relations behind it. To really understand
architecture *today*, therefore, you must follow the money.

The occasion to write this book coincided with the fallout from the
economic collapse after 2008. This may or may not prove to be the
end of a particular era in the West, that turn to free-market neoliberalism after the 1970s, but it is, at least, a significant marker. It has
given me, like so many others, pause to think.

This book is, in part, a very personal story. It is an attempt to
explore and understand the buildings that I once fell in love with, that
have surrounded me as I have grown up. The Wowhaus is *my* architecture. My life so far – born in the 1970s, an adult in the 1990s – almost
too neatly coincides with the turn to free-market neoliberalism and
the rise of this new architectural landscape. The society and landscape
into which I emerged, that of the welfare state, has withered away,

replaced by younger models. Like so many others, I mourn the passing of the old world. I am nostalgic. But I am also an optimist. I am an enthusiast. I am inquisitive about the new. I want to understand it. I want to hear what it is saying to us. In order to do this I have had to travel far, and far back in time. Architecture is exceedingly slow. Ideas take decades to realise in built form. The architecture being built right now has been influenced by changes in economics and taste in the 1970s, the 1960s, the 1950s, the 1940s – even as far back as the nineteenth century. You cannot understand what is happening now without knowing what was happening then.

It is also an attempt to understand the city I have lived in for more than twenty years, London, and my place in it. Over those twenty years, I have witnessed at first hand London's transformation from the grimy city I first moved to in the 1990s, battling it out with Paris and Frankfurt to be capital of Europe, to today's sparkling 'world city' at the planet's crossroads, the meridian line between east and west. What is particularly fascinating is how the value of land in the city, and especially the central city, has risen to such extraordinary heights. The city has been gentrified. What was once of less value has become valued again. And valued so much that the very nature and purpose of such a city is coming under question. The right to the city has been replaced by the right to buy the city. So expensive are property prices and the cost of living in London, those with insufficient wealth are having to leave, or are being forced out. We have become used to neighbourhoods gentrifying; but an entire city? Like so many millions of others in this dazzling city, my family is hanging on to its place in it by our fingernails.

When I moved to London after university, my father said a very strange thing to me. 'So, you're moving *back* to the big city.' Strange, because I had never lived in London before, or any big city. *He* had, though. In fact, the Dyckhoffs had lived in London for centuries, ever since they arrived, like so many of this city's population, as immigrants, off the boat from the Netherlands. 'Why did you leave, Dad?' I asked him. And so he told me.

My journey, therefore, begins in London, in Britain – my home city, my home country, the places I know best – but also travels to the places that have perhaps reinvented themselves most fervently along free-market lines since the 1970s. After all, if we are to explain what we see around us, we must trace the source of the power and money – and both, over the past seventy years, have come from across the Atlantic. The USA succeeded Britain as *the* world power decades ago, reinventing capitalism as it did so, and while its influence still dominates the world, it has dominated and continues to dominate the UK and its cities more than most.

This book, though, has a far wider remit than me, London, Britain or even America. Few landscapes have escaped these recent fundamental shifts in geopolitics. The book may begin in the UK, but soon after widens its scope, taking in America, France, Canada, Italy, the Middle East, Spain, country after country, region after region, as the city of spectacle has risen from the ashes of the old, and has done so in every corner of the world. For this is not *just* the journal of a professional tourist, nor merely an attempt to understand the landscapes that he has seen, nor even an account of the fading of a love affair as the naive tourist uncovers more and more about the objects of his youthful affection. It is all of these. Together, I hope, they combine to create a faithful eyewitness account of the spectacular rebirth of that great invention of the Renaissance, the Enlightenment and the Industrial Revolution – the western city – before it finally expires for good.

CHAPTER ONE

THE VIEW FROM HERE

'It looks like an Easter egg to me.'
'It doesn't look anything *like* an Easter egg. It's a glass bollock.'

Two men looking at London's City Hall, overheard on the
commuter train to Charing Cross Station, London

Upon Westminster Bridge

The sun is glinting off the bubble carriages of the London Eye as it
slowly, almost imperceptibly rises on one side, and falls on the other.
And every other second, these blazing reflections are matched by
flashes from within, as the occupants of the carriages photograph the
views all around them. To those of us watching from below, the London
Eye sparkles like a gigantic silver bracelet.

The London Eye has been called iconic since it was a glint in its
architects' eyes. And it has gone on to fulfill this prophecy. It is world
famous. Rare is the day when there is not a lengthy queue at its
entrance. The building has performed for the nation as the framework
for fireworks displays at significant events, and has stolen scenes in
famous films and live theatrical acrobatics, such as the unfurling of
political banners by demonstrators brave enough to scale its height; or,
in 2003, the balancing upon one of its carriages by the magician David
Blaine. The Eye has even received the ultimate accolade of modern
celebrity – emulation – having being cloned in cities all around the
world. Facsimiles also appear in miniature within snowglobes or on

china plates commemorating Historic London, sold in the tourist shops underneath it, a modern interloper beside familiar olde worlde icons such as the Tower of London.

All around me, on the pavements of Westminster Bridge, tourists are sharpening their elbows for the best position from which to photograph it. There is quite a throng among the Peruvian trinket-selling hustlers and the busking bagpiper. About halfway across the bridge there is a sweet spot where the canny photographer can get the best shot of both the London Eye, and, if he or she nimbly swivels, that other sightseer's icon, Big Ben, without shifting position. The tourists ignore the less picturesque prospect to the south, of luxury apartment complexes that have sprouted upriver in recent years, which also take advantage of the spectacular views, though more permanently, and rather more expensively.

In recent years, Westminster Bridge has become less a crossing, and more a promenade suspended over the Thames. The London Eye is an extension of this promenade, only circular and constantly rotating, almost infinite. On some days, so thick are the crowds on Westminster Bridge that tutting Londoners hurtling to get to important meetings at the Houses of Parliament or St Thomas's Hospital spill onto the road to get past, swerving to avoid the buses and lorries. The pavements on the bridge have become the sole habitat of tourists wielding selfie sticks and smartphones who, if you stand back and observe them, enact a curious kind of performance en masse. The photographer of the party crouches, or stands on one leg like a flamingo, bends this way and that, trying to squeeze into the image both the view and their friend, their mum, their entire family or school group – who, in turn, strike whatever witty pose comes to them, which must make sense viewed through the camera lens but looks perverse to the world outside. One man is trying to line up the London Eye so that it forms a halo around his friend's head: 'Left a bit . . . That's it, that's it, ha! Now, look like a saint.'

Westminster Bridge, with its constant supply of tourists, has become the very epicentre of world city London, city of icons, city of spectacle. It is a strange place. Let me show you around.

Let's follow the crowd off the bridge, as it swirls past the London Eye and eddies in its shadow. In the two decades I have lived in London, a vast landscape of amusement has been built from here right along the south side of the Thames, entirely given over to encouraging the crowd to experience . . . anything: taste, touch, smell, sight, sound. It is a route of permanent *passeggiata*. A tide of humans flows from here downriver with the water from dawn till dusk and into the night, experiencing the thrills put on for their benefit, set against the picturesque background of the sights of London on the other side of the river, obligingly lit by the southern sun, like one of those painted backdrops on old movie sets.

When I arrived in London in the 1990s, the river was mostly ignored, unsure of its role now that the trading heart of the British Empire no longer bobbed with clippers and watermen. Well-meaning articles in newspapers would implore us to use the river better. In 1986, the famous architect Richard Rogers came up with plans for riverside piazzas, promenades and café-bars, called 'London as it could be'. And now it is. It soon became the policy of local and national governments to encourage this promenade, and extend it, ever since Margaret Thatcher, having abolished London's administrative government, sold its historic seat beside the London Eye, County Hall, to the Japanese that same year. County Hall now houses the kind of souk of attractions you might find on a seaside pier: an aquarium, pubs, a McDonald's, amusement arcades, bowling alleys, shops selling trinkets and sweet treats, bumper cars and Death Trap, a 'Live Horror Show'. Only the Japanese tea house offering a 'Zen Universe' seems out of place.

But the unexpected is ordinary in this landscape. These tourists haven't come all this way for the kind of humdrum they can get in their everyday lives. How about a giant, upturned inflatable purple cow housing comedy events? Of course. Outside it, living statues dressed as Captain Jack from *Pirates of the Caribbean* and other popular shows entertain the crowds; one dressed as Yoda from *Star Wars* tickles ladies dressed in burqas with his light sabre; a half-dressed Phantom of the Opera, off duty, off his makeshift stage, smokes a cigarette through his mask; a headless giant fluffy duck, sweating in the sunshine, is groomed by his or her partner.

One could, perhaps, date the emergence of this landscape to the 1951 Festival of Britain, which turned a bombed-out old industrial neighbourhood here on the South Bank into a festival of modern design, illustrating new directions for the country after the Second World War. As it turned out, though, the new direction for the country proved not to be what was contained *inside* the pavilions – efficient modern methods of sheep farming and coal mining – but what was created *outside* them, the act of visiting and experiencing: the very act of festival itself.

Today, all manner of kiosks and pop-up installations on our Thames promenade, sponsored by various corporations, offer entertainment both temporary and permanent for all sorts of festivals – world poverty, dance, poetry. There is food from every corner of the world. There are lurid banners encouraging to you 'Touch. Explore. Play', or ones offering visitors' smartphones websites and apps to improve their promenade with multimedia fun. The more up-to-the-minute visitors, possessed by Pokémon Go, dart about like flies, hunting virtual phantoms only they can detect in the physical world through augmented reality games on their phones. Even alienated urban youth can enjoy the public theatre. A cave of concrete beneath the Queen Elizabeth Hall is home to things which in most places are now actively discouraged – graffiti, skateboarding, brutalist architecture – but which here, officially sanctioned by the cultural elite, are, for the time being, permitted.

At moments the melee of festival reaches fever pitch. But it's only ever a street or two deep. Walk back from the promenade and you're enveloped back in the undazzling city of brittle new loft apartments and hulky council flats. And there are moments, just moments, where even in this landscape of spectacle, the dun-coloured dreariness of ordinary life kept at bay by this new urban skin surges forth again: say, when the Thames is at low tide, revealing its riverbed of rubble, shopping trolleys, traffic cones and mud; or when you happen upon an occasional, un-regenerated building dating from one of London's gloomier periods, such as the 1970s, when the city seemed destined for a future of motorways and concrete, until a brighter, shinier future was fixed upon.

The city of mixed metaphors

But let's not look that way. Let's cast our eyes instead across the river to the north bank of the Thames, where the tourists' cameras are pointing at that film-star backdrop. London's centuries-old financial district, the City, has lately been fashioning itself a new skyline, building new speculative office developments in all kinds of shapes. Judging from the number of photos being taken, this dazzling new look is a hit with festival-goers on the Thames promenade, its image destined for countless Instagram, Twitter or Facebook accounts. Viewed from this side of the river, these unusually shaped new additions to the skyline look unreal – cut, pasted and Photoshopped – like dinky ornaments lined up on a mantelpiece, or a huddle of toiletry bottles on the bathroom shelf. You could almost reach out and grab one.

These new arrivals all have nicknames. There's 'the Gherkin', of course (or 30 St Mary Axe, as it is officially known). Everyone knows the Gherkin. Norman Foster's skyscraper opened for business in 2004, and is now reproduced on adverts, television programmes and T-shirts as an instantly recognisable symbol of modern London, financial powerhouse. Muji, the Japanese homeware shop, includes it in its 'City in a bag' toy town, alongside Big Ben. The skyscraper's fabulous, crystalline zenith, seemingly floating in the sky, is used to entertain high-end corporate clients. Foster has, rather grudgingly, learned to accept its nickname.

A nickname for a building used to be a sign that it had entered popular culture, been accepted by the general public. Nowadays, though, buildings – especially ones likely to be controversial, such as a skyscraper – often come ready-equipped with them courtesy of their developer's marketing department. Nearby, developer British Land is sticking to the rather dour 'Leadenhall Tower' for the Gherkin's neighbour – 'the Cheesegrater', a 48-storey wedge fashioned by Norman Foster's former business partner and his British rival on the architectural world stage, Richard Rogers. A few streets away looms Uruguayan star-architect Rafael Viñoly's 'Walkie-Talkie' (real name 20 Fenchurch Street) – an oddly old-fashioned nickname for a 160-metre skyscraper that looks more like a curvaceous smartphone. That's right, a skyscraper shaped like a smartphone. Anything goes in spectacular London!

There is logic behind its strange shape – economic logic, naturally. Skyscrapers commonly narrow with height, out of aesthetic tradition and engineering sense. But, since the rental price of upper storeys is greater, thanks to the views, such shapes, despite the demands of gravity, do not make economic sense in these financial times. So Viñoly, a most commercially savvy kind of architect, has reversed convention: his skyscraper bulges at the top to maximise premium rentable space. 'The curve that's ahead of the curve,' toots the building's advertising slogans: 'The building with more up top.' Apparently, and stretching credulity somewhat, 'the slight curves of the facades', explains London's *Evening Standard* newspaper, 'complement those of the river and follow the geometry of the medieval streets.'[1]

Those futuristic, concave curves, however, turned out to reflect not only the historic neighbourhood, but also the sun in high summer – down onto the streets below in what newspapers came to dub the 'Death Ray', when a reflected beam of light reached such a temperature that it melted the bodywork of a parked Jaguar. The Walkie-Talkie was renamed the 'Walkie-Scorchie', the 'Fryscraper'. Media outlets sent their reporters to fry eggs using nothing more than the reflected power of Viñoly's architecture. '[I] didn't realise it was going to be so hot,' the architect explained to the *Guardian*. 'When I first came to London years ago, it wasn't like this . . . Now you have all these sunny days.'[2] The building has been fitted with sunshades to prevent such a regrettable incident from ever happening again. After all, the building's tenants are some of the City's most prestigious insurance firms. Anticipating risk is their stock-in-trade, though they didn't see the Death Ray coming.

A skyscraper so dazzling it melts Jaguars – in spectacular London, sometimes the truth is stranger than fiction. In that same *Evening Standard* article cited above, Peter Rees, for two decades the City of London's chief planner responsible for the skyline's new look, explained his 'fruit basket' approach to town planning here in London's ancient heart, encouraging in the architects whose buildings he approved or rejected an eclectic, fruity kind of design, and a variety of architectural metaphors – walkie-talkies, gherkins, cheesegraters, helter-skelters – all on the same stage. He is the man who decides what fruit to put in the bowl, which ornament to put beside the next on his urban mantelpiece, which showstopper to put on this most public of stages. But why adopt this approach at all?

The City was once the unassailed centre of Britain's financial industry. Since Canary Wharf was built further east in the late 1980s, though, it has had to cope with a local rival that can offer nomadic global finance all the space and privatised bubbles of wealth it needs. The ancient heart of London had to get with the programme. It began doing so before Canary Wharf even existed. In 1986, when the 'Big Bang' first modernised financial transactions in the UK, it ushered in huge new trading floors, which wedged themselves, sometimes uncomfortably, in the City's protected tight-meshed medieval street pattern. A third of the City's land was redeveloped during the 1980s, forcing a clash between the two poles of conservative politics. Encourage the free market and allow developers a free hand? Or conserve the status quo of the past and protect the City's heritage? Skyscrapers – too reminiscent of the flashier sort of capitalism – were discouraged in what, for all its technological reforms, still remained a bastion of tradition; in their stead were built 'groundscrapers' – vast, squat developments that contained these new trading floors without troubling the skyline.

Three decades on such thinking seems quaint. These days, places in

Britain – even ones within the same city, such as the City and Canary Wharf – compete for investment and property taxes not only with next-door neighbours but also with investors from Tennessee to Uzbekistan. Modern-day international capitalism needs elbow room, and freedom to build and rebuild as it sees fit – creative destruction. Heritage and sentiment just gums everything up.

The City not only needed more space, it required a new look. Downriver, Canary Wharf offers its corporate tenants a steel, glass and marble facsimile version of downtown Anywhere: comforting, its luxurious, bland, international-style magnolia minimalism demanding little acclimatisation for financiers swooping in from either Notting Hill or more distant time zones. During the Noughties, the City, in response, has encouraged international property companies to redevelop the Square Mile likewise, with quality materials and designs deployed in little utopias of untroubling luxury. Old developments from times less concerned with public relations have been demolished, or, in the case of the once concrete-fronted London Stock Exchange, given a new, glassier, sparkling skin. The City already beats Canary Wharf in terms of heritage and authenticity, vital commodities to a certain connoisseur class of international capitalist. Now it has an updated, instantly recognisible skyline, too, to beat Canary Wharf's dull blocks.

The City, though, has a new rival much closer to home. Just across the Thames, in an entirely separate (and considerably poorer) local borough touting for international business and collecting its own property taxes, there is a building to beat them all. For now.

One shape fits all

The Shard began life when it was first proposed in the early Noughties as plain old London Bridge Tower. But then it got a marketing strategy. The building began to Tweet. On 28 May 2012 at 10.09 a.m. I received its first message, informing me that 'The Shard is designed to reflect London – "shimmering" in the London skyline like a shard of glass.' The Shard sent a few more Tweets that morning. 'The Shard will redefine London's skyline and become a symbol for the capital,' said one. 'How far away can you see me?' enquired another, asking followers to send in pictures demonstrating just how incredibly visible this 1,016-foot-high spike of glass was. As if you could miss it. Up close, set within a street pattern that dates from before Shakespeare, and with no nearby rivals, this skyscraper is so breathtakingly huge as to be laughable, ridiculous, mesmerising. But then I don't have to live under its shadow.

Renzo Piano, Italy's most famous architect, once told me his 'shard', such an aggressive metaphor, was in fact inspired by the sea: he sketched for the tower's developer when they first met, he said, a 'sail' on a menu of a local café as a nod to those trading sailboats that once crowded the Thames, below. (Architects and developers like that myth of a scribbled eureka design; it adds to the mystique of creation.) In later accounts, though, Piano explained the shape not as a sail but as a homage to the spires of Christopher Wren's City chuches. At its opening he likened it to a 'sparkling spire flirting with the weather', flickering, ethereal and ghostly, as if trying to downplay what is in fact a gigantic hunk of concrete, glass and steel. Quite what a shard of glass has to do with either sails or spires is a moot point in this city of mixed metaphors.

No matter. Once its developer, Irvine Sellar, got past the dreary London Bridge Tower name, he embraced Piano's 'Shard', emblazoning, during construction, the zenith of its rising stump with that one graphic word – SHARD – making it ever more visible across London. Owing in part to its sheer size, but also its media campaign, the city has obediently admitted the Shard into its popular culture. I pass by it on the suburban train most days and eavesdrop on the conversations fellow passengers have about it: Do you like it? Why? Why not? Look, Mum, it's the Shard! Did you hear about the fox that broke into the building site and made its way to the top? What's it like up there at the top, high in the sky?

Scenes on the Shard's hoardings as it was being built depicted its imagined future: well-dressed power couples supping cocktails in glossy rooms during the permanent twilight common to artists' impressions, the glittering lights of the city behind, the unmistakeable shape of the London Eye grounding it in some real place outside the developer's imagination. The caption? 'Inspiring change', as if the Shard's very existence might do just that. Perhaps. This is the 'trickle down' ethos behind modern capitalism, modern regeneration politics and modern architecture: the idea that investing in one spot of excellence will spread its largesse liberally and pull the neighbours up out of shabby penury. At the very least, the existence of the Shard is the sizeable pound of flesh demanded by the developer to contribute to the rebuilding of London's oldest and grubbiest railway station below, through a custom in Britain's urban planning called 'section 106'. Such is the horse-trading of modern urban politics.

The building contains, says its promotional material, 'world-class office space, an exclusive collection of residential apartments . . . the highest residential apartments in the UK, a five-star (plus) Shangri-La Hotel and spa, restaurants and public viewing galleries'. The architecture was declared 'iconic' even before it was completed; the piazza in front, naturally, is 'stunning'. On the day in 2010 when, still being built, it became the tallest building in Britain, it even trended on Twitter – a rare feat for a building. Its developer, Irvine Sellar, liked that. 'I think Londoners will learn to love it,' he said. At the opening day's celebratory shindig, the then London mayor, the ever-colourful Boris Johnson, agreed: 'If you want a symbol of how London is powering its way out of the global recession,' he announced, 'the Shard is it, rising confidently up to the heavens . . . and is destined to become as iconic a landmark on London's cherished skyline as the Gherkin, St Paul's or Big Ben.' It is interesting to note that, before being elected, Johnson was vehemently opposed to the skyscrapers then being encouraged by his left-wing predecessor, Ken Livingstone. But there's nothing like experiencing first-hand the cut and thrust of urban governance to make one reassess once firm-held opinions.

Irvine Sellar bought the land under the Shard in 1998, the year before the UK's 'New Labour' government – of which Livingstone was a rather contrary member – pledged to encourage high-density development of architectural distinction as part of its planned 'renaissance' of the country's cities, blighted with post-industrial angst: John Prescott's 'Wowhaus'. It tallied with New Labour's wider economic approach: encouraging free-market, private investment in the hope of trickling down to you and me a little more in the way of benefits than was managed in the 1980s and early 1990s. Iconic, Wowhaus architecture had become an economic necessity, and, therefore, government policy.

When the world's economy began to wobble in late 2008, the Shard, like the Walkie-Talkie – like so many of the UK's physical assets – was bailed out with still-buoyant Middle Eastern money – a consortium of Qatari investors. London has been encouraging investment in property by international finance for decades, but since the global economic downturn began foreign money has poured into London like never before. A Cambridge University study in 2011, 'Who Owns the City?', discovered that 52 per cent of the offices in the old financial heart were now owned by foreign investors; in 1980 it was 8 per cent.[3] In some of London's richer postcodes only one out of three purchases is made by Britons. The city's property market in these spots has experienced in recent years what has been dubbed 'supergentrification'. Spaces like the Shard have been created for London's new, nomadic super-rich citizens, or, if you are willing to pay £25 for a temporary pass to the viewing gallery at the top, for you and me. And these days, prestigious architectural trinkets like the Shard are traded on international markets like gold and futures. Like any commodity.

The building was inaugurated in 2012. It was, naturally, quite a spectacle. The streets below were locked down to all but its glamorous international invitees, including Qatar's prime minister, Sheikh Hamad bin Jassim bin Jaber al-Thani, the governor of its central bank, Sheikh Abdullah bin Saud al-Thani, its ambassador to the UK, Khalid

Rashid Salem al-Hamoudi al-Mansouri, plus a scattering of dignitaries, including Prince Andrew and the then Conservative chancellor
of the exchequer, George Osborne. Waiting for a train on the con-
course at London Bridge Station, I could peek past the security guards
at the immaculately dressed greeters lined up with goody bags, as
if this were the Oscars. Ever since Dubai's Burj Khalifa was christened in 2010 with 10,000 fireworks and a choreographed and themed
sound and light show, opening ceremonies for buildings have had to
raise their game beyond cutting a red ribbon. And so, in the evening
of the Shard's inauguration, guests were treated to a live laser show
with online simulcast broadcast around the world, with dazzling
beams firing from the building's zenith to light up other monuments
in the city, such as Tower Bridge and the London Eye. The soundtrack?
'Fanfare for the Common Man', by Aaron Copland. No irony
intended. In spectacular London, sometimes the truth is stranger than
fiction.

The Shard is fascinating not just because of what it actually is, but
what it has come to represent. This tower of many metaphors can be
anything you want it to be, depending on your position. For London's
pro-growth capitalists, such as its former mayor Boris Johnson, it
opened at a delicate time, with many arguing for greater regulation of
the city's financial industry; the week after the building opened, the
rate-rigging Libor scandal engulfed Barclays, a few miles away in
Canary Wharf. The Shard, by contrast, was a far more uncomplicated
symbol of blind economic optimism, and, therefore, to be welcomed.
For Rob Lyons, deputy editor of website Spiked, 'I like to think it's
saying "screw you" to those who want us to settle for the little we've
got.' For Angela Brady, then president of architecture's industry body,
the Royal Institute of British Architects, it 'proves the validity and
power of Gt Architecture,' she Tweeted. 'We need quality architecture
to enliven our culture and future aspirations.' Others, though, compared its pyramidal form to the Ministry of Truth in George Orwell's
dystopia, *1984*: 'it is almost exactly the same height,' reported London's *Evening Standard*.[4] For Greenpeace activists scaling its walls to

unfurl a protest banner, it was just a great big billboard, a mechanism for leveraging Tweet-able publicity. The *Guardian* called it 'a perfect metaphor for how the capital is being transformed – for the worse': a town of £50-million apartments suspended in the clouds for the hedge-funders to enjoy, and to which we get occasional access – 'the Tower of the 1 per cent'.[5]

For some it is a thrilling symbol of London's status as world city extraordinaire, for others an emblem of capitalism's evil empire. The state of the world is encapsulated within one building. The Shard, whether it looks like a shard, a sail or a spire, is a shapeshifting metaphor for whatever you want it to be.

Hipster urbanism

Back down at street level, let us walk from the Shard, past the cheese-graters and gherkins, half an hour to the north of the City to Old Street roundabout. There you'll see one peculiar-looking building. For a moment words fail me. What can you say about a huge apartment block of steel and glass entirely made up of two interlocked spherical segments, like a pair of disembodied buttocks squashed against a bar?

The Old Street roundabout is not a lovely place. It's the kind of gnarly spot estate agents euphemistically describe as 'gritty'. In recent years it's become the hellish gateway to London's most fashionable districts – Hoxton and Shoreditch. Clinging to its glum flanks are hundreds of new technology companies, pulled here by relatively cheap rents (well, once upon a time) and that nebulous quality so prized these days – 'urban buzz', emanating from its bars, art galleries and clubs. It has been nicknamed Silicon Roundabout, or Tech City, though most days it looks decidedly un-futuristic. Commuters hurry around, en route to their offices, faces pinched against the droning traffic, scything wind and general foulness. Nobody lingers. At night they are replaced with hundreds heading to those fashionable bars.

The roundabout's two rival kebab shops are kept mightily busy at closing time.

This used to be my neighbourhood – until 'grittiness' became too expensive. Hipsters aside, it's an ordinary bit of inner London – of inner Anytown, really – a mash-up of people, buildings and activities, anything, everywhere, as if assembled by a blind chimpanzee: there's some intelligence underneath, though from its appearance it's hard to fathom. Edwardian social housing abuts office block in jazzy 1980s blue-mirrored glass abuts 1960s slab abuts Victorian terrace of betting shops and cafés abuts ventilation shafts for the Tube station beneath my feet, habitually grafittied in Banksy-style street art.

The roundabout itself was built in the 1960s as one tiny part of a car-mad dream common for that age – an inner ring road for London. But, typical for this city of chaotic individualism, only fragments were ever built, so today more drivers than could ever have been imagined when the roundabout was designed crawl round it at 12 m.p.h., if they're lucky. Giant billboard adverts have been built to entertain them, tempting them with mobile phones, face creams, navigation devices and the promise of happiness: 'You are not stuck in traffic,' croons one. 'You are traffic. Break free.'

Those gigantic beer bellies won't escape the commuters' eyes either. They seem designed for that very purpose; though in the general urban chaos, the fundamental strangeness of a giant, tinny building made from interlocking spheres is rather lost. It seems normal; one more shouty object in a landscape of shouty objects designed to grab our attention. Its name is Bézier, a 'luxury' apartment block, its banners proclaim. At its base, promotional hoardings, replicating its singular architecture two-dimensionally as the apartment block's logo, are dotted with photographs depicting aspirational scenes that could take place inside, should you choose to abandon your sluggish car and sign on the dotted line: a pair of hands slicing at an appetising plate of food, some disembodied sushi, a line of crisply ironed shirts, a seductive martini for 6 p.m.

Today's visionaries re-imagine Old Street roundabout as a 'growth node', designated by London's mayors as a place abandoned by the state, failed by such collective enterprises as ring roads, and surrendered to the private sector to improve. Old Street stubbornly resisted such 'improvement' throughout the economic boom of the late 1990s and 2000s, but once London became high on average annual property price rises of 25 per cent, speculative developers, at last, pounced. Flushed with the extreme optimism only such developers emanate, Old Street is now becoming a landscape of Béziers. To the north, high-rise luxury apartment blocks are sprouting in globules and spikes. At the other end of Old Street, meanwhile, the latest branch has long been planned of European boutique hotel chain art'otel – purveyors of expensive, culturally inspired shelters for the world traveller in formerly artistic quarters. 'Hoxton', said its blurb, 'is the ideal location for an art'otel, given its close proximity to the artistic influences of Hoxton Square,' as if 'art' were contagious, floating in the air like a miasma. It replaces, inevitably, a community-run artists' centre, although the hotel will preserve the old building's graffiti by Banksy for authenticity. Still, the blurb continues, the end result will look 'stunning' – of course it will – an eighteen-storey, gold-lamé drum, the windows of which, the blurb continues, were 'inspired by the punch cards used in the textile industry that were historically located in the area'.

The circus comes to town

An amusing series of Tweets did the rounds the day that Britain entered the second plunge of its double-dip recession, the first of its kind since the 1970s. 'London has a giant ferris wheel and a high-altitude cable car,' went one. 'And a clown for a mayor,' replied another, alluding to the self-conscious media buffoonery of its then mayor Boris Johnson. 'The Barnum Conspiracy?' questioned another Tweeter. 'London is being circusified.' Bread and circuses has long been a hackneyed metaphor for political attempts to quell the seething masses with treats and theatrics, ever since the tactic was used repeatedly by the emperors of ancient Rome. But London of late does seem to be taking it rather literally.

In order to see the circus, we must leave Old Street roundabout and get onto the Tube. Northern Line to London Bridge again, then Jubilee Line to North Greenwich. The circus's big tent is easy to spot. What was once called the Millennium Dome is now the O2 Arena, after its sponsorship deal with the telecommunications giant. The Dome, and the exhibition built inside for the 2000 millennium celebrations, the Millennium Experience, its budget approaching £1 billion, was such a colossal, monumental, iconic failure that it haunted the then new, fresh and optimistic government of Tony Blair for years to come. However, since then, in private hands, it has become the most financially successful music and entertainment venue in the world. This icon, a failure in its first life, has been rehabilitated. The project is ongoing. The Dome's latest wheeze is Up at The O2, the most recent in a new breed of what might be called architectural extreme sports – such as climbing the Sydney Opera House – in which from the 'Base Camp' you can scale the heights of the Dome, and gaze, from the top, at the landscape all around.

What you can see from up here, the Greenwich Peninsula, was once dubbed the 'black hole of London', a marshy land of gas works and gravel extraction plants, some of which stubbornly refused to disappear to make way for the festival future planned for it for more than twenty years. This project is also ongoing. At night, the area around the Dome comes into its own, like a salaryman who lives for Friday nights. The landscape inside and out is transformed into lights fantastic, son et lumière and videoscreens all themed to the act performing onstage in the big tent. It is a landscape of hyperactivity, designed to get visitors in the mood. During the day, though, a sleepier air descends. It seems mostly populated by parties of school children and East Europeans from local building sites, both groups munching sandwiches on the vast shade-less plazas, though never the twain shall meet. Despite such thrills as Up at The O2, and the legion of superstars that perform within it, the Greenwich Peninsula has never yet quite escaped that forlorn air that clings to it, attractive only to lovers of melancholy, estuarine landscapes.

As if to compensate, the O2 has spawned a landscape of wide-eyed urgency, like an overdressed wallflower trying to catch the eye of dancers at a disco. Office blocks are plastered in gaudy walls. A gigantic prong of twisting metal, apropos of nothing, simply announces its own existence and place in the world. They are what town planners and developers call 'markers' or 'gateways', three-dimensional exclamation marks. The state continues to pour money into the Greenwich Peninsula to court private investment – cleaning up its contaminated past, building a Tube line, a model village, the world's most successful entertainment venue; there is no end to the largesse. They come, but – a little like those who came to the Millennium Experience – never quite in the numbers expected. Almost two decades on, the O2 is still mostly surrounded by hopes rather than buildings. Like much of the east of London, the retreat of industry in the 1960s and 1970s has left behind so much land there's not quite enough future-with-a-viable-business-plan-attached to fill it. Maybe the newest plan will do the trick. In 2012, the peninsula was bought by Hong Kong developer Knight Dragon for around £786 million. 'The idea is to create a hi-tech village for arty, foodie, design-savvy Londoners,' the *Evening Standard* explains.[6]

The latest addition to the circus is, with perfect economic symbolism, a high wire act. That high-altitude cable car is open for business. Though business is not quite booming.

It is hard to know what to call the Emirates Air Line, as the cable-car is called. Is it a piece of public transport? Or a themepark ride? Or both? The (historically richer) half of the capital west of London Bridge has dozens of river crossings; the other (historically poorer) eastern half of London has just one bridge, two tunnels and a ferry, all the product of nineteenth- and twentieth-century industry. This part of town needs river crossings. But it is not altogether clear that the Emirates Air Line is quite right for the job. The first new crossing over the River Thames since the millennium cost about £60 million, more than half of it funded by the Dubai-owned airline, the rest by public funds. Such overt private sponsorship of public infrastructure has become commonplace in cities. Someone has to pay for the public life. Though there are strings attached.

In theory this cable car can transport 2,500 people an hour. If only they would use it. In July 2014, London radio station LBC found that just forty-four people got on board during an average rush hour. To reach it from North Greenwich Tube station involves a dash of several hundred metres across sun-bleached or rain-soaked car parks. And maybe Emirates knows something I don't about the future prospects of this patch of London, because right now all this multimillion pound chain of steel seems to link is one giant empty car park in a neighbourhood where very few people live to another giant empty car park in a neighbourhood where very few people live. Defending his creation, the then mayor Boris Johnson, as always, protested too much: 'On school holidays, later in the day it absolutely starts heaving. This thing already covers its cost. The cable car is still sensational value . . . It is a howling success.'

If Emirates wanted to invest in London's transport network, I'm sure most Londoners could have suggested something more useful. Round here a bridge would come in handy, for instance. But that would be to mistake the actual point of the cable car. It exists not so much to be useful as to be talked about. There was some disquiet when the Emirates brand name appeared on the London Underground map, a design classic dating from 1931, a time when the state was stepping up its role in the management of public life after another period of speculative excess by the corporate world. The cable car itself, though, is branding in three dimensions, not two. This is not so much about getting from A to B quickly, the harried commuter's clear aim, as about branded thrill-seeking. It is a fairground attraction, a theme-park ride, thinly disguised as a piece of public transport. Very thinly disguised.

Around £9 pays for a return trip of fifteen minutes or so. Or, for £88, you can exclusively hire a whole cabin, for a (very brief) birthday celebration, perhaps. At the ticket office, you are greeted with a huge banner: 'See London like you've never seen it before.' Before you travel, you may visit the 'Aviation Experience', a flight simulator. The brand-aware illusion of airflight is rigorously enforced throughout. The stations at either end are called 'terminals', the tickets 'boarding passes'. Another billboard invites you to 'Share the view from your journey' on Twitter, using the hashtag #MyEmiratesView. As if to reinforce the point, each of the cabins is covered in Emirates advertising: 'Experience a new way to see Mumbai.'

The cable car itself is impressive: three thrilling towers of twisting metal, 295 feet high. The sights you can see from the top! I get on with a mother and two middle-aged daughters down in London for a day trip. They are very excited. 'If I start hyperventilating, grab me.' 'I hope it doesn't go upside-down.' The cabin rocks free of terra firma. 'Ooooo!' 'I'm a bit scared, actually.' 'At least there's no sharks in the Thames.' 'Oh my God, we're really dangling in thin air.' The cabin steadies. The phones come out, poses are struck. 'Could you get my slim side, please?' 'I don't much like the Millennium Dome, so I'm not taking a picture of that.' 'Me neither. Those sticky-out things look like they're made out of pipe cleaners.' We arrive, a little quicker than expected. 'Is that it?' 'I think I preferred the London Eye.' 'So where's this then?' A very good question. They stay for a coffee, gaze at the expensive apartment blocks, and briefly peer into the Crystal, another brand experience disguised as public service, in this case 'the world's largest exhibition about our urban future' courtesy of electronics firm Siemens, though our urban future seems pretty obvious from the landscape around. Then, with nothing else to tempt them, they get back on the cable car for the return journey.

The party's over

The athletes, watching hordes and international TV crews are long gone, but in the town centre of Stratford, host neighbourhood of the world's biggest spectacle, the 2012 London Olympics are still ever-present. You can even spot the odd banner yet to be removed several years later, as if the place is hanging on to the memory for dear life, like the last person to leave the party.

The Olympics are not really over. They never can be. After all, world city London, city of icons, city of spectacle is, these days, a city of permanent festival.

Stratford was once an everyday sort of suburb, hardly the most obvious spot to be chosen as the site for an Olympic Games. It had its moments of post-industrial beauty: walking the canal on a Sunday afternoon perhaps, sun glinting off the surface of the water, blooming weeds bursting from the verges. But it was not a place used to sporting superstars and the glare of international TV crews. Sure, you would get the odd film crew roaming its streets looking for that precise East-End-gangster-meets-post-industrial-apocalypse look that only a landscape of pylons, canals and Victorian viaducts can conjure up. But before the Olympics, it was not somewhere used to the limelight. Where you now see stadia, plazas and iconic sculptures such as Anish Kapoor's ArcelorMittal Orbit, another landscape existed quite happily for thousands of years, keeping itself to itself: a landscape of odds and ends. Every city has its Stratford, a spot where things that don't fit in elsewhere, like sewage works and scrapyards, find their place. It was the archetypical hinterland – London's backroom, where all manner of things went on quietly, far from public gaze.

During the Games, though, Stratford put on its party frock. Olympic legacy – the pay-off to a place for inviting the world's television sets to focus on its streets – comes in many forms round here. There are new benches and avant-garde bollards, new coats of paint to brighten up the social housing. A fringe benefit, not part of the official Olympic bid, now comes in the form of the new apartment towers in alluring skins and various shapes – wedges, shards, slabs – that have mushroomed up in the years since, their marketing still fuelled by Olympic magic dust ('Go for Gold in these spectacular apartments'), though affordable housing might have been of more use here in one of the poorest boroughs in London. Stratford also has its share of prongs, markers and gateways announcing its presence. One has been erected by Swedish furniture multinational Ikea beside its development, Strand East. During construction, its hoardings positioned the tower alongside the Eiffel Tower, the London Eye and the Seattle Space Needle: 'All these Monuments were created to celebrate important moments in history. For us, this moment is Strand East.'

There is the Olympic Park, of course, renamed after Queen Elizabeth and slowly making its tricky transition from a stage set, designed to be viewed through a camera lens in our living rooms, to an actual place in which people live, buy groceries, take kids to school and squabble with the neighbours. But the most immediately noticeable Olympic legacy, and one of the strangest, is the Stratford Shoal, a flotilla of gigantic metallic scales in all sorts of colours that wraps around the concrete body of the Stratford Centre, a 1960s shopping precinct. The Shoal is the thing that first catches your eye as you emerge from the Tube station. This is its point. It is a building reduced to a billboard, a new skin that wraps around a building presumably deemed too ugly and outdated to appear on TV screens around the world. During the Games, social housing tower blocks from the embarrassing recent past around the Olympic Park were also turned temporarily into billboards, their vast concrete flanks hidden from view by adverts for running shoes, in case the cameras should pan their way. This screen, however, has remained.

Behind the Shoal, though, the Stratford Centre seems much as it was before the Olympics. What was once, in the 1960s, a vision of another future for Stratford, is now a reminder of a past its modern-day visionaries want to forget. It is still awaiting an Olympic legacy. Inside, its malls are lined in 99p or Cash 4 Gold shops, Lithuanian food stores and indoor market stalls selling ripe plantain and yellow yams and pumping out 1970s soul music for passers-by. The homeless, heavy bagged, scour the bins for food, and wash in the toilets where they can read cardboard adverts touting motivational speakers – 'Grasp the future' – and solicitors – 'Visa problems?'

Yin to the Stratford Centre's yang is directly to the north. Westfield Shopping Centre was built in time for the Olympics by its powerful Australian developer, as a gateway to the Olympic Park from the Tube station through which two thirds of visitors to the Games passed. Barriers and security guards ensured there were no short cuts to avoid its parade of brand names. Today, it is now the most visited shopping mall in Europe. This is Stratford's latest vision of the future. From the outside, its collage of boxes offers a variety of flat-faced surfaces, sheen, glittering mirrors — filigree glass for upmarket John Lewis and faux weatherboarding for Fat Face, symbolising the homely authenticity of the surfer slacks it sells. But nobody is taking photos of the outside of Westfield. It's the inside that counts.

Inside, as on London's South Bank, a vast landscape of amusement has been built for its aspirational tourists, entirely given over to encouraging the crowd to experience . . . anything: taste, touch, smell, sight, sound, only here it has been built from scratch. Like the South Bank, it is a route of permanent *passeggiata*. Here too a tide of humans flows from dawn till dusk and into the night, experiencing the thrills put on for their benefit, set against the picturesque background. Here too the unexpected is ordinary. These tourists haven't come all this way for the kind of humdrum they can get in their everyday lives.

The architecture of Westfield, its very solidity, seems to have dissolved into a succession of glittering surfaces, constantly and frenetically moving. Columns are backlit with streams of light, surfaces not covered in gigantic brand names or advertisements are coated in glossy copper, bronze, gold and chrome. Pulsing media screens every ten paces sell you celebrity chefs and the latest blockbuster, like those annoying pop-up adverts on the internet. Indeed, walking through Westfield is a little like what I imagine it might feel like to leave behind the physical world, and, like Alice through the looking glass, push past the screen and continue into the digital world. It is like walking in a blizzard of light and words and images, every fragment vying for your attention, flung into your retina. Clintons. Sizzling

Summer 3 for 2. Vision Express. WH Smith. M&S. New series starts July on Sky Atlantic. Gucci. Grab our latest gaming deal. Win your dream car. Vacation is a state of mind. Park all day & shop till you drop.

Have you seen enough of my dazzling city? Then it's time to retrace our steps.

CHAPTER TWO

CITY OF THE DEAD

'Over the country depression lay like fog . . . [It was] a land passing though some strange metamorphosis . . . What next? The roping, the selling, the plundering?'

Margaret Drabble[1]

Bob Hoskins, town planner

We are in a very different London, sometime in the summer of 1979, and Harold Shand, a one-time East End gangster trying to go straight, is on board his luxury yacht, powering down the River Thames with various dignitaries on board, all invited for the launch of Shand's Big Vision. They are a motley crew, including a crooked local politician, Alderman Harris, Parky, a policeman on Shand's payroll, and, as guests of honour, a group of American businessmen whom Shand is banking on investing in his most lucrative deal yet, one he hopes will catapault him and his patch of the city out of a grubby past into a future of more yachts and more canapés.

Shand begins his big speech in Churchillian mode. 'Our country's not an island any more. We're a leading European state. And I believe that this is the decade in which London will become Europe's capital, having cleared away the outdated.' He's in his stride now. 'We've got mile after MILE and acre after acre of land for our future prosperity. No other city in the WORLD has got right in its centre such an opportunity for profitable progress. So it's important that the right people mastermind the new London. Proven people, with nerve, knowledge, and expertise.'

To prove his point, he gestures to this land, his decrepit backdrop, 'outdated' acres upon 'outdated' acres, where London's immense docklands once fuelled the import–export business for the largest empire the world has ever seen. Now these acres are silent and largely empty, but, just minutes from Tower Bridge, the shells of their buildings are set to be, in Shand's Big Vision, replaced by venues for the 1988 London Olympics, venues he plans to build with a little help from his American friends. Inside his yacht, a large architectural model gives form to Harold's ideas, to tempt potential investors with stadia, cafés and restaurants, and marinas for the kind of yachts he already owns, and luxury apartments of the kind he already lives in; and, I'm sure, if we could study the model in more detail, there'd be an art gallery or concert hall or two, a concession, perhaps, to his cultured, upper-class girlfriend. He promises his American investors 'instant planning permission', before, *sotto voce*, leaning on Alderman Harris: 'The Yanks think we're a cock-handed corner shop over 'ere, you know what I mean? Exude efficiency.' Shand, you see, has seen the future. The future is spectacular, for those willing to embrace a change in the order of things.

Many will remember the film *The Long Good Friday* (1980) as the movie that created, with its melding of graphic violence and British humour, the template for a certain type of cockney geezer gangster film. Many will remember it for launching the careers of Bob Hoskins, as Harold Shand, and Helen Mirren, as his high-class moll. Trivia fans will remember it for a cameo by a young Pierce Brosnan playing an IRA terrorist whose sensibilities Shand inadvertently offends. But when I, a teenager obsessed with town planning, saw the film, all I was interested in was the architecture.

The London that *The Long Good Friday* depicts has disappeared. It could just as easily be the London of *Gaslight* or *Sherlock Holmes*. It is a London before the Shard. You won't find Canary Wharf in it, or the Gherkin. Instead you'll see a London that today exists in fleeting fragments, a city of outdated 'acres' of quietness and emptiness, of warehouses not lived in by bankers, but ruined and decaying, of waterfronts not crowded by luxury apartment complexes, but going spare. Viewing the decay, Shand gets momentarily dewy-eyed. 'Used to be the greatest docks in the world, this.' His unsentimental American investors sharpen their gaze. 'Things change, Harold. Don't get nostalgic.'

Indeed. A very American way of doing things was at that time about to be imported to Britain. There is no room for sentiment as the 1980s begin. This is London on the brink of transformation, from the shabby old city of Empire into today's glittering world city. You can see it in the clothes of the guests aboard Harold Shand's yacht as he makes his speech. Some are still wearing floaty, floral dresses and brown flares, as if it were 1975 and the Carpenters were in the pop charts. But a few, like Shand and his girlfriend, and those American businessmen, are wearing sharp suits, maybe Armani. They are drinking mineral water. The old brown world is giving way to something shinier, more crystalline. Shand proposes a toast: 'Hands across the ocean.'

Shand's Big Vision came to pass, in a manner of speaking. He was out on the London Olympics by twenty-four years, but there was plenty of 'profitable progress' in the acres he surveyed from his yacht. The derelict wharves behind him, the keen-eyed Londoner will spot, were magicked into Shad Thames and Butler's Wharf, in part by design mogul Sir Terence Conran, before the late 1980s property crash. The wharves are derelict no more, but house expensive apartments, cafés and restaurants, such as Le Pont de la Tour, where, one sunny spring evening in 1997, the newly elected British prime minister, Tony Blair, entertained US president Bill Clinton with seared tuna, stuffed squid and a bottle of Bollinger against the picturesque backdrop of Tower Bridge. On the site of the vast old warehouses of the Royal Docks, where Shand paces out his Olympic dream, London City Airport now zips businessmen to Zurich and other European cities.

Like Harold Shand, I get nostalgic. Though I live in this new

London, surrounded by Shand's Big Vision, I can still see the old one underneath. This was the London I first saw in the 1970s, and it wasn't what I expected from my first visit to the big city. Instead of Buckingham Palace or Big Ben, I remember ruined wharves, buddleia blooming from the cracks. I knew nothing then about why – the state of the nation, punk, No Future, J. G. Ballard, Derek Jarman or the imminent collapse of the country. I knew nothing of deindustrialisation, the oil crisis, the unions, the blackouts, stagflation, squatting, the power cuts, the bail-out of the UK by the International Monetary Fund. I just remember the ruins. I remember London, a city I only knew from *Mary Poppins*, as quiet. Which puzzled me. I thought cities were meant to be busy and bustly. This city was silent and empty. Where was everyone?

This was the London my father showed me. He, like Shand, was a working-class Londoner trying to better himself. He was no gangster, though he talked occasionally of being a Teddy Boy teenager with a flick-knife, whose blade he said he used for nothing more violent than cleaning his nails as he hung around on street corners. Dad's approach to social mobility was to marry a middle-class Lancastrian whom he met on a seaside pier, and to get the hell out of the city. They saved up for the smallest of mortgages, got a job in one of the factories tempted out of London's fading inner city to a modern 'green-field' site, and left at last the rented flat they shared with Granny. And so I was born in a new starter home on the edge of the suburbs on the edge of a town on the edge of London, the edge of the edge of the edge.

My father, though, couldn't leave London behind. I wonder if he missed it, and what it was he missed. There wasn't much left to miss by the mid 1970s. The London he'd left behind wasn't there any more. Still, he'd take me to visit the city he'd grown up in – not the obvious touristy places to entertain a child, but Wapping, Rotherhithe and Bermondsey, places he remembered from his teenage years in the 1950s, when their docks and industry still clanked and hollered. These silty riverbanks were our family's patch. Dyckhoffs are recorded in the archives Dad studied in the local record offices he visited on our trips, as he retraced the steps our ancestors made. We were a family of water-men, truckers of the Thames, shifters of gravel, refuse and goods up and down the river; a family whose fortune, modest as it was, depended upon the trading fortunes of the city, the nation and empire in which it found itself. We shifted the stuff that came into and out of the docks up and down the Thames, until there was no more stuff to shift, and no docks to shift them from. Between 1974 and 1981, 20,000 jobs were lost in the docks; London's East End lost 41 per cent of its manufacturing jobs.[2] Dad got out just in time.

On our trips, we'd wander down silent streets of Victorian walls and padlocked gates, peeking into dank warehouses, like those in Shad Thames – now apartments for City workers, but then of a decrepitude I'd never seen before. Where I was born, on the edge of the edge of the edge, might have been suburban and mundane, but at least it was new. Here everything was old, sooty, muddy, drippy, dark and quiet. We came upon hubbub just once – a busy street of horses and carts, men in caps, women in bustles and corsets amid instant London fog puffing out of a smoke machine: a crew filming a costume drama in this ready-made film set. It took little imagination to conjure up Fagin and Sherlock Holmes in the real streets.

After hours traipsing round the ruined past, we'd usually end up in Covent Garden. In the Fifties, Dad hung out round here with his Teddy Boy pals. Now this neighbourhood was also empty and quiet. Covent Garden's famous old fruit and flower market, like everything else in the city, it seemed, had closed down and moved out of town, along with its porters and hullaballoo. Building after building was boarded up and graffitied. There were some stirrings of life, however. A few warehouses had been painted in jolly colours. I remember gardens, rough around the edges. There was a café selling coffee beans. I'd never seen coffee beans before. And there were shops that Dad called 'boutiques'. I'd never seen boutiques before. Covent Garden, it appeared, was changing.

Fear city

Writing these words today, London's skyline sparkling with new towers, its population higher than at any point in its history, it's hard to imagine a time when people were thinking of giving up on the place. But they were; and they did. Dad's story was hardly unusual. From 1939 to 1979, London's population dropped by 2 million – a quarter;[3] from 1961 to 1971 alone, it dropped by 600,000. Many went to new towns, thanks to a government policy to 'de-slum' the inner city by reducing its density. Some gave up on the entire country, and joined the hippy trail to America. In the 1970s, Britain's population fell for the first time in centuries, as hundreds of thousands of people, fed up with recession and that sense of doom that seemed to hang over the whole country, left the UK for more optimistic climes.

London's story was far from unique. At exactly the same time, cities all over the western world were also in crisis. This was a moment when we all, almost, gave up on the very idea of the city. Today we fret over shrinking cities, such as Detroit, where nature is reclaiming blocks and sidewalks. But our old cities have been shrinking for decades. Eight out of the ten biggest American cities, for instance, have lost at least a fifth of their population since 1950;[4] while six of the sixteen biggest – Detroit, Cleveland, Buffalo, New Orleans, Pittsburgh and St Louis – have lost more than half their population. As the economist Edward Glaeser writes, 'the age of the industrial city is over, at least in the West'.[5]

Cities have existed for millennia, of course, as places of manufacturing and consumerism – production, trade and entertainment. But the Industrial Revolution, and the invention, in Britain, of the industrial city, with its vast agglomeration of factories and factory workers, tipped the balance. Western cities became, first and foremost, places for industrial production, cramming unprecedented populations in unprecedented densities to feed the labour demands of enormous factories. Until, that is, they weren't.

With hindsight, I can see flashpoints in my own childhood. My teenage years in the 1980s were soundtracked by news reports worrying about 'the inner city', after riots in Moss Side in Manchester, Brixton in south London or Toxteth in Liverpool, caused by industrial closures and savage unemployment. A decade earlier, my 1970s are filled not only with daytrips with Dad to the urban apocalypse, but with bulletins about strikes, more riots, more factory closures. The 1970s was an anxious decade; and that anxiety was most manifest in our cities. In the UK, after a brief economic boom, the oil crisis of 1973–4 provoked either dystopian nightmares or utopian dreams, fed by E. F. Schumacher's *Small Is Beautiful* (1973), about escaping the city for a more bucolic, ecological future. As Andy Beckett puts it in his alternative history of the 1970s, *When the Lights Went Out*: '*Watership Down* was published in 1972. Laura Ashley's peasant dresses sold in great quantities. Led Zeppelin and other hard-rock bands softened their albums with folky interludes. People watched *The Good Life* on television and spent their weekends visiting villages in the Cotswolds. They tried home brewing. They moved out of tatty cities to East Anglia and the south-west, the only two English regions to show significant population growth.'[6]

One flashpoint in that anti-urban decade, though, stood above the rest. In 1975, New York City – Gotham, the modern world's very definition of what a city should be, with the largest urban budget in the world – came close to bankruptcy. The films of the time – *Mean Streets, Taxi Driver, Dog Day Afternoon, Serpico, Escape from New York, The Taking of Pelham 123* – no longer portrayed the world's greatest city as the world's greatest city, its carefree sidewalks trodden by Jimmy Stewart or Cary Grant, but one riven by crime, unemployment and amorality, its dangerous streets kerb-crawling with Travis Bickle cleansing the city with tough love. During its fiscal crisis, New York became 'Fear City', where robberies, rapes, car thefts and assaults were everyday events, where the murder rate doubled, where junkies lurked in shadows and neighbourhoods went up in flames each night; a place whose decaying infrastructure had become a metaphor for a crumbling social order. Half a million manufacturing jobs were lost in New York after 1969. For 200 years, industrial cities like it had depended on being engines of growth, generating income that was ploughed back into the city. Now the greatest of these cities was no longer paying its way.

Cities were changing, though, long before New York's fiscal crisis. The change began in America – by now the driving force behind the capitalist world – but it quickly spread to cities across the West. Beneath the surface, like ocean currents, international economics and geopolitics had shifted, subtly at first, but with an irresistible force that would, in time, break apart the economic structures that had governed western nations for centuries. As a result, the shape and purpose of the industrial cities that had grown out of these economic circumstances changed radically.

In the late 1960s, a few American economists noticed a subtle but ominous trend. After the boom years of the 1950s, during which it seemed US factories couldn't produce enough dishwashers, Chevrolets and suburban houses to satisfy the American consumer's demand, the rate of profit accumulation in the US economy began to dip. From 1966 to 1970, it had fallen around 6 per cent to just over 4 per cent.[7] The rate of industrial production fell too. Subtle changes, perhaps, but significant ones. Companies began looking at how they worked. They began to cut costs. They began to restructure.

As American workers produced less, businesses began to hunt for cheaper, more eager labour. This might come in the form of increased automation, that age-old tale of the Industrial Revolution: replacing a human with a machine. But it also came in a new form, one, today, that has become a normal way of life: the wholesale shifting of production lines out of the city – first to the suburbs, but eventually out of the country entirely to distant nations, such as Mexico, Hong Kong, Taiwan, Singapore and South Korea, where land and labour were cheaper still. So cheap, in fact, that, combined with grants from central government and sweeteners from new host nations, they outweighed the cost of building new production lines, training a new workforce and shipping goods to consumers back home.

By the time that rate of profit accumulation had dropped in the second half of the 1960s, factories, offices and the people who worked in them had been leaving the old city for fifteen or twenty years; even earlier in the exotic new landscapes of the Sunbelt states in America's south-west and West Coast. The old model for a city – a European one inherited from former colonial powers and maintained by millions of European immigrants in the nineteenth and early twentieth centuries, of dense streets of factories, theatres, cinemas and workers' homes – was giving way to a new one: the American suburb. Los Angeles, not New York City, had become the city of the future, the city to emulate. As the architecture critic Peter Reyner Banham wrote in his 1971 ode to LA, *Los Angeles: The Architecture of Four Ecologies*, 'Los Angeles cradles and embodies the most potent current version of the great bourgeois vision of the good life'.[8]

A new landscape was being built in Los Angeles for a new way of life lived behind the steering wheel of a car, fuelled by a growing legion of middle-class consumers, a landscape of new-fangled things, such as shopping malls, freeways and drive-in diners. Space at last. The USA's postwar economic surplus was in part spent on creating this new living environment. Federal policy and state subsidies encouraged Americans to leave the city; the Federal Housing Administration guaranteed up to 95 per cent of mortgages for middle-incomers; mortgages became tax-deductible; and pioneers such as construction tycoons William and Alfred Levitt placed the mass-produced suburban home within reach of more consumers than ever before. Cheap oil allowed middle-class suburbanites to live further and further apart from one another, and from their place of work. It was a certain kind of freedom. In 1900, only 5 per cent of Americans lived in suburbs, 20 per cent in the central city.[9] By the 1950s, those figures were reversing.

The booming American suburbs, however, created a problem: the old city. It was not in good shape. The middle classes had expressed their consumer preference for suburbia, but the dense, industrial city of the past they had left behind remained. Ever since Franklin Roosevelt's New Deal programme in the 1930s, attempts had been made to improve it, eradicating 'skid rows' and slum tenements with early housing projects, such as Fort Greene Houses, a vast estate of thirty-five almost identical thirteen-storey apartment blocks in Brooklyn.[10] Two decades later, though, skid row was still there, and getting bigger. As fewer and fewer people lived in the old city, its problems escalated. Traditional economic theory about cities predicted that such decline would 'bottom out', and that old neighbourhoods would be left to a blue-collar population who, over time, would nurture them. Only, plagued by the first inklings of what would turn out to be deindustrialisation, this blue-collar population was having its own problems.

Those left behind in the old city were usually poorer and less able than the middle classes to express their consumer preference by moving elsewhere. They experienced more social problems. They tended to be from ethnic minorities, less welcomed in the new suburbs: there was a distinct racial component to suburbanisation – 'white flight' – one that worsened after a succession of so-called 'race riots' in the 1960s, feeding middle-class anxieties about the city, and, in turn, propelling them even more speedily towards the comfort of the outer districts. The old city became shabbier. Its physical infrastructure – often antiquated – still needed maintenance: a city, like a grand, old house, is an expensive thing to run. And yet with fewer businesses left in the centre, and a poorer population, there was less money from local property or business taxes to pay for these expenses. The city began its vicious spiral.

Even in the 1950s, the decline of the old city had become a cause for concern in the US, first among experts in the booming disciplines of urban economics and sociology, and then among politicians, buttonholed by voters and lobbyists with investments there both financial and sentimental. Why, at a time of optimism and economic growth, was downtown America such a downer? At first, American town and city governments addressed the problem with the most obvious medicine. The suburbs were booming; ergo, turn the old city into a suburb. Give people what they want. Build freeways, build shopping malls, build houses, build office parks.

'Urban renewal' it was called. It took many forms – social work, improvements in civil rights, the building of social housing 'projects' or plain, old-fashioned property development. The state, pressured by chambers of commerce, downtown businesses and landowners, intervened where consumer economics were failing, to stimulate a resurrection in the old city. Urban renewal came in all shapes and sizes, but it tended to have the same effect: making the old city more like the suburbs. And yet, urban renewal did not arrest the decline, a decline that continued to reveal itself on front pages in various ways into the 1960s: from crime rates (the murder rate in New York City quadrupled from 1960 to 1975[11]) to social unrest; from race riots (those in Watts, Los Angeles, in the summer of 1965 or Detroit two years later left scores dead) to protests in the streets on subjects as diverse as the Vietnam War, civil rights or the preservation of a neighbourhood's historic buildings.

Urban violence, though, only hastened the departure of those with money. And as the fortunes of the old American city spiralled further downwards, it was confronted with a new threat: that crisis of declining productivity and profitability in the American economy. In the late 1960s, with deindustrialisation tightening in America and Europe, and suburbs sprawling ever outwards as the new promised land for a generation of aspirational migrants, citizens protesting their various causes marched on the streets of old cities from Paris to Detroit (though rarely did they march in shopping malls, designed to be the new 'town squares' of the suburbs). And as they marched, the old city was both dying beneath their feet, and being reborn.

Hanging in the balance

It's half past nine in the morning under the portico of St Paul's Church in Covent Garden, London. A street performer called The Great Escape, half in character, is supping a Red Bull. It's going to be a long day. There's no audience yet bar a gaggle of bored Belgian goths, gawping at their laces. This is the Covent Garden I scurry through, head down. Until recently, you'd still come across useful things here, hardware shops like F. W. Collins, where you might pick up paintbrushes, mops and steel-toe-capped boots. The shop has gone, replaced by a fashionable clothes boutique, though Collins' metal sign remains. A ship's chandler survives from the past – Arthur Beale's, its shackles, hooks and ropes of every persuasion surreally beached amid Neal Street's trainer shops and cafés. Covent Garden is mostly full of big brands these days: Diesel, Carhartt, Dior, Apple. It's full of hen parties, tourists giggling and off to see *Dirty Dancing*. Too many Aussie bars, Canadian bars, South African bars. Too many shops selling room fragrances. Too many street performers. Too many crowds.

Fifty years ago, though, the Covent Garden my Teddy Boy father lurked in was a rather different place. It's impossible to imagine today, as I elbow past Covent Garden's crowds, but even in 1970, as *The Survey of London* put it, today's tourist honeypot was considered 'a little bit out of the way'.[12] Trafalgar Square might have been round the corner, and famous roads like the Strand, Charing Cross Road and Holborn thundered past on all sides. But they formed a moat, beyond which Covent Garden remained a secret garden. There were few reasons for Londoners, let alone tourists, to cross this moat, unless you were hanging out, like Dad, in Covent Garden's louche corners, or you were off to the Opera House or the ballet; or maybe you were here for work. For this was still a part of central London where people made things. As late as 1968, Covent Garden was home to 1,700 firms and 34,000 workers,[13] including glass blowers, potters, musical instrument workshops, light industrial workers, printers, publishers and stamp dealers.

And at the neighbourhood's heart, Covent Garden's market, hundreds of years old, set the pace. Grainy film footage of the market in the 1960s shows its narrow streets piled high with wooden crates, fruit and veg of every variety, and market porters, with their flat caps and six-foot-long wheelbarrows, nipping between large modern delivery lorries that were now squeezing themselves between the buildings. I'm in Covent Garden now to meet three retired porters. Bobby Parker spent his late teens here in the 1960s. 'It was a bloody good life,' he remembers. 'You'd get up of a morning and actually enjoy coming to work. You had such a variety of people over here from all walks of life. You had your toffs, you had your tramps. You could literally say there was no two people the same. There was arguments and a bit of fisti- cuffs now and then, very rare. What I really think made this [place] unique was the caffs, the pubs, the theatres. You'd come out and see all the ballet dancers. I used to call them "ten-to-twos". All their feet were at ten to two.'

Parker's friend, Reg Hudson, remembers the odd spot of demi- monde glamour in Covent Garden's grimy streets. This was, after all, London's infamous swinging Sixties. 'Not every night, you know, but you had one or two stars walking through. Film stars. "I know that face!" I came here a shy boy, went away a little bit blasé, you know.' By the time my dad started hanging out here in the Fifties, Covent Garden had already been touched by bohemia. The coffee bar and rock'n'roll scene was mostly a ten-minute walk away in Soho and Denmark Street, but Covent Garden's hidden world and illustrious past, and its buildings of faded grandeur, also attracted people 'a bit apart', to places like the Arts Lab, where a young David Bowie per- formed, or Middle Earth, where, early in their careers, Pink Floyd and The Who played in its huge winding basement of gloomy pillars and where counter-cultural happenings, like the first meetings of the Gay Liberation Front, lit up its shadows.

This dense neighbourhood of alleys and alehouses had already experienced rollercoaster fortunes. It was laid out, by the Fourth Earl of Bedford, as seventeenth-century luxury housing for aristocrats, using the most famous architect of his day, Inigo Jones. But a century later, its star had fallen. By the 1750s the aristocrats had moved on to newer, fancier neighbourhoods. Artists and men and women of letters, though, had already taken their place: Covent Garden became Lon- don's first gentrified neighbourhood, what city mayors would now probably call a 'creative' quarter, populated by eighteenth-century hipsters. Its list of inhabitants is a roll call of Britain's Georgian intelligentsia: Daniel Defoe, Jonathan Swift, Alexander Pope, Robert Walpole, William Hogarth, Oliver Goldsmith, Henry Fielding, Samuel Johnson, James Boswell, Richard Sheridan, Jane Austen, David Garrick, J. M. W. Turner, Thomas De Quincey; it was a vibrant era of thriving coffee houses, lively taverns and packed theatres.

Soon, though, Covent Garden's reputation for bawdiness, brothels, gin houses and gaming rooms spiralled out of control. Arch satirist William Hogarth set his 1751 print *Gin Lane*, with its scenes of debauchery and its prostitute, high on gin, inert to her baby's fate, beside St Giles's Church. Covent Garden was, if anything, 'de-gentrifying'. Industry expanded. Mechanics began repairing coaches in garages on Long Acre; stained glass was mass-produced on Endell Street. Nearby, Seven Dials became the most notorious slum in London, and in every corner even today you'll still spy Victorian philanthropic housing for the deserving poor, gothic almshouses and industrial buildings from the age of rickets and Fagin. Skip a century, and by the early 1960s, Covent Garden's star was in the gutter. It was a slum, skid row.

It had been government policy in the UK ever since the Second World War to take advantage of the opportunity presented by bomb sites strewn across so many British cities to rebuild them for the new era of the welfare state – with modernist housing estates, roads that anticipated an American-style future of greater car ownership and in orderly, lower-density plans that removed for ever the scourge of slums and overcrowding. Car ownership in the UK soared from 2 million cars in the late 1940s to 5 million in 1960 – 30 per cent of British households owned one, far more than any other European country (only Sweden came close); by 1969 it would rise to 10 million.[14] In Britain, the rebuilding of cities was called 'comprehensive redevelopment', not urban renewal, but it amounted to much the same thing, compelling hundreds of thousands of people to move to new suburbs and towns built in the countryside. Whether by state action or consumer choice, the end result in Britain by the 1960s was exactly the same as in America: people and jobs were leaving the old city.

In Covent Garden, for instance, two-thirds of its mostly working-class population had already left by the 1960s. Those who remained were older; they were mostly tenants, there for cheap rents in poor housing; only half of its households had exclusive use of hot water, a bath and an inside toilet.[15] These people were well-rooted, though: a third had family in the neighbourhood, 43 per cent had lived there for longer than twenty years and almost a third worked in the neighbourhood. 'A high degree of neighbourliness exists,' found a report on the district by the Greater London Council, 'and a large majority want to stay.'[16]

Life at the fruit and veg market, though, was becoming difficult, remembers porter Bobby Parker: 'Once the juggernauts come in, and supermarkets started coming in . . . The lorries were too big, you've seen the streets. You could not cope. You were in a position where you would either have had to knock buildings down, to try and give us space to work, or we had to move, and to be fair, the only way was to move.' And so it was. An act was passed in 1961 by the Conservative national government to move the market from Covent Garden to more spacious parts of the city. A firm of management consultants, Fantus, was employed to consider the neighbourhood's future.[17]

The sheer scale of redevelopment plans for Covent Garden soon emerged: once the market left its 14-acre site, the whole neighbourhood, a site more than five times larger, was to be entirely rethought. Similar urban renewal or comprehensive redevelopment projects were planned in many other cities, from San Francisco to Boston, Paris to Amsterdam, where old markets and factories were being moved out of town. Covent Garden's labyrinthine streets of shabby, if illustrious, buildings – anathema to city planning lore at the time, with its emphasis on neat and tidy zones of activity, not chaos and mess, however lively and picturesque – were ripe to be 'improved'. As the capital's government, the Greater London Council (GLC), was to describe it, it was 'the last soft area in central London',[18] 'soft' enough to be remoulded.

Town planner Geoffrey Holland was on the city's Covent Garden Planning Team at the time, set up by the GLC and the local Westminster and Camden Councils to oversee this mammoth redevelopment. I met him on the roof terrace of the Royal Opera House. Holland is retired now, but every inch of those streets below us is etched deep in his memory. 'It was clear that there would be a burst of development taking place,' he recalls. 'And if this was going to take place, what the council felt was it could jolly well produce some benefits for London. Some social housing for people. They could get more road space. And space for new projects.'

As soon as the decision to move the market was taken, property developers began buying Covent Garden's rundown plots of land for a good price – a practice called 'site assembly' – lumping them together in large plots, the better to create large buildings in the future, whatever that future held. These developers could play the long game: sitting on land until the time was right. As they did so, they neglected their properties; why keep up with maintenance if the building was to be demolished? Rental leases for local residents were not renewed; more people moved out. The slum slumped even further.

Government planners like Holland then had a lot of power; they saw themselves as mediators between the private developer and ordinary people, using control over land and planning law and powers such as compulsory purchase for 'comprehensive redevelopment' or urban renewal to cajole private developers into creating things 'for the public good', a rather nebulous 'good' that planners themselves defined, and the public had to accept. Holland spent much of the mid 1960s trying to work out exactly what form this 'good' would take in Covent Garden's renewal: 'a new beating heart for London, of some kind', says Holland; 'We didn't know what at that stage.' When the heartbeat of an old city disappears, what happens next? Now that money, people and industry had left, what was the point and purpose of somewhere like Covent Garden?

The shape of London's 'new beating heart' was finally made public in 1968 in the GLC's *Covent Garden Area Draft Plan*. In 1967, the city's first Conservative administration for thirty-three years had taken power, led by Desmond Plummer, keen to demonstrate the kind of innovative business thinking it had seen in American urban renewal.

The plan for Covent Garden, with its then-novel partnership between the public and private sectors, would be its flagship. They had, says Holland, learned from the mistakes of the worst kind of inhumane rebuilding that had taken place across European and American cities in the past two decades – 'concrete jungles and so forth'. This plan was to be gentler. It spoke glowingly about the 'special flavour' of the area, its charm and family businesses, its 'long and distinctive history still subtly expressed in its present character'. At Covent Garden's heart, 'strips of character', its old buildings, would be preserved in the new plans, a forward-thinking touch at a time when most of Covent Garden's buildings were not legally protected. The city council itself, remembers Holland, was not bothered about old buildings. 'I mean, they'd knocked the Euston Arch down [in 1961–2, to opposition from only a few architectural historians]. Buildings were just not valued in the same way by the establishment, by the public, by everybody; that came later.'

I met Holland's then colleague, Brian Anson, over a pint of Guinness in the Opera Tavern. He has a very different account of their plan, one he now calls 'a very beautiful monster. I mean, we were terrific draughtsmen. [We were thinking] At least it's not like most of the bloody plans they're building now. It's all sort of nice and cuddly.' The *Draft Plan* is, indeed, a beautiful thing: 118 pages in modish graphic design, its 'artist's impressions' influenced by pop art. One image in particular, created by Anson himself, depicts one public square, Cambridge Circus, as a 'People's Place', in the form of a groovy blizzard of neon signs and brand names like Slazenger and Champion, Las Vegas-style.

'But', Anson adds, 'nonetheless, it was incredibly destructive. I knew we'd done big, big deals with property speculators. So, it was a beautiful monster. But it was a monster.' With the private sector contributing £110 million of the development's £150 million cost, deals were being struck between the GLC and corporations such as Bovis, Laing, Prudential Assurance and Taylor Woodrow. The precise nature of these deals was delicately balanced. As Ralph Rookwood, the

GLC's planning team leader, put it in 1969, in typical planners' jargon: 'How can we make redevelopment profitable enough to attract large-scale private investment without driving out the low return uses that are essential to central area diversity and character?'[19] In other words, how do you please private companies, which, after all, are funding most of the renewal, without destroying the qualities of a place? How do you protect both Geoffrey Holland's 'public good' and private profit?

British towns and cities might have been new to this kind of public–private urban redevelopment imported from America, but they were learning. City planning in Britain was at the time still dominated by the orderly apparatus of centralised state control enshrined in laws such as the 1947 Town and Country Planning Act. These laws had been slowly established over half a century to cure the ills of the nineteenth-century city – overcrowding, say, or poor housing – ills brought on by the very absence of regulation, the *laissez-faire* economics of the Victorian city. Now these laws began to be loosened. Concerned that the new housing, schools and hospitals promised after the war had not materialised on any scale six years later, the Conservative national government that took power in 1951 began untightening the regulations behind their construction. It looked across the Atlantic, where public–private partnerships were already driving urban renewal, and turned for help to private building contractors and developers, in return for a more relaxed attitude to development. 'The people whom the government must help are those who do things,' declared its minister for housing and local government, Harold Macmillan: 'the developers, the people who create wealth whether they are humble or exalted.'[20]

In 1953, for instance, the previous Labour administration's 'betterment' – a levy on increases in land value after redevelopment, to pay for further improvements to towns; essentially a 100 per cent tax on development profits – was abolished. Controls on the construction of offices 'effectively lapsed'[21] and developers swiftly exploited loopholes in regulations, building office towers 'for export purposes', say, to avoid planning controls. Banks and insurance companies were encouraged to assist property developers, whose enormous profits went almost untaxed for years. Restrictions – such as those governing the height of buildings – were loosened. In London, height limits were still set at 24.4 metres, to protect the visibility of St Paul's Cathedral. But by 1961 the Shell Centre on the South Bank was completed, 107 metres high: a tiddler compared to the skyscrapers of Manhattan, but a nod to the American culture that was now sweeping across the Atlantic.

A different kind of property developer emerged soon after to take advantage of these newly favourable conditions; a type markedly different from the old aristocratic estates that had stewarded Britain's urban development for centuries, whose efficacy, after the Second World War, was now hindered by onerous inheritance taxes. The new generation of developers was interested in the short term and the bottom line. They were more than happy to help the government deliver urban renewal, mass housing and bold new road schemes, reconfiguring town centres for the age of the car – for a price. If a town wanted to buy land to create new housing or roads, for instance, it had to compensate the owner of the land; so developers became skilled at buying plots close to mooted state developments to profit from compensation or deals in kind. In a typical piece of horse-trading, developer Harry Hyams was allowed to almost double the height of London's Centre Point skyscraper, so that the city could build half a roundabout.[22]

By the time the plans for Covent Garden were published, the way in which we build towns and cities had changed utterly. Britain's urban landscape had been irrevocably altered. And its new breed of private developer had got rich. Harold Samuel, for instance, built his Land Securities Investment Trust, today one of Britain's biggest developers (creator of the Walkie-Talkie skyscraper), from nothing in 1944 to profits of £11 million in 1952 and £204 million in 1968. Central government tried reintroducing regulations on private development throughout the 1960s. But it was too late. The genie was out of the bottle.

So it is hard, today, looking back at the scale of urban renewal that was planned for Covent Garden in 1968, to see exactly where the delicate balance was between Geoffrey Holland's 'public good' and private profit. For the balance of power had already altered. There is much debate today about the privatisation of public space and assets in towns and cities, as if this were somehow a new phenomenon. It is not. This new kind of city was sweeping in from America half a century ago, and Covent Garden was where it would take root.

Gentle these plans were not. They were, as Brian Anson said, a monster. The nineteenth-century market buildings would be restored, yes, but for a new life as a shopping mall, their iron roofs replaced with a version in then fashionable plastic. Inigo Jones's Piazza would be entirely redeveloped: the historic Floral Hall and Jubilee Market would be demolished, replaced by a huge complex of office blocks and walkways, high-rise hotel and conference centre, 'something that most European cities [then] felt they ought to have', recalls Holland. The entire northern half of Covent Garden, where most of the remaining working-class population lived, was to be rebuilt as office and apartment blocks.

Across the higgledy-piggledy neighbourhood; Holland, Anson and their team scored new roads, to efficiently feed its new office blocks, shopping malls, hotels and conference centres. Colin Buchanan's 1963 *Traffic in Towns* was then the planner's bible, with recipes on how to make American-style road-building squeeze into Britain's tight-knit towns. A 'box' of motorways was already planned by London's city council to encircle central London, part of which was close to completion in Notting Hill, after considerable local opposition. Covent Garden was to have its own 'box', a four-lane ring road replacing historic streets such as Maiden Lane, Earlham Street, Drury Lane and the medieval courts and alleys off St Martin's Lane. With hindsight, the 1968 plan's intention was clear: to turn Covent Garden into a suburb.

At first, remembers Holland, his design was well received. After all, such large-scale redevelopment to retrofit old neighbourhoods for a suburban future was utterly normal at the time. 'The *Evening Standard*

[London's most important newspaper] produced a piece saying it was all lovely and great,' Holland says, 'and the first major improvement in getting away from the concrete jungles and all this kind of thing.' But that optimism wouldn't last long. The rise of private finance and urban renewal wasn't the only change that had taken place in the old city in the 1960s. Public opinions had changed too.

A curious reversal

In 1963, a sociologist at University College London called Ruth Glass noticed something rather strange happening in her city. London, like so many other cities in the West, was changing. The old industrial city had long been studied by people like Glass; it was, by now, understood. It was predictable. Now, though, it was behaving oddly. Glass was editing a collection of essays about this very topic, *London: Aspects of Change*.[23] Today, of course, we understand what was happening: London, like American cities before it, was evolving as global economics and politics began to shift. The old city was dying, or, perhaps, becoming something else. But in the early 1960s, academics like Glass knew no better. They were simply puzzled by what they observed, and could not explain.

One phenomenon Glass found particularly puzzling: why were some middle-class people now choosing *not* to move to the suburbs? London, like most other west European cities, had been obediently following America's lead and suburbanising. Almost all experts on the city for the best part of a century had been predicting and prescribing that towns would and should increasingly disperse, become less dense, or even die altogether, for the health and social well-being of their citizens. But now the opposite was starting to happen. 'It was mainly the poorer sections of the metropolitan working class', she wrote, 'who wanted to stay behind in "good old London".' That was, until after the Second World War, when, thanks to comprehensive redevelopment even these were moved out of town, though not always out of choice. The old city they left behind, though, emptier, more rundown in parts, or being transformed into Los Angeles in others, was not entirely dying, noted Glass. London, for instance, had its shabby parts, its skid rows, or 'twilight' zones 'of transition', she called them. But there was beginning to emerge a new 'gleam of affluence';[24] 'it shows itself in an abundance of goods and gadgets, or cars and new buildings – in an apparently mounting flood of consumption . . . The shops are crammed with personal and household paraphernalia . . . The wrapping and labelling of commodities . . . have a new gloss.' Glass's description is startlingly prescient.

In this city of growing affluence, a curious reversal was taking place. Some of the middle classes were choosing not to move to the suburbs as their parents had once done. They were staying in the old city. 'One by one, many of the working-class quarters of London have been invaded by the middle classes';[25] note the word 'invaded' – Glass, a Marxist, did not mince her words. 'Shabby, modest mews and cottages . . . have become elegant, expensive residences.' Casually, she coins a word for this strange phenomenon. 'Once this process of "gentrification" starts in a district, it goes on rapidly until all or most of the original working-class occupiers are displaced, and the whole social character of the district is changed.'[26] Glass's brief description of what would become the most significant force in western cities in the second half of the twentieth century – 'gentrification' – is almost throwaway. Little did she know how significant it would become.

Why was gentrification happening, though? Glass offers an explanation. After years of postwar austerity, in the late 1950s and early 1960s Britain was at last having a taste of American-style consumerism. The average wage had doubled during the 1950s; consumption per head rose by 20 per cent.[27] White-collar work was booming nationwide, but especially in London, whose city council had increased the amount of allowable office space from 1.7 million square feet in 1951 to 5.9 million square feet in 1955.[28] It was still national policy to move jobs and people out of the city, but since Britain's government had begun loosening its planning system to encourage the private sector to pay for urban renewal, the free market had spoken. And it seemed to say: 'Stay in the city.'

As offices, conference centres and shopping centres sprung up to 'save' towns and cities in the late 1950s and early 1960s, just as they had under America's 'urban renewal' programmes, the people who built them – the developers – and the people who worked in them – a new, more affluent middle class – competed for property. Hence property prices boomed. 'London may quite soon be a city which illustrates the principle of the survival of the fittest,' wrote Glass. 'The financially fittest.'

But this didn't entirely explain gentrification. Why were these middle-class workers *living* in the old city as well as working there? Why didn't they just commute in from the suburbs? Glass searches for answers. Her final theory was the most intriguing. There was, she noted, a change in the *attitudes* of the middle class: 'Their anti-urban bias, in particular, has been substantially modified.' Tastes had changed. Some of the middle classes were learning to love the city again.

Who was teaching them? Few then were extolling the virtues of urban, rather than suburban, life; but those few became immensely influential. They emerged, notes historian Raphael Samuel in *Theatres of Memory*, in cities across the West, as the landscape of each was rapidly altered during and after the Second World War. They came from the political left and right, the avant-garde and the reactionary; but what united them was both the experience of seeing their towns and cities destroyed, whether through wartime bombs, deindustrialisation or property developers, *and* an urge to protect what was left. They shared a love for values inherent to the dense, historic city, whether its aesthetic form, its layers of history, its ability to somehow encourage neighbourliness or its sheer excitement – values they considered lacking in suburbia. They were, for now, writes Samuel, 'self-consciously minority tastes, even a kind of eccentricity'.[29] This eccentric minority, though, would grow in power.

In Paris, for instance, 'Situationist' intellectuals such as Guy Debord praised the crumbling old city, in whose overlooked nooks, they hoped, Marxist revolution would one day emerge. Avant-garde architects in

Europe, such as the prolific Team X collective, had been scandalising old-guard modernists since the early 1950s by opposing Le Corbusier's approach to the historic city, which had reigned supreme since the 1920s: don't demolish the old, they proposed, renew it from within. Learn from it. Learn from the slums.

More reactionary sentiments were also bubbling up. Britain, for instance, had embraced modernist architecture and culture far later than most European countries; now that it had acquired a mania for modernisation, some were having misgivings. Nostalgia was a logical sentiment when so much was new. It was the very recent past that was so alluring – the Victorian age, after all, had only ended fifty years ago, and it was largely Victorian Britain that was being demolished in the rush to rebuild. In 1958 the Victorian Society was established to defend the period's architecture, with eminent architectural historian Nikolaus Pevsner in the driving seat, and poet John Betjeman as its bard. But nostalgia took all forms. In 1962, the illustrator Geoffrey Fletcher published *The London Nobody Knows*, 'unusual wanderings' and 'strange adventures in this reserved, esoteric city', highlighting its finer details – such as the last Yiddish theatre – now 'vanishing at an accelerating speed'.[30] The designer Laura Ashley, who would become the doyenne of nostalgia in the 1970s, notes Raphael Samuel, 'was printing her tea-towels ("with a characteristic Victorian motif") as early as 1953';[31] while 'Roy Brooks, the fashionable left-wing estate agent . . . was pioneering a new market in run-down period properties'.

Concerns about the future accompanied this nostalgia, especially the future being built by property speculators in partnership with the state. Embedded in these worries was a scarcely hidden anti-Americanism – common throughout Europe in the late 1950s, as American money and culture flooded across the Atlantic. In 1955, *Architectural Review* magazine's popular critic Ian Nairn criticised the American-style 'subtopia' being created in Britain. In Ruth Glass's own 1964 book of essays, *Aspects of Change*, eminent modernist architect William Holford worried about the 'consistent trend towards . . . greater anonymity of appearance'[32] in urban landscapes; 'the small, the individual, the eccentric, and the flamboyant buildings are disappearing; large, impersonal, repetitive and much less interesting buildings are taking their place'. Skyscrapers, he predicted, could be 'run of the mill buildings' by the end of the century.

Even in America, dissenting voices began to be heard against the new landscapes of the city, whether the suburbs or the 'downtown suburbs' being created through urban renewal. William H. Whyte's best-selling 1956 book, *The Organization Man,* challenged the importance of America's new corporate and office-based culture, criticising its detrimental effects on individualism and identity. It sparked a succession of critiques of suburban life and its landscapes – anonymous office towers, out-of-town factory campuses – *and* the universalising corporate mentality and hidden controls beneath this new form of capitalism. In 1961, Richard Yates published the critically acclaimed *Revolutionary Road*, a tale of the stifling effects of married life 'among all these damn little suburban types' as protagonist Frank Wheeler puts it,[33] a man forever hankering after a more fulfilling life in the old bohemian Manhattan he'd left behind. In 1970, the sociologist Richard Sennett published his study of the contemporary American city, *The Uses of Disorder*. Sennett explained the flight to the suburbs as the latest incarnation of 'a fear of the richness of urban society'.[34] Throughout history, humans living in cities have dealt with their sociological diversity, inherent instability and the anxiety these induce by wearing masks both psychological and cultural, projecting almost theatrical identities while the authentic self retreats. But the expansion of the suburb, with its 'purified community', suggests Sennett, was now leading to a physical or geographical 'withdrawal from complexity'[35], as people retreated from cities more chaotic and unstable than for decades. But suburbs were not, he found, making people happier. There was 'an emotional poverty'[36] lurking there, 'a pessimism, an undercurrent of despair about the social consequences of abundance.' He saw this despair especially among the young. They were, he observed, 'refusing to be bored'.[37] They were seeking escape, back to the city, back to a less ordered, more anarchic way of life.

Back in that old city, not far from the West Village streets romanticised by Frank Wheeler, the warehouses of SoHo – emptying out as the garment industry, which once employed more than Detroit's car industry, began to wither – were by the late 1950s being occupied by abstract expressionist artists, such as Robert Rauschenberg. They used the vast spaces both as cheap places in which to work on canvases too large to squeeze into a garret, *and* as places to live, extolling a version of domestic bliss similar to that being pursued in the suburbs – individual freedom – but in a radically different form, with dirty old industrial walls scarred by history, and vast, open-plan, almost modernist spaces. A few blocks away, in Greenwich Village, beatniks congregated not at the new civic agoras planned for them in shopping malls by developers, but hugger-mugger in jazz and folk clubs, in the dark, atmospheric basements of nineteenth-century terraced houses.

Meanwhile, a few blocks away, a bespectacled journalist tapped away on her typewriter, composing her own love letter to the unsuburban city. *The Death and Life of Great American Cities*, the most influential book on cities for the next fifty years, was published in 1961; fortysomething Jane Jacobs, though, had been crusading against urban renewal for a decade. Indeed, she was chair of the Joint Committee to Stop the Lower Manhattan Expressway, a slum-clearance project planned for Greenwich Village. As correspondent for *Architectural Forum* magazine she sourly criticised both urban blight and its so-called panacea, urban renewal. She took on 'big guns', whether celebrated buildings, such as Manhattan's Lincoln Center, or celebrated designers. Interviewing eminent city planner Edmund Bacon beside one of his developments, Jacobs was dismayed by its lifelessness. 'I said, "Where are the people?" [Bacon] didn't answer. He only said, "They don't appreciate these things." '38

They, like her, appreciated a different kind of city. And she put her money where her mouth was. In the early 1950s, before we knew such things existed, Jane Jacobs became one of Ruth Glass's gentrifiers, moving with her husband, architect Robert Hyde Jacobs, into an old storefront building on Hudson Street in Greenwich Village. In a 1955 letter to the mayor of New York, Robert F. Wagner, she explained her eccentric passion: 'My husband and I are among the citizens who truly believe in New York – to the extent that we have bought a home in the heart of the city and remodeled it with a lot of hard work (transforming it from slum property) and are raising our three children here'.[39] She may have been swimming against the suburban tide, but she was not alone. In 1958, she wrote an article for *Fortune* magazine, 'Downtown Is for People', which, its editor Holly Whyte said, garnered 'one of the best responses' ever;[40] her 'minority' tastes were beginning to gain followers.

Soon after, she was approached by the Rockefeller Foundation to study her attitudes in more depth. The Foundation was concerned at the lack of rigour in a discipline, city planning, that was comparatively new in America yet increasingly powerful, reshaping towns and cities across the continent;[41] it began funding research that interrogated the assumptions upon which urban renewal was being carried out. The first project, by artist György Kepes and his student urbanist at MIT, Kevin Lynch, looked at how humans perceive the built environment. The results, published by Lynch as *The Image of the City* (1960), are fascinating not just because they valued the importance of human *experience* of the urban landscape, unusual at a time when the building of cities was dominated by questions technical (the correct width of road) or political (how many housing units to supply). What is pioneering about the book is its radical suggestion that buildings and cities should, in the future, be built to somehow enhance this human experience of the urban landscape, make it 'beautiful and delightful',[42] 'soaked in memories and meaning'[43] and 'sensuous enjoyment'. A beautiful, sensuous environment, suggested Lynch, provides 'emotional security' and social cohesion; the corollary being that an ugly, alienating one, perhaps that of the dull suburbs or the 'renewed' downtown, might cause social breakdown.

The Death and Life of Great American Cities followed a year later in the same vein, seeking 'scientific' explanations for the apparently subjective appeal of urban life in the old city. Jane Jacobs's key contention was that suburbanisation and urban renewal may have had good intentions – the eradication of poverty, perhaps, or modernising a city's infrastructure – but that the cure was worse than the malady, leading to the break-up of established communities in the old city and social isolation in the suburbs. As Jacobs told a reporter from *Mademoiselle* magazine in 1962: 'Suburbs are perfectly valid places to want to live, but they are inherently parasitic, economically and socially.'[44]

The future of the city could be found, instead, in the past. The so-called 'redundant' patches of the kind of dense inner city – like her own Greenwich Village, and later Covent Garden – then being all-too-easily demolished contained values vital to human culture, Jacobs proposed. She praised what she called 'generators of diversity', devices and designs that encouraged social mix and, to her eyes, a positive experience of urban life: a certain density of people, for instance, stimulated social interaction; street blocks should be not monolithic but small, human-scaled, filled with all sorts of activities; architecture should come from a wide range of ages and styles. The very purpose of cities, right from their roots in ancient Mesopotamia, she wrote, was direct human exchange and interaction, qualities now being threatened by 'anti-urban' planning and suburbanisation.

In the decades since, Jacobs's critique has been lauded, but also criticised for ignoring issues of race or class, and for her suggesting her own experiences of cities were somehow 'scientific', 'natural' and 'universal'. Nevertheless, for all its faults, *Death and Life* for the first time powerfully expressed to a relatively *mass* audience, not just 'eccentric minorities', the precise qualities of the old city that were worth celebrating. The avant-garde – whether Situationists or cutting-edge architects – might have been extolling similar virtues. But Jacobs broadcasted them. Her book sold several hundred thousand copies – not bad for a treatise on town planning.

What Jacobs seemed to be suggesting, and Lynch before her, was that those in charge of our dying old cities, in their rush to revive them with office towers and freeways, had forgotten why so many people loved them. They had forgotten about the importance of subjective human *experience*. They had forgotten about beauty and delight, memory and meaning, sensuous enjoyment. People didn't love cities just because that was where the work was or the traffic flowed efficiently. They loved them because it was where their grandmother lived or where they went to boxing club with Uncle Bill, because of the way light fell on a church tower at 9 a.m., because of a particular dirty old jazz club they went to with their friends that played the *best* music, because of Mrs Williams behind the counter at the grocery store, with her annoying chitter-chatter, because of all the qualities town planners, politicians and developers didn't notice, let alone value. They loved the supposedly overcrowded, inefficient old city *because* it was overcrowded and inefficient. People no longer *needed* to work and live there as we had in the past; but some were *choosing* to do so, precisely because of the sensory and emotional experience they could find amid the 'intricate ballet' of the streets, but could not in the suburbs or on an LA freeway at 50 m.p.h. The old city might have been on its deathbed, but it wasn't dead yet. Some people detected a pulse.

The last paragraph of *The Death and Life of Great American Cities* was extraordinarily prescient: 'Dull, inert cities, it is true, do contain the seeds of their own destruction and little else. But lively, diverse, intense cities contain the seeds of their own regeneration.' Town planners, architects and city politicians would learn from Jacobs, though not in the form she might have chosen. And not yet. Instead, during the 1960s, that last paragraph became the rallying cry for an army of activists who took to the streets to protect those very streets from politicians, planners and property developers, at first across American towns and cities, and then in those across the Atlantic; an army, at first, not just of Glass's middle-class gentrifiers, but a coalition of interests, each defending their own experience of the city – as a place of traditional work, the heart of an established community, as a place for individual creative freedom, and, especially, as a place embodying those newly prized qualities Jacobs identified: 'liveliness', 'diversity' and 'intensity'. However, whether and in what form this coalition held together would determine whether and in what form the old city would hold together too. A decade after Jacobs published her book, events came to a crux, in Covent Garden.

Taking to the streets

All, for the moment, was quiet. After the plans for Covent Garden's urban renewal were published in 1968, they were, as was normal, examined by lawyers and subjected to 'public consultation' with local landowners and businesses – though not all local residents. By now, American cities had learned, through bitter experience in the 1950s and 1960s battling Jane Jacobs and her disciples, to allow those who actually *lived* in a place to be involved in what happened *to* it. Britain had yet to learn that lesson. It was about to do so.

During this hiatus, land values in the neighbourhood rocketed to around £1 million an acre, with the expectation of millions of pounds of private and public money pouring in. Landowners put up rents. Those small family firms that the 1968 plan had praised as integral to Covent Garden's character began to be priced out, replaced by fashionable shops, bars and restaurants for tourists and new office workers, eager to get a foothold in London's new 'beating heart'.

Change stirred in the country, too. In 1970, unexpectedly, the left-of-centre Labour government was replaced by the Conservatives, led by prime minister Edward Heath. Heath, like his counterpart in the GLC, Desmond Plummer, was a Keynesian politician. Most were back then – even business-minded right-wingers. Heath believed in regulating capitalism through state planning, to make business more efficient and long-term in its thinking. He formed a new Department of the Environment for big infrastructure projects to modernise the country, such as an airport in the Thames Estuary to replace Heathrow and a tunnel beneath the English Channel. The plans for Covent Garden fitted in nicely. But Heath was also keen, as his government's slogan put it, to 'go for growth' with a new business-minded agenda.

He brought into his administration businessmen such as Peter Walker, head of Slater Walker, a new type of enterprise efficient at 'corporate raids' and 'asset stripping' of inefficient public companies and nationalised industries. Walker was made secretary of state for Heath's new Department of the Environment, in charge of city planning, and keen to bring modern business thinking to the kind of partnerships between private enterprise and public institutions now key to urban development. The future of Covent Garden was in his hands.

That new business agenda soon got results. London's financial district, the City, was eager to position itself as the economic engine of the European Common Market, which the UK had just joined. Peter Walker once again began loosening British planning laws. Office development permits, which controlled spiralling land values and rent, almost ceased; planning permissions were freely given. Bank lending rules were eased and interest rates cut. Developers used newly lax credit to amass land in ever-larger sites, mortgaging and remortgaging and leasing land back from mysterious subsidiary companies and pension funds to spread the risk.

A national scandal had already bubbled up about the fortunes amassed by these developers as more and more of our towns and cities fell into their hands. Today, bankers and financial institutions are the bogeymen of popular culture. In Britain in the late 1960s and early 1970s, it was property speculators, with their wealth and shadowy practices, who were rarely off the front pages. In 1967, financial journalist Oliver Marriott published *The Property Boom*, a lively account of this new breed of developer. Christopher Booker and Bennie Gray, under the alias Counter Information Services, began investigating the collusion between government, city councils, financial institutions and property developers, published as *The Recurrent Crisis of London* in 1973. As a property journalist then on London's *Evening Standard*, Simon Jenkins returned continually to this shift in power from the state to private developers, 'another of the great historical exchanges in the control of London's land', he wrote. 'New institutions of property ownership have taken vast tracts of London under their wing and are in a crucial position to determine what happens . . . in the future.'[45]

While lawyers pored over the plans for Covent Garden, indeed, the biggest property scandal in postwar Britain was playing out. John Poulson had emerged in the 1950s and 1960s as the canniest of architects, whose firm, one of Britain's largest, had got rich largely by adopting modern, American-inspired management techniques. Poulson, through his network of subsidiary companies, streamlined and sped up design and construction for his developer clients, the very ones increasingly being asked by British governments to help rebuild towns and cities through public–private partnerships. Poulson had on his payroll a long list of local politicians, the better to win lucrative contracts – most infamously in the northern city of Newcastle-upon-Tyne, whose equally canny council leader, T. Dan Smith, wanted to reshape the city through urban renewal to become, he said, the 'Brasilia of the North'. In 1968, the Inland Revenue began legal proceedings against Poulson for his tax affairs; a year later his business began heading towards bankruptcy. By 1972, the police were investigating him for fraud, sending shockwaves to the very top of national government: Reginald Maudling, Poulson's friend and business associate, but also home secretary in Edward Heath's government, was forced to resign. In 1973, Poulson, T. Dan Smith and Scottish civil servant George Pottinger (a recipient of Poulson's lavish gifts) were arrested for corruption, and later jailed. The 'business agenda', it seemed, did not always work for the 'public good'.

In Covent Garden, 'suddenly it all changed', remembers planner Geoffrey Holland. 'We were the worst thing since the Nazis. "The GLC's throwing people out of their homes and relocating them to Dagenham." Which was not the case at all. But nobody believed it.' What had happened during the hiatus was simple. Taste had changed. Public opinion had changed. And, in the meantime, the people who actually lived in Covent Garden, that deep-rooted community the planners so praised, but which, in their 'public consultation', they had declined to consult, had finally read what was in store for them. People like John Toomey.

Toomey's great-grandfather had come from Ireland in the 1840s during the Great Famine to work in Covent Garden's market, followed by his grandfather, his uncles and cousins. Toomey, eighty-two years old when I met him in the churchyard of Inigo Jones's St Paul's, was born and raised 200 metres away from the market on Neal Street. He'd moved away now, but still visited his brother here every week. When Toomey was growing up, 'the market belonged to us. This was our football pitch. In and out the market . . . we played.' His family's daily life was etched into the streets. He points to the Piazza: 'I can see my mum there, me walking with her. Lots of people have got those sorts of memories. My brother always used to say, "The people in Covent Garden, they weren't blood-related, but they were a tribe." It's the same with buildings, the fabric, it belongs to us. That's what made the community.'

This community, though, was about to be re-planned. When Toomey found out, 'I thought it was disgusting. People like me, we don't read *The Times*, or the little print on planning applications. Nobody knew about it in Covent Garden, not ordinary people like us. It was all cut and dried. I thought, "My God, this is going to happen to the place I was born in, where my mum and dad were born, where my grandparents lived. They're going to destroy it, and are not even going to talk to us about it."' He is still angry, decades later. His voice is hoarse, but firm. 'The Greater London Council coming in here and telling Covent Garden what it's going to be like! People who didn't know one street from another. The arrogance of them. But *we* knew the pavements we were walking on, they were part of us. Not just to make money out of the bloody place. These bureaucrats, I'm not saying they're evil or wicked, but they never thought of ordinary people. I used to go to meetings and half the language, they could have been talking French or German. But gradually we caught on, you know.'

In the summer of 1970, Brian Anson, the very planner who had helped Geoffrey Holland draw up the plans for Covent Garden, began to have misgivings himself. He was, he says, on a 'learning curve'. 'I realised what planners sometimes do is tell lies. These were lies. So I said to my colleagues in the [planning] team, "Look, we're doing it wrong, let's stop, and start again." Most of them were sympathetic, but they probably thought, "Well, I'm not going to sacrifice my job." '

Anson, though, thought differently. He began his own covert form of public consultation. 'I'd spend every night in this area, talking to people, the housewives, kids, the market porters.' He began to cross a line. He began not just talking to the residents, but influencing them, telling them, 'You're going to be screwed.' Few residents had visited the exhibition about the plans; but Anson, sifting through its comments book, found two, and wrote to them. One, Jerry Coughlin, replied and, in early December, Anson met him, John Toomey's brothers Terry and Paddy and local resident Sam Driscoll to begin hatching their own plans.[46]

That second letter, though, was returned to sender, and, before Anson could retrieve it, was propelled to his bosses. Anson wasn't sacked, but he was removed from the Covent Garden team. He'd broken an unwritten rule: he'd talked to the people whose lives he was planning. Anson's boss Geoffrey Holland was also uneasy about their plans, but felt duty-bound to maintain the planner's traditional 'objectivity', mediating between private and public sector. 'We were working for the council,' Holland says, detached to this day. 'Who were we to challenge the elected members? We were just hired to do the job.'

Anson, though, continued to act like a double agent. By day, although off the Covent Garden team, he tried to get intelligence on the latest plans; by night he passed it on to local residents. In March 1971, Anson received a phone call from a man called Jim Monahan: 'Jim said, "Is your phone tapped?" ' remembers Anson. 'I said, "I don't know." I'm not naturally a melodramatic person. He said, "We've got to meet. We've got to go public." And so we did.'

Anson and Monahan were strange bedfellows. Anson was a working-class Liverpudlian in his early thirties, a Marxist, whose account of the time, *I'll Fight You For It!: Behind the Struggle for Covent Garden*, is soaked in the romance of working-class struggle and 'folk heroes' like John Toomey. Anson equated Covent Garden's struggle with the kind of class wars happening all over the world, with Cuba, say, or the Republican cause in Northern Ireland. To him, he wrote, 'the Cockneys of London and the working class in the North face the same issue – the defence of their traditional culture, a culture anti-pathetic to that of the middle-class invaders now taking over Covent Garden and the centres of all our cities'.[47] Monahan, though, was a middle-class socialist in his early twenties studying at the nearby private Architectural Association School of Architecture. As any historian of that time's left-wing politics will tell you, though, being on the same side of the political spectrum did not equal consensus. When I met both, forty years later, neither wanted sight of the other. Monahan, acknowledging Anson's 'bravery', believes he was fundamentally wrong: 'As far as Brian was concerned, everything was black and white, working class against established class.'

At first, though, they pulled together, united by one belief: Covent Garden's urban renewal was wrong. With Anson's fiery rebellion, and Monahan's gift for publicity stunts, they set a date for the first meeting for all those opposed to the plans: 1 April 1971 at Kingsway Hall, headquarters of the Methodist Church. 'They said, "Will you speak on behalf of the residents?"' recalls John Toomey. 'I thought it was in one of the *rooms* in the Kingsway Hall, but it was in the *main hall*! There were six or seven hundred people there. I got up and spoke and the place erupted, because I was just an ordinary working-class bloke. They said I spoke from the heart or something. But I just got up and said what I thought.'

That night, the Covent Garden Community Association was formed. It usually met in a dark basement on Neal Street. 'We didn't have any money,' says Anson. 'The cellar had no heat; it didn't even have a staircase. And there we were, candlelight all around us, plotting revolt against the biggest local authority in Europe.'

'It was so exciting,' Monahan remembers. 'There was a coalition, an amazing variety of people from businesses to students like me to theatrical people.' Within this coalition sat him and Anson, advisors to the committee; Canon Austen Williams, of St Martin-in-the-Fields

Church; prominent Methodist minister Donald Soper; John Wood, owner of the famous Rules restaurant; Fred Collins, who ran his hardware shop at Seven Dials and refused to budge for the developers; David Bieda, a youth worker; Simon Pembroke, a lecturer at nearby London University; Christina Smith, a local businesswoman; and residents like Jerry Coughlin, the Toomeys and the Driscolls. It was, for the moment, that rare thing: a true alliance of people and classes.

They had to move fast. Developers, let loose by Peter Walker's business-minded policies in central government, continued to buy up Covent Garden. Monahan, though, kept pace. 'We'd put posters up saying "This building will be demolished." That came as an extraordinary surprise to the people who were living in it; even the owners sometimes didn't know.' Each road, street and alley in the neighbourhood was assigned a CGCA member to watch over it. The demonstrations began. 'We carried a coffin over Waterloo Bridge,' remembers Toomey. 'That was Covent Garden, and we took it to County Hall, with the roll of a big drum. And we said, "We've brought Covent Garden over, and this is the burial."'

Covent Garden's protestors became renowned for their innovation, energy and media savviness, much of it down to Monahan. He'd learned, he says, from anti-Vietnam War protests and countercultural campus radicalism. Protestors used 'community guerillas' to acquire 'intelligence', as if this were the Cuban revolution. The 'carnival of the streets' of May 1968 was still fresh in the memory, and urban protests similar to Covent Garden's were ongoing in Paris against the demolition of Les Halles, and in Amsterdam against the redevelopment in the Nieumarkt district. And he borrowed tactics from those original rebels against urban renewal: Jane Jacobs and her followers. Jacobs had been arrested for disorderly conduct in 1968, still fighting the Lower Manhattan Expressway.

There were rallies, of course, marches and occupations, but also sketches performed on the streets. Bogeymen, such as London's millionaire developer-architect Richard Seifert, were lampooned in papier-mâché models. Monahan cultivated relationships with journalists in nearby Fleet

Street, heart of Britain's newspaper industry, who were eager for Covent Garden's spectacle. 'We'd invade press conferences,' says Monahan. 'We were young. You believed you could change things. Things mattered.' As the journalist Paul Foot put it in *Private Eye* magazine, 'There is a fire and militancy in Covent Garden not seen . . . for decades.'[48]

Because the Greater London Council needed to compulsorily purchase vast areas of Covent Garden, the grand plan had to be heard in a public inquiry, a quasi-legal hearing in a court. It became the longest in British history. Anson finally crossed the line for good. He resigned from the GLC's planning team and began coaching the Community Association for the inquiry, armed with his intimate knowledge of the enemy's plans. By now Covent Garden was taking up whole pages in national newspapers like *The Times*, with headlines like 'The Revolt in the Cities'. Taking to the court's witness stand were opponents as eminent as poet laureate John Betjeman. But to Monahan, the whole public inquiry was a joke. 'The planning lawyers just wanted to rabbit on tediously about "plot ratio densities"', while 'we were talking about community and messy things and humanity and children; these were anathema, they just didn't fit in.'

Covent Garden continued its slide into dereliction. By the following May, in 1972, a sixth of its buildings were either demolished or derelict. In anticipation of victory at the inquiry, the city council began relocating social housing residents – the Community Association estimated 700 longstanding locals were moved out. Mysterious fires destroyed empty buildings. Developers with anonymous names – Trafalgar House Investments, Amalgamated Investments, Town and City Stock Conversion – continued to build vast office blocks on its intricate streets. Meanwhile, a scandal: the press revealed that the leader of the GLC, Desmond Plummer, had £20,000 invested in development companies behind the proposed rebuilding of Piccadilly Circus, that symbol of London undergoing its own planning battle a few blocks away.[49] All the time, Covent Garden's land values rose higher and higher – to £5 million an acre.

At last, in July 1972, the planning inquiry decided. The city council had won. 'Several witnesses', the planning inspector concluded with a disapproving sniff, 'were clearly disciples of Jane Jacobs: their "bible" her thought-provoking book *The Death and Life of Great American Cities* . . . I am not convinced that her treatise can be so readily applied to London.'[50] In the court of public opinion, though, the jury was still out. Monahan knew his rebels had popular sympathy, so he banged the drum even louder. Covent Garden was no longer the forgotten-about neighbourhood it once was. As Brian Anson wrote, it 'had been *discovered*'.[51] It was in the national press, the international press. A pro-testor doused prime minister Edward Heath in black ink at Brussels Airport, crying, as she did so, 'That's what you're doing to Covent Garden.'[52] At the end of 1972, stars of stage and screen joined Peggy Ashcroft and Laurence Olivier on the street, protesting against the demolition of Covent Garden's theatres.

Anson, though, was becoming uneasy. This wasn't exactly class war. He blamed the celebrities, the media, Monahan's publicity stunts. In his book, *I'll Fight You For It!*, Anson recounts discovering a 'secret' meeting between Monahan and the celebrated Labour politician Anthony Crosland, shadow secretary of state for the environment; by now, Covent Garden had reached the Houses of Parliament. He burst into Monahan's flat: 'Jim and his girlfriend were sitting drinking wine with Crosland and his wife,' he writes. 'To my disappointment John Toomey was also there . . . Jim, livid with rage, leant across the table to grab my hair, hissing his anger. Also incensed, I warned him, "Never do that again." The rift between us two . . . seemed to be complete.'[53]

The following January, though, in 1973, after months of feuding, Anson and Monahan buried the hatchet, and prepared to up the ante. On the evening of 10 January, Anson, Monahan and eighteen of their most trusted lieutenants met at the Opera House Tavern to plot their most audacious act yet, planned for the following Thursday: to break in and occupy the city council's Covent Garden headquarters on King Street. Anson, though, wanted more.[54] This, he believed, was his moment of revolution. He wanted 'an indefinite occupation', one that would at least enable the rebels time to rifle through the city council's records for crucial intelligence.

Five days later, Peter Walker's replacement as secretary of state for the environment, Geoffrey Rippon, held a press conference to announce how plans for Covent Garden would move forward. He made a magnificently political decision. Rippon endorsed the 1968 plan's 'general objectives' and granted the city compulsory purchase powers, but only if there were 'substantial modifications'. First, Rippon called for its road scheme to be rethought. Second, 'more of the existing fabric should be kept, and the scale of new development more closely related to the present character of the area'. He instantly protected around 250 buildings.[55] Finally, Rippon called for 'full public participation'. He said yes to the plans, but also no. Rippon could not oppose tainted city council leader Desmond Plummer, a fellow Conservative; but, with London elections in April, he needed to reflect public opinion.

That very evening, Anson, Monahan and their crack team met in the Opera House Tavern to make final plans for Thursday's assault. They were to assemble at 'precisely 5.25 p.m.', with assigned 'units' to secure different parts of the GLC's building, before jamming the telephones and busying themselves by printing posters and leaflets 'declaring COVENT GARDEN IS AT WAR'.[56] On Thursday, though, just a few minutes before the rendezvous, Anson received a phone call. The police were already inside the building. The occupation was off. That is when 'it all fell apart', remembers John Toomey. 'Someone informed, you know. I'm not going to name names, but there were suspicions.'

That evening, instead of starting his class war, Anson went to the pub. 'I sat drinking pints of Guinness,' he recalled, 'just staring into space.'[57] Revolution would have to wait. His comrades, he says, even folk hero John Toomey, had 'no stomach' for it. Anson recounts confronting Toomey at a community meeting soon after: 'This very room is full of people who will screw each other to get a piece of Covent Garden for themselves,' he cried.[58]

The coalition of rebels had lost its most radical member. Before Brian Anson's eyes, the very thing he was fighting for, that meant so much to him about the old city – Covent Garden's working-class community – was slipping away. New legislation from Edward Heath's business-minded government allowed the uncontrolled conversion of industrial buildings into offices, and removed protection for historic local trades. In Covent Garden, white collar replaced blue collar. New businesses took advantage of government grants for renovating old buildings. They were Ruth Glass's gentrifiers – or, as Anson called them, 'cuckoos in the nest'. Bistros, boutiques and wine bars opened in old warehouses, with studios for advertising agencies or photographers above. Tastes had changed. Dense old Covent Garden, once regarded as worthless, had become fashionable. In the Community Association, working-class residents were being outnumbered, and while their causes, such as keeping rents low, were still high on the agenda, others, such as architectural preservation, rose up the ranks. 'The artists, for instance, didn't want the warehouses to be knocked down,' says Anson, 'because you know, where would they get their great studios? But they didn't give a damn about the [market] porters, or the tramps sleeping on hotel grilles.'

The following April, in 1973, the Conservative Party was routed in London's elections. Covent Garden and the power of private developers had become a political hot potato. A new Labour city council, with a decidedly left-wing agenda, took control. It swiftly published more modest plans for Covent Garden: 'no skyscrapers', 'more rented housing', 'no new roads', no more offices, a bigger conservation area and 'human scale' development. As the oil crisis exploded in autumn 1973, though, the entire western economy was plunged into the most serious recession since the Second World War. The 1968 plan was now simply unaffordable. Who would be driving on its roads when oil prices had risen fivefold? The following autumn the Conservative Party was narrowly beaten in the national elections. Property prices crashed. Living standards plummeted for the first time since the 1940s. Emigration soared.

And yet for now, in the midst of this crisis there was for some a curious kind of freedom. London was for the first time in decades free of grand plans. This was the city in ruins I visited as a boy with my dad, a city of decay, but also experimentation. In the cracks of its inner city subcultures sprouted: punks, feminists, anarchists, gay liberators. Covent Garden's warehouses housed not only modish boutiques, but squats and Warhol-ish galleries, underground presses and punk clubs. On 11 November 1974, surrounded by dereliction, Covent Garden Market sold its last box of apples, and finally closed. 'It was at *this* time', remembers Jim Monahan, 'that the community was most active. Everybody got to know each other. Parties in the street. We changed from just being a protest group. We built a community centre, we built a sports centre, we had a local newspaper, we set up a housing cooperative.' Community gardens were planted on derelict sites; youth clubs were set up; Covent Garden's old buildings were given grants to be restored for community use. And Rippon's ruling that new plans had to be done with 'full public participation' – by now normal in the US, but a landmark change in the UK – was bearing fruit.

By contemporary standards the new plan for Covent Garden agreed in November 1976 by the Labour city council – after its novel bout of public consultation with residents – was remarkably progressive. Top of the agenda were public ownership of facilities, low rents and more family housing. The future 'purpose' of the neighbourhood was to be – astonishingly at a time of mounting deindustrialisation – light industry, plus a few shops (local shops, mind, not fashionable boutiques) and plenty of affordable housing. Preservation not demolition was the default position. There were to be no new roads, and a 'firm restraint' on offices. The community appeared to have won, for a few months at least.

For on 5 May 1977 the Conservative Party swept to victory in the London elections. It immediately approved the new Covent Garden plans, but put at the helm of the committee steering them Alan Greengross, a key figure behind the plans of 1968. Greengross spoke ominously of Covent Garden's 'tremendous untapped wealth', its 'opportunities'; 'the possibilities are immense, very exciting'. He was not talking about punk clubs, or community gardens. As the landlord controlling much of the district, the city council, in these tough economic times, now had to – by law – maximise its income on any available patch of land. If there were to be offices in the neighbourhood, he declared, 'make them as profitable as possible'.[59] 'Let's face it,' Greengross signed off, 'nothing's immutable.' The Conservative GLC was looking for new inspiration in how to run a city. It looked, again, across the Atlantic.

CHAPTER THREE

PEOPLE POWER

'Today successful cities, young or old, attract smart entrepreneurial people, in part, by being urban theme parks.'

Edward Glaeser[1]

The entrepreneurial city

In 1972, American president Richard Nixon declared his country's urban crisis over. He slashed public funding for urban renewal projects; new federal rules required cities to develop comprehensive plans – almost like business plans – to manage growth. Nixon was a little premature. The crisis in American cities was, in fact, in full swing. Indeed, it was joined by many other crises – Watergate, Vietnam, the tottering national economy and that emerging decline in corporate productivity and profits. With less and less in the federal budget, Nixon decided to apply some tough love, with the help of William E. Simon, a new treasury secretary who had recently joined the administration.[2] Simon was a former Wall Street bond trader with a fearsome work ethic and a crusade to bring modern business thinking into the stuttering US economy, just like Edward Heath's 'go for growth' drive, only with rather more chutzpah, and a very different ideology. Simon argued for stringent public sector cuts, and a greater reliance on competition and the free market. He viewed the public sector with disdain, driven by a belief – increasingly popular among a strident new establishment in the US – in the 'monetarist' economic theories of Milton Friedman and Friedrich von Hayek of the Chicago School of Economics, a belief that would be redoubled by the oil crisis. These theories insisted that economies should be administered by controlling the amount of money in the system, not by old-style Keynesian state investment. The private sector should deliver that investment instead through economic growth, with the activities of the state severely restricted to merely stimulating or attracting that private investment. So deep were Simon's cuts in America's public sector in order to 'free' the market, they earned him a nickname: William the Terrible.

It was William the Terrible who would decide the fate of New York, as the city hurtled towards bankruptcy. After a late 1960s office-building boom similar to that in London, New York's mayor, John Lindsay, just like Britain's prime minister Edward Heath, tried to buy his way out of crisis with pay rises and high taxation, cobbled together with short-term loans. By the mid 1970s, though, all this plan had created was a pile of debt – at least $5 billion. William Simon had other plans. At the height of New York's fiscal crisis, the city's new mayor, Abe Beame, turned to Washington to back its bonds. President Gerald Ford was persuaded to take a somewhat hard line. On 29 October 1975, after months of headlines, strikes and chaos in New York, the president went before the National Press Club in Washington and declared the city's 'day of reckoning' had come, pointing the finger at its vast public spending and massive welfare bill. New York was no longer paying its way. Ford promised to veto any bailout. The next day, America's most read newspaper, the *New York Daily News*, printed its infamous front page: 'Ford to City: Drop Dead.'

A month of tense negotiations followed. The city had already had to swallow massive budget cuts to balance the books: a sixth of the city's workforce had been laid off, and unions had had no choice but to accept deep cuts in salaries and working conditions for the rest. Now they would face more. William Simon agreed in late November to back New York to the tune of $2.3 billion a year for the next three years. But the terms were harsh: years of cutbacks. Simon told a Senate hearing, 'I would urge . . . that the financial terms of assistance be made so punitive, the overall experience be made so painful, that no city, no political subdivision would ever be tempted to go down the same road.'[3] 'The city had lived beyond its means for years,' he later wrote. Simon was a Travis Bickle, cleaning up the streets with the toughest of love.

Attitudes towards the decline of the old city had hardened since the oil crisis. Money was tight. Even before, in 1972, architect Oscar Newman's immensely influential book, *Defensible Space*, had called for a response to the violence and decay engulfing cities by employing defensive tactics in design to protect your 'turf'. In 1974, director Michael Winner's infamous film *Death Wish*, hugely successful at the box office, brought its own interpretation of defensible space. Vigilante architect Paul Kersey, played by Charles Bronson, broken by the murder, rapes and moral degeneration of New York, wreaks revenge on the streets with his gun. It is one of a series of films in the 1970s, from *Dirty Harry* to *Taxi Driver*, that depict chaotic, depraved cities being brought to order by the administration of various forms of William Simon's tough love.

For decades, wealth had bled from New York City. Now it needed a transfusion. Money needed to be attracted back to the city, even if, to do so, methods seemingly curious for free-market adherents were employed. As writer William Menking points out,[4] soon after the urban crisis had peaked, a concerted effort began to use state intervention and even public money to lure the middle classes back to New York City. In 1981, for instance, the new mayor Edward Koch began various programmes which, en masse, sought to gentrify the city. 'His ideas about the future of the city', writes Menking, 'seemed to be grounded not in the needs of the current population of the five boroughs, but in his childhood memories of the city before the Second World War, when it had a large, white middle class. Koch wanted these middle-class residents back in the city, and he was not shy about promoting his vision. In 1984 he declared, "We're not catering to the poor anymore . . . there are four other boroughs they can live in. They don't have to live in Manhattan." [5]

To sweeten the pill of such changes, though, softer tactics were also required. The year after its bail-out, New York State hired an advertising agency, Wells Rich Greene, and a hot graphic designer, Milton Glaser – famous for his psychedelic poster of Bob Dylan that accompanied the 1967 *Greatest Hits* album – and set about marketing itself with a now famous logo: I ♥ NY. From now on, cities would have to think differently. They would no longer be able to rely upon public money. They would have to compete for private investment. They would have to be entrepreneurial. They would have to regard themselves as businesses. They would need to sell themselves. Cities would have to fight – and fight one another – to survive.

Sweetening the pill

The geographer David Harvey has long chronicled this change within western cities. As the economy of the world shifted in the 1970s, he wrote, in *The Condition of Postmodernity* (1992): 'The grim history of deindustrialisation and restructuring . . . left most major cities in the advanced capitalist world with few options but to compete with each other, mainly as financial, consumption, and entertainment centres.' [6] To achieve this, he wrote, they relied on 'a public-private partnership focusing on investment and economic development with the speculative construction of place'. By 'the speculative construction of place', what Harvey means is that as the world globalised and the market was 'freed', with factories and workforces moving to wherever conditions were least onerous and most profitable, declining towns and cities – each, remember, with less state money to run them, and, thanks to disappearing populations and businesses, less private money too – embarked on a new kind of urban renewal. This renewal would not only change their image, it would become a way of making money in itself: bold office towers housing newly important financial industries, perhaps, or flamboyant shopping malls and art galleries to encourage consumerism. These buildings not only signalled a change in a place's public relations, they became profitable enterprises in their own right.

As the world shrunk, as globalisation and a new form of capitalist society took hold across the world during the 1970s focused on service economies and the international flows of money required by the free market, places didn't end up all looking the same, as you might expect. The opposite. Towns and cities now *had* to look different from one another. Places had to distinguish themselves; they were competing with one another for investment and employees in the newly 'liberated' market that William Simon and his colleagues were fighting for. They had to stand out from the crowd.

The precise qualities that made a place attractive to investors and their increasingly mobile workforces, that made them stand out, suddenly became far more important: the lifestyle a town could offer employees, for instance, the quality of its schools, the things that could be bought in its shops, the buzz of its nightclubs, the quality of its streets, the look and feel, even, of its architecture. These qualities that made a place a place, of course, were exactly the ones Jane Jacobs had fought for in Greenwich Village two decades earlier: 'liveliness', 'diversity' and 'intensity'. Back then they were just subjective qualities hankered after by Raphael Samuel's minority of 'eccentrics'. They didn't have an economic value then. They did now. Now that Jacobs's message had spread, now that fashions had changed and intensity of the love for the declined city's qualities had been demonstrated in revolts against urban renewal across America and Europe, politicians, businessmen and economists began to take note. Perhaps there was money to be made from the old city – and not by turning it into a suburb. The gentrifiers had arrived.

Indeed, after the economic shock of the oil crisis, people with serious money began to look for alternative, safer investments, to spread the risk – in areas such as property and material objects; 'and so began the vast inflation in certain kinds of asset prices,' writes Harvey: 'collectibles, art objects, antiques, houses, and the like. Buying a Degas or

Van Gogh in 1972 would surely outstrip almost any other kind of investment in terms of capital gain. Indeed it can be argued that the growth of the art market (with its concern for authorial signature) and the strong commercialisation of cultural production since around 1970 have had a lot to do with the search to find alternative means to store value.'[7] The newly fashionable old city would do nicely.

David Harvey focused much of his research on Baltimore, on America's East Coast, where, after riots following Martin Luther King Jr's assassination in 1968, city politicians and businessmen brainstormed novel ways to attract investment and improve the city's image, tarnished like so many industrial cities by urban unrest. It launched a festival, the Baltimore City Fair, celebrating ethnic and neighbourhood diversity, attracting 340,000 people in its first year, 2 million by 1973. By the end of the decade, Harborplace had been completed, a massive waterfront development including a science centre, convention centre, marina and hotels. It was, notes Harvey, different from old-school urban renewal. It was fun: 'an architecture of spectacle', he writes, 'with its sense of surface glitter and transitory participatory pleasure'.[8] Baltimore, though, was far from alone.

In 1972, for instance, on the other side of the continent, Portland, Oregon elected its first Democrat mayor in forty-two years, with the largest majority in the city's postwar history – the 32-year-old Neil Goldschmidt, a hip civil-rights lawyer who promised a very different kind of urban renewal. Portland's Downtown Plan was created with advisors such as Jane Jacobs and Kevin Lynch, and realised in three dimensions the kind of beauty and delight, memory, meaning and sensuous enjoyment that Lynch had called for in *The Image of the City*, and the 'liveliness', 'diversity' and 'intensity' so dear to Jacobs. Widened sidewalks were dotted with public art, and lined with restored historic monuments and humanely scaled new architecture. By the end of the decade a new City Hall, designed by the then modish 'postmodern' architect Michael Graves, came in the symbolic form – literally – of a gift-wrapped present to the city. Four years later, Portland won first place in Quality of Life Indicators in 'US Metropolitan Areas: A

Comprehensive Assessment', one of a new breed of 'liveability' leagues that America's entrepreneurial cities now used to measure their appeal and competitiveness. Portland had become 'a new kind of city', said *The New Yorker*,[9] 'the Lazarus of American cities', wrote *Architecture* magazine.[10] Its population 'more than doubled' from 1940 to the early 1980s.[11] New arrivals came to work in its booming service sector, for firms like sportswear brand Nike. It was a younger population: 15–34-year-olds rose from 22 per cent of the population to 33 per cent. They were gentrifiers.

It was back on the East Coast, though, that the most influential example of this new, more appealing kind of urban renewal was created. In 1968, Benjamin Thompson – head of architecture at the prestigious Harvard Graduate School of Design – delivered a lecture, 'Visual Squalor and Social Disorder: A New Vision of a City of Man'.[12] Thompson, like many, was horrified by the unrest and decay in American cities. He had his own theory, he told his audience, about 'this chaos we see around us like a rising plague'. The cause? 'The disintegrating quality of modern environment.'[13] Echoing Jane Jacobs, Thompson saw urban renewal, with its 'treeless streets' and 'impersonal buildings'[14] as the problem. An aggressive, impersonal environment had produced an aggressive, impersonal society. Like Jacobs, Thompson used science to support his subjective opinions, in his case recent ideas in psychology. 'Sensory monotony', he proposed, 'inhibits the workings of the higher brain . . . Chaos (too many disorganised sensations) shuts down the brain system to preserve its equilibrium . . . Sensory variety', on the other hand, ' . . . is a biological need as real as hunger.' Improving the urban landscape wasn't just about aesthetics or 'taste'. There was, he contended, a biological impulse behind that demand in people for the qualities that Jane Jacobs had identified almost a decade ago; people were attached to the old city, said Thompson, because their bodies compelled them.

Thompson had his own solution for the urban crisis: build 'the city the "rioters" are subliminally crying out for', with a stimulating environment and 'positive values' transformed into 'felt experience'.[15]

Beauty could stop the streets from burning. His inspirations, he said, included Venice and Paris, with their 'visual nourishment', but also Copenhagen, whose Tivoli Gardens had 'amusement areas, theatre, puppets and refreshments for every purse . . . for if a city is not *just* a park, it could *work* like a park'. A city as a theme park. He called for 'an intimate city by day and a radiant city by night', full of 'exciting vistas' and 'recreational enjoyment . . . The city then is no longer a prison from which to flee,' he concluded, 'but a prism aglow with a million different lives . . . What is necessary is merely a working model.'[16]

He soon had one. For Thompson was not just an idealist; he was an entrepreneur. In 1953 – an early gentrifier just like Jane Jacobs – he had opened a shop, Design Research or D/R, in a renovated, weather-boarded townhouse in Cambridge, Massachusetts.[17] Thompson's shop both educated Americans in good design, through exhibitions and events, and sold it to them. He wasn't alone in this, but his retail strategy was quite distinct. He had no background in shops, relying instead on an architect's instinct for what made *experience* a *pleasure*. The shop to him was a stage set. 'I felt D/R should be a natural-feeling place,' he said, ' . . . the kind . . . they might imagine themselves living in. The thought was, "Let's make a house that is a store but feels like a living place." '[18] He favoured for his shops bustling, urban locations in the city, so that the intensity of the street would flow inside to his design 'bazaar'. With his notorious, impromptu 'walk-throughs', Thompson kept a sharp eye on the customer's experience. His shops were designed to feel like homes, with tricks such as wafting the smell of fresh coffee through the stores. Nowadays we'd say Thompson was selling a 'lifestyle', but in the 1950s this was novel stuff. It worked. D/R soon became a destination store for design-savvy consumers. By 1965, Thompson had opened two more shops in New York, garnering annual profits of $2.2 million.

It was his fourth store opening later that year, though, that would be the breakthrough. Thompson chose San Francisco – an obvious spot, with its liberal population, gentrifiers and booming service economy (with the embryonic 'Silicon Valley' close by). But it was the site he chose *in* the city that was so influential. Ghirardelli Square had

opened the year before as that rare thing in the 1960s, a shopping
centre not in the suburbs and, rarer still, not in some sparkling modern
mall, but in an old factory.

When family chocolate manufacturer Ghirardelli's was bought out
by a conglomerate in 1962, production moved, inevitably, to the suburbs. However, city businessman William Roth and his mother
Lurline, a shipping heiress, had fond memories of the old factory.
They were more of Raphael Samuel's 'eccentrics' – sentimental, like
so many, about the fading old city; but these eccentrics had a lot of
money. To stop Ghirardelli's being replaced with condominiums, the
Roths bought the entire site. At the time, wealthy people like them
did not characteristically regard derelict factories as worthy investments, especially because of their architectural quality. The vogue for
the 'industrial style' had not yet arrived. In 1962, few other than Andy
Warhol and the avant-garde saw industrial buildings as desirable places
to inhabit, rather than unsightly, unhealthy blots to be shifted as far
out of town as possible. Ghirardelli's was, however, at the picturesque
end of industrial, with nineteenth-century neo-gothic architecture
and a dinky clock tower – more Willy Wonka than smelting plant.

To convert their factory, the Roths brought in architects Wurster,
Bernardi & Emmons and landscape architect Lawrence Halprin, who,
fresh from landscaping the 1962 Seattle World's Fair, was making a
name with public space projects designed around how people experienced and moved through space, influenced by his wife, Anna
Halprin, an avant-garde dancer. Halprin had become fascinated with
the theatrical potential of urban space. At Ghirardelli Square, Halprin
restored the old buildings and in between choreographed a kind of
'urban park', with open spaces and picturesque nooks to encourage
exploration and the kind of intimacy lacking in the kind of vast, 'modernist' plazas most cities undergoing urban renewal were building at
the time. A series of theatrical 'scenes' were dotted across the terraces
that Halprin tumbled down the steep site, housing cafés, restaurants
and what were then called 'speciality stores', not big retailers but small
independent shops appealling to its target clientele, local gentrifiers in

Pacific Heights and Nob Hill. It was, thought many, very 'European'-feeling. Key to Ghirardelli's appeal was that visitors should have a pleasurable experience. A world away from the monolithic malls of the suburbs, it was like the rest of the old city that lay beyond its walls, only more beautiful, more controlled and choreographed, without any hint of decay or threat. It was like the real city, only art directed.

Benjamin Thompson recognised like minds at Ghirardelli Square. This was exactly the kind of city he was searching for. A city as a theme park. Thompson converted the lower floor of the factory's clock tower into his latest store, restoring its original oak flooring and knocking down walls to create open-plan rooms. It was like those artists' lofts in SoHo, only slicker, for rather less bohemian and more bourgeois visitors. Unlike his other stores set in houses, one housed in a former factory would obviously lack homeliness. Instead, Thompson would conjure up the energetic feel of a marketplace. Markets were, in design terms, innately full of 'liveliness', 'diversity' and 'intensity' of experience, especially when their less picturesque elements – dirt, mouldy potatoes or chaotic crowds – had been designed out.

Back home on the East Coast, however, Thompson had grander plans. In 1966, he launched his own architecture firm, with eyes focused on a site in downtown Boston. Faneuil Hall, a collection of old, Greek-revival market buildings, was, like Covent Garden, facing redundancy, after a new market had opened out of town. A few years ago, city planners might have suggested building the kind of landscape that had already risen around it: on one side a waterfront freeway, on the other, the concrete City Hall. Typical urban renewal. Times, though, had changed. By 1966, Jane Jacobs's opinions were mainstream in more liberal cities like Boston, if not, yet, in Oklahoma or across the Atlantic; with an eye to this shift in public opinion, Boston's city administration had already begun restoring old waterfront piers on the other side of the freeway, as leisure attractions, rather than demolishing them as they might have done a few years ago. Maybe something similar might keep Faneuil Hall alive, too.

Thompson thought so. He adored the historic market's elegant old buildings, lovingly photographing their little details, such as the old traders' hand-painted signs, or the way sunlight fell on its cobbles. They provided that 'visual nourishment' he thought was lacking in the modern city. His love was shared by two local architectural preservationists – Frederick A. Stahl, trustee of the Society for the Preservation of New England Antiquities, and Roger Webb, founding head of Architectural Heritage, Inc., a new firm 'combining a preservationist's vision with a businessman's sensibility', its website proclaims to this day – who that year had managed to persuade the Boston Redevelopment Authority, the city's urban renewal agency, to fund both a report into the condition of Faneuil Hall, and a $2 million grant for its restoration.[19] All well and good. But what would be *inside* the buildings? Thompson worked up his own plans: to replicate Ghiradelli Square on a grander scale. That marketplace vision had worked wonders in his store. Could you repeat it writ large?

Few private investors in the late 1960s, though, were spending money on something as crazy as a leisure destination in the declining downtown, certainly not one in decrepit old buildings, however beautiful, and certainly not on this scale. The city tried to tempt property developers to become partners; they, in turn, tried to tempt financial institutions to invest; but to no avail. No wonder. The business plan didn't make sense. The cost of renovating Faneuil Hall's historic buildings was always going to be greater than demolishing and starting anew, so why keep them? Why not build a brand-new downtown mall on top, business as usual?

One developer, though, bit. James W. Rouse had no pedigree in investing in old cities. Quite the reverse. He was one of the many developers who'd got rich on their decline, with twenty-six suburban shopping malls to his name, an entire suburban new town, Columbia, and form advising the American government on urban renewal and suburban expansion. He was no Jane Jacobs. Like any developer, he was simply interested in what would make him money. But he shared Thompson's interest in the importance of customer experience. Suburban malls usually pushed convenience as their big draw – how easy they were to drive to, say. James Rouse, though, promoted *his* malls through their convenience *and* the stimulating experience inside. Shopping, he said, should be 'enjoyable', even 'entertaining', a leisure activity, not just a chore.

Understandably he had his reservations about Faneuil Hall. Rouse, though, was nothing if not astute. He had, he said, a 'belief' that there were 'great opportunities in the downtown centres of cities'.[20] He just needed a big enough site, not 'tiny little islands in the midst of jungles', like Ghirardelli Square. Faneuil Hall might be just the place for his own little experiment. Sure, it would be an expensive venture. But, said Rouse, Boston 'is a city that is still strong in its heart'. Like Baltimore, Boston had already embarked on a waterfront revitalisation strategy. 'But', said Rouse, 'downtown needed a revitalised core to be . . . the final burst of energy to make everything really wake up.' Returns could be good. There were, after all, 20,000 people living within walking distance of Faneuil Hall, 20,000 people with money: gentrifiers. Not driving distance, note, but walking distance. Gentrifiers preferred to walk, so as to better experience that buzz of the city so precious to them. Beacon Hill, with its tree-shaded streets wall-to-wall with eighteenth- and nineteenth-century townhouses, was already gentrifying; North End, a historic blue-collar neighbourhood, South End and Bay Village were hot on its heels. Rouse sniffed a business opportunity.

By the early 1970s, a decade after Ruth Glass had casually noticed the phenomenon in London, gentrification was in full swing in North American cities. It took another decade, though, before its character was studied. David Ley, a Welsh-born geography professor, began observing gentrifiers in 1970s Vancouver, to analyse, he said, 'when hippies become yuppies'. He called them a 'new middle class', one which had grown up in the 1960s immersed in that decade's individualism and sensitivity to the nuances of constructing personal identity.[21] That was exactly what the new middle class was doing by living in the old city, said Ley, displaying 'a mark of distinction in the constitution of an identity', marking their territory and distinguishing their tribe from the traditional – square – middle classes of the suburbs. And, as sociologist René König wrote in 1973, the very thing that distinguishes the bourgeois 'is distinction itself',[22] those little details setting you apart from others, such as finding value in tatty old downtown, a value that suburbanites just couldn't see.

Artists had demonstrated *their* freedom from convention a decade ago by moving into old downtown warehouses and industrial buildings, bringing a new version of domesticity to once non-domestic spaces, and distinguishing themselves from mainstream society by doing so. Now this new tribe, gentrifiers, wanted to live their version of that emancipatory life, to distinguish themselves from their parents' generation. The old declining city, for them, was a landscape of freedom, far from the supposedly conformist suburbs, where they could express their changed tastes and value systems. In San Francisco, for instance, Manuel Castells studied gay culture in the Castro, where one kind of emancipation was playing out, the creation of a space apart for sexual liberation, perfectly chronicled by Armistead Maupin's 1978 novel *Tales of the City*. Studying 1970s Toronto, Jon Caulfield described how emancipatory its gentrifiers found living in the inner city: 'Old city places offer difference and freedom,' he wrote, 'privacy and fantasy, possibilities for carnival.'[23] As another academic, Brian J. L. Berry, put it in 1985, 'These persons favour lifestyles associated with aesthetics, the excitement of central-city living.'[24] The dying city was their playground.

This new middle class, though, shared two attributes with the old middle class it shunned: money and social insecurity. Many had increasingly comfortable incomes working in what sociologist Daniel Bell in 1973 had christened the 'Post-Industrial Society', in services, information, data, finance, culture; they were also as keen as every other middle-class tribe in history to bolster their collective identity by broadcasting their superiority. In 1899, Thorstein Veblen's influential *The Theory of the Leisure Class: An Economic Study in the Evolution of Institutions* proposed 'conspicuous consumption' as a key bourgeois behaviour – the buying and displaying of things non-essential to life to demonstrate wealth, and the freedom bought by it. Seventy years later, this new splinter group of gentrifiers behaved exactly the same. Uncertain of its place now that it had detached itself from the suburbs, it wanted to put down roots, to mark its territory. And nothing did the job better of simultaneously rooting you, distinguishing you, emancipating you, investing your money in something safe, but risky enough to stimulate dinner-party conversation – *and* displaying it for all the world to see – than buying a shabby little warehouse or town-house downtown, and getting the builders in.

With this new generation on its doorstep, then, Faneuil Hall had a business plan, albeit a risky one, but enough for James Rouse and Benjamin Thompson to secure a symbolic, if modest, $10 million investment from the city, state and federal governments. Restoration work began in 1972, repairing the buildings' architectural set pieces, such as the huge dome in Quincy Market, and those subtle period details so attractive to Thompson. New canopies were added along the sides of the buildings, to shelter the diners and coffee drinkers Rouse and Thompson hoped to tempt down from Beacon Hill. Even as the buildings threw off their shabby appearance, though, it took two more years to convince private investors to pitch in; Rouse had to rifle through his little black book, twisting the arm of ten Boston financial institutions and old business partners like Chase Manhattan Bank who'd once backed his malls in the suburbs. After all, Rouse did have excellent form.[25] Maybe this crazy plan had legs. Suddenly, with petrol prices soaring after the oil crisis, a shopping mall you could walk to didn't seem quite so stupid.

Work could begin. Rouse and Thompson's design restored the his-toric buildings, the old market's signs, stone floors and cobblestones – all those characterful details – and filled them with neither big-brand shops nor the 'anchor stores' of conventional malls, but independent speciality stores like Crate & Barrel, gift shops, craft boutiques and small cafés – a lively, diverse mix replicating the higgledy-piggledy intensity of the old market, with the drama ramped up and the dirt removed. The *experience* of shopping was to be as big a draw, if not bigger, than the shops themselves; shopping would be as pleasurable a leisure activity as eating in Faneuil Hall's restaurants, drinking coffee in its cafés, admiring its architecture. You would consume them all. One innovation was re-using the old market's carts to house small retailers or craftspeople. 'We hired a bright young woman', Rouse told the press, 'who went out all over New England identifying artists and craftsmen and small entrepreneurs with narrow specialities'.[26] It was about creating the right atmosphere, sending out the right signals, to attract those gentrifiers up the hill. They didn't shop in malls. They didn't live in the suburbs. They wanted something different for their urban playground, something unique.

What Faneuil Hall offered at the time *was* unique. It monetised the urban qualities community activists like Jane Jacobs had been fighting for for years. It sought to realise in three dimensions Thompson's vision of a city of pleasure and enjoyment, not decay and riot. But its business plan was incredibly risky. The cost of re-using an old building was high. There were no major 'anchors', reliable names like Sears or Macy's, that guaranteed visitors. Quite the reverse. This shopping mall's USP was that it had *no* chains, that it was unlike other, squarer shopping malls. Its picturesque small retailers had unreliable credit histories, and a tendency to go bust. The entire development was built on risky foundations.

Rouse and Thompson's gamble, though, paid off. Faneuil Hall was an instant and immense success. By the summer of 1977, a year after it had opened, it had attracted more than 12 million visitors. Eyewitness reports breathlessly describe its 'thronging' crowds, 'beset' by 'temptations'; 'the area continues to overflow with human vitality'. There's one fascinating article on Faneuil Hall at the time in the American magazine *Architectural Record*[27] – 'The Case for Design Quality in Today's Marketplace: Four Studies of Collaboration Between Architects and Developers that Explore the Arithmetic of Excellence.' 'The arithmetic of excellence' is an interesting phrase. The article doesn't quite come up with a financial equation behind Faneuil Hall's novel design – a delicate balance, perhaps, between the financial risk to developers, the amount gentrifiers will pay for 'liveliness', 'diversity' and 'intensity' in their city, precisely how far they will walk to find these qualities, how much 'edginess' in the inner city they will tolerate – but it's not far off. By 1978, Rouse and Thompson's gamble had a retail turn-over of $54 million.[28] This was the newly freed free market in action, in, of all places, a market.

Market forces

Across the Atlantic, the free market was about to be unleashed. After the 1973 oil crisis, Edward Heath's big dreams of renewing the UK through massive infrastructural projects had given way to smaller, more pragmatic policies. After the International Monetary Fund bailed the country out of defaulting on its debts in 1976 – negotiated, interestingly, by William Simon – it insisted on what were for the time savage cuts in public spending, with road building and new social housing taking some of the biggest hits. The Labour government that succeeded Heath's had already begun to dabble in a new kind of pol-itics and economics, stimulating the economy with income tax cuts, rather than Keynesian public spending, and, crucially for Covent Gar-den, removing controls on office buildings in inner cities, to encourage a white-collar recovery by attracting small businesses. Enterprise might regenerate the emptying hearts of towns and cities, now that the state no longer felt able to.

While vast amounts of urban land were still owned by the state, and some left-wing local boroughs experimented with new ways of building – innovative cooperative or self-build housing, say – other public institutions, such as British Rail, were now required to act like private companies, improving the state's bank balance by selling off their assets. The Port of London Authority, for instance, one of the biggest landowners in London, began selling redundant property in the emptying Docklands to wily developers who, in turn, took their own punt on which way the wind was blowing. For it was beginning to blow in a very different direction.

It began to work. In the second half of the 1970s, before the famous 'winter of discontent' in 1978–9, industrial action, inflation and unemployment were all falling, and disposable income rising. House prices doubled. In 1977, the gap between the rich and the poor was smaller than it had ever been, and ever would be again. The working day had shortened, and there were more paid holidays than ever before. Was the leisure society that many had predicted since the 1960s finally arriving? The Conservative opposition party didn't think so. It was pushing for something more radical. Its leader, Margaret Thatcher, had become interested in the new pro-market economics being pressed on America and its cities by William Simon and all those in thrall to the theories of Milton Friedman and the Chicago School. Thatcher was still a way off convincing her own party, let alone the whole country, to follow this new political and economic path. Like Benjamin Thompson's vision for the future of cities, what was needed was a working model. She found it in London.

Horace Cutler, a flamboyant Thatcherite, had swept to power in the city council in 1977. Cutler was a property developer, with, his 1997 obituary noted, 'an eye for derelict property with a development potential'.[29] As soon as it arrived at County Hall, Cutler's administration began on a path that is familiar to us today, but in the late 1970s was novel indeed: assets were privatised or sold off; tenders for contracts were put out to the private sector; council houses were sold off to their occupants at cut-price rates. With hindsight, London's governance in the late 1970s appears to have been a trial run for the country as a whole.

But what of Covent Garden? The Thatcherite spirit was coursing through its streets too. After all, the man running the Greater London Council's committee for its new neighbourhood plan, Alan Greengross, was keen to make the district work hard for its resurrection. It had to earn its place in the newly entrepreneurial, free-market capital city, by maximising profit for its owners so they, rather than the public purse, could maintain its expensive historic streets. Nonetheless, Greengross had to work within the limits of the progressive 1976 plan passed by his Labour predecessor, one which proposed for the area low-rent family housing, the protection of the existing population, a 'firm restraint' on the creation of offices and the preservation of the historic fabric – things expensive to the public purse, and anathema to Friedman-esque economics. As Greengross had said, nothing was immutable, but neither could the city risk another decade of controversy in Covent Garden, controversy that might jeopardise its revival by putting off potential private investors; particularly when there were, as Greengross noted, such 'opportunities' in the neighbourhood.

No, the city council would have to tread carefully. In the new spirit of monetarist economics, it would have to dispense public funds judiciously – paying for the restoration of old buildings perhaps, but only to house a viable future use – in the hope that they would attract the right sort of private investment. Environment minister Geoffrey Rippon's 1973 ruling that Covent Garden's redevelopment must have proper public participation was crucial. As Rippon had astutely observed, public opinion had changed, the more so after the oil crisis. Big plans, certainly ones that *looked* like big plans, were neither popular nor affordable. However, this public participation was a certain kind of people power, for certain people. For as the economic value of once-hidden, once-decrepit spaces like Covent Garden rose, alongside rents and property prices, what Ruth Glass had predicted a decade earlier had came into play: 'Once this process of "gentrification" starts in a district, it goes on rapidly until all or most of the original working-class occupiers are displaced, and the whole social character of the district is changed.'[30] The face of Covent Garden was now preserved in law. But under the skin, new blood was running through its veins.

The gentrifiers who had moved into the area, to the disdain of Brian Anson, were now demonstrating that 'liveliness', 'diversity' and 'intensity' paid. These qualities of place were also, of course, those that Jim Monahan, Brian Anson and John Toomey had fought for, if for different reasons. Only, unlike the gentrifiers, they had no money to invest, just time and energy. They did not own land. They might have valued it, but they were powerless to do anything with it. Covent Garden was ruled now not just by big property developers, but little ones: gentrifiers. They did have money to invest; not, at this stage, a lot of money, but enough, with that little grant from the government, to renovate an old warehouse and open an attractive boutique. Like the cities in which they invested, these gentrifiers were entrepreneurs now. Tastes had changed. The old city was no longer ruinous and old-hat. It was edgy. It was hip. And people were willing to pay to live, work, shop and party in it. Horace Cutler, with his developer's eye for derelict property, was the right man at the right time to make the most of – and from – Covent Garden.

Such attitudes were already paying dividends in other parts of London, such as St Katherine's Dock, beside the Tower of London, where architect-developer Peter Drew had found a new use for Thomas Telford's 1828 dock. The land was leased by the city council to the Taylor Woodrow construction group for 125 years, for a modest £1.5 million, less than it had cost Telford to build it.[31] Why so little? The bother of restoring and maintaining the old buildings and infrastructure was removed from the public purse; the risk in making the redevelopment a success was the developer's. Win-win. So went the new thinking. The developers' recipe for success was clearly modelled on waterfront revivals in American cities like Baltimore, with its combination of leisure attractions for the masses and investment opportunities for the rich. Its old warehouses were restored as fashionable apartments for sale or on short lets as crash pads for City businessmen; another became the Dickens Inn, cashing in on the contemporary fashion for costume dramas and heritage attractions; the dock itself housed both promenades for the hoi polloi, and exclusive moorings for yachts.

Covent Garden, though, needed quite some work. Its central market building, once the heartbeat of the neighbourhood, was a ghost, boarded up since 1974. Plans for it had been left vague. The 1968 designs had envisioned it with restaurants, pubs, exhibitions, shops, studios, art galleries and 'speciality shops'. For a time flats were planned for its upper floors, but they proved too hard to squeeze in. A report published in November 1977 sheds some light. The building, it said, 'had to establish itself in the public imagination as somewhere of a quite distinct nature'.[32] Distinct. It had to capitalise on the qualities of place that made Covent Garden Covent Garden. The next year, a marketing firm, Donaldsons, was employed to focus minds. It would be a difficult building to transform, with tiny internal spaces – built to store fruit and vegetables in a time of carts and horses – and the historic fabric to respect – now legally protected, and vital to the USP of the development. Not, it seems, that they needed to have worried: 800 businesses applied to move into thirty-seven spaces. Indeed, the challenge was less would anyone want to move in, more would the right *kind* of businesses move in?

Covent Garden Market opened to the public on 19 June 1980, a year after Margaret Thatcher had arrived in Downing Street as Britain's new Prime Minister. The result? Well, if imitation is the sincerest form of flattery, Benjamin Thompson and James Rouse should have blushed. Even Thompson's idea of re-using old market carts as business units for small entrepreneurs was copied; 'a slightly more casual trade such as this', wrote architectural historian Robert Thorne, 'helps preserve, in polite guise, some of the animation which used to fill the place'.[33] A series of 'speciality stores' appealed to the area's gentrifiers: Hammick's Bookshop, Thorntons chocolates, the fashionable new Covent Garden General Store, the Punch and Judy tavern, The Body Shop, health food shops, Culpeper's. Copying the tactic of revived American cities, street performers were encouraged, providing ambience and 'liveliness', for free. And, novel for a time when Sunday trading was prohibited and shops still closed early on Wednesdays, the building opened late into the evening.

Thompson and Rouse's 'festival marketplace' had arrived in Britain, and didn't we love it? Four million people visited in the first year. So crowded were Covent Garden's streets again – with shoppers these days, not demonstrators or market porters – one reviewer found his 'way barred by a film team focused on [British TV personality] Angela Rippon'. The building, too, he concluded, had become 'a celebrity'.[34]

It was, said another commentator, 'so American'. Across the Atlantic, *The New Yorker* also recognised one of its own: 'It's Faneuil Hall Marketplace without the fast food.'[35] The first American-style suburban shopping mall in Britain, Brent Cross, had only opened four years earlier. Now the country had fast-forwarded to the latest model: Rouse and Thompson's vision of the city of pleasure.

Not everyone, though, liked the new Covent Garden. 'I hate being back here,' growled Brian Anson when I met him almost thirty years later. 'I don't see any tramps getting warm on the gratings, because tramps as far as I know aren't allowed in Covent Garden any more. I don't hear people saying "love", like the market porters might. I see the shell, but I don't see the love any more.' Brian Anson's revolution never happened. A different revolution, though, did.

Jim Monahan, too, is resigned to the Covent Garden that has risen up around him. There is only so much you can fight against, and an entire shift in western political economies was, perhaps, rather too big a foe for the Covent Garden Community Association to vanquish. What happened in Covent Garden was the canary in the coal mine, an augur of the changes that would sweep across London and cities around the world over the next forty years: the coming of the city of spectacle, a gentrified city built on the values fought for by him, Anson, Jane Jacobs and countless other 'eccentric minorities', but one in which not everyone would profit, or profit equally. A shift in power had taken place.

It was a battle of values, and he, like Anson and so many others, lost. Monahan is magnanimous in defeat. He has to hand it to the victors. They played the long game. 'The developers learned very quickly that they could still make a huge buck out of Covent Garden, just in a different way.' Monahan knows what went wrong: 'We never got our hands on the land.' For a moment, he almost agrees with his old friend and foe, Brian Anson. They lost control of the land beneath their feet. Maybe the old Marxist was right all along. If only they'd gone ahead and occupied that building; if only someone hadn't informed the police; who knows what might have happened?

John Toomey, though, is quiet and tearful, not angry or resigned. 'I come down here two or three times a week, and I have a couple of hours with my brother, and a cup of tea. And do you know, to me Covent Garden's empty. I don't see a soul I know, anyone I lived next door to, or went to school with. We saved all the lovely buildings. But it wasn't only buildings, it was people, and I think they got forgotten. People wanted to come here and make money out of Covent Garden. They used to say to us, "Do you know how much the price of land is you're walking on?" I said, "Do you know I've walked on that all my life? That land belongs to me, and I'm not a Marxist. My mother and father walked on that land. My grandparents, my great-grandparents." But they couldn't see your point of view. I couldn't see their point of view. And do you know, I walk along and I touch the sides of the buildings. I think, "This was mine one time," but it don't belong to me now. It don't belong to ordinary people now. It belongs to financiers in Zurich and New York, places like that.'

Six years after the revived market opened, London's city council – by that time back in Labour hands under the then flamboyantly radical 'Red' Ken Livingstone – was abolished by Margaret Thatcher. Its assets were sold off, or passed to quangos, or leased – including those in Covent Garden. Nowadays Covent Garden Market is leased to CapCo, a huge pension fund. 'As well as a dedicated property team,' its website toots, 'there is also a high-profile branding and marketing team focusing on fashion, culture and the arts.' In the past few years CapCo has been trying to increase further the revenue of the land, by attracting bigger international brands to the development and capitalising on its distinct urban character. The neighbourhood has not just been gentrified; it has been supergentrified. It has succeeded. Dior, the Apple Store and Chanel have all moved in. Making money from the city of spectacle is, these days, a serious business.

CHAPTER FOUR

SELLING THE CITY

'The inventiveness of so many new American buildings, the lines, the details, the materials, the shapes, the general structure, fascinate me.'

Margaret Thatcher[1]

What sells?

I'm standing on floor 42 of Tower 42. I still can't get used to the name. Until relatively recently, it was the National Westminster Tower, named after the British high-street bank (and famously designed with its logo running through the floorplan, like a stick of rock). The tower was the tallest building in western Europe in the 1980s, 183 metres high, until a new breed of skyscraper erupted around it. But this old-timer still gives you a good view. Britain's financial heart, the City, is laid out before me and I'm up here with the man who sells it.

Bradley Baker is head of central London tenant representation at top UK estate agents Knight Frank – a.k.a. the man who sells the city, and the City. He sells the land beneath our feet, and everything above it. He sold, across the street, the Gherkin skyscraper for its landlord, insurers Swiss Re. He did the deal for Rothschild's bank HQ down the road, and the Bank of Tokyo round the corner. He sells land like a haberdasher sells fabric, by the metre, the square metre, and he sells it in one of the most competitive, dog-eat-dog square miles on the planet. Bradley Baker is the king of estate agents. If anyone knows how to sell a square metre of space, this is the man.

So, Bradley, what sells? 'It starts with the basics: location – there's no point having a fantastic-looking office building in the middle of Timbuktu. Transportation nodes are important. Once you have those two, occupiers are looking for usable space, efficiency, natural light.' And, of course, 'it depends which tenant you're talking about. Swiss Re were keen to have something strong and quite – not flamboyant – but iconic. Whereas some of the north American banks are happier to have a more confident, less shouty type of image. So they're more restrained in their appearance.'

You have to remember, he says, that for developers, buildings aren't just buildings, solid things occupied by actual people. 'Investors are really buying an income stream from that building. So if a finance company is taking a twenty-year lease, what the investor's really buying is that income stream over that twenty-year period.' Property developers are, after all, a business with shareholders to please. They need to get their return, even if, in this line of work, it's a slow return over a couple of decades, not the flash-in-the-pan profit that stock-market traders *inside* these buildings survive on.

They've been at this game for a long, long time, since at least the first half of the seventeenth century, when King Charles I began loosening the reins of royal power over land, in contrast to his autocratic opposite number across the Channel in France. The speculative developer was a product of these early days of flexible international capitalism, in London, Antwerp and Amsterdam, in places where autocracy was being nibbled away by the rising middle classes and their clever ways of making money, by such tricks as repackaging and rebuilding on the same square metre of land over and over and over again.

For centuries afterwards, though, most land in Britain, and in London in particular, was owned by aristocratic estates such as the Duke of Westminster's Grosvenor, or the Church of England – landowners who treated their land, if not always their tenants, with patrician care, 'stewarding' it over centuries, a run far longer than the twenty-year return today's investors demand. A new breed of less gentlemanly,

more rapacious, commercially minded developer, such as Land Securities and British Land, emerged in the 1950s, when the Conservative
national government first began to stimulate the property market.
These developers could help the state, for a cut, to build the huge
postwar programme of schools, hospitals, social housing and, increasingly, offices and shopping precincts. Until relatively recently, though,
property development was mostly a home-grown affair. Not any
more.

'Since 2008 and the financial downturn,' explains Bradley Baker,
'the biggest issue has been development finance [the up-front investment developers need to get going], which has been extremely
difficult. So we're now seeing sovereign wealth funds providing the
finance, and pension funds; the finance is slowly but surely creeping
back in.' These joint venture agreements, partnerships between developers and often international investors, are a fairly new invention.
'International flows of money are coming into London buying these
buildings,' Baker continues. 'American money, Asian money, the Far
East is investing heavily in London. Russian money. Also it depends.
Certain countries come in in certain times. So for a while we had Irish
money but now there's no Irish money, but there *is* Far East money.
Investors invest in Britain because of the stability; politically it's very
stable, economically it's very stable and it's predictable. Right now it's
the world's number-one financial centre just above New York, with
Hong Kong rising behind it. Its time zone, its ability for labour, the
language aspect doesn't harm.' (Britain's vote to leave the European
Union in 2016, sending jitters through the country's prime property
market, though not – yet – seriously undermining it, is exactly the
kind of unpredictable curveball developers hate.)

Take, for example, Lend Lease, an Australian developer, which has
partnered with Southwark Council, just south of the Thames, to
redevelop Elephant and Castle. This central London neighbourhood
was blighted, in the cold-eyed logic of real estate values, by (to them
and their potential demographic) 'unattractive' postwar social housing, pounding roads and decades of underinvestment, all things the

developer seems eager to reverse. Another Australian, Westfield, provided the vast, eponymous shopping malls in Shepherd's Bush and
Stratford. The Malaysian group SP Setia bought the site around Bat-
tersea Power Station, its outline famed for a certain generation for its
starring role on the cover of Pink Floyd's album *Animals*. Its bulk has
lain empty, slowly degrading, since it was decommissioned in the
1980s, tempting few takers, despite the repeated banging of its drum
by national governments – so great is the investment required to repair
and find a new life for its huge, iconic bulk. Various business plans and
visions have come and gone. In recent years, though, so many international buyers have wanted a home in central London, a developer
has at last been found to take a gamble, one with enough up-front
wealth both to restore the building and fill it and the vast acres of land
around it with a viable use as luxury apartments (that is a *lot* of space,
a *lot* of luxury homes, and a *lot* of up-front wealth).

It's the Qataris, though, in the form of the Qatar Investment
Authority, headed by Sheikh Abdullah bin Mohammed bin Saud
al-Thani, that, since the 2008 financial crash, have forged the most
visible buying spree, taking majority stakes in an assortment of London's more famous assets, such as Canary Wharf, Harrods, the 2012
Olympic Village, the Shard, the US Embassy in Mayfair, assorted
blue-chip apartment complexes, as well as half of the Walkie-Talkie
skyscraper. London, many say, is becoming Londoha.

In turn, however, Middle Eastern money is slowly being overtaken
by the latest new arrivals: the Chinese. A 2016 report in the *Guardian*
claimed that 'a new wave of investment is just getting under way'.[2]
The investors behind it are not just the superwealthy. So vast is China's
middle class now, even relatively ordinary citizens have enough surplus wealth to invest in property around the world. A huge network
of companies has sprung up to direct these smaller investors to property
developments in London, but also other British cities like Liverpool,
Manchester and Birmingham. The inflation this has in large part caused
in property prices has created a huge domestic political crisis of housing
affordability; ordinary Londoners or Mancunians are now competing

with ordinary Chinese for homes in Southwark or Salford – an extraordinary situation. Some administrations, in Australia or Hong Kong, for instance, pressured by citizens increasingly unable to afford a place in their own cities, have begun to intervene in this international market, installing brakes to protect prices for nationals. Perhaps London will follow suit. In 2016, London's new mayor, Sadiq Khan, at least promised an investigation into the city's international property investment market.

This, though, is hardly the first time foreign money has bought up Britain's landscape. Murray Fraser and Joe Kerr, in their outstanding 2007 study of the links between British and American architecture, *Architecture and the 'Special Relationship'*, chart the flow between the two countries of ideas and money since the mid nineteenth century. The result on either side of the Atlantic is, they say, a 'hybridised' form of both architecture and the economics behind it.

The two countries, thanks, perhaps, to their common ancestry, have long embraced one other more tightly than they have other nations, in politics, culture, economics – and in architecture. But the strength of that embrace has changed. Once, Britain was the world power; since the Second World War America has surged ahead. Mind you, the US overtook Britain in terms of per capita GDP as early as the 1870s. With cash to play with during the boom after the Civil War, the US for the first time looked beyond its borders and frontier economy for investment opportunities. Cheaper grain and meat from the Prairies flooded into Britain, depressing the price of agricultural land in the UK, and the wealth of its aristocratic landowners. Many of these aristocrats sold off assets to compensate – often to the very Americans who had caused their decline in fortunes in the first place. Mayfair, London's most prestigious neighbourhood, was one favoured spot for this transatlantic shopping spree. Its Georgian townhouses were soon joined by American-style neighbours as plots of land traded hands and new-fangled building-types from across the Atlantic were imported, such as luxury hotels, multistorey car parks and apartment blocks containing exotic innovations like electric lifts.

American money funded – and American technology helped build – the expansion of London Underground in the early twentieth century, Britain's first steel-framed tall (for these shores) buildings in Liverpool and London, and its most forward-thinking production lines and factories in Manchester and Glasgow. And after the Second World War, with more money than ever to spend, America made Britain not only the largest recipient of Marshall Aid, but subject to another enormous influx of both investment in the built environment (in the form of even more new breeds of exotic buildings, such as office blocks and shopping malls), and in the management and financial techniques of the businesses that built this new landscape. By the mid 1970s, write Fraser and Kerr, 'Britain was still the location for 40 per cent of US investment assets in Europe'.[3]

In the years after the 1973 oil crisis, though, with American capital flows to the UK slowing somewhat, new kinds of foreign investor jumped into the gap. First came the newly triumphant OPEC (petrol-exporting) countries, with their petrodollars. In the early 1980s, though, Thatcher's revolution in the British economy – with tactics such as abandoning onerous exchange controls, and creating a low-wage, flexible and decreasingly unionised workforce – attracted foreign multinationals from ever further afield to invest in its economy, and in its landscape.

In the City, its historic government, the Corporation of London, encouraged a huge boom in office building, after finding itself ill-prepared for the new enterprise economy. In the mid 1980s, New York had twice as much office space as London, Tokyo two-and-a-half times as much.[4] By 1987, though, London had increased its office space by twenty times the square metreage of 1982.[5] Such was the demand for it, rents for office space soared from £35 or £40 per square metre in 1985 to £60 in 1988. This boom was financed by increasingly international backers. Paternoster Square, beside St Paul's Cathedral, for instance, was paid for by British Greycoat Plc, American Park Tower Group and the Mitsubishi Estate Company of Japan. The City's new rival, Canary Wharf, was funded first by a consortium of Credit

Suisse/First Boston and others, but finally Canadian conglomerate Olympia and York, then the world's biggest commercial landlord.

The American influence still dominated, though. Indeed, say Fraser and Kerr, by the 1990s there were more American banks in the City than in New York.[6] These new financial institutions, after the 'Big Bang', required a particular kind of space to work in – 'the latest generic model of American office design,' say Fraser and Kerr. 'Floor plates of 3,000 square metres on every level; distances of 12–20 metres from the core to perimeter; only 20–40 per cent of interior space as cellular offices for senior managers; ceilings of 4 metres in height; and super-abundant service voids for cabling and air conditioning.'[7] The old, custom-built British office of corridors and cell-like rooms was dead. The flexible economy required flexible space, built, of course, flexibly.

American construction firms had, since the end of the Second World War, far better knowledge about how to build the new breed of steel-framed office and retail buildings required for Britain's new consumer-led economy; the US, after all, had not suffered the onerous rationing of building materials experienced in Europe. These construction firms began to employ novel management techniques to speed up the often slow process of building, techniques cribbed from such innovations as the 'just-in-time' methods used in the Japanese car industry. Work on building sites, for instance, would begin even before the architectural designs were finished; components were added to the rising building as soon as they arrived on site, rather than being stored, expensively, on precious land. The quicker the building could be built, after all, the quicker its landlord could make money from what went on inside it – and from the very building itself, as the property market of the 1980s and 1990s established its now familiar pattern of booms and busts.

The nature of these investments, too, became ever more diverse and complex – not just 'sovereign wealth funds', and 'joint venture agreements', but from investors once not known for their interest in land and property. Developers took on unusual shapes – pension funds, for instance, such as Capital and Counties or CapCo, which now owns the site of Earl's Court, a vast old exhibition hall in west London which it plans to replace with new expensive housing, and which in recent years has taken control over most of Covent Garden. Land, and what goes on top of it, has become an international market as complex and fast-moving as any other traded on the stock exchanges of the world, and one with its own convoluted rules and methods.

Modern-day property development may not be a science, but it has an economic logic, albeit an inexact, slightly fuzzy one. For instance, very few new buildings both in the city below me and Bradley Baker on that day or in towns and cities across the western world are now built 'bespoke' for the owner of the land. Most are speculative; in other words, a developer leases a plot and creates a building on top which they then rent out. Property developers, wherever they are, take a huge risk buying land in an extremely expensive market, forking out a fortune on creating a building and, most often, at the end of it all they don't even know exactly who'll occupy it.

So great is the financial risk they take, developers have to know their stuff about plot ratios, building regulations, planning law, all the details. They know about the constraints they have to work within. And they instinctively know what sells, too, or how they can redevelop that square metre of space in a way that might appeal to their mysterious future tenants. Each patch of land in the world has its potential market. Here in the prime streets of the City of London, for instance, these tenants might be an insurer, a trader, a law firm, or, perhaps, those new arrivals, a tech or media company. Each has their own proclivities, their own ways of occupying offices. 'Traditionally,' explains Baker, 'most lawyers still occupy portioned offices. The financial community pretty much always want open-plan. A financier's dream floor plate really would be a very nice square one that they can cram as many people in as possible. Some firms, for example a media company, will be fairly forward-thinking in the way that the building could look; maybe an accountancy firm would be less forward-thinking.'

However, unless a building is created specifically for one kind of tenant – a risk, as it limits the potential market for your building in the future – it is best to hedge your bets, to create a space that is not too much one thing or another. Make it, as Bradley Baker says, 'flexible'. Flexible because they don't know exactly who is going to move in: the space has to appeal to a tenant from anywhere around the world, with a business doing almost anything. This rule exists at the top of the market, and the bottom. My local council gym, for instance. Presumably to remove assets expensive to maintain from the increasingly stretched local government budget, the gym, built bespoke in the 1930s and owned by the council, was demolished and sold off. The Stairmasters and Swiss balls stepped and bounced a few streets away into leased space in a new private housing development. This space, though, should even tougher public finances dictate the gym's closure in a decade or so, can mutate; so 'flexibly' has it been designed that a supermarket, a night-club or a call centre could move in in its place. The building, like the property developer who creates it, has to be a shapeshifter nowadays, its very form designed to nimbly adapt to the changing circumstances inherent to advanced capitalist society.

So what does this 'flexible space' look like? Imagine a great grid of relatively abstract space, constrained by the edge of your plot – a gigantic open-plan shed, if you like, whose empty space inside can be rearranged, like a stage set, for whatever tenant moves in. Then stack as many of these sheds on top of one another as local planning rules on the height of buildings will allow, each 'shed' served by the latest in communications, lighting, plumbing and air conditioning, as well as cutting-edge lifts, lobbies and bathrooms. This flexible space is called the 'shell and core' model, a three-dimensional blank sheet, ready to be written on by whoever moves in.

Only in its communal areas and the overall external look of the building does architecture make an appearance, says Baker. 'Appearance' is an apt word, because in such buildings design quality is reserved for the superficial look or feel of the space, he adds: people arriving 'will see the outside, have an image as to what that building is as they walk in and approach the receptionist. Those first impressions are really crucial, and it will be made up of what's the material on the floor, lift cars, what's the lift lobby like on the twentieth floor, does the ceiling match the one on the ground floor, is the same quality there?'

The architect, in this process, is reduced to a decorator. All too often today, the architect designs just the skin of a building, perhaps 1 metre deep, whether it's a prime development in the City, or an office block in a provincial market town. What lies beneath the skin is abstract flexible space predetermined by the economic logic of speculative development. Buildings today are mostly designed by economics. Architects interfere with this at their peril – and only *if* it doesn't affect the developer's bottom line *or* if this interference in the business plan actually makes the developer more money. As Baker says, straightforwardly, 'At the end of the day, there's no point in a building looking wonderful if it's not actually meeting the reason it was put there in the first place.' And the reason is: making money.

There are, though, occasions when messing with the economic logic of repetitive, standardised flexible space makes sense for the developer. Baker points down, and we put our noses south-westerly to the glass and squint at a new building in the middle distance. It's easy to spot. For a start it's beside St Paul's Cathedral, and you can't miss that. It's also rather unusual looking. Unlike the buildings around it, of varying ages but all covered in higgledy-piggledy period details, and with recognisable roofs and walls, this building is smooth with green glass; its walls and roof meld into one another in a series of facets, like a gemstone, or a stealth bomber come to land in one of the most protected patches of land in the country. Views of St Paul's Cathedral – thanks to its position as an uncriticisable national icon, wrought, in part, from being centre stage in a famous photograph from the Blitz showing it resolute beneath the bombs – are heavily protected, both immediately beneath it, but also from distant viewpoints, such as Greenwich Park. St Paul's Cathedral must, say the planning laws of the land, always remain visible to the nation, its symbolism unobscured by the grubby glass towers of mammon. So landing a weirdo stealth bomber of a building, under the radar of planning regulations and slap-bang beside this icon of icons, was quite an achievement for the developer. Must have taken some effort.

Baker continues: 'If you look at One New Change [for that is this strange building's name], a speculative building, Jean Nouvel is the architect, it must have been an expensive building to build. But actually it's extremely successful, a good example where you can spend a lot of money on the design but the investor gets his money back because people recognise it's a world-class building so they'll pay a world-class rent for it. Retailers will want to be in that building because it is so good. Developers are very good at recognising that if they get a world-class architect on board that architect can enhance the value of that site by creating something truly iconic. It's a win-win situation; and you end up with a product which is really exciting for the public to look at.'

Baker swings my vision to the east. He points to a more familiar shape. 'When we were acting for Swiss Re back in '97 when the Gherkin deal was struck, they wanted something special, something unique, something that would not necessarily be delivered by the normal marketplace. And so it was quite a brave shout to go for a building which was that tall. They wanted to raise their profile in the City, to add something to London and make something reflective of them, world class.' The Gherkin caused a lot of controversy when it was proposed, thanks to its shape and height. But, adds Baker, 'because it's been so popular and an icon for London, I think it's caused people to realise tall buildings can be great for the city'.

So world-class architecture by a superstar architect like Norman Foster or Jean Nouvel, expensive and difficult to achieve though it is, does have a market. But this market demand, says Baker, is limited. There are only so many customers out there across the planet who want to rent space in 'world-class architecture'. Most simply want their flexible, blank-slate square-metreage wrapped up blandly and un-controversially in plain glass, melting into the background of the skyline. 'Tenants want something that looks good, that's going to attract staff, that's going to be good to work in. They don't need it to be avant-garde and crazy. If it's too wacky then it is fair to say people might shy away from it.' There is only so much appetite for aesthetic risk in a business risky enough as it is.

The views of the building can add to its allure, though, and, therefore, its bottom line. After speaking to Bradley Baker, I met a handful of office workers in the Gherkin on their lunchbreak, who all, to a fault, spoke of their pride in working in the building. 'Everyone knows it,' said one, 'I can tell my friends where I work and they know it instantly, and every day as I set off to work, I do think, "Look where I work!"' Though most of all, especially for the lucky ones with a desk by the window on an upper floor, it was the view *out* that counted. The owners of that 'iconic' stealth bomber of a building beside St Paul's Cathedral – One New Change – can charge more rent for its offices and restaurants because they overlook a seventeenth-century 'icon'. And there is no surprise that at the very top of the Gherkin, the best view of all, housed in a dome of glass at its pinnacle, is reserved for a luxurious restaurant in which blue-chip clients are entertained by blue-chip companies.

Just how valuable is that view, though? How much will people pay to look at a stimulating landscape or building? Just to the south of the Gherkin is an even more unusually shaped buillding – Uruguayan star-architect Rafael Viñoly's 'Walkie-Talkie' – one that bulges at the top. The rental price of the upper storeys of buildings is generally greater, thanks to the views they afford; so Viñoly, a cunning, most commercially astute kind of architect, in a eureka moment, created a building that bulges at the top to maximise its premium rentable space. Oliver Gardiner, head of London development for Land Securities – which funded the building in partnership with the Canary Wharf Group international consortium – is pleased as punch with it. 'People immediately go up the top of a tall building and look out at the view,' he says. 'There's a tangible position to take on the price of an upper floor in a tower with the view that it takes . . . How much you can scale that from zero with no view from the basement, say, all the way to the top is market-driven. You put your more valuable floors towards the top. People like the views of historic London, the Thames, the Palace, landmarks, the Palace of Westminster. Big Ben, Tower Bridge. The ability to see the skyline in as much vista as possible attracts a greater degree of rent.' His clients, he says, 'might put their "wow" space or entertaining space into those views' or their main board room for the big deals to impress their clients. Best of all, he says, is 'if you've got a view across the river. Then you've really got an uninterrupted skyline across a wonderful vista. You can say you've got a view across the River Thames or you can see the Shard. Because the river isn't going to get built on. Or,' he adds, ominously, 'shouldn't be for many years.'

Bending the rules

Never meet a town planner. Not if you're predisposed to melancholy. Allthough, in that case, you might part company with your mood lifted. At last! Someone worse off than me. You see, the once noble profession of city planning has been under the cosh for decades. The rise and rise of the entrepreneurial city of spectacle has relegated planners to the role of dealmakers and negotiators – they are all that stands between you, your home and a property developer that wants to build a skyscraper at the end of your street. They are the last and only line of defence. Only these dealmakers are infantry troops with their arms tied behind their backs and their eyes gouged out.

Western countries each have their own culture and laws of city planning, honed from centuries of experience about what works and what doesn't in their towns, and customised, through democratic process, to suit the nuances and norms of the population that lives there. The laws of planning – governing, for instance, how built up we want our neighbourhoods to be, which buildings or styles or kinds of open public spaces we want to preserve or protect, how wide we want our pavements, how efficacious our drains – exist as a series of commonly agreed standards that we expect from the environments in which we live. What unites them, though, is a commitment to regulating the free market in land and property in order to protect the commonly held values each society holds dear.

In the UK, for instance, much, if not most, of the culture and laws of city planning date from after the Second World War, when the vast, orderly apparatus of centralised state control, established in laws such as the 1947 Town and Country Planning Act, were brought in to cure the ills of the industrial city – to curb the loosely governed suburban sprawl that had worried many in the 1920s and 1930s, and to eradicate the slums and overcrowding blighting the old city. Planners were emboldened and empowered to plan the futures of their fiefdoms according to these planning laws; they were the guardians and enactors of the 'public good', even if, as the saga at Covent Garden showed, their interpretation of what this 'public good' looked like was not always shared by the public itself.

However, this period of town planning triumphant was just a blip. British planning in particular has for centuries been ad hoc, 'patchwork, more polycentric', says Michael Hebbert, professor of town planning at University College London. We don't easily do the detailed zoning of Manhattan, the neat, statist *grands projets* of France. We have, since property speculation first took hold here in the seventeenth century, depended heavily on private money to deliver public good. The rise of the entrepreneurial city has simply allowed this state of affairs to return to its default position. The free market in land and property has, after its postwar flirtation with state control, been deregulated.

Rules, though, still exist. Not everything has been deregulated, save in a few experiments such as 'development corporations' or 'enterprise zones'. These were introduced in the 1980s by the government of Margaret Thatcher in troubled patches of British cities experiencing the after-effects of deindustrialisation, after factfinding trips to precursors in American cities. Development corporations are run by a board of directors, much like a company, with huge powers over a designated swathe of land. They usually have compulsory purchase or 'eminent domain' powers, and can override local governments, despite being directly unelected. Enterprise zones are more powerful still, perhaps the most extreme manifestations of the new entrepreneurial city: whole neighbourhoods run according to the economic logic of the 'monetarist' theories of Friedman and von Hayek, that the private sector should deliver investment, with state activities limited to efforts to attract that private investment in the first place. In the UK, thousands of hectares of land have been offered up as 'enterprise zones' since the 1980s, pulling in private investors big or small with tax breaks and the suspension of planning laws. You can build almost whatever you want. In London's Docklands, the Isle of Dogs enterprise zone has, since it was established in 1982, attracted private investment worth six times the £7 billion state subsidy ploughed into it, albeit from investors who arrived there with little intention of speaking to, much less employing, the neighbours who already lived there.

These are exceptions. Nonetheless, the past twenty years have seen the vast structure of planning laws across Britain nipped and tucked, usually in the name of attracting business to stricken areas, and 'loosening' restrictive laws to 'free up' private enterprise so it can ride into cities experiencing decline, and save the day. Local government in general has been disempowered over the past thirty years following a series of stand-offs in the 1980s between Conservative central government pursuing American-inspired monetarist, business-led policies and so-called 'Loony Left' town councils with very different agendas. Policies such as rate capping (limiting the amount local councils can raise from property taxes), and restrictions on the amount of money central government doles out to towns and cities (with politically motivated conditions attached) have, in effect, kneecapped local democracy. City or town governments are even more dependent upon central government, and even more reliant on the swift, international flows of private investment. They are forced to become beauty queens on a stage, flirting for attention, in the hope that some promiscuous investor might look their way.

To adapt to this new old way of doing things, policies that

deregulate how we create our landscapes have been incorporated into city planning since the 1980s, many originating from across the Atlantic. The outsourcing of roles and jobs in the public sector to the private sector is now default. The selling off of public assets, such as former social housing estates like New Era in north London – whose Boudicca-like residents were adopted as a cause by the comedian Russell Brand – is the norm. Once-novel practices such as the selling of 'air rights' above low buildings, like train stations, to build ever upwards, are now merely commonplace. Business improvement districts, another American invention, have proliferated in British cities: organisations set up and funded by businesses (whether multinationals or a local dry cleaner) to 'improve' a neighbourhood in myriad ways from picking up litter to employing private security or street 'ambassadors' to orchestrating gigantic redevelopment schemes.[8]

The effects of this privatisation of public space in our cities have been brilliantly documented by writers from Mike Davis, whose *City of Quartz: Excavating the Future in Los Angeles* (1990) unpicked early tactics in 1980s LA, to Anna Minton, whose *Ground Control: Fear and Happiness in the Twenty-First-Century City* (2009) reveals the democratic cost of losing public control over land. In such developments, explains Minton, 'rather than being unconditionally open to the public, like the rest of the city, it is up to the owner to decide who is allowed in and what they are allowed to do there ... Now, a generation later, what began specifically to serve the needs of business has become the standard model for the creation of every new place in towns and cities.' Private estates can abolish ancient rights of ways through 'stopping up orders'. They can demand compulsory purchase orders, if they can prove the new development is of public benefit. And in 2004 the very definition of 'public benefit' was altered to give greater emphasis on the economic impact of a scheme, not just its social or environment impact.

These Faustian pacts may have delivered spruced-up neighbourhoods, but the costs – whether overzealous private security guards stopping amateur photographers, or devices, such as 'anti-homeless spikes', to deter particular populations – have become ubiquitous, one more symptom of the entrepreneurial city. Cash-strapped town and city governments sell off chunks of public land not only to raise money, but to cede its control and administration (from what gets built to who empties its bins) to the private sector.

Planning laws, of course, slow everything down, and interfere with the fleet movement of international investment finance. But you can only deregulate them so far. As with the financial industry and its regulation, it is the precise balance between the free market and its regulation that's the key. Regulate too tightly and developers say the state is strangling them; too loose and liberties are taken – common standards of civic life are threatened, and demonstrators arrive on the streets, as they did in Covent Garden. Like making a loaf of bread, a few milligrams here or there can make all the difference. So efforts to untighten these restrictions, or to speed up their administration, have to be delicately planned. Their impact, though, has been far from delicate.

As I said, never meet a town planner. In any case, I have saved you the bother. Over the years, while doing my job, I have met hundreds. There are many that have so completely accustomed themselves to the business agenda of the cities whose landscape they administrate they might as well go and work for Accenture or Citibank and earn a ton more money. Most, though, do this as a vocation, like teachers or nurses. They are there to defend those commonly held civic values. They are like Canute before the waves. They know this.

Planning whistleblowers are as rare as planning millionnaires. This is not Watergate, after all. No planner wants to lose their job for revealing menial, quotidian, minor scandals involving drains and pavement widths. Nobody wants to do a Brian Anson. Off the record, though, they are more candid. One, for instance, told me once of his fear of being labelled: 'Anyone who speaks out is lambasted or gets a reputation as "unhelpful", or not considering the wider public interest because we aren't allowing business to do what they want, which is ridiculous because there might be problems with the way planning laws are in this country, but they are there, at least, to *protect* the public interest.'

Planners are well aware of their denuded powers, of their David status against the Goliaths of international property development. They are also well aware of how their role is changing, as central governments, lobbied by property developers, try to loosen and speed up the planning process. In the UK, for instance, the coalition government of Conservatives and Liberal Democrats published the National Planning Policy Framework in 2012 – in theory a well-meaning document designed to reduce bureaucratic red tape: a thousand-plus pages of policy have been shrunk, by magic, to sixty-five. Planning offices in British towns, underfunded and undermanned from decades of underinvestment though they are, now have strict time limits on how quickly they must process planning permissions, so as not to hinder the flows of finance.

The balance of power has shifted in the entrepreneurial city. Cities, after all, need jobs and investment; they need property developers to make things happen. It is in their interest to tempt the private developer and give them as much freedom as they can. It all comes down to the nuances of the deal they make; and, trained and professional as they are, local planning officers are usually no match for a property firm with legions of lawyers. 'We are essentially paper pushers, we shovel shit,' one told me in a moment of existential angst. 'We have no actual power other than to negotiate before democratically elected planning committees, whose members often don't even have to have any background in or knowledge of planning, urbanism or architecture.'

More fundamentally, though, another planning officer once admitted, 'We don't plan any more. We are not planners. We respond to the plans of others. We have a fuzzy document, a local plan, that hopes for so-and-so here or there, but it's really just an invitation for private developers to come in. We can steer them one way or another like cattle ranchers; but we haven't got much fencing, what we have is pretty crappy, and the bulls are a lot stronger than us.'

There is fencing; there are rules. But where rules still exist, they can be bent. Let's take one of the biggest rules of all: section 106 of the Town and Country Planning Act 1990, the British equivalent of

America's 'planning gain'. This is a levy on new development, and its exact size is negotiable. The more cynical might call it a bribe. Section 106 agreements demand of developers a financial contribution to local government, designed to offset the negative effects a new development might have on an area, such as an overbearing building, downdrafts from a skyscraper or increased traffic or pedestrian flow on the streets. It is the 'hidden hand' or 'trickle down' of capitalism in action, and can come in a huge number of forms: a new public health centre built as part of a development, more pavement width, a square open to the public (although owned and managed by the landlord on its terms), a new playground or park.

At London's Spitalfields Market, for instance, a shopping mall plonked gracelessly by developer Hammerson and architect Foster & Partners in the shell of a historic market, section 106 'design gifts' come in the form of 'sensitively' stepping the profile of the office tower above it so it doesn't glower over the pedestrians, or as 'community gifts', which Hammerson proudly displayed in the form of local schoolkids' murals or polemical banners declaiming, communist-style, the good that the developer has brought with it. One hundred and eighteen 'social houses' [sic] built! Two new community centres! £1 million for environmental improvements!

Section 106 is the latest in a long line of such rules, a very fuzzy and grey line. From rebuilding the City after the Great Fire of London in 1666, to rebuilding Manchester after the 1996 IRA bomb, there is always, says Michael Hebbert, professor of town planning at University College Londen, a 'tortuous process' negotiating the give and take between the property owner or developer who owns the land and wants to do whatever it wants with it, and the state in all its forms, which hopes to cajole or extract from it some form of collective good.

There is an inherent problem to section 106: the bigger the development, the larger the contribution. This encourages cash-strapped local governments and cash-rich developers to think big, the latter so they can make more profit, the former so they can siphon off more section 106 contributions: taller buildings, fewer affordable homes, fatter buildings, though all crammed with ever-smaller offices or homes. The bigger the better for all concerned. But, if a developer can reduce their obligations, of course, they will. Once again, it all comes down to the deal, the negotiation, the Faustian pact it agrees with the city or town. In a typical bargaining tactic, a developer might, for instance, ask to reduce the amount of affordable or social housing it is required to have in a development, if it promises to increase its section 106 contributions. Affordable housing mixed with free-market housing in the same building can, say many developers, reduce the amount they are able to charge for the latter; the rich do not like mixing with the poor. Already the twain are characteristically divided in new housing developments, with separate entrances – so-called 'poor doors' – and circulation systems, so they need never meet. Such is the current inflation in Britain's high-end residential market, that if a developer can reduce or eradicate the amount of social housing it includes by increasing its section 106 contributions, it can achieve a far higher price in the homes it sells. This profit may far outweigh the amount it would have had to spend on its 106 contributions. It makes perfect business sense.

Indeed, a whole industry of planning consultants has developed, whose job is to find out how developers can avoid or bend section 106. This is a little like the worldwide industry of tax 'managers' there to find loopholes in the law for the rich, in the form of tax havens or complex Houdini-like financial structures. Planning consultants examine what is being asked of a developer to see if it is 'viable' or not. What this slippery term means is that they decide whether the level of regulation or the amount or nature of section 106 contributions being asked of the developer is damaging the business plan of their scheme: if it is making it economically 'unviable'. In the development industry, though, profit margins of 20 per cent are standard, so what 'unviable' means in practice is that the company may not be making quite as much profit as they are used to.

Demonstrating 'viability' in planning negotiations is an intricate art involving smoke and mirrors, cloaks and daggers. Once again, the dice are loaded in favour of the developer. They are able to plead a lack of viability using the most expensive planning lawyers and consultants. Planning officers, though, do not have equal access to such resources. They may on occasion, though, in a fit of Janus-faced politics only possible in the entrepreneurial city, use the very same firm of business consultants to disprove 'unviability'. However, thanks to commercial confidentiality, they will not have the same levels of access to the developer's business plan as the developer itself.

If planning permission is refused, then developers can always appeal – it is an expensive process, but worth it if the stakes and potential profits are high. Or they can avoid an appeal by paying for special treatment. Planning performance agreements mean that a developer can purchase a dedicated part of a city's planning team to deal with their application, if it is large and hefty enough, like a kind of fast-track scheme for the rich; another way for local government to acquire more money from a developer, while simultaneously ceding power to it. Or they might choose to go straight to appeal rather than wasting valuable time stuck in the democratic process quibbling with planning committees. At least in appeal it's a matter of who can afford the best planning lawyers. I think we know the answer. As one senior planning officer told me, 'Developers simply hold a gun to our heads. They have all the cards. "Let us in, or we'll take our money elsewhere." Which means no investment, no regeneration, no new housing or public facilities for us.'

Negotiating deals in the entrepreneurial city, though, can get complicated. It can easily drift into John Poulson-like corruption. Or, more likely, into the murky realm of lobbying, where the private and the public sector can get very cosy indeed. The satirical magazine *Private Eye* revealed that, just before granting to Australian developer Lend Lease a very favourable planning permission to redevelop the Elephant and Castle Heygate estate, the leader of the borough of Southwark, Peter John, was treated to various perks of the job, sponsored by Lend Lease, such as a pair of tickets to the 2012 Olympic opening ceremony and a luxurious trip to the MIPIM property fair in Cannes.

Multitudes of Investors Prepared to Invest Megabucks

Could anything be sleazier-sounding than a trade fair for property developers? An arms-industry trade fair? Or perhaps the porn festival which often follows Cannes's annual Marché International des Professionels d'Immobilier (MIPIM) in the South of France. But the four March days of MIPIM sure give the arms and porn industries a run for their money. The tans are just that bit more unreal, the dark suits (for this is mostly a male affair) are a bit showier – flashing a few pinstripes – the money rather newer. The whole town feels as if it is coated in a light slick of oil.

You might think that this is little more than a town planners' convention, with its nerdy talk of square metreage, net to gross, retail offers and mixed-use development, a place where wearing the right lanyard is your passport to meeting the surveyor of your dreams. Not a bit of it. This is big business. The number of beefed-up yachts in the marina and burly pony-tailed security guards at the Russian stands is proof. Cannes in early spring is not a bad place in which to plot the future of the world's cities. The air is sweet, the weather more clement than most places on the planet. You can sit on the Croisette with a café au lait and a cigar in the twinkling sunshine and think yourself king of the world. And an awful lot of people here are just that.

MIPIM has seminars on responsible development, sustainability, 'the way forward', 'the future of the city' and all that, but that's just window dressing. Everyone knows the real reason for MIPIM, even in leaner years: making money. Cannes might be more famous for its film festival in May, but it's MIPIM where most money is exchanged, and which, of its 150 or so yearly trade fairs, the town most prizes.

Events following the 2008 economic crash became a little more muted, though there's always money to be made; it's just a matter of less or more money than usual. In 2007, back in the good old days, almost 30,000 turned up – property developers, politicians, architects, property lawyers, agents and consultants, car-park companies with the latest concept in making the car-parking experience more beautiful, firms with dodgy land to flog, and some here perhaps just for the free cigarettes and Russian vodka that are routinely doled out. There was a feel to the place even more crazed than usual. The models of future buildings and cityscapes had that much more extra bling, and even the stand for the city of Manchester, whose filthy streets were once trodden by Friedrich Engels while exposing the excesses of early Victorian capitalism, displayed scale models of its future property developments with facades coloured in gleaming, unironic gold. Worries, though, about market 'corrections' lurked behind the PR's bright smiles. The mood here was like the British weather: changeable, capricious.

MIPIM's visitor numbers dropped by a third after the financial crisis, to a rump, some of whom turned up just to show they hadn't gone bust. There were stands 'Specialising in Distressed Assets and Investments'. Insolvency specialists visited, to take devalued property off your hands for the right price, such as toxic housing estates in busted Ireland, or whole towns of empty apartment blocks in Spain. Even Dubai's stand became, briefly, a little less ostentatious, compared to those crazy years in the mid-Noughties when beaches chilled by sub-sand refrigeration, archipelagoes in the shape of the world, a skyscraper a kilometre high . . . *anything* seemed possible. Now, though, there are other Dubais, such as Russian cities nobody in the West seems to have heard of; Tula, perhaps, with its dreams of giant domes and swooshing skyscrapers.

There are the famous architects, specially jetted in by this or that central Asian country, to schmooze. There are also the hordes of less-famous architects, here to summon up the courage to speed-date developers and cities. City mayors come – such as London's Ken Livingstone and Boris Johnson (who, with his journalistic talent for a quip, once memorably called the event 'Multitudes of Investors Prepared to Invest Megabucks'). Famous property developers are ten a penny, such as the Tchenguiz brothers, unable to attend in 2011 owing to Vincent Tchenguiz's arrest for investigations into dealings with Icelandic bank Kaupthing before its collapse in 2008. Government ministers are here, too. In 2005, John Prescott, then UK deputy prime minister in Tony

Blair's administration, had to fight off accusations from the right-wing press about 'taxpayers' hard-earned money' being spent on the jacuzzi in his Carlton Hotel suite. The London Borough of Croydon – for, yes, even lowly local councils come to Cannes, often 'sponsored' by property developers, since the cost of coming can reach £500,000 – had to follow suit in 2010, defending, in tough economic times, spending £160,000 of taxpayers' money on a trip. They come because they need what the likes of the Tchenguiz brothers can supply. They need investment. And so they, in turn, invest in a Ryanair plane ticket and an architectural model or two. Whether they get it back in actual built projects is a moot point. But that, in theory, is the plan. That is the trickle-down theory of the new breed of entrepreneurial city.

The architects are here to get their concepts and theories built. So many architects these days will stop at nothing in the process. Some, though, seem to find the whole thing beneath them, if you read the architectural press. As one property PR suggested in an advice column: 'If you find four days of schmoozing in the South of France too demeaning, then you probably won't be able to stomach a long-term relationship with a property developer.'[9] Some are here as promotion: that 'taxpayers' hard-earned money' is often spent paying for the more colourful, infamous architects to get there and be chauffered around with their entourage. They are the meat being marketed, dressed, as ever, in black. You want corporate minimalism? Post-pop architecture? Neo-modernism? Just plain bling? They are there to provide developers with that elusive modern-day requirement of cities: 'buzz'.

This is not a place for Marxists to visit. Or maybe it is? What a place for latter-day Engels to do their research into the wilder excesses of modern-day capitalism. Buildings here are products, akin to financial products, best viewed from high above, from afar, in the form of gigantic plastic models suspended in the bubble of a trade fair in the French Riviera. Buildings here are safe deposit boxes in which the world's rich can store their bullion, as Peter Rees, the City of London's former planning supremo once put it. It is in this bizarre spot that you can best witness the deals that make our cities what they are, that fuel the churn of creative destruction that makes and remakes the places we live in, that demolishes and rebuilds, and reinvents the same old patches of land again and again. That old Will Rogers quip, 'Buy land; they ain't making any more of the stuff,' is rendered obsolete. Here land is endlessly extended and augmented upwards and outwards in the form of buildings whose extravangance knows no end. Nothing is deemed impossible, so long as engineering can make it happen. The planet contains roughly the same amount of space it's ever had, but at MIPIM it is continually renewed, extended and rebranded in order to produce money.

Whole areas are devoted to actual places, with banners shrieking 'Bristol!' 'Lille!' 'Rio!' With their slogans – 'Stunning', 'Astonishing' – old cities on their uppers shore themselves up against young pretenders. Places are relaunched, with the help of celebrity chefs or gigantic art installations. Each place sells its USP: high technology, the finest wine, the best surfing opportunities, *the* location for the most pleasant of lifestyles. Commentators and speakers in the auditoria, though, talk of these places not as places you and I know, places where we brush our teeth, eat, sleep and watch box sets. Instead they are investments, companies almost. The 'top 300 cities'; who's up, who's down, like the Nasdaq or the FTSE 100. It's all a question of how much risk you want in your investment. What are the stakes? London is usually a safe bet; that's why the Qataris have bought half the 2012 Olympic site, and why the city is subject to apocraphal tales of Greeks arriving with suitcases of euros. Sure, it's expensive to invest in, and the return on your investment will be slow and steady, but this city ain't going anywhere. Britain's vote to leave the European Union, though, has put a spanner in the works. But you might plump for Tula: an autocratic regime is tricky, admittedly, but imagine the return if you succeed! Indeed, Russia's tent, these days, tends to be the largest and most extravagant, if you can get in past the blonde models in short skirts dispensing those vodkas. And, of course, there's always China.

Even in the boom years, though, there is a slightly desperate air to MIPIM, an air of neediness, like a singles' night. There are those who need, and those who can supply. Architects and city governments need cash, but they can supply land and government grants and aesthetic and engineering sparkle and those all-important intellectual 'concepts'. Developers and investors and the shadowy pension funds and financial organisations who own the urban land beneath our feet – we call them 'stakeholders' these days – have the cash to offload, money to launder, but need something to spend it on, property development whose design will be alluring enough for tastemakers and politicians to overlook any democratic deficit. And so they all come to Cannes.

These participants perform a delicately nuanced mating dance, the free vodka and complimentary cigarettes helping to get them in the mood. First there is the display of prowess. In the 'Bunker', the euphemism for the Grand Palais, itself a now-outmoded vision of the future, a gigantic hall awaits, an informal city of stands of varying sophistication for places, companies and architects to strut their stuff in front of the money men. Some turn heads with CGI fly-throughs of possible visionary cities mainlined to one's retina on virtual reality headsets, as visually sophisticated as the latest superhero movie. So sophisticated is CGI, and so ubiquitous here at MIPIM, it is almost impossible to distinguish what is real and what is unreal and yet-to-be. That is exactly the trick the sellers are hoping to pull off.

But the good old-fashioned physical model is still king, giant models on huge plinths and table tops displaying architectural zoos, their hermetic dreams in Perspex cubes, unsullied by the air outside. Whoever makes miniature model trees and tiny humans and cars must be making a killing. Some stands are loaded up with euphemisms. There are 'vistas' and 'icons' and 'mixed-use' spaces with 'connectivity', in shapes that are generally 'dynamic' and always with 'vision': there is a lot of vision in Cannes. Other stands stand for frankly I've no idea what or who or where, or whether they're buying or selling, and no amount of my questions can unravel the truth; they are probably, therefore, landlords to the universe.

The next stage in this mating dance is the courtship. The participants might repair to the Café Roma, or the art-deco Hôtel Martinez.

The champagne flows like water. Oysters are supped in private parties on the yachts, or up in the villas in the hills above, where hairpin bends, pool parties and copious booze are not a good combination. The journalists, though, aren't invited, and we repair to the beachside bars, where, by 6 p.m. the Eurodisco music starts pumping out and tales begin to swirl. Use your imagination. Who knows if they're true or not? They call the thing MIPIM sells 'real estate', but not everything about it is real. It is part fact, part fiction. The most fabulous tales are told these days about our cities of spectacle. The trick is working out which are the true stories, and which are the fables.

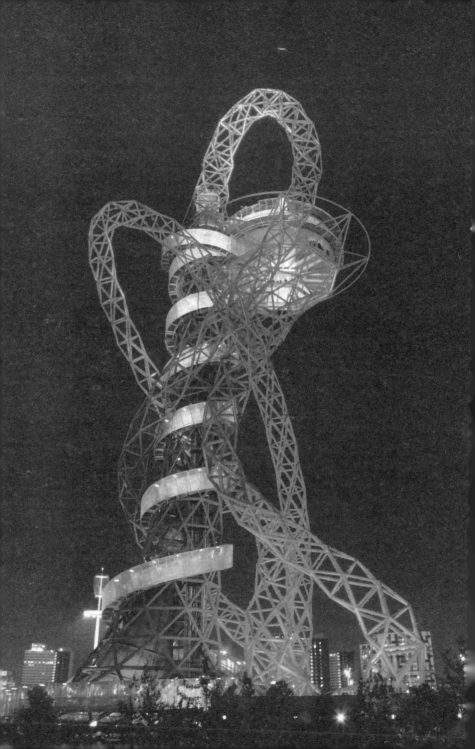

CHAPTER FIVE

BRANDSCAPES

'Junkspace is overripe and undernourishing at the same time.'

Rem Koolhaas[1]

Image problems

The architect Will Alsop nips outside for a sly Benson & Hedges. Inside, Rita Davies, Toronto's executive director of culture, is waxing evangelical about her 'Culture Plan for the Creative City', before Canada's great and good: 'We're a born-again city. Hallelujah. Toronto CAN be a global cultural capital.' She brags about her city of a hundred languages, where every seventh worker is in the creative industries, adding $9 billion to the city's GDP. *This* will be the Year of Creativity, she decrees. The audience whoops.

Alsop is guest of honour at the baptism of born-again Toronto, his new building, the Sharp Centre for Design (nickname: 'the Flying Tabletop', its slab of steel sailing, improbably, over the city's rooftops) phase one in this town's new creative life. Hitherto, notes Davies, Toronto has been somewhat lackadaisical with its culture. 'Our competitors spend us into the ground.' Its neighbour Montreal (boo, hiss) forks out $26.62 a head. San Francisco, $86.01. Toronto, a meagre $14.65. For the kind of creativity Rita Davies is talking about, you see, is not a question of canvases, concepts and suffering artists. It's about investment. These days, a city's 'creativity' is what sells it on the global stage. Culture has become public relations.

Cities, after all, are now brands. Ever since the rise of the entrepreneurial city, selling its space by the square metre, the idea of
promoting a place as if it were a product – a toaster, say, or a brassiere –
has become utterly normal. Places are businesses; they have public
images. They are brandscapes.

'Place marketing', for example, brands settlements according to
the specific qualities of the town or city, or the dreams of what it
may become; or, rather, what dreams it promises its potential inhabitants and investors. A place's creativity is simply one attribute in a long
line – such as its sports facilities, the efficiency of its transport infrastructure or, in the case of Glasgow's 'Smiles better' campaign in the
1980s, its nebulous 'happiness' – used to distinguish one place from
another on the earth's surface, and better attract income and
incomers.

Architecture is central to this urban rebranding, the skin on a town
or city's face. Since the 1992 Olympic Games, Barcelona has famously
used the striking nineteenth-century architecture of Antoni Gaudí to
promote itself. Glasgow has followed suit, milking its Charles Rennie
Mackintosh heritage for all it's worth. But contemporary as well as
historic architecture can be employed to cultivate an image for a town,
too, as Jørn Utzon's Opera House proved for Sydney in the 1970s, and
Frank Gehry's Guggenheim for Bilbao twenty-five years later, attracting tourists to post-industrial cities, and promoting them in adverts
circulating around the world.

Since Bilbao, indeed, contemporary architecture has been used in-
numerable times to give places a 'new face', as the clichés put it, help
them 'turn over a new leaf', be 'transformed' or have 'new life' breathed
into them. The physical shape of the city sells the city. 'Does Melbourne
need an iconic structure to put it on the tourist map?' asked a headline
in *The Age* in 2006.[2] 'Liverpool is the new Barcelona,' Martin Jackson,
partner in estate agents Knight Frank, told the *Guardian* as the city
prepared to become the UK's Capital of Culture in 2008.[3] 'Apart from
the weather, obviously, there is a lot of comparison.' In Helsinki, a few
years earlier, 'Deputy Mayor Pekka Korpinen would like to see an

example of jaw-dropping architecture in the capital.'⁴ A decade on, the competition to design a new Guggenheim art gallery for the Finnish capital has been won by a small firm of young architects. The design of their building, though, will be modest and low key, certainly by comparison with Frank Gehry's mould-breaker. These days even 'anti-iconic' architecture is a kind of brand.

City halls around the world grasp Richard Florida's book *The Rise of the Creative Class* as if it were Mao's *Little Red Book*, an ABC to an enlightened and profitable future city peopled entirely by loft-living tech entrepreneurs. Florida has made a career out of quantifying the qualitative attributes of that once-nebulous noun 'creativity', suggesting that culture can make or break a town whose factories have long since slunk off to China. San Francisco, Austin, Texas, Sacramento or 'world cities' like London, he proclaims, are the new (post)industrial hubs, not Pittsburg or Preston. Michigan's Department of Labor and Economic Growth even employed a 'Cool Cities Coordinator'. Every town from Beijing to Nuneaton wants to be the world's creative capital. No wonder, thinks Florida, who found that 30 per cent of the American workforce and half the country's income came from the 'creative class'. Who wouldn't want them in your town?

Florida breaks down his 'creative class' into various sub-categories, such as 'rational innovators', and the 'creative middle'. He has, though, a rather broad definition of creativity, with the kinds of people and activities you might expect – artists, writers, even advertising executives – making up a 'Super-Creative-Core' of about 12 per cent, while those included in the wider category of 'creative professionals' extend to fields not usually associated with conceptual art or the post-feminist novel, such as sales, management, finance and law.

Florida's recipe for creative success, though, is a little more precise: 'The 3Ts', he explains: 'technology, talent and tolerance'.⁵ The old tools of cities to attract new people and money – a convention centre, perhaps, or a new stadium, are no longer enough. The creative class – or gentrifiers, as Ruth Glass might have recognised them – demand liberal values, tech hubs and like-minded creative neighbours; they innately gauge how high a town scores on the 'bohemian index', the edginess of a place that gives it the kind of street cred so appealing to the creative class.

Toronto, though, lacks that street cred, despite being the city in which Jane Jacobs chose to end her days. For much of its history it's been a conservative, uptight, insecure place, a big town with a small-town mentality, a city of clean air and spotless sidewalks, which, it's joked, are rolled up and packed away each evening. When Bono visited, he said he was almost niced to death. It shows. 'No offence,' begins *Time Out*'s guidebook to the city, 'but Toronto isn't the most visually impressive city you'll see.' 'You think New York, an image comes to mind,' says Joe Fiorito, columnist for the *Toronto Star*, here for Rita Davies's revivalist meeting. 'You think Toronto and what?' We gaze across its collection of bored skyscrapers. Well, there's Mies van der Rohe's cool, dark Dominion Centre. Too minimalist. The CN Tower? Just Seattle's Space Needle on steroids.

This won't do at all. Nice doesn't cut it in the premier league of world-class cities. Toronto needs ego, fast. Its new architectural clothes are therefore designed to quash all insecurity as it shuffles onto the world stage. The city's underachieving landscape now bristles with cranes promising a hundred new condo towers, each muscling up to the next in a show of height. The city is filling its cultural lacuna with new or nipped and tucked cultural venues from opera houses to a film centre. And every world-class city, of course, needs a building by Frank Gehry and Daniel Libeskind, especially one that's hometown to Gehry, and to Libeskind's wife and business partner, Nina. The prodigal sons have duly delivered their usual brands in makeovers for Toronto's top cultural income generators, the Art Gallery of Ontario and the Royal Ontario Museum.

For more edge, though, Toronto has turned to a very naughty boy. Will Alsop – with his behind-the-bike-shed cigarette habit, down-the-pub demeanour, shaggy art school lecturer clothes and tendency to swear on live TV – cuts an unpredictably bohemian figure among the suits in the audience today. His Sharp Centre for Design at the Ontario College of Art and Design (OCAD) follows suit on the skyline, supplying all the eccentric ego a city could want. The Flying Tabletop is genuinely eyepopping. Numbers here at North America's third largest art school are ballooning. In order to supply the creative city with its future creatives, Alsop has provided both space, and space to think, with bright window recesses, deep-cut, he says, to be 'places to daydream'. Its jazzed-up box, spotted like a Dalmatian, sails, 26 metres above the ground, clean over its Victorian neighbours on twelve tottering legs coloured like felt-tip pens. OCAD, like all of Alsop's buildings, is high on energy, a cobbled-together collage of forms and colours. Set against the dull skyscrapers on Toronto's skyline you can't miss it. Job done.

Toronto, though, has tough competition. Formerly nice but dull, or ugly and poor cities and towns around the world have all had a creative makeover. Even cities in America's Midwest, not a region renowned for bohemian values, have been on a building spree, local philanthropists funding new temples to creativity mostly by European architects at the spectacular end of avant-garde. In Minneapolis, grain silos that once inspired Le Corbusier now overlook Jean Nouvel's Guthrie Theater, whose massive balcony is dotted with tourists admiring the skyline, newly perked up by a flamboyant public library by Cesar Pelli, Michael Graves's Minneapolis Insitute of Art, a Frank Gehry in the Frederick R. Weisman Art Museum and Herzog & de Meuron's extension to the Walker Art Center. In another Midwestern city, Akron, Ohio, Coop Himmelb(l)au's extension to the art museum is three times larger than the old building, a cuckoo in the nest, its explosion in glass and steel fatally embracing the sober old redbrick original. In Denver, Daniel Libeskind has added an equally hyperbolic extension to its art museum: 'They have an ambition', he said, 'not to be just a cow town in the Rockies.'

And then there's Cincinnati. Cincy is a ribs 'n' beer kind of place. It takes its baseball very seriously. You get the message the instant you arrive: two vast stadia crouch over the downtown riverfront like guard dogs. In town, a public art programme – Bats Incredible! – fashions sculpture from baseball bats. Jerry Springer is a former mayor; Larry Flynt its infamous local 'book' store proprietor. Cincinnati is your archetypical down-home middle America. But Cincinnati was cosmopolitan enough to display Picasso's *Guernica* in 1940; and it was Cincinnati that successfully defended in court the city's First Amendment rights to see Robert Mapplethorpe's photos in 1990. And it's modest Porkopolis, not Paris, London or Manhattan, that in 2004 built the Contemporary Arts Center (CAC), the first major work by that most self-consciously avant-garde architect, the late Zaha Hadid.

Hadid and the Midwest made an unorthodox couple. But there was method in the madness. ' "Contemporary", "art" and "museum" are three of the scariest words to the average American,' says Charles Desmarais, the CAC's urbane director. 'We want to demystify them. We did a lot of thinking about our brand, our relationship with the audience. Our mission became "experiences outside boundaries". Art wasn't even in there. Most of our visitors won't be deeply informed about art. They come because they want to see things through someone else's eyes. If someone's only interested in sport then we've got a problem. But if they like sport and other stuff too we hope they'll drop by here after the game.'

The building is designed like 'an urban carpet', Hadid explained to the press, one end of which lies across the sidewalk at the busiest intersection in town like a trap, ready to yank unsuspecting Reds fans past the front doors for a dose of Sol LeWitt. Inside, the carpet rolls through the entrance, up the back wall, marked with light bands directing you like airport landing strips to the walkways, up which you clamber like a kid on a climbing frame, bouncing from artwork to artwork. Ten thousand people spilled out onto the sidewalk for the opening party. Even the rude boys in their bling-bling old black Caddies, 50 Cent on the stereo, check out the building. But those Reds fans? Here's one, sixty-ish, red baseball cap, checked shirt, gawping at the galleries hovering high above the sidewalk. 'I don't know if it'd tear me away from a game. Not even beer, ribs and a naked lady'd do that. But I'll be sure to give it a try.' High praise from a Cincinnatian.

In rebranding such cities, it is the *impression* of creativity that is most important, rather than actual cultural production. Decades before Bilbao, for instance, Paris – a place you'd think would not need to prove its creative credentials – underwent its own image transformation in 1977 with the opening of the Centre Pompidou. Renzo Piano and Richard Rogers's culture factory, with its pop-industrial looks – all its guts, plumbing, electrics and air conditioning draped on the outside in DayGlo colours – was designed specifically not to 'fit in' with the mansard roofs and bistros of the fourth arrondissement. It was designed to be different. It was designed to signal 'change'. Following the decidedly uncreative suppression of the 1968 student riots, the building was commissioned by France's president as a kind of healing aid for the nation. Rogers, then doused in left-wing politics, almost refused to enter the design competition in solidarity with the rioters, until pragmatism got the better of him. When his building emerged, its striking looks and novel programme – 'where artists meet the public and the public becomes creative', said its first director, Pontus Hultén – gave the impression that Paris remained a creative force, even if its politics said otherwise. 'Le Freak, C'est Chic', went one newspaper headline.

Proof of a place's true creativity, though, can be a nebulous thing to quantify, for all of Richard Florida's number-crunching. You can perhaps count artists and art galleries.[6] New York in 1945 contained a few galleries, with two dozen or so prominent artists regularly exhibiting; by the mid 1980s, the city had 150,000 'professional' artists, 680 galleries, and 15 million artworks created a decade; compared with 2,000 or so artists in mid to late nineteenth-century Paris, producing 200,000 art works. Perhaps the amount of money these artists generate is proof of a town's artistic worth. Though 'there's still somehow the *impression* the creative industries are intangible', says John Sorrell, co-founder and chairman of the London Design Festival, with which every autumn, alongside London Fashion Week and the Frieze art fair, London anoints itself creative capital of the known universe. 'Other cities all want our crown,' he says. London, though, he thinks, still reigns supreme. 'There'll always be those who think [the creative industries] are airy-fairy.' How can a nation that once made sturdy things like ships and empires now support itself on branding consultants and directional interior decor? What do all those website designers and fashionistas *do* all day? Make money, of course. A survey for London's mayor by Creative London, a body uniting creative industries, unearthed 525,000 people working in the sector. That's one in five. A Tweet in 2016 from the UK's Department for Culture, Media and Sport tells me the creative industries contribute '£84.1 billion' to Britain's economy.

Some, though, need convincing. The big creative money still stays in Milan, Paris and New York. It comes to London Fashion Week not for the deals but to hoover up graduates from London's much-envied art school system, which trains about a quarter of the world's designers. 'When I started there were no big design companies,' says Sorrell. 'Now there are hundreds. In sheer commercial terms, that's the sign of a maturing industry. But we're just not good enough at shouting loudly.'

All this talk of brands and returns is anathema to many who have made 'Creative London' what it is, not so much because of snobbery at getting their hands dirty with multinationals, but the worry that as London's creative industry gets serious, the very thing it has going for it, its informality and creative chaos, will disappear. 'You can see it happening already,' says fashion designer Shelley Fox. 'We survived Cool Britannia, but now everything's being packaged up together. Controllable. There's so much blandness out there. But the whole draw of London is its easygoingness.' And don't even mention property prices. Sorrell sympathises. 'It's a bit like when areas gentrify, the designers and artists are the pioneers, then all the chains moved in. We were one of the first people in Covent Garden in the Seventies, but when the local pub installed a lightbox for photographers to use, we knew it was time to move out.'

Barcelona and Bilbao propped up their 'creative' urban renaissance with decades of state planning, infrastructure, rent controls, and – important, this – invested not only in international iconic architecture to get them noticed by tourists, but architecture and culture thoroughly rooted in place, in their citizens. When Lille in France – another declined former industrial city – became European Capital of Culture in 2004 it asked its citizens what they wanted out of the year. Very 1789. Lille got *grands projets*, but it didn't forget about *petits projets* too. It built Maisons Folies, twelve grassroots community arts centres, many by local architects, and packed them with the equipment necessary to create and sustain the new 'creative city' – such as IT training centres and free recording studios. The point, said its project director, was to celebrate that very French thing, '*l'art de vivre*', the weaving of culture into local, everyday life – rather than its equivalent in Britain, 'lifestyle'. After all, creativity is not just a brand. But nor is it the cure-all for urban decline, concluded a report by British think tank the Institute for Public Policy Research: 'It is no substitute for a strong economy . . . Creativity and cool are the icing, not the cake.'

A message from our sponsors

Time for an ad break. Some trivia: the world's largest billboard is not in Ginza, Times Square or Piccadilly Circus. It is, says *The Guinness Book of World Records*, at King Khaled International Airport, Saudi Arabia: 820.2 feet long, 39.3 feet tall, advertising the wares of electronics company LG. It is not, though, the most lucrative billboard in the world. That *is* at Times Square, unveiled in 2014, and no tiddler either: eight storeys high, wrapped around an entire Manhattan block. Unlike its Middle Eastern rival, it is a *digital* billboard, made up of 24 million pixels. At its unveiling (even billboards have social diaries these days) a dazzling light show of swooping shapes and abstract images entertained the crowds. TV footage of the event shows a very postmodern scene: a film of a smartphone filming a billboard. Three hundred thousand people visit Times Square every day, and for that kind of 24/7 advertising exposure for your brand, we're talking $2.5 million for four weeks. The first advertiser to rent space? Google, who you would think wouldn't need the publicity: internet advertising, after all, is what is meant to be the future – and, after all, is kind of what Google does.

But, it seems, even in this age of digital media triumphant, one of the oldest forms of media – architecture – still has some worth. In 2014, the total annual spending on outdoor advertising was $7.2 billion in the US, £1 billion in the UK. These days, though, the outdoor sector, unlike the internet or social media, is not where the cool cats of advertising hang out. The sector is regarded as dull but steady. It has, after all, been around a few millennia – 'brands' in ancient China and Greece used wall posters to advertise – and most billboards are not in Times Square, but on average side roads in ordinary towns without 24 million pixels to play with, just paper and ink, just as they did thousands of years ago.

Nonetheless, there is something about the dull unavoidability of outdoor advertising that still makes it attractive to advertisers. You can ignore adverts on the internet, fast forward them on TV, turn the page in magazines, but you can't (yet) block out the space around you. Now that our waking hours are fought over by infinite media 'platforms', each demanding milliseconds of our attention, those idle minutes waiting for the bus or speeding along the motorway with nothing but asphalt to watch – that's a lot of lucrative time and space going spare that only three-dimensional advertising can invade.

Outdoor advertising might be old-fashioned, but it's being taught 21st-century tricks. Today's niftiest billboards are not just digital, but can even interact with their audience, broadcasting, through hidden cameras, the faces of those, in turn, gazing up at the big screen. They can connect with your smartphone, texting you offers from the advertiser. Advertising giant M&C Saatchi has installed billboards with hidden cameras that can 'read' viewers' emotions, adapting its adverts accordingly. We are not so far from that scene in the film *Minority Report* (2002) when John Anderton, played by Tom Cruise, strolls past digital billboards that coo, 'John Anderton, you could use a Guinness . . .'

The worth of each outdoor advertising spot is calculated according to its position, and, through this position, the nature of the audience that it commands – just like any advert. Some spaces, because of their fame, location and audience, command high prices – the equivalent, perhaps, of the SuperBowl spot on American TV, or a full-page advert in *Vogue*. Other spaces are more akin to a pizza delivery flier shoved through your letterbox. In the UK, the curved digital billboard of Piccadilly Circus, owned by property developer Land Securities, is the most famous and prized; 2 million people are thought to pass by every week. They even visit, as they do at Times Square or Ginza, to look *at* rather than avoid the adverts. Advertisers here therefore change hands rarely: Japanese electronics firms Sanyo and TDK displayed their adverts here for almost thirty years, and Coca-Cola has rented a space since 1955.

The M4 motorway corridor from Heathrow Airport to central London is another high earner, the most famous stretch of roadside advertising in the UK. Today, the drive to and from the airport is peppered with billboards on buildings for its captive audience, and even structures purpose-built just to contain a billboard, some of which push aesthetic ambition beyond a plain rectangle. One is designed by Norman Foster. Another looks like New York's Chrysler Building.

One of the most lucrative spots on it, though, is where traffic slows down, descending from flyovers into the dense streetscape of west London, and coming to a complete stop at some traffic lights. Cars and their inhabitants queue impatiently here day and night, so it's the perfect spot for a billboard; what else are the drivers going to look at? Here, one of Europe's biggest outdoor advertising firms, JCDecaux, planned a show-stopping billboard designed by one of the world's most famous architects: the late Zaha Hadid. Artists' impressions show metal ribbons and embedded lights curled around a screen, whose display, proposed a press release from Hadid's firm, was 'capable of blending into the form, enhancing the form and moving beyond the traditional rectangular advertising format . . . Its distinctive features can act as an iconic focal point to an area that is currently uninspiring and suffering from an overall sense of neglect and dearth of identity.'

This 'striking built form', continued the press statement, 'crosses the line between media platform and public art'.

It is a fine line, and it has already been crossed. Advertising is a lucrative way for the city of spectacle to raise money – not by selling off space to developers, but by leasing its most eye-catching square metres to the highest bidder. In doing so, though, towns and cities confront their obligations as collective entities protecting public good. Various regulations exist across the world governing the display of advertising in public places – such as America's 1965 Highway Beautification Act – regulations that vary according to local attitudes towards the ethics, aesthetics or road safety implications of outdoor advertising. In some places less predisposed to rampant commerce, for instance, such as the French city of Grenoble, with its Green Party mayor, advertising in public spaces has been banned. Grenoble declined to renew its contract with JCDecaux in 2014, denying the city €645,000 in income. The removed panels were to be replaced with trees and community notices.

In 2006, a more politically conservative mayor in São Paolo, Brazil, Gilberto Kassab, removed adverts in his city, one of the largest in the world, and replaced them with a campaign against pollution. He fought challenges in the courts, and, inevitably, a billboard campaign from outdoor advertising conglomerate Clear Channel ('Outdoor media is culture,' ran one of its slogans). Within a year 15,000 billboards had been removed, adverts on public transport were gone and shop signs had shrunk. Online photography sites show the results: the ghostly shadow of now departed famous logos and names, literally branded by sunlight or grime onto the sides of buildings, and still, ironically, recognisable. There were other unintended consequences. Removing advertising revealed parts of the city hitherto hidden, such as unknown *favelas* and the living conditions of migrants inside them. And São Paolo's stance has become an unintended advertisement for the city: 'The city's now got a new language, a new identity,' said a reporter with *Folha de São Paulo*, Brazil's largest newspaper. Just as people travel *to* Ginza, Times Square and Piccadilly Circus to *see* advertisements, they come to São Paolo *not* to.

In other places *more* predisposed to rampant commerce, though, the opposite holds true. The UK, for instance, has stringent rules on the placement, content and size of advertisements, governed by the Town and Country Planning (Control of Advertisements) Regulations (2007). However, in the era of the entrepreneurial city, with public budgets under pressure, these rules are often bent. As more services once run by the state are sold off or outsourced to private contractors, so branding and marketing has entered spaces once considered non-corporate, such as museums, hospitals, schools or parks. The selling of 'naming rights' to public spaces, for instance – utterly normal in the US for parks, rest-stops on freeways, bridges or roads – has become common in the UK. The appearance of the Emirates branding on London's Tube map in 2012 was not the only perceptible shift in what has been deemed acceptable in recent years. Under Boris Johnson's mayoralty from 2008 to 2016, London stepped up raising money through outdoor branding. Christmas lights in London's West End routinely depict characters from the latest blockbuster. Urban branding, though, can be, if not more subtle, then more under-the-radar. The ArcelorMittal Orbit is a bright red, tongue-twisting, metal-twisting 115-metre-high sculpture-cum-observation tower by artist Anish Kapoor in London's Olympic Park. It came into existence, it is alleged, after a very brief chat in the cloakroom at the World Economic Forum in Davos, between Johnson and Lakshmi Mittal, CEO of the world's largest steelmaker, ArcelorMittal. Johnson hoped it would become 'an icon to match the Eiffel Tower'. There was no functional need for it, of course – though you can hire it for wedding ceremonies, and book to abseil down it – so one cannot help but think of it as a gigantic three-dimensional logo for a multinational masquerading as high art, a patch of London sold off, displaying the scantiest fig-leaf of 'public good', and all done on the spontaneous whim of a mayor rather predisposed to spontaneous whims. This whim, though, is permanent, and rather hard to miss on the skyline.

However, this is one brandscape in danger of failing, a marketing campaign gone rogue. Unlike other structures in London, like the

Gherkin or the Shard, its shape has become the subject of press and public ridicule. The ugly duckling waits in vain to be adopted as a kooky national treasure. Visitor numbers have been disappointing: since 2012, just 300,000 people paid to ascend the tower. The latest wheeze to revive its fortunes has been to allow the Orbit to finally become what its shape alludes to, the helter-skelter ride it has always wanted to be. Courtesy of another artist, Carsten Höller, a huge slide has been added to the Orbit, the world's longest, no less, whose thrill-seekers reach speeds of 13 miles an hour. Maybe that will do the trick.

More ubiquitous city branding, though, came in the form of Boris Johnson's 'Boris Bikes' cycle hire scheme, which began with sponsorship from Barclays Bank for, it is thought, £25 million – a bargain for what must be, in sheer square metreage, one of the largest corporate-branding exercises in the world. Barclays got its name and blue livery on every bike and docking station, and hundreds of miles of 'Barclays Cycle Superhighways', painted in the same unmissable blue. (In Paris, by contrast, where the modern-day model for urban cycle hire schemes began, Vélib bikes are run by advertising company JCDecaux, but corporate branding is discreet, and the bikes and docking stations a demure beige, slipping quietly into Paris's equally beige cityscape.)

Transport for London (TfL) not only operates the cycle hire scheme alongside its vast network of buses, Tube and tramlines, it operates through them one of the biggest outdoor marketing contracts in the world. For hire by advertisers is space in 270 Tube stations, 83 London Overground stations, 39 Tramlink stops, 45 Docklands Light Railway stations and, when it opens, 40 stations on Crossrail, a new high-speed railway crossing the capital. TfL claims an annual audience of 1.5 billion people. Today, the interior spaces of London Underground stations are emblazoned in billboards and videoscreens from your train seat to the pavement: companies can block-book entire stations to offer Tube customers a totally immersive brand experience. In 2011 there was even talk of Tube station names being sponsored. Australian winemaker Oxford Landing, for instance, was recently in talks to rename Oxford Circus Tube station 'Oxford Landing Station'.[7] In

2012, Madrid sold off the sponsorship rights of many of its metro stations. However, London's station names – from Piccadilly Circus to Paddington – have more global recognition and currency.

When Barclays was given the largest ever fine by the UK's Financial Services Authority in 2012 for manipulating interest rates, the perils of brand alliances became apparent. Barclays cut short its sponsorship of the 'Boris Bike' scheme, and today the bicycles are sponsored by another bank, Santander, in a seven-year deal worth £7 million a year, their livery now in bright red, although the city's cycle highways remain stubbornly blue. At the launch of the new bicycles, the then mayor pressed home the importance of brand loyalty: 'If anyone still persists in calling them "Boris Bikes" rather than Santander I will change my name to Santander Johnson.'

Cultural deserts

Dubai is a place where taps aren't just gold, but encrusted with diamante; where a herd of gilded horse statues on your hotel forecourt is commonplace; where nobody thinks twice about carving coastlines into a map of the world, or building underwater hotels, revolving skyscrapers and office blocks shaped like iPods. In this city of superlatives, the irony is that nothing ever shocks you. Until now. For this freakshow city's latest trend is truly bizarre: Dubai wants to cultivate a more tasteful image.

Before the 2008 crash, Dubai began courting the avant-garde. Jean Nouvel designed an opera house; Snøhetta came up with a 'gateway'. Both were stymied by the downturn. Zaha Hadid, though, completed her Opus building, a hole-hearted block containing a 'design hotel' and apartments. This serious list of stellar architects marks a shift, says Dubai's director of planning, Rashad Bukhash. 'We want to change what people think of us. Dubai would like to be taken seriously.'

It wasn't just that Dubai's streetscape was beginning to look the wrong side of bizarre. It wasn't just the logic of building a megalopolis where daily temperatures of 50°C require air-con, and carbon footprints, on a Herculean scale. In the late Noughties reports came in of poor working conditions in Dubai's labour camps, home to the hundreds of thousands of workers, largely from south Asia, who actually build its icons. Chief among critics was Mike Davis, who in *Evil Paradises: Dreamworlds of Neoliberalism* called Dubai 'a nightmare of the past: Speer meets Disney on the shores of Araby'.[8] 'Dubai is the achievement of a certain fantasy or utopia', he said in one interview, 'of a society in which the corporation, private ownership and the state are all collapsed into one another.'

'Dubai's been hurt by the criticism,' says Khalid Al Malik, CEO of Dubai Properties Group. 'But we don't ignore the screams. We're working hard to change. We have one great advantage: we are a city of bedouin nomads – we can change direction in an instant.' The most obvious volte-face concerned the environment and the labour camps. Since the UAE signed the Kyoto treaty in 2005, Dubai has developed CO_2 recovery technology, solar power, water recycling and massive desalination plants, insists Bukhash, while new codes introduced last year mean 'all new skyscrapers will be green', though doubts as to the inherent ungreenness of the whole concept of Dubai still linger. The labour camps have also improved, he claims: 'These are five-star hotels, not labour camps. The government's had a lot of attacks. Originally they were right, but we are trying.'

It didn't help that Dubai's neighbour was attracting rather more positive headlines, courtesy of its own architectural reinvention. In 2006, the French government concluded months of diplomatic negotiations about creating a branch of the Musée du Louvre in Abu Dhabi, a deal that French newspaper *Libération* called the 'most novel and controversial deal in the history of French cultural politics'. Rumour had it that Abu Dhabi paid more than £500 million to the Louvre. In a straight swap the French government received money for the export of its greatest cultural prize – minus all art containing nudity or religious subjects likely to cause offence to Abu Dhabi's citizens (which wipes out quite a chunk of western art) – in a new museum designed by France's most famous architect, Jean Nouvel, in the shape of a vast umbrella punctured with holes, raining light onto a mini-city underneath.

It promises to be just one showstopper on an entire island of show-stoppers. Abu Dhabi's royals always seemed to cast a slightly sniffy eye at their brash upstart neighbour, Dubai, with its malls and glitter. Their response? Saadiyat Island, a haven of instant civilisation and, at £28 billion, by far the biggest cultural project in the world. Instant creative credentials, albeit with a mammoth price tag. Alongside the inevitable artificial ski slopes, golf courses and the 'iconic seven-star' properties will sit, on artificial promontories, Nouvel's Louvre, Norman Foster's National Museum and Zaha Hadid's triffid-like Performing Arts Centre. But stealing the show will be something from the man who came up with the very template for the modern iconic art gallery, Frank Gehry: a new version of his Bilbao Guggenheim, on a far vaster scale. Stretching credibility somewhat, it is suggested that this, the largest of the island's projects, 'echoes Gulf architecture'. Pull the other one. This is as North American as McDonald's, Gehry's own brand as recognisible as the golden arches.

Such exporting of museum branches is nothing new: Tate Gallery has been doing it for years within the UK; the Guggenheim brand has long been so internationally ubiquitous it was nicknamed McGuggenheim. In 1999 councillors in Liverpool – then one of the poorest post-industrial cities in Europe – tried to court the Guggenheim Foundation. 'We are offering the Guggenheim Foundation a prestigious position on a world heritage site on the banks of the Mersey,' explained councillor Flo Clucas.[9] The Guggenheim, to little surprise, picked the oil-rich Abu Dhabi instead.

Dubai's rapid response to both bad headlines and Abu Dhabi's local competition is oiled by the state being effectively ruled by one man – Sheikh Mohammed bin Rashid – son of the leader who in the 1970s began transforming Dubai from fishing village to world city, Sheikh Rashid bin Saeed al-Maktoum. What 'Sheikh Mo' says goes, through the Hydra-headed conduit of Dubai Holding, whose myriad subsidiaries control the city's various facets. 'Dubai, Inc.' is basically old-fashioned oligarchic state planning, with gold-plated sheen.

But is this image change more than just PR to appease the delicate consciences of one of Dubai's key markets – rich, holidaying western-ers? 'Yes, of course,' claims developer Al Malik. 'This is Dubai's survival instinct. Unlike other parts of the Gulf, we have never had much oil. The only thing we have is ideas. We trade on our wits. Behind the jokes, the real Dubai is beginning to emerge,' helped, he says, by seri-ous planning to make Dubai 'a proper city', with a hinterland beyond the 20-mile strip of Premier League footballer hideaways, and a diverse economy with eggs in many baskets, what Bukhash calls 'the pillars of the city, the serious stuff'. The Dubai stock market opened in 2005, Jebel Ali port doubled in size, and Dubai's new international airport swarms with visitors. New roads and bridges are being built, a metro and light rail system to curb the city's reliance on the car, plus entire quarters dedicated to finance, the media, research, universities, IT – Dubai Internet City, already packed with companies from Nokia to Microsoft – and healthcare.

Dubai even wants its own 'creative city', to get up there with Lon-don, Barcelona and Abu Dhabi. Sheikh Mo made one of the largest charitable donations in history, £5 billion, to establish the Moham-med bin Rashid al-Maktoum Foundation, to foster, he said, a 'knowledge-based society'. It began with the International Design Forum, where against a background of studded white designer leather, creative luminaries such as Rem Koolhaas, Karim Rashid, Paola Antonelli from New York's MoMA and 'uber-curator' Hans-Ulrich Obrist lectured the locals about how best to bring the artistic set to a city not known for bohemian credentials. There are plans for a college of innovation and design, its looks modelled, perhaps, on a scrubby East End warehouse, only gold-plated and 120 storeys high.

Until Damien Hirst moves to the Burj Al Arab, though, the aes-thetic reinvention of Dubai is in the hands of its newest visitors, star architects. At the International Design Forum most display their standard formulas. Rem Koolhaas, though, has a cannier tactic: what he calls the 'anti-icon'. Koolhaas identifies 'the Dubai icon paradox, that when everything looks so wildly different, it ends up looking all the same. They cancel each other out.' His solution is architecture that is 'generic, completely abstract'. Porsche Towers, designed for the car manufacturer, is a simple, massive, cylindrical tower and a hollowed-out slab. Another design, Waterfront City, is a perfect, 1 billion-square-foot artificial island of generic skyscrapers, offset by vast megastructures of monolithic shapes – an 82-storey spiralling cone, recalling the ninth-century minaret at the Great Mosque of Samarra, Iraq, a 44-storey sphere, already nicknamed the Death Star – alluding to the heroic visions of eighteenth-century architect Étienne-Louis Boullée. The shapes have a silent, sombre, negative energy. 'When the world is clamouring for attention,' says Koolhaas, 'do the opposite.' And thereby become more noticeable.

For Koolhaas, Dubai is the 'generic city', a 'post-global' city in a permanent present, designed for international nomads. Developer Al Malik agrees. The UAE's long-term plan 'is to become *the* hub', he says, 'between Europe and the Far East', reaching a potential market of 2 billion, for whom Dubai, Inc. is whatever you want it to be: a place for a cut-price boob job, for sunbathing in January, skiing in June, and now for avant-garde architecture. It is the ultimate free-market city, though one, ironically, built by an oligarchy. Dubai is a true mirage, and a perfect business plan. Joke? I reckon the joke's on us.

White-knuckle architecture

If I make it to 225 years old, I'll expect a damn good present. Vintage Aston Martin, place in the Seychelles, cashmere suit hand-stitched by Hedi Slimane. So Cristina Nardini was being positively thrifty when she commissioned a mere €7 million bespoke building by one of Italy's most renowned architects. Cristina is celebrating the 225 years her company has stayed in the family. She shows me the family tree. There she is, beside Francesca. There's papa Giuseppe, who pops in and out of the office to keep an eye on the kid. You can follow the branch down the trunk to the root – Bortolo, who, in 1779, built a small distillery and osteria beside River Brenta in Bassano, northern Italy, and started making his new invention, Italian firewater: grappa. Bassano soon became a pitstop for businessmen heading from Milan to Venice. Italy is still run on a quick espresso and a shot of grappa. *Aquavite*, they call the latter: water of life.

Cristina is following a tradition begun by Bortolo: investment in the future. He planted the first vines. She's planting vines of the future, two giant glass bubbles designed by Massimiliano Fuksas. 'We have plenty of tradition in Italy,' she smiles. 'Time for something new.' Designer wineries and distilleries have become quite a thing since the mid 1990s, when Dominus Winery in California commissioned Herzog & de Meuron to build their offices as a 'filigree' of translucent 'stone wickerwork'. Since then, there has been a steady outpouring of big-name architects – from Norman Foster to Santiago Calatrava – designing high-concept spaces for high-end drinks companies. American 'carver of light' architect Steven Holl created Loisium, a visitor centre, spa and hotel for Langenlois vineyard in Austria. Frank Gehry made a new building for Kathryn Hall vineyards in Napa Valley, and for one of Rioja's most famous bodegas, the Marqués de Riscal, in his trademark vortices of titanium and glass, somewhat cheesily coloured in pink, gold and silver (in honour of the wine and its bottle's protective netting and foil).

They are the luxury end of a market that has boomed in the past few decades: experiential architecture. In modern art galleries, the building is often now said to be as part of the creative experience as the art it contains. We visit 'white-knuckle' architecture in droves, specifically designed to make us experience bodily thrill as efficiently as a fairground ride – viewing platforms with glass floors, say, like the skywalks of Tianmen Mountain in China's Zhangjiajie National Park; entire landscapes, like Norway's National Tourist Routes, dotted with architect-designed buildings such as the Stegastein viewpoint, to augment the sublime views; or structures, like Sydney Harbour Bridge or London's O2, that we can now clamber over in 'visitor experience' attractions transforming you into a mountaineer, crampons and all, for sixty minutes. Buildings like the London Eye have proliferated, lifting us to the heavens for a god's eye view of the planet as a detached, picturesque visual experience. The city of spectacle needs such apparatus these days to enhance our experience of it.

Just as cities use such experiential architecture to enhance their image, extract income and form a bond through experience with inhabitants and tourists, so other brands follow suit. Fuksas's blobs are essentially architecture as high-class advertising, in which the sensuous, three-dimensional experience of the space cements the visitor's relationship with the brand behind it. Top-drawer alcohol falls into the same category as Prada or Calvin Klein. At these prices, for these discerning consumers, brand image has to be immaculate, down to the architecture. Hence Miuccia Prada commissions Herzog & de Meuron and Rem Koolhaas to create her store concepts. Buying bottles of booze, for people who don't shop for Sainsbury's £4.99 reliable rioja, has to have the same seamless consumer experience as stimulating as swallowing the product itself. As the marketing blurb for Steven Holl's Loisium winery puts it, 'wine is a wholly sensual experience', even at its designer checkout.

Nardini's new addition is, Cristina admits, part present, part marketing. The futuristic look of the new buildings is pointedly chosen. Nardini has 25 per cent of the Italian market, but Cristina is eyeing up new markets in the Far East, where the look of the new blobs, she hopes, will go down well. One bubble houses a laboratory and quality control, putting the 'purity' of the product literally on a pedestal for all to see. The second houses a corporate entertaining suite, to indulge those who buy several cases of the Pope's aged grappa (very smooth; they let me sniff a millilitre). Both bubbles perch upon a plinth housing a visitor centre for the company's cultural programme. 'This is also a present to the people of Bassano, to Italy,' adds Cristina, playing the latest role in a line of beneficent Italian elites, from Roman emperors to the Medicis of Florence, who have attempted to merge public and private good.

Massimiliano Fuksas is, with Renzo Piano, Italy's biggest architectural name. Both play with the language of the hi-tech architecture they grew up with. But where Piano injects its machine-age looks with humanity – all wood and cosiness – Fuksas injects it with energy. 'Function anyone can make,' he says. 'People come to me for emotion.' For his luxury clients, Fuksas turns emotion into form. For Ferrari's new Product Development Centre in Maranello, he created not only an appropriately precision-engineered building, but one with a sense of humour, its first-floor volume floating unsupported for 7 metres, as if levitating. In Milan's 750,000-square-metre Milan Trade Fair campus, Fuksas infects its cool, rational, glass and steel sheds, vast as an international airport, with craziness – rising here like a lacey hanky caught by the wind, or, there, sucked down to earth by a vortex.

For Cristina he's created another fantastical landscape, on the theme of a bubbling spring, a 'journey', Fuksas says, from darkness to light. You begin by descending underground down a stepped ramp which doubles as an auditorium for events, into a deep cave of concrete carved with faceted walls. It feels like a Bond villain's lair. The ceiling is punctured with skylights gurgling with water on the other side, through which you can see the giant bubbles high above. 'Don't you feel the water around you?' Fuksas enthuses. Next you ascend to the giant bubbles through a twisting staircase or a glass funicular, which pops through that fizzling water, revealed as a pool on the ground surface.

Only up close can you see the sheer craft and finish of the bubbles. One of Italy's foremost glass manufacturers lovingly created the panels, each as exquisitely made as Murano glass. It is close to impossible to create impeccable concave glass with curves in all directions on an architectural scale; harder still to then place them, without cracking, in a setting of sharply detailed steel lattice, purposely designed so that, from the outside, you can't see what's holding the glass up. You can draw such blobs on computers, easy peasy. But actually creating them? Fuksas's blobs, though, are perfect. This is, afer all, Cristina's present; no expense has been spared. 'She came into my office and Cristina, she say, "I want architecture." That's it.' Fuksas guffaws. 'I say to them, "Tell me the budget." And they say, "Tell *me* the budget." I wait all my life for this kind of client.' I bet.

'It's all about the impression, the effect it has on you,' says Fuksas. 'And that comes to you in the heart,' he adds, suddenly serious. 'Giuseppe, the father of the company, he came to me last week and he said, "I am crying." Now here is a strong man, a hard businessman. And I have moved him to tears.'

The experience economy

Nothing sticks in the memory like experience. We have old saws that tell us so. Once bitten, twice shy. Learn from your mistakes. Experience is the mother of wisdom. And experience itself tells us so. There is nothing like going through something yourself – schooldays, childbirth, parenting, illness, death, the highs and lows of life – to sear it upon your soul. These days we even buy experiences as gifts: a day in a Formula One racing car, maybe, or bungee jumping, white-water rafting, a day in a luxury spa. We humans have always craved experiences – pleasurable ones as well as those just the right side of dangerous – but today they are offered up to us like never before. Where once – during my childhood, perhaps – we were lucky to have a holiday a year, today we feel inadequate if we have not, this week, experienced husky-sledging in the Arctic, or artisan sushi-making in Kyoto. Live concerts these days outsell recorded music; people want a communal, HD experience of Taylor Swift.

The most popular art today, too, appears to have become that which is most interactive with the audience. Director of Tate's galleries in the UK Nicholas Serota picked up on this in 1996 in his book *Experience or Interpretation: The Dilemma of Museums of Modern Art*, noting the then-novel 'growing curatorial inclination to favour . . . "experience" over "interpretation"'.[10] This inclination gathered pace a year later with the opening of Bilbao's Guggenheim, a building habitually criticised as

being more spectacular than the art inside. Today, the 'relational aesthetics' that critic Nicolas Bourriard identified in the participatory
nature of so much contemporary art, and the demands on curators 'to
generate a condition in which visitors can experience a sense of discovery', as Serota puts it,[11] means that this inclination has become
unstoppable. Serota, indeed, has encouraged it with spaces like Tate
Modern's Turbine Hall, which has routinely hosted art installations
that demand interaction or inhabitation from the visitor, such as Carsten
Höller's *Test Site* (2006) with its theme-park slides, or Olafur Eliasson's
The Weather Project (2003), whose gigantic, orange sun mesmerised
thousands into a catatonic state.

But let's get lowbrow. Companies and brands have also long identified that the physical experience of their products was something
intense and visceral enough in their customers to merit attention. That
wily old fox of communications theory in the 1960s and 1970s, Marshall McLuhan, hit the nail, as ever, on the head: 'Everybody experiences
far more than he understands,' he once wrote, 'yet it is experience,
rather than understanding, that influences behaviour.'[12]

Walt Disney became the most infamous early adopter of that powerful link between the experience of the consumer and a brand's identity.
He was obsessed with city planning and architecture – particularly in
his later years – poring over the spaces of his theme parks as meticu-
lously as he plotted his films. Much has been written on the tactics of
his 'imagineers' to transfer the qualities of his fictional environments
from the big screen into real life, from Anaheim's Disneyland in 1955
via the EPCOT Center to the 'real' utopian community of Celebration. As Anna Klingmann writes in *Brandscapes*,[13] 'Disney sought from
the beginning to make Disneyland a soothing alternative to [the]
urban decay and suburban sprawl' of the urban crisis in the 1950s.
That, though, was not enough: in the company's suburb, Celebration,
as Naomi Klein writes in *No Logo* (1999), 'For the families who live
there year-round, Disney has achieved the ultimate goal of lifestyle
branding: for the brand to become life itself.'[14]

The term 'experience economy' was coined in 1999 in B. Joseph

Pine II and James H. Gilmore's *The Experience Economy*,[15] in which they chart the rise of experience in consumerism as a way of promoting a brand, by sweetening the route from a consumer's intent to purchase a product to the use *of* the product; for instance, through the intricately staged 'striptease' choreography technology giant Apple builds into the packaging of its products. It coincided, Pine and Gilmore say, with the shift in western society from standardisation to one of customisation and individualism; we no longer expect our lifestyles to resemble the cars that popped off Henry Ford's conveyor belt – any colour so long as it's black. We expect our lives to be constantly fulfilled and custom-built to suit our every whim, and companies are happy to oblige, for the right price.

A company defines itself by a set of 'brand qualities' – sleekness, quality, energy – connected to various cultural allusions (red equals danger and sexual pleasure, a Scottish castle equals rugged romance, a swooping logo indicates speed and litheness, etc) built through tradition and repetition, which then define how it presents itself to the world, from the precise nature of its logo, to the colours it dresses itself in, through to the spaces it surrounds it and its products in. These brand values must then connect with the consumer. I understand you. I am you. I will fulfill you. That age-old promise of consumer culture: I will make your life better.

The experience of space is one tactic in this arsenal used by brands today to distinguish themselves from one another, and to communicate and bond with us, the consumer. The immersive, sensory nature of architectural space – the fact that you can't escape it, and that it pulls on so many senses – helps brands make that connection with us in their environments, whether showrooms, shops, event spaces or offices. Brand qualities are embodied in the architecture, right down to 'storyboarding' the narrative of a place as if it were a film or an advertisement, a method routinely employed in the design of theme parks, casinos or shops.

These are not, of course, new tactics. Architecture has always been used to immerse and bond with us. In the eighteenth and nineteenth centuries, for instance, British aristocrats employed eminent architects and landscape designers such as Humphrey Repton and 'Capability' Brown to design country estates like Stowe as theme parks for the intellect and emotions, picturesque landscapes to promenade through during periods of leisure, punctuated by follies – gothic pigeon houses, Chinese pagodas, faux ruined temples – to stimulate allusions and a rush of beauty to the head. Same tactics, only today, a different patron: consumer brands.

Some brands create a communication system – including architectural spaces – powerful enough to appeal to a wide audience, as Apple has done with its sleek, minimalist products, carried through to their stores, offices and marketing. But few brands these days are able to create a language that appeals so widely that it needs little alteration for local or individual culture or tastes. Instead, multiple experiences are developed to be sold to different niches and sectors of the population.

You can spot the use of architectural branding in all sorts of mass-market products – the design of McDonald's restaurants, perhaps, or the faux-homeliness of a Starbucks. But it really comes into its own within one niche: luxury. Architecture is, after all, an expensive business. It takes a lot of investment. You must be sure of your return. That is why wineries and distillers, such as Nardini Grappa, have spent millions creating environments augmenting the sensory experience of consuming their high-end product. They distinguish themselves by doing so, recognising that those consumers fortunate enough to afford it distinguish *them*selves by knowing of and selecting their brand and its associated qualities. Just as their consumer is educated, tasteful and distinctive enough to recognise the quality of taste in the brand's product, so they will be educated, tasteful and distinctive enough to recognise the quality of the spaces in which the brand surrounds itself.

BMW, for instance, has used the contemporary architecture it wraps its expensive cars in as an extension of its own brand qualities. In Munich, it commissioned Austrian avant-garde architects Coop Himmelb(l)au to create BMW World – a tornado in glass symbolising speed, modernity and cutting-edge credentials. Here you can experience 'brand qualities' in a cultural centre, or collect a car, whose finer details (colour, quality of trim, mod cons) you have selected yourself. You, the customer, can immerse yourself in the essence of BMW, as it has defined itself. In Leipzig, BMW spent £37 million on Zaha Hadid's Central Building for its mammoth production plant. All workers must pass through; it's where the canteen and other collective spaces are housed; it is where the boffins and management work, where the bigwigs are entertained, and where the products are show-cased. This is where you buy your BMW souvenir rubbers. Hadid's architecture embodies and projects brand values of modernity and movement. First, literally. The building is built around the production line, which is hung and displayed from the ceiling, loaded with cars, coursing silently and relentlessly and bathed a little theatrically in blue floodlight, as if posing for a car advert. Modernity and movement are also embodied metaphorically, the building's ultra-modern architec-ture of interlocking lines, dizzying ramps, terraces and stairs and tricky perspectival games creating the impression of movement within solid concrete.

The key thing about the experience economy today, though, as Pine and Gilmore pointed out, is that it is no longer *just* about sweet-ening the route from a consumer's intent to purchase a product to the use *of* the product. Experience in the experience economy can *be* the end product, another service to be consumed, for which we will pay handsomely. What you pay on the turnstiles of football stadia like London's Wembley will guarantee a particular kind of environment, down to the authenticity of leather trim on your seat. Airlines today carefully calibrate the luxury or economy of the experiences they sell to customers, down to a millimetre of leg room, or the precise feel of seat fabric. The function of travel is no longer just to get you from A to B safely and quickly, but to do so with a certain kind of experience that will distinguish both you and the brand you have chosen.

And today the symptoms of this experience economy occur not just within the spaces controlled and used by private companies, but in public spaces. After all, notes urban theorist Sharin Zukin, buildings and cities today are 'produced under nearly the same social conditions as consumer products' and 'follow the same patterns of both standardisation and market differentiation'.[16] As our entrepreneurial cities and towns have adopted the tactics of private companies, so they have donned their dress, using branding and experience as a way to distinguish themselves.

Take bridges, for instance. Bridges don't just bridge any more. They must have other tricks up their sleeve. They have to be symbols, of course – Tower Bridge, Sydney Harbour, the Golden Gate. But nowadays bridges are built that seem more symbol than bridge, and which turn the getting from A to B into a transformative experience. The Millennium Bridge, in Gateshead, northern England, was one of the first to be honest about how important it was not just as a bridge across the river, but as a symbol *and* a thrilling experience. Its primary purpose is to transfer promenading tourists between Newcastle and Gateshead, ensuring the success of those waterside bars crucial to national economies these days. But look how its architects Wilkinson Eyre do it. Like other bridges, it uses a light, elegant, arching form to give the impression of movement. Yet there's more. The bridge's walkway isn't a straight line, but a long curve. It gets you from A to B not as quickly as possible, but by slowing you down. It invites you to promenade, take in the views. Not only that – the bridge itself performs for you. Whenever a tall ship approaches, the bridge's twin arcs rotate, rising and falling and rising again like a blinking eye. Even the drinkers in those waterside bars go silent, for a second.

Anyone who has ever crossed a bridge anywhere in the world understands that to do so is a particular experience – the feeling of being suspended over a void, or rushing water; that release, perhaps, of being out of the ordinary for the time it takes to cross. The experience is a pleasant by-product of the main function of the bridge: crossing. Today, though, the function of crossing has become the necessary by-product of experience. No bridge can sit there quietly, keeping itself to itself. It has to be interesting. For years, you could barely move on London's Millennium Bridge for people bouncing up and down, slightly disappointed that Norman Foster was compelled to remove the wobbles that caused it such bad press when it opened (an experience too far, perhaps).

In Paddington, west London, for instance, three curious small bridges have been created as part of the infrastructure of Paddington Basin, a speculative apartment-cum-office development. The bridges have the serious job of funnelling its 20,000 daily office workers over the canal to Paddington Station. But, in doing so, each hopes to elevate the commuter's rat race into a pleasant experience. They are an 'enlivener of spaces', says Sandra Percival, director of the Public Art Development Trust, which commissioned two of the bridges, 'to add layers of complexity, expose the less visible', and give this bland, glassy-eyed development some identity.

Artists Ben Langlands and Nikki Bell describe their bridge, a great white-etched sheet of steel and glass, as 'a suspended room,' says Langlands, 'where people and place become suddenly visible' – an eyrie, if you like, abstracting you momentarily from the melee. A few hundred metres east, a cylindrical bridge bound with a metal helix is imagined by its artist, Marcus Taylor, as 'a playful device, a poetic event', he says, in which 'you are constrained, which forces you to contemplate the rest of the world around you with more force. It's not just a question of getting across this span of water but how.' The very act of passage from one side to the next becomes dramatised.

The bridges are designed to be looked *at*, as much as looked *from*. Langlands and Bell's is inspired by a cinema screen: it flickers with the shapes of those who use it, 'silhouetted', says Langlands, 'in a semi-ghostly way, like shadow puppets'. Taylor's bridge looks inert. But it creeps. 'I was thinking', he says, 'about making a bridge into an event. And I wanted a non-traditional way of making the bridge move, not simply up and down.' The bridge looks like a screw, and moves like a screw, rotating on its helix.

Between the two, the bridge designed by the internationally renowned Thomas Heatherwick is more dramatic still. Not that you'd suspect. On first impression it looks, he admits, 'beautifully boring, very, very simple' – a mere gangway. One flick of a switch, though, and the gang-way comes alive. The handrail, fired by hydraulic pistons, unlocks and flexes like a backbone, rising into the air, curving into an arch and then a ball. It can remain still at any given point. Heatherwick's favourite position lets it hover just above the bank, 'as if it's doing yogi flying meditation'. The irony is that Heatherwick's bridge is utterly pointless: it saves you from walking an extra 10 metres. Its pointlessness is my point. Even the banal, the useless, has today become an experience.

Such 'performing' bridges are essentially follies in the city of spec-tacle, a theme park in which experience is all. The mechanism uniting such follies is the 'city promenade'. Promenades and viewpoints have been a feature of resorts for centuries. But now that all towns and cities are resorts, at least in part, promenades have proliferated, from that along London's South Bank, to Paris Plage, the urban beach along the Seine that has spawned a thousand, rather less illustrious, imitators worldwide, to perhaps the most successful of our age: Manhattan's High Line. The High Line was once a derelict freight viaduct, where, in less gentrified times from the 1970s to the Noughties, the artists of Chelsea, the Meatpacking District and Hell's Kitchen would escape the city's grind by breaking past razor wire into a secret garden, acres of wilderness and weeds thrust up into the air. As property prices rose around it, though, 1.5 miles and 6.7 acres of magnificent emptiness – coursing through twenty-two blocks of prime real estate – left to rot and bloom in one of the densest cities on earth seemed almost fabu-lously obscene. It could never last. The most obvious thing to do was to demolish an eyesore cursed by landlords for depressing local prop-erty prices, and replace it with more of what lay around it: real estate. It was, after all, privately owned space; its owners could do what they wanted. Freelance journalist Joshua David and artist Robert Ham-mond, though, had other ideas, setting up the Friends of the High Line in 1999. To them and their fellow 'friends', the High Line wasn't any old real estate. It had cultural value, experiential value, as well as latent financial value as something other than a site for condomini-ums, values that they set about releasing.

The Friends of the High Line didn't own the space, but they could claim a kind of collective ownership of it by celebrating its potential. The High Line, after all, passed through a landscape heavily populated with creative brainpower; surely its artists could imagine a better future for it? Yes, it could become dumb old real estate, same as every other Manhattan block. Or it could become . . . cow pastures? A rollercoaster? One giant long skinny swimming pool? These were some of the 720 entries of David and Hammond's ideas competition in 2003. But in David and Hammond's minds was another bright idea from across the Atlantic, in Paris.

In 1998, a derelict railway viaduct, following Avenue Daumesnil from the Place de la Bastille 3 miles across the twelfth arrondissement, reopened as the Promenade Plantée: below, its street-level arches were given over to fashionable shops, artists and workshops; on top an urban park, unwrapping once-hidden views of the city, a Paris just below the rooftops. The Promenade Plantée was a revelation for the pair, doing what all good urban spectacles should do, particularly in this archetypical city of artists: making a familiar landscape suddenly unfamiliar, surreal almost, allowing furtive glances into *appartements* or *hôtels*, unusual views of places you thought you knew. Paris was a city reinvented in the mid nineteenth century as *the* precursor of the city of spectacle, infamous planners like Baron Haussmann reconfiguring its landscape with vast *boulevards* and *places* the better not only to circulate armies to quell the revolutionary masses, but to circulate the bourgeoisie past Paris's sparkling new shops and attractions. Here, though, was the boulevard reinvented, turning the city into an experience to be consumed, and its visitors, rich or poor, into flâneurs and modern-day surrealists.

Back in New York, though, the question was how to convince the city to back such fripperies. The gentrification of the neighbourhoods around the High Line became Joshua David's weapon. On the one hand it gave him powerful local friends, supporters such as Hillary Clinton, artist Cindy Sherman, actors Harvey Keitel, Glenn Close and *Sex and the City*'s Cynthia Nixon, who would attend the Friends' glamorous yearly fundraiser, hosted by film star Edward Norton and designer Diane von Fürstenberg. On the other, it allowed David to appeal to those age-old Manhattan qualities: greed, elegantly fused with civic altruism.

The Friends handed the city a study showing how turning the High Line into a public asset rather than demolishing it would result in property prices in the neighbourhood rising even higher, higher than if it were replaced by apartment blocks. The then mayor, Michael Bloomberg, was embarking his urban planning policy of beautifying a now thoroughly bourgeois Manhattan with parks, cultural centres and contemporary architecture, a far cry from the Fear City of the 1970s and, indeed, the more confrontational approach of his predecessor Rudy Giuliani (famed for his 'zero-tolerance' policing, and all for the High Line's demolition); helped, no doubt, by the fact that, owing to his own riches, Bloomberg's election campaign did not have to go cap-in-hand to the power brokers of Manhattan, its real estate community. Bloomberg instead brought in energetic staff, like city head of planning Amanda Burden, keen on loosening, slightly, the zoning rules that have rigidly segmented New York since 1916, to release land for developers, though without overly alienating Manhattan's powerful community activists.

'The High Line [was] such a magical space,' says Burden, 'ugly, but with a unique character. I always said that if ever I got into a position of power this would be my highest priority.' The trick with the High Line, though, was to make the 'magic' work for everyone, to open up the space for people other than artists or property developers. 'This is a real-estate driven city,' adds Burden, 'and developers are always looking for the bottom line. But then the mayor has always insisted architecture is a great economic developer.' The answer? With one hand the city protected against eviction through gentrification the hundreds of galleries that today line the High Line by creating an 'art and culture' district better 'connected', says Burden, to the rest of the city by turning the viaduct into an urban promenade open to all; the city rewarded developers whose buildings gave public access to the High Line. With the other hand, the surrounding area was rezoned from mainly industrial to residential, pleasing developers by suddenly releasing the potential for 4,200 new apartments. Owners of properties near the High Line were able to sell 'air rights' to new developers to build taller buildings along 10th and 11th Avenues, while keeping roofs low along the Line, protecting its surreal views through the cityscape. Solomon himself couldn't have made a defter judgement.

Today, the once-shabby viaduct has lost much of its romance. It is no longer a secret garden. It has opening hours like any park. Its gardens have been beautifully tamed and tousled by landscape designer Field Operations, its weeds replaced by horticulture. Its structure has been patched up and added to by architects Diller, Scofidio & Renfro. They call the result 'agri-ecture', 'a post-industrial instrument of leisure, life and growth', weaving together hard landscape – sinews of undulating concrete boardwalk arching high and meandering low through slashes revealing the street below, and over galleries, market places, a public swimming pool, beach, and a daringly cantilevered amphitheatre – and soft vegetation, here woods, marshland, wilderness, meadows, there graphically bright and preened municipal borders; ending by the Gansevoort Meat Market in a cantilevered gallery building and staircase, with a glass wall that turns butchering into a spectator sport.

Once city mayors talked of the 'Bilbao effect', after the miraculous effect Frank Gehry's Guggenheim Museum had on the economy of the Spanish city; now they talk of the 'High Line effect'. From its reopening in 2009 to 2014, 20 million people walked this promenade, sharing an experience of the city – something akin to the feelings of 'intensity', 'liveliness', 'sensuous enjoyment', beauty and delight called for by Jane Jacobs and Kevin Lynch – once the preserve of artists and the adventurous. No wonder cities around the world want to copy it. A body in London, for instance, as well connected as the Friends of the High Line, wants to build from scratch a verdant clone, a 'Garden Bridge' across the River Thames, created by the designer of that performing bridge in Paddington Basin, Thomas Heatherwick. Despite high-powered friends, however, Heatherwick's bridge has proved harder to realise. It lacks the very things crucial to the High Line's business plan: greed, elegantly fused with civic altruism. Straddling water, rather than real estate, it is harder to bribe locals underneath – seagulls? Canada geese? – with promises of compensatory property price rises.

The High Line effect comes in many forms. Along the flanks of the High Line, as the Friends predicted, property prices have duly catapulted. Tourists come in droves. The feeling of freedom and aesthetic novelty the artists that scrambled up its sides experienced in the 1970s has been efficiently, sometimes beautifully packaged up for all to share. For some, these feelings are available on a permanent basis. New, often avant-garde apartment blocks have risen beside it; they loom, offering their wealthy residents views up and down its length, just like those that once rose around Central Park. Some of these views are not, shall we say, of horticulture; a subculture of voyeurism has developed along the High Line. Residents in some of those new apartment blocks, or in high-class hotels like the Standard, which straddles the promenade with stout concrete legs, are said to offer the High Line's ever-present audience of tourists below a different kind of display, involving *tableaux vivants* of naked, gym-taut bodies.

Designed thus, with urban promanades and attractions, the city of spectacle becomes exactly what the architect of Boston's Faneuil Hall, Benjamin Thompson, prescribed in the 1960s for the failing modern city: 'for if a city is not *just* a park, it could *work* like a park'. The city of spectacle mimics in concrete, steel and glass the precursors Thompson so admired, the estates of those eighteenth-century British stately homes, theme parks for the intellect and emotions, picturesque landscapes for the leisured to promenade through. It is a landscape to consume, with all the senses, but with the sense of sight most of all.

CHAPTER SIX

THE RIGHT TO BUY

'The Ladies' Paradise, with its furnace-like glare, seduced her completely . . .
it was burning like a beacon, it alone seemed to be the light and life of
the city.'

Émile Zola[1]

Consuming passions

'Excited?' the billboards ask. 'You will be . . . Birmingham will never
be the same again.' The entire city quivers with anticipation. It is
2003, and two days remain until the new-look Bull Ring shopping
mall opens. The old concrete bruiser of the 1960s has been replaced by
a new concrete bruiser, only this one is covered in glittering glass. The
press is predicting a stampede. First stop will be Selfridges department
store – part of, yet pointedly distinct from, the main shopping centre,
a brand powerful enough in its own right to be given its own independent presence on the city skyline. Its hourglass figure curves in all
the right places and a design inspired by Paco Rabanne's chainmail
number has been tempting passers-by since the scaffolding came
down. This is one shop that needs no adverts. The architecture does it
for free. People eyeball it, calling it all manner of names. One seems
perfect: the Boob Tube.

Nothing gets a crowd going like sex and shopping. Émile Zola
described it in *The Ladies' Paradise*, a novel set in a Parisian department
store, based on the world's first, Le Bon Marché, established by

Aristide Boucicaut in 1852. Paris gave birth to modern consumerism: its eighteenth-century *passages* foresaw the mall, and, when Zola wrote, Baron Haussmann was reshaping the city in wide boulevards lined with alluring boutiques. Boucicaut made shopping profitable with new tricks, the biggest of which was making sexy what was once a mundane activity left to the servants. He practically invented the kind of *double entendre* that still sells anything from cars to ice cream. For Boucicaut, shopping was seduction, selling you desires you didn't know you had, magically lit with futuristic gas lighting; goods were freely available to be touched by shoppers for the very first time, without pressure to buy from pushy shop assistants. Zola describes his department store as a 'remorseless' and spectacular half-machine-half-beast, picking your pocket, in the most pleasurable way.

I meet Selfridges' Boucicaut, chief executive Peter Williams, inside his own machine of seduction. He looks the part – jazzy paisley shirt, rogue's moustache. 'The grandness of it all!' he exclaims. 'It's an exact repetition of what was done 100 years ago: architecture as a billboard for the business. It distinguishes us from everyone else.' His sweeping hand flicks dismissively towards Debenhams, his lesser rival. 'You wouldn't be here otherwise.' True. 'We can't be boring. We have to provide something *more* than the product. There's got to be buzz.' Welcome to the Ladies' Paradise, twenty-first-century style.

It's not a complete coincidence. The building's architect, Future Systems' Amanda Levete, was given the novel by Vittorio Radice, Selfridges' former director, who plucked the ageing company from faded grandeur by returning to what Boucicaut and, indeed, founder Harry Gordon Selfridge knew best: shopping as spectacle. In the early twentieth century, Selfridge used Daniel Burnham, then America's hottest architect, to build the columned giant you see today on London's Oxford Street, still the street's grandest building. He stuffed its shop windows with products lit by electric light, and treated customers to novelties like a crèche and ice-cream sodas. 'You know why they come here?' asked Selfridge. 'It's so much brighter than their homes.'[2] For his part, Radice courted high-class brands, top architects and

artists to turn the same building into a modern-day bazaar to tempt
blasé metropolitan eyes. Birmingham's Selfridges is his legacy, a whole
building that reinvents the department store by taking it back to its
root: seduction.

This building is flashy, quite literally. Flashiness is its function.
Shops need few exterior windows beyond those at street level (retailers
want 'black boxes,' says Williams, enclosed like theatres, so their constantly changing stage sets can bedazzle the shopper). Future Systems
has made a virtue of this. The building is an almost windowless blob,
with no conventional roof and walls but, rather, one whole skin, created
by spraying concrete onto metal mesh – like papier-mâché – painting
it Yves Klein blue, then covering it with 15,000 anodised aluminium
discs, specifically tested to shimmer alluringly against Birmingham's
deadpan skyline. There is no shop sign. 'The building *is* the sign,' says
Levete. '"Your shop will be on postcards in every shop in the city," we
said,' adds her partner, Jan Kaplický. It dutifully appears on Barclays
Bank adverts, and billboards tempting tourists in London to visit the
UK's second city.

Inside, the machine-beast sets to work on its shoppers. Look up
through the atrium and each floor is marked by fat, white polished bal-
ustrades, like the ribs of a monster, stepped back to the skylight. A
second, smaller atrium, is a plump-lipped ovoid penetrated by thick,
rounded shafts of escalators: 'The sensuality is very overt sometimes,
isn't it,' says Levete. Each floor is designed by a different architect with
different tricks – acid colours here, light shows there, but always sensual,
always fun fun fun. For Radice's retail hunches to be proved right, its
expensive spectacle must help it outsell a conventional shop. 'If they sell
more knickers per square metre,' says Kaplický, 'we'll be happy.'

But there's a lot more at stake than knickers. Zola called *The Ladies'
Paradise* 'the poem of modern activity'. In the city of spectacle this activity has seeped outside the shop to encompass spaces from art galleries,
railway stations and airports to – thanks to internet shopping – the
bedroom. Shopping is, wrote architect Rem Koolhaas, a little cynic-
ally, 'the last remaining form of public activity', one of the few that

still binds almost everyone on the planet, the more so today. Governments follow retail performance figures as if lives depend on them; they do. The entrepreneurial city is built today not on factories, but on buildings like Selfridges: consumer experiences, whether shops, malls, offices, entertainment complexes. 'More people will pass through here than Tate Modern,' glows Amanda Levete. 'This building questions the nature of a public building.' Shops in all their manifestations, Koolhaas argued, are the architectural form of our age, just as cathedrals were in the fourteenth century, factories in the nineteenth. It's in this kind of 'junkspace', he wrote, that we spend most of our time. Birmingham, at least, has a cathedral of junkspace. Most other towns just have junk.

The seeping of this activity, though, can be more insidious, more subtle. The privatisation of a city's space, its transformation in recent decades into the entrepreneurial city, has changed the very way in which we define the spaces inside it. It changes how these spaces work. It changes what we do in them. It changes even the way in which we talk and think about buildings, the very words we use.

New kinds of spaces have been designed, like ultra-modern shopping malls; but old kinds of spaces, too, have been completely rethought. For the culture of consumerism now lords it over not just shops and malls, airports and railway stations, but civic spaces like schools, parks, libraries — rebranded as 'one-stop shops' or 'idea stores' — and even private spaces like our homes, upon whose rising and falling fortunes so many millions of households depend.

Once there was relief from consumerism, spaces you could enter, having paid your taxes, where you were not being sold something. That is no longer an option. As the state has receded from public life, and as public activity has become increasingly contracted out to or owned by the private sector, so all spaces today come with a business plan. Architecture, after all, has to pay its way.

Architecture's evolution from modernism to postmodernism is neatly encapsulated in three buildings in the City of London: the former Commercial Union Building by Gollins Melvin & Ward (1969), the Lloyd's Building by Richard Rogers Partnership (1986) and 30 St Mary Axe – 'The Gherkin' – by Foster & Partners (2004)

Designing 'experiences' is the defining role for architecture today. This example is at the Top of The Rock Observation Deck and NBC Experience Store, Rockefeller Center, New York

At the inauguration of the Shard in London, a live laser show shot dazzling beams from the building. The accompanying soundtrack? 'Fanfare for the Common Man', by Aaron Copland. No irony intended

'This was mine one time, but it don't belong to ordinary people now. It belongs to financiers in Zurich and New York, places like that.' Covent Garden Market, London

'The airport is now a shopping centre.' Zurich Airport. Where isn't?

Cities around the world all seem to want the so-called 'Bilbao effect':
bringing them back to life through the glorious power of architecture.
Guggenheim Museum Bilbao, by Gehry Partners (1997)

Photograph by Phillip Maiwald

'All work conditions in China are not what you'd desire,' says Jacques Herzog. 'But you wear a pullover made in China … Engagement is the best way of moving in the right direction.' The Bird's Nest Stadium in Beijing by Herzog & de Meuron (2008)

The 'fluid space' of Zaha Hadid's architecture is best experienced as you are experiencing it right now: at a distance, in an image. Station, Nordpark Railway, Innsbruck by Zaha Hadid Architects (2007)

Learning how to shop

Growing up in 1970s St Albans, we weren't short of thrilling retail experiences. But in March 1976, something altogether more glamorous appeared on the horizon: Brent Cross. The fountain! The dome! The escalators! The air conditioning! Open till 8 p.m. – almost all week, too! No half-day closing here. America had come to Britain.

This was a simpler age: the United States was still exotic, and our family's twice-yearly visit to a new-fangled McDonald's was luxury indeed. Brent Cross's winning formula was that behind all American-style capitalism: give 'em what they want and pile it high. The mall was beige, comforting – as undemanding as daytime telly. Demanding nothing of you was its point: cars would carry you from home to entrance, doors opened automatically and, inside, no rain fell. It was a glimpse of the easy life that America had promised since the 1950s, preying, like Big Macs and big cars, on our laziness and greed. I was in love. So was Britain.

Before Brent Cross, the UK had shopping *centres*, but not shopping *malls*. Mostly we had postwar shopping *precincts*: a bit 'age of austerity'. We had arcades too, imported in the nineteenth century from Paris, though the magical cocktail of consumerism and voyeurism philosopher Walter Benjamin identified in Parisian *passages* didn't always translate quite so alluringly in Bolton or Birmingham. The opening in 1956 of the world's first enclosed mall – Minneapolis's Southdale Shopping Center – upped the ante. Architect-developer Victor Gruen's rationale? Minnesota is either too hot or too cold; so huddle shops round an atrium, add heating/air-con and watch the customers come: comfort architecture, in big boxes covered in logos, to be viewed at 60 m.p.h. from the freeway, but lingered over inside. Gruen, an Austrian émigré, was dismayed by the individualism that car culture was inflicting on American life. Malls, he said, would be the agoras of the suburbs.

It took just five years for two Yorkshiremen – Arnold Hagenbach and Sam Chippendale, Arn and Dale – to import his idea into Britain, plonking Arndale Centres in towns reinventing themselves as American-style motorvilles, and simultaneously importing a notion exotic in Britain: shopping as a joy, not a chore. Each Arndale outdid the next with spectacle and size, though, like many British takes on America, they seemed a little feeble beside the real thing. It took Brent Cross and its air conditioning to really teach us how to shop pleasurably.

In the years after, as Britain under Margaret Thatcher learned to spend, malls like Brent Cross multiplied on the edges of towns. Brent Cross, though, was small fry beside Birmingham's Merry Hill, Sheffield's Meadowhall, Essex's Lakeside or Manchester's Trafford Centre, each outmanoeuvring the other with novelties. Meadowhall was Britain's first mall to open on Sundays. Gateshead's Metro Centre brought in a firm of American mall consultants, who advised adding to its mix cinemas, a bowling arcade and theme park. Across the Atlantic, after all, malls had already ballooned into miniature cities. Canada's West Edmonton Mall, for years the world's largest, contained a vast amusement park. Minneapolis's Mall of America entertained its 1 million weekly visitors with nightclubs, theme parks, an aquarium, even a wedding chapel.

It seems astonishing that a British government, usually so besotted with Americana, outlawed out-of-town malls in 1993; more astonishing still that it was a Conservative government, usually so besotted with free-market Americana. Planning Policy Guidance 6 was designed to silence that part of the Conservative Party less in love with it, especially when it concreted over the green and pleasant countryside near their homes. This law, though, didn't stop malls. It moved them, and changed their shape. British suburbs today are dotted with big boxes and retail parks, smaller than out-of-town malls, but, en masse, just as enormous. Meanwhile the 'town centres first' or 'urban renaissance' policy of Conservative and Labour governments since 1996, designed to revive city centres, simply encouraged megamalls to move downtown, under the guise of 'retail-led regeneration'. Not even the 2008 financial crash could kill the mall. In Bradford, a northern post-industrial city, Australian mega-developer Westfield paused its city-centre mall mid-flow; the land it demolished was nicknamed 'the Hole', and, wrapped in hoardings, became a literal and metaphorical inaccessible empty heart, until work resumed. There's nothing a developer likes less than unfilled land. When the mall finally opened in 2015, its developer, strangely enough, decided not to name it the Hole, choosing instead something altogether more untroubling: the Broadway.

Today, despite online shopping and the decline of traditional high streets, 'retail-led regeneration' continues. Why? Because architecture can still offer something that online shopping can't: physical experience. Where developers spot fat wallets, they go for the wow factor. In other towns, though, with a different, poorer, demographic, 'retail-led regeneration' can be the last economic hope, requiring the council to sell land to the first developer that turns up, then turning a blind eye to the lumps they build, packed with risk-free clone stores, and draped inexpertly in thin, gaudy architecture to both hide their bulk and get them noticed.

Pick a town. Let's try Plymouth. This city on Britain's south coast has a noble maritime history. Its strategic importance meant that it was heavily bombed in the Second World War; since then, it has struggled to get its mojo back. It was rebuilt in postwar architecture, pleasant enough, but too plain to get it noticed in today's frantic global market-place. So, enter stage left, its rebuilt, rebranded heart: Drake Circus shopping mall. This will get Plymouth noticed; though not necessarily for the right reasons. For Drake Circus is so bizarre-looking, it's hard to imagine what went through the architects' minds. First, two parting waves of mammoth terracotta sheets, set, edgily, at post-earthquake angles; followed by a huge pregnant bulge of latticed wood; bringing up the rear, a block of checkerboard stone is topped with gridded metal panels in tree patterns and finally the two gigantic brick drums of the car park, which look like the cheeks of the monster's booty. I'd laugh, if I didn't think of poor Plymouth having to suffer it every day. With some irony, across the street is Plymouth University's architecture faculty. They must have very bad karma.

Drake Circus is a freak, but it's not a one-off. Massive malls like it have been built – and are still being built – in town centres across the

UK. Exeter has Princesshay, developed by the Crown Estate and Land Securities. Liverpool has Liverpool ONE, a 42-acre development of 160 shops, owned and developed by the Duke of Westminster's property company, Grosvenor. Portsmouth has Land Securities' Gunwharf Quays. In Leicester there's Highcross, 'an awe-inspiring mix of fashionable stores, stylish restaurants and true city centre living'. In Bristol: Cabot Circus. Nottingham, York, Portsmouth, Canterbury, Cardiff, right down to little old St Austell . . . few towns have escaped 'retail-led regeneration'. The return on commercial property, especially in town centres, has far outstripped that on gilts or equities. A safe bet. And, on the one hand, good news. Money has returned to town centres. The problem, as always in the entrepreneurial city, is how it's done, exactly how the deals are brokered. Like banks or big supermarkets, big mall developers – usually mammoth corporations such as Westfield or Land Securities, paired with trusty dullard architects like Chapman Taylor – have a lot of clout. They bring to cities the promise of cash tills ringing. Naturally they want the biggest return for the least investment and least hassle. It's up to the city to look them clean in the eyes and negotiate.

The science of sparkle

Westfield Shopping Mall, west London, measures itself in the millions or billions: 1.5 million square metres in size, £1.6 billion in cost, 23 million visitors in its first year. Ten years in the planning, it had the misfortune to open in 2008, the very month after the worldwide economic crisis began. This does not appear to have held it back. Westfield has stared global recession in the face, and blown a raspberry.

Westfield sells itself as a new kind of mall – not out-of-town, but hip and urban; not a destroyer of neighbourhoods, but their salvation; not a 'privatised' space, but a 'third space', melding public and private life. As a spokesman put it from the architectural firm that designed the space, Westfield is 'a continuation of the street fabric', with 'a sense of being outside without being outside'. But it's a particular kind of

street fabric, he continues, one with 'a certain feel of elegance and luxury. We want our customers to feel pampered. Studies show that the
longer people spend in an environment like this, the more they're
likely to spend . . . Seduction', he adds, 'plays a big factor.' You don't
blow £1.6 billion without being sure of a return; the mall's demographics have been precisely worked out. This is a mall for everyone
(with money), from the uber-posh enclaves of Notting Hill and Holland Park across the street, to the media hipsters of Shepherd's Bush,
to the 4x4s of suburban Buckinghamshire up the M40. 'Indulgence',
the mall's blurb promises, 'is no longer the preserve of the very rich.'

Westfield's arsenal of seduction has something to appeal to each
demographic niche. There are chain stores, but also artisan cheese
shops and Dior boutiques. You can shop, but also eat in every corner
of the planet, see exhibitions, car shows, movies or impromptu 'happenings' from its events team. It is like a chunk of the city – diverse,
intense, lively – only not. It is privately owned. And there are 'lively'
things you can do in cities that you can't do here: smoke, rollerblade,
hold political protests. Though that didn't stop hundreds in 2014 from
staging a mass 'die-in' against the deaths of black men by American
police officers, Instagrammed around the world. All publicity is good
publicity, but the unexpected is not welcomed by Westfield's owners.
They want you to enjoy a certain kind of choreographed spontaneity,
and have designed the mall down to the doorknobs to nudge you
exactly in the right direction.

Westfield mall is owned by Westfield the conglomerate, the world's
biggest, most innovative mall developer and operator. It started out in
suburban Sydney in the 1950s, but now owns more than 100 malls
across the world and hones its craft astutely. Its research 'Lab' in San
Francisco updates those lessons developers took from that city's Ghirardelli Square in the 1960s: how physical space can be a USP, even in
this age of online shopping and globalised sameysameyness. It merges
real and digital spaces, testing inventions – such as gigantic smart
screens where you can order online, then collect for real – in its San
Francisco mall, before unleashing them on us.

There is a very precise recipe underlying each of its malls, their shape honed according to data on demographics, customer flow, retail sales targets and so on. Across town, for instance, is a twin – east London's Westfield mall, Stratford City, whose very different design targets its particular demographic. Its senior marketing manager April Taylor told the *Evening Standard* newspaper in 2010 about its 'industrial' ambience: 'We want to harness that edgy, eclectic east London feel.' Artists such as Tracey Emin, reported the newspaper, sat on its 'cultural committee'.[3] Back in wealthier west London, though, there is no 'edgy, eclectic' feel. Instead, glamour is the name of the game.

Like any corporation, Westfield holds its cards close to its chest. But we have a spy with us who can prise some of them away. Dr Tim Holmes is a neuroscientist who has long studied how shops use neuroscience to encourage us to behave in particular ways: it is called 'neuromarketing'. Mall environments are designed to stimulate our senses, and, through them, our cognitive response and behaviour, all monitored by inconspicuous CCTV, to ensure we are doing as our environment surreptitiously tells us.

Tim and I sit on a sofa high above the crowds. 'A lot of people think that they're in control of their attention,' he says. 'But in an environment like this you're not. The environment is manipulating your visual attention.' Holmes can see things I cannot. To pull the wool from my eyes he gives me a strange pair of hi-tech glasses. They record both the direction in which my pupils look *and* what they look at; the data is then transmitted to image-crunching software in his laptop. He sends me off with an errand. On my return, we examine the results.

First: the most obvious. The most infamous trick retailers perform is the 'Gruen transfer', named after the inventor of the modern-day mall, Victor Gruen, who, in the 1950s, began inducing confusion in customers with continually changing, labyrinthine layouts. The aim is to make us feel lost and vulnerable. 'They're trying to mess with your ability to navigate,' says Holmes, 'because this is what makes you susceptible to the visual cues that are thrown your way.' I have fallen for the trick. Holmes studies his laptop, and its record of my eye movements. 'The only reliable navigation tools that you were looking at were the store names.' The mall has information signs and maps, but they're 'very subtle, they don't make it easy for you to see them'. Instead, navigation is by brand name. 'It's bang, bang, bang with the brand names,' he says. I can see dots representing where my pupils move laid on top of film footage of what they were looking at. They leap from shop sign to shop sign as I feel my way through the mall.

Sheepishly, I notice too that my pupils keep landing on the scantily clad male and female figures used in shop windows. Am I *that* obvious? I am. 'That is biological,' Holmes reassures me. 'We look at other faces to see if they are potential mates, aggressors. We can't help but do it. You have neurons in your brain that will move your eyes towards a face. It's unavoidable. This is what marketing is: it's about appealing to our basic biological instincts.'

Throughout the mall, I notice groups of sofas, rugs and coffee tables, under more subdued lighting, like a living room plopped into this least domestic of spaces. The intention is obvious, says Holmes: the more like home an environment is, the less threatening it is, and the more likely you are to feel emotionally attached to it. 'This is one of the ideas of "third space",' says Holmes: 'to give you a place that feels like home but that's not your home.' Every time I sit down or pass through a 'home zone' my eye movement relaxes. I stop scanning shop signs and adverts. Every sofa, though, is packed. There are not enough of them. For there is a limit to how homely and relaxed you are meant to feel. The mall-designer calculates, precisely, the correct number of seats to create the impression of homeliness without causing us to rest for too long. The chairs are backless and only just comfortable enough. 'It's about keeping you moving through the mall,' explains Holmes. 'If you *are* going to sit, sit in one of the coffee shops, [or] the food hall and spend some money.'

Because the single most important job that the mall designer must accomplish is to get you moving. They want you to shop, truly, until you drop. Customers must continually circulate so they are exposed to as many brands as possible. A trick as old as the Gruen transfer is the 'anchor store', with favourite shops in key positions to tempt us to move between them, past smaller fry. These days, though, retailers have more sophisticated tricks up their sleeves to get us moving. Those shoppers beached on sofas are not encouraged to stay long, not least by the frantic environment. Muzak is loud, adverts on video screens jab your retina. The crowds course around them like river rapids, an effect exaggerated by patches of bright light passing over from on high. Above us, the mall's ceiling is designed with opaque and transparent glass panels. As the sun and clouds move, randomly scattered patches of light move in the mall too.

This disco-ball effect, like everything here, is not unintentional. The roof has been designed to let light in, natural light being a well-known method of energising mood. But designing it to also project moving spots of light is a strategy, says Holmes. Our eyes are innately drawn to movement. 'We are looking for predators. If something's moving, we need to check it out.' Our eyes are also drawn to light, especially fast-moving spots of natural light – sparkle. My pupils prove it, says Holmes, 'skipping around the points of light. Your eye is constantly on the go,' meaning 'you're very susceptible to anything that they'll throw at you to grab your attention.' The mall's sparkle encourages my eye to scan its environment more widely and quickly, so that I am more likely to sweep my eye across brand names, adverts, or products in the windows. Even the Gruen transfer encourages my eyes to sweep: the more lost you are, the more your eye scans the scene to work out your location. And the mall does all this without me even noticing. 'It doesn't make for relaxed shopping,' says Holmes, but then that's not the point.

There is some relief, though. Westfield London contains a mall-within-a-mall: The Village, full of luxury brands, where the architecture plays a subtly different tune. The light is lower: 'It's a glowy light, more flattering,' says Holmes. Shop fronts have faceted glass panels, their refractions creating a glittering effect. But it is a different calibre of sparkle – less in-your-face. Surface materials are more luxurious; there is a better class of fabric on the sofas; colours are less garish. The environment, says Holmes, is saying to me, 'This is a world you'd really like to be part of.' He can see it in my eyes: I am calmer. I slow down. I have more time to gaze at the chandeliers and the expensive products in shop windows. A mall with two kinds of experience, for two kinds of people? 'This is not a democratic environment,' says Holmes.

Malls without walls

Ironically, though, in the land that invented it, the mall is metamorphosing once again. US mall building has slumped since 1990. Trashier malls are being 'de-malled', their arcades opened to the air and shops installed with entrances onto streets. It's all about 'lifestyle centres' now, like New Jersey's Xanadu, mixing shops, restaurants, theme parks, even schools and churches around a 'Main Street' – like the very thing malls were meant to replace: downtown. They're cheaper than conventional malls to build and maintain, and their 'retail experience' is judged more stimulating by America's easily bored consumers, who now demand places like 'mom-friendly' malls, tailor-made for their demographic niche. Meanwhile, in the old downtown, developers buy up swathes of the conventional streetscape to create 'malls without walls', or group businesses together to manage the space as 'business improvement districts'. And there's always China. In 2004, Beijing's five-storey Golden Resources Mall, all 6 million square feet of it, knocked Canada's West Edmonton Mall off the top spot as the world's largest. It, in turn, has been knocked off the top spot several times since. Each of China's myriad cities tries to out-bling its neighbour. In 2006, for instance, half a million people witnessed the opening of Guangzhou's Grandview Mall, containing the world's tallest indoor fountain.

Wherever the mall, the result is much the same: 'Downtowns have become veritable "entertainment machines" . . . catering to urban dwellers and suburbanites seeking something new and different.'[4] To fight off the siren call of the internet, the experiential thrill of these brandscapes has to be ever more unforgettable. Each has to outdo the last on Instagram.

We owe such malls-without-walls to one man: Jon Jerde. James

Rouse might have popularised the 'festival marketplace' mall as the saviour of downtown in the 1970s, but, soon after, Jerde brought in the showbiz. He learned his trade well. In 1984, after an apprenticeship, like Rouse, designing suburban malls, Jerde was commissioned with graphic designer Deborah Sussman to design the look of the Los Angeles Olympics. The only catch? An unOlympian budget: $10 million. How do you dress up an entire city for the world's TVs with a few bucks? There was no money for conventional Olympic building. Instead, Jerde turned to Hollywood, designing with Sussman stage sets for the camera crews that looked fabulous in living rooms, but, in the actual, real LA streets were so insubstantial they could be packed away when the circus left town. The Los Angeles Olympics became famous for two rare feats in the Games: leaving few traces and turning a profit.

It was a lesson Jerde never forgot: pump up the melodrama *and* the bottom line. Jerde's company today makes some grand claims: a billion people shop every year in one of their malls; their developments can raise property prices. 'We put people', Jerde once said, 'in a popular and collective environment in which they can be most truly and happily alive.'[5] But what was that environment? Like Jane Jacobs, Jerde adored the theatre of the street. He grew up, he told the *LA Times* in 1988, in Oklahoma, Louisiana and Texas, 'rather lonely places', he said, without hubbub.[6] His first visit to Europe with its dense old cities, Jerde said, was 'a revelation'. Here were places that *appeared* successful. And perhaps their success might in part be attributed to their design. So what if you could design, from scratch, a neighbourhood offering its visitors 'destinations', says Jerde's website, 'that pulse with life through a carefully orchestrated procession of public spaces, shops, parks, restaurants, entertainment, housing and nature'?

The year after the LA Olympics, down the coast in San Diego, Jerde designed another urban 'stage set' for developer Ernest Hahn, to lure people into its declining heart. Horton Plaza was a chunk of city – complete with speciality shops, offices, cinemas, a hotel, four department stores and an outdoor theatre – only privately owned. It was designed for 'conviviality', said Jerde, mimicking the haphazard feel of a city by having its parts designed by different teams, like a game of exquisite corpse. Put into the architectural blender were allusions to souks and piazzas – anything foreign, exotic and bustling. Twenty-five million people visited in its first year.

Jerde's malls shared common qualities. They were spectacular, not only visually: built-in sound systems raised the sonic mood. He liked design that encouraged visitors to explore; he liked contrasts in experience. He used curves 'to draw people in', suggested Jerde in a book about his work, *You Are Here*.[7] People are intrigued by curved paths, he thought; they can't help but follow them to the end. His friend, the famous science fiction novelist Ray Bradbury, worked with Jerde to imagine the 'storyline' of the new spaces. 'We threw conversational confetti to the air,' Bradbury once remarked, 'and ran under to see how much each of us caught. We blueprinted cities, malls and museums by the triple dozen, threw them on the floor, stepped on them . . . I felt honoured to be allowed in as an amateur Palladio with my meagre experience but Futurist hopes.'[8] The formula was repeated, with a different 'look' again and again: CityWalk at Universal Studios (1993), which aimed to boil the experience of the city down to a single mall (why bother with the real thing?), the Fremont Street Experience (1995) in Las Vegas, and then around the world to Seoul, Shanghai, Hong Kong, Budapest. And, in 2006, Istanbul.

Istanbul is a city with its fair share of in-built liveliness, and the kind of urban richness, accumulated over millennia, that does not, you'd think, require much intensifying. But this didn't stop Jerde – in a spectacular feat of taking coals to Newcastle – from opening a downtown megamall, Kanyon, designed to fast-track into the twenty-first century a city famous, from its Grand Bazaar to its picturesque street markets, for a rather more old-school approach to retail.

Inside Kanyon, in Istanbul's northern business district, Levent, niche high-class boutiques target the demographic of Turks who read *Wallpaper** magazine – 'personally hand-picked,' says Kanyon's MD Markus Lehto, 'no, almost curated.' There's Le Pain Quotidien, with its gentrified brioches, Mandarina Duck, Furla and Camper, a rooftop branch of London's chic Chinese restaurant Hakkasan, plus smarter Turkish brands such as Ottoman Empire, purveyors of skinny T-shirts to Istanbul club-bers. Istanbul received its first malls in the 1980s, a decade in which they've hitherto remained. With Kanyon, though, says Lehto, 'It's like going straight from black and white to digital plasma screens,' and that involves training its users in how to be modern consumers – 'learning to walk into an Apple Store and play with an iPod,' he adds. 'Learning to queue for Wagamama. Turks just aren't used to that.'

It's not just the novelty brands causing a stir. The architecture is spec-tacular, designed, as its name suggests, as a deep, open-air canyon, arching round – in one of Jerde's trademark curves – a bulging multi-plex cinema, and lined with four floors of stone-faced terraces, to mimic, says David Sheldon of Jerde Partnership, the hills and ravines of the city's geography. Kanyon has urban ambitions, Sheldon proposes, as 'a quality, mixed-use space' (there are posh flats and offices in the high rises above) which he hopes will catalyse Istanbul's chaotic, creaking urban form. 'Istanbul in its Islamic heyday was a glorious urban experience – the gardens, the mosques, the fountains. Now if you've got money you leave.' Kanyon, he thinks, will restore the glory. He likes to call it 'a place in the city with all the perks of the suburbs'. Despite the ambitions, though, it remains essentially a privatised mall for the right kind of citizen, with airport-style security at the gates. Hijabs are thin on the ground. Shopping bags are not. 'Istanbul's an intense urban experience,' adds Lehto. 'There are no places where you can walk and shop safely in a nice atmosphere, without people coming up and beg-ging or hassling you.' Kanyon is a high-end safe space within a frantic city for those with deep pockets. So far, so conventional. But what if your clientele has no money and the product you are 'selling' is free?

Idea stores

Generations have tried to save Poplar. Its East End London streets are encrusted with the accumulated remains of successive waves of do-gooders trying to drag it out of the gutter. Over there is a Victorian board school, one of thousands that for the first time introduced free education for all in the late nineteenth century. Behind it, the Salvation Army. Across East India Dock Road, the 1930s Poplar Public Baths, from a time before power-showers became standard, is now decrepit, awaiting deep pockets to reimagine it, perhaps, as a luxury spa for local gentrifiers. Poplar is still waiting to be saved. Each building uses the language of civic improvement of its day – morality and education for the Victorians, a bracing dose of physical activity in the 1930s. Today? Commerce. Two doors down from the pie-and-mash shop, next to Jones Quality Meat, the next generation has come to save Poplar. It's a library. No it's not. It's an Idea Store®.

Libraries are old news. To get the masses reading these days, you must speak their language. And their language is definitely not crusty old libraries. In our collective memory, libraries come cast in antique form. In the UK, for instance, most are products of the 1850 Public Libraries Act, one of numerous waves of social reform in the second half of the nineteenth century directing towards public good the powerful currents of the Industrial Revolution. These Victorian stalwarts come fronted in pillars, raised on monumental staircases, carved with the names of their wealthy philanthropists – Passmore Edwards, Carnegie. Inside, their interiors remain lavish by today's standards in sheer materials alone: parquet floors, cast-iron Victorian radiators, intricate joinery. Such wealth. Today, though, after decades during which library funding – like so much from the public purse – has been increasingly reduced, these old-timers have adopted that character common in the less vigorous parts of the UK: faded grandeur.

The rate of fading has quickened recently. Libraries, like so much of life today, have been overwhelmed by technological advances. Now that one can find anything on the internet, what role is there for these fortresses of knowledge, in which the appearance of wi-fi can still be a rare and wondrous event? Libraries have often resisted change, embodying an inherent tension in them between extending knowledge to the masses, and extending *just* enough of the *correct* kind of knowledge. Britain's first public libraries divided their readers through architecture: serious scholars in reading rooms, women in 'magazine rooms', and the working class in 'newspaper rooms'. There was out-rage among some in the early twentieth century when closed-stack systems – in which material is locked away, retrieved for you by librarians – gave way to open-access systems, in which the user does it themselves. The cultural stereotype persists of the fierce, tight-lipped librarian, guarding their stash of information.

Not fierce enough, though, to counter the savage cuts to library funding in the UK since 2010, when Britain's coalition government reduced local council budgets as a response to the 2008 economic down-turn, forcing each to prioritise which of its public services to keep or cut. Hundreds of libraries have closed; hundreds more have passed to volunteers. Even Birmingham Library, an uncharacteristically large and lavish new arrival, unveiled with full symbolism in 2013 by education rights activist Malala Yousafzai, had to substantially cut its opening hours and services two years after its launch. As councils have taken dif-ferent choices, so across the country you find some areas in which libraries are just surviving, and others where few exist at all. This, too, at a time in the UK in which child illiteracy is still an issue, more than 150 years after the Libraries Act. And as libraries become a rarer sight in communities, so fewer use them or acquire the habit. Libraries are engaged in a battle for survival worthy of a pot-boiler novel, brought on by the collision of circumstance and their own innate character flaws.

Such cost-cutting, of course, has been a long time coming. When the entrepreneurial city was born in the 1970s, it was decreed that the civic heyday of the Victorians or the 1950s and 1960s was over. The city had to earn its keep. Town centres were abandoned to shopping malls, caretakers were outsourced to private firms, council estates were sold off or thrown to the dogs, and what few new school or hospital buildings were built were built not just with our taxes, but using a new invention from across the Atlantic – the public–private partnership. Investment products spawned by this new invention, such as the private finance initiative (PFI), essentially ask the private sector to help pay for, build and often ultimately own public buildings.

The state cross-subsidises the investment with our taxes, and the public institution that occupies it – a hospital, a local leisure centre, a library – becomes a tenant. Public and private, private and public. Smoke and mirrors. So many of the advances and improvements in western towns and cities in the second half of the nineteenth century – sewage systems, water provision, transport networks – were also accomplished by private companies in partnership with the state. Only there is a sense today that the balance of power has subtly shifted.

Poplar's wider neighbourhood, Tower Hamlets, once had more libraries per head than any other London borough. By the late twentieth century, however, only 20 per cent of its population ever set foot inside them. Wrapping themselves in grand doors and columned porticos was no longer an appropriate strategy for libraries. The masses will not come. They will sit at home on PlayStation, or nurse lattes surfing the net in Starbucks. A report in 2014 commissioned by the UK's Conservative culture minister Ed Vaizey found that this habit of Poplar's citizens was repeated more widely: only 35 per cent of people in England regularly used their libraries. The other 65 per cent, though, have been well trained; we are exercising our consumer 'choice' *not* to go to libraries. We will not put up with their capricious opening hours and hard oak seats, no matter how beautifully made. Interestingly, though, the report found that 50 per cent of poorer or immigrant populations *did* use libraries regularly. Perhaps the coffee shops in their neighbourhoods were full.

Some libraries are already rebranded in the bureaucratic thoughtspeak of their day: 'learning resource centres', 'hives', 'community hubs'. The government's report, though, proposed that libraries needed to improve their 'offer' further, in a 'retail-standard environment'. To be understood and used, libraries, like so many public institutions today, must be rebranded with the most popular language of our age, one that truly unites the nation – shopping. Hence the Idea Store. In 2003, Tim Coates, former managing director of UK bookstore Waterstones, issued a grim warning for Libri, a library charity. Coates gave libraries fifteen years, and prescribed a culture change: longer opening hours, more events, fewer bureaucrats and off to the charity shop with those dog-eared novels. But then he would. Coates oversaw the painful reinvention of his high-street bookshop as a *Friends*-style coffee hangout. It worked. In 1979, two and a half times more books were loaned from libraries than bought. Today the balance has tipped the other way.

'The idea that libraries are dead is laughable,' says David Adjaye, architect of Poplar's Idea Store. 'It's the 100-year-old environments they're housed in that are dead. An Ikea looks better than most libraries. They're intimidating. Those regimented rows of books two metres above my head aren't about making me feel comfortable. Architecture has these subtle visual codes and hierarchies that distinguish classes and communities.' Adjaye has confidence in spades, touted as the next big thing since he began designing homes, boutiques and bars for London's art and media crowd in the 1990s. Now he *is* a big thing.

His great aim, he says, has always been to build 'the architecture of the post-city'. You what? What he means – I think – is a new public architecture that avoids the visual language nineteenth-century architects used for their institutions – portly columns and gothic plucked from stately homes and cathedrals – in favour of something, he says, in that buzzword *du jour*, more 'inclusive'.

It was Adjaye's retail design experience in his early career that caught the eye of Heather Wills, Idea Store programme director at Tower Hamlets council. 'Our residents want us to use the language of retail rather than the language local authorities used in the past. And they wanted libraries on the high street, so they could pop in while shopping.' Out go old-school libraries; in rolls the 'Idea Store brand', says Wills. Idea Store even has an ® next to it, as if it were Disney or BMW. A pilot 'store', by architectural firm Bisset Adams, opened in 2002 off Roman Road in Bow, east London. Its melange of library, the inevitable café, 'surfing space' and adult education classes has a hyperactive interior like the set for a Saturday morning kids TV show. Visitor numbers have trebled.

Adjaye's Idea Stores, too, have adopted this 'retail-standard

environment'. Poplar's is positioned in a shopping mall; its neighbour
in Whitechapel jostles with a centuries-old street market on the high
street. The exteriors of both, though, are twenty-first-century, not a
column, pediment or portico in sight; instead they're decked out in
swish double-height entrances in eye-catching blue and green glass
stripes, and escalators to lure punters inside. The glassy exteriors, says
Adjaye, are not just about transparency, letting light in on the closed
book that libraries have become for many. Their stripy appearance, at
once transparent and opaque, is, he says, designed to shimmer and
intrigue the curious, 'a mirage that turns out to be real. In a harsh,
seriously defensive neighbourhood, surrounded by fortress buildings,
you counter with delicacy and beauty.'

Inside they're photogenic, like one of Adjaye's chic boutiques. But
it's more than style. It is, he says, an exercise in 'dissolving the monument', creating an accessible space without sacrificing subtlety. No,
there are no vast book stacks, but curly-wurly plywood units on wheels
instead, arranged as an intimate maze to wander through, and kept
low, so you always feel as if you're in one big room. Surfaces juxtapose
often peculiar, or recycled materials – a typical Adjaye ploy – such as
cheap paper acoustic panels, or 'junk plywood' wall fins and ceiling
joists. Adjaye says he likes using 'shitty materials elevated till they're
beautiful'. The effect is warm, homely, humble, the detailing either
intentionally or unintentionally a little DIY, with rough wood or
paper-thin laminate surfaces, another departure from the rich (in
every sense) interiors of their Victorian predecessors. You do wonder,
though, if they will wear well.

For there is an inherent contradiction within public–private partnerships. The private companies that engage in them quite rightly owe the
public sector nothing – they are accountable only to their shareholders.
So, to persuade them to build what the public needs, a government
needs to dangle a tasty carrot: the prospect, say, of making money with
a plum building contract for a new hospital or a renovated village hall.
But the end result depends, as it always does in the entrepreneurial city,
on the deal – on who blinks first.

In the UK, for instance, there was a brief public-sector building boom under Tony Blair's Labour government after 1997. Britain built more schools, hospitals, health centres, even more social housing than for decades. Labour created its own 'watchdog', the Commission for Architecture and the Built Environment (Cabe), to enforce design quality in these new civic buildings. Libraries got a new lick of paint, town squares received smart bollards, sleek stainless-steel seating and expensive paviers, parks were cheered up, new hospitals were built. Things got better. Slightly.

But in 2007, Cabe, in its first audit of the new generation of affordable and social housing – a key pledge of the government – found that 21 per cent was 'poor'. A mere 18 per cent was rated good or above. The year before it found that eight out of ten new secondary schools were 'mediocre' or 'not yet good enough'. Classrooms were too dark, prone to overheating; communal areas were too noisy. And a year before that it found that a third of new houses being built were of such poor quality they should have been denied planning permission. For every flagship public building like Adjaye's Idea Store, there are countless others that fall short. It all depends on the deal.

Still, for now, in Poplar at least, a minor miracle has taken place. It's Monday afternoon, the sun's blazing outside while, inside the library – sorry, Idea Store® – the spaces teem. I can report genuine teenagers reading genuine books.

Home economics

Homes, for those lucky enough to have one, have always been symbols as well as shelter. We use them to impress. We use them, like we use our clothes or anything else we consume, to display to all who we are, or who we want to be, whether we are Louis XIV in Versailles, Kim Kardashian and Kanye West with their multiple Los Angeles pads, or just you and me. For homes today in the entrepreneurial city are no longer just homes, places of residence, of memory and meaning. They are income generators. Many homes earn more, in yearly property price rises, than the occupants inside. Even if they don't, they can be easily rented out to strangers by the hour, as holiday homes or workspaces while you are at the office, through websites like Airbnb and Spacehop.

This is hardly a new idea. Homes have been used to generate income for centuries. Exactly when domestic property development was 'invented' is a moot point, but by the Great Fire of London in 1666, it was in full swing. The previous 150 years had been a period of un-settling social change across Europe. That new breed, the middle classes, the bourgeoisie, or what were called, in England at least, the 'middling sort', were bubbling up in nations less predisposed to autoc-racy. Early capitalism might have been born among the money lenders of Florence, but it truly flourished in Flanders, the Netherlands, the ports of the Hanseatic League and the British Isles, places where the wings of monarchs and monks had been clipped, but those of mer-chants allowed them to soar. Some of these middle classes were in professions regulating the new capitalist economy – law, perhaps, or government; most, though, were in the capitalist economy itself, as merchants or manufacturers. But the activity of all was governed by one thing: the buying and selling of commodities, even if those com-modities could not easily be packed onto a ship destined for the Orient – commodities like a home.

In England, for instance, Tudor and Stuart monarchs had relin-quished power to unruly parliaments or to curry favour among key allies by buying them off with gifts of land and title. Henry VIII's Protestant Reformation famously not only transformed England's religion, it also revolutionised its pattern of property ownership, as lands grabbed from the Catholic church were given to families who found themselves suddenly yanked up the social ladder. The self-made man – and, occasionally, woman – is the key theme of the age, find-ing, today, its archetype in Hilary Mantel's portrayal of Thomas Cromwell in *Wolf Hall*, a blacksmith's son who becomes, through his ability to wheel and deal, the second most powerful man in the coun-try, chief minister to the capricious Henry VIII.

You didn't have to be newly ennobled, though, to deal in houses. The crumbs that fell off wealthier tables were feverishly traded by the new middle classes, too. Fortunes could be made, land amassed. Property developers like Nicholas Barbon, son of a leather seller, got rich on the rebuilding of London after the Great Fire, and have continued to get rich on endless rebuilding ever since. There was only one rule for the middling sort as it wheeled and dealed in homes: get hold of the land. Land is, after all, a finite commodity, yet by constantly repackaging it in new architectural forms or interior design trends, a perpetual income stream could be produced.

A time-travelling First Earl of Bedford or Nicholas Barbon might not recognise the homes we build in our cities today. But they would still understand the economics behind them: the monetisation of dreams, of how we want to live, of how we want to be seen. At the Geffrye Museum of English domestic interiors in London's East End, 'model' rooms displaying the domestic and interior design trends of their age are displayed from medieval times to the present day. The Tudor mansion, the Georgian townhouse, the Victorian villa, the art-deco semi, the 1950s high-rise flat. Each displays the aspirations and fashions of its age.

The last room is the latest, the '1990s home'. It is the loft, a warehouse apartment, of a gentrifier. Every detail of modern-day domestic aspiration is in place: the double-height 'space' (never a room), the wooden floor, the white walls; the Matthew Hilton Balzac armchair (displaying the owner's modish, and mandatory, interest in young British design); the casually placed copy of *Wallpaper** magazine; the designer kitchen – olive oils, *River Cafe Cookbook*, Smeg oven – for impromptu dinner parties with creative friends.

It wasn't meant to be like this. In their original form, in those patches of the city abandoned by industry during the urban crisis of the 1960s and 1970s, lofts and warehouses were cheap (or, even better, squatted) dives for those opting out of a 2.4 kids existence. Think of Robert Rauschenberg's loft, or Andy Warhol's Factory. Their style was no style, 'spontaneous' or 'as found', which, since they were usually former industrial spaces, meant exposed pipes, acres of rough brick walls and huge steel windows. The kind of open-plan space inside was rooted in an alternative, potentially radical model of living, in which you could reject the nuclear family and nine-to-five job and live an individually – or collectively – fulfilling, creative life. You assembled the form and contents of your life just as you assembled the form and contents of your home in the free, open-plan space of the loft.

Such bohemian ideals didn't last long in the entrepreneurial city. They were monetised. Owning your own home and the land beneath it, once a minority habit among the middle classes, expanded through-out the first half of the twentieth century in Europe and America. It fuelled the expansion of the suburbs. The idea of the home as more than a shelter, as a demonstration of your taste and social position, *and* a financial investment, became entrenched. Now, though, that taste had shifted. The middling sort were buying homes in the city again.

The return of the middle classes to the city, of course, could only take place with major changes in politics and economics. Ruth Glass's pioneers in the early 1960s would have become just another historical footnote had not national and city governments in America and Europe in the decades that followed taken decisions and passed laws encouraging, say, small grants for the restoration of rundown proper-ties, popularising sources of easy credit, or selling publicly owned homes to their residents well below market value. It could only take place by widening the definition of who was middle class. Govern-ments took these decisions for multiple and complex reasons, but they coalesced as one unstoppable change: more and more diverse people owned land, more and more of them owned land in the city, and, therefore, more and more of the city was owned not by the state, but by entrepreneurs both vast and small.

This latest in history's great transfers of property and power began in earnest in the 1970s, as the great selling-off of public assets began. Forward-thinking governments were eager to get the decaying city off its books. The invention of that new financial instrument, the modern-day mortgage, meant that for the first time on any scale not only were millions of the middle classes able to buy their own home, blue-collar manual workers could too. Millions of miniature property developers were created. My mum and dad were two of them. I was born in a starter home in the suburbs in 1971. Later that year, though, we moved to an old house in the city centre, which Dad spent most holidays renovating. We had become gentrifiers. Ten years later we moved to another. And then another. And each time we moved, we found our home had miraculously doubled in value. Millions across the West discovered the same. We found that we were no longer citizens of the city; we had become stakeholders in it. The fortunes of my family were manacled to the land beneath our sofa, and to the city beyond our living room.

There are two broad theories behind the mechanics of gentrification and the return of the middle classes to the city. One is called the 'production side' explanation: how we 'make' cities through buying and selling their land had changed, principally through what's called the 'rent gap' – property prices in inner parts of the city had to be low enough to present an economic opportunity. The other theory is called the 'consumption side' explanation: there was a change in how people with economic power 'consumed' or used these inner parts of the city. Tastes in the middle classes altered from suburban to urban. Both theories, however, must work together, and must do so supported by government laws and economic decisions on a mammoth scale. There's no point in having cheap land if there is no desire for what it contains.

Sharon Zukin's groundbreaking 1982 study of 1960s and 1970s New York gave this shift in economics and, most importantly, middle-class domestic taste its now-hackneyed name – *Loft Living: Culture and Capital in Urban Change*. Although gentrification took place in anything from the Victorian townhouse we lived in to an eighteenth-century blacksmiths in Covent Garden, it became *most* associated with the formerly industrial warehouse, or 'loft'. Zukin's story sprang from buildings in her own block in Greenwich Village – the very neighbourhood, of course, celebrated two decades before by Jane Jacobs – which swiftly metamorphosed from industrial sweatshops via squats to 'developed' luxury homes for lawyers and accountants who had followed the artists back into the city. To Zukin, loft living was another symptom of the lurch of the western city from one form of capitalism – manufacturing – to another – service industries and consumerism – encouraged by a city eager to kill several birds with one stone (such as gentrifying 'declining' neighbourhoods and reviving cities in crisis) at little cost to itself.

Zukin's history begins in the late 1960s, with New York's pre-eminence in the art world and its economic shift towards cultural production and consumption. Thanks, in part, to the initial spark of Andy Warhol's Factory, the lifestyle of what were once eccentric artists living in decrepit industrial spaces became fashionable and, by the 1980s, sellable. Likewise the story of the warehouse apartment in Britain starts when it takes over from New York as the centre of the art and design world in the late 1980s. True, there had been British artists 'doing a Warhol' in disused industrial spaces before. Apeing their New York colleagues, creatives in the 1960s and 1970s, such as op-artist Bridget Riley, settled in declining industrial pockets, such as Covent Garden, Wapping and Limehouse, Rotherhithe and Shoreditch. But their lives certainly weren't the stuff of popular mass aspiration – not yet. Not until 'Britart'. When Damien Hirst hosted the Goldsmiths College art show, Freeze, in a disused industrial space in Bermondsey in 1988, he unwittingly kick-started a shift not only in Britain's artistic culture, but in its domestic culture too. Our art changed shape; but what we expect our homes to *look* like and *do* changed as well.

Charles Saatchi, the most prominent collector of Britart, had already imported the industrial 'SoHo loft' aesthetic to his gallery in Boundary Road, St John's Wood in 1985. There were practical reasons: the work he collected – installations, abstract expressionism, and, now, Britart – was physically large, and disused industrial spaces were big and cheap: that's in part why the abstract expressionists in the 1950s had turned to the abandoned warehouses of New York's Garment District in the first place. But the Young British Artists (or YBAs, as they came to be dubbed) that Saatchi was to court were to make this new kind of domestic space desirable on a scale never seen before.

Almost within a matter of days after Freeze, the YBAs were cool, or, rather, their *lifestyle* was cool – a decadent lifestyle not in Manhattan's SoHo, but in *London*'s Soho. The spaces where they hung out were cool. It didn't matter whether or not the Britartists themselves actually lived in lofts or warehouses. Some did – like Gary Hume – some didn't. What mattered was that the right tastemakers – wealthy collectors, pop stars – were seen *in* loft-style spaces, whether galleries, homes or bars, and that the glamorous package was paraded in the media as that new thing, a lifestyle brand. It didn't matter, either, that Britartists were hardly counter-cultural. What mattered is that they were perceived as counter-cultural – free spirits to be envied from our office desks. The disused industrial space became the landscape of decadence in the late 1980s, where Britart was shown, where illegal raves took place. It was dangerous, and, therefore, attractive. The decrepit had become desirable.

The business plan of the warehouse loft was honed after the 1987 financial crash and its high-profile property collapses. Big developers learned from their mistakes. They changed their shape. They rebranded. Instead of the 'anything goes', 'pile' em high' property speculation of the 1980s, developers learned from the gentrifiers, those small entrepreneurs. They saw that tastes had changed. 'We were more cautious, more discriminating,' says Harry Handelsman, chairman of the Manhattan Loft Corporation, the most renowned of Britain's loft moguls. His first property was a former 1920s printers on Summers Street in London's Clerkenwell, a once-industrial area north of the City. Its lofts went on sale in 1992, the day after the Black Wednesday stock market wobble. And instead of waiting for a reluctant government to help them (the usual template), developers like Handelsman were, like the political climate, more entrepreneurial, risking investment in areas where there was an existing, if shabby, infrastructure, and, crucially, where gentifying 'pioneers' had already settled: still edgy and urbane, but not too far from civilisation.

By the time the first warehouse apartments were sold in the UK, British audiences had already learned the language of their brand from across the Atlantic. Tastes obediently changed. In the 1980s, 'loft apartments' featured as spaces of domestic aspiration in countless Hollywood films, especially those, such as Joel Schumacher's *St Elmo's Fire* (1985), starring the Brat Pack generation of fashionable young American actors such as Demi Moore and Rob Lowe. People with money still moved to the suburbs, as they'd done for decades, centuries, but the suburbs were no longer the landscape of aspiration they once had been. Instead, on sitcoms and soap operas, they were places to be mocked for their pretensions. Advertisements depicting scenes of social mobility or financial success were now located in the city, not the suburb, often around warehouse apartments – such as a popular 1980s British TV advert selling Halifax bank's new ATM service, in which a handsome fellow awakes, cashless, in his Victorian warehouse only to discover a new-fangled cashcard in his wallet, all to the soundtrack of The Commodores' 'Easy Like Sunday Morning'. The association between free-flowing money, free-flowing lifestyle and the free-flowing space of an open-plan loft apartment was sealed.

In a warehouse loft you could be anything you wanted to be, went the mantra. They were the entrepreneurial city in built form, the physical embodiment of the new, neoliberal society, brought into being by millions of micro-entrepreneurs drawn back to the city in search of those elusive qualities identified all those years ago by Jane Jacobs. The suburbs themselves, of course, had, since their birth, sold their own lifestyles as a kind of freedom – a freedom *from* the city. The inner-city warehouse loft, though, freed you from the suburb. The suburb's form of individual freedom became a byword for stifling conformism – 'keeping up with the Joneses'. But the urban warehouse loft was no less conformist. In it, you conformed through being non-conformist, a kind of mass-marketed individualism. Your interior design had to mimic the interiors of those artists in decades before who had enough free time and creative latitude to rifle through skips for old dentists' chairs and 1930s office furniture.

Loft developers soon sold this creative individualism as a brand, through the glossiest of marketing campaigns. Take the blurb written in the 1990s for the Beaux Arts Building in Islington, north London: 'Freedom of expression', runs the headline: 'You are in control . . . You can do whatever you like . . . You end up with more personality.' Personality was for sale. One way the loft liver could demonstrate individualism was through their warehouse apartment's unsuburban architecture. 'Authentic' period detail, especially iron columns and other reminders of past, particularly industrial, uses, attracted a premium, as did 'authentic' history. The Beaux Arts Building's brochure notes the area's history of nonconformism, as a 'bastion of free-thinking eclecti-cism', equating the purchaser's consumer choice with radical politics.

The neighbourhood was a key part of the brand. Like a game of cat and mouse, developers followed gentrifying pioneers, their new bars and clubs, the warehouse raves (sometimes mimicked in launch parties for developments), places colonised by new media industries. Harry Handelsman's first loft development, on London's Summers Street, for instance, was ideally placed. In the early 1990s, 'Clerkenwell was not an obvious residential area. But there were the seeds: the growing design, graphics and media industry; we had the Eagle [a gastropub], the Quality Chop House [a 'progressive working-class caterer', in its own words, selling classic British food at non-working-class prices] and Viaduct [a modern furniture store]. There was a slight infrastruc-ture that we could sell to our punters.'

The final ingredient in the brand was the risk, for both you and the developer. These neighbourhoods and buildings were perceived as physically and socially rundown, dangerous, far from the conven-tional centre of things: you both took a risk in buying. Yet you were tantalised by this. So you weighed these perceived dangers against the potential profit you might make should gentrification take hold. And, to sugar the pill, you were portrayed, and portrayed yourself, as an urban pioneer, a frontiersman, doing good in a lawless country, saving the city from dereliction.

In 1990s Britain, Handelsman was cleverest at packaging all this as a lifestyle brand. As journalist Caroline Roux noted, 'His activities have generated more column inches than any other developer this decade. Harry didn't invent "loft living", but he did put the quote marks round it.'[9] Just look at the company name, for a start. No matter that Handelsman was born in Munich, and grew up in Belgium and France, his company, in iconography, design and name embodied the concept of 'New York loft'. By buying from him, you were close, but not too threateningly close, to the decadence of 1970s SoHo.

It was hard at first to convince anyone else to invest in lofts: government, banks, local councils were all cautious after the 1980s property collapses. They didn't understand this new product. By the mid 1990s, though, they'd caught on, recalls Handelsman, demonstrated by a more relaxed attitude to property development on the part of cities and towns which, in the new entrepreneurial era, were now only too eager for developers' interest. Loft living effectively became urban regeneration policy.

The noisiest promoters of gentrification, though, were neither developers nor governments. Sharon Zukin and Andy Warhol could not have imagined the proliferation of lifestyle media in the 1990s, the sheer number of magazines, TV programmes and column inches selling endless dreams of consumption: from the loft-living magazine king and queen, *Wallpaper** and *Elle Decoration,* to bottom-shelf DIY handbooks. This proliferation marked, for self-appointed style guru Peter York, how the shift in mass-market taste from the country to the city truly became mainstream between the 1980s and the 1990s: 'Thus a range of English Country Dreams titles (*Country Living, Country Homes* and *Interiors* etc.)', he wrote, 'is now fiercely opposed by the Chuck Out the Chintz brigade – *Elle Deco, Wallpaper** etc.'[10] Industrial style, stripped wood floors, open-plan living, Eames chairs and Ikea for those who could afford no better were now the norm, in fashion terms.

Media coverage of this new urban lifestyle was indistinguishable in its enthusiasm from the marketing brochures of warehouse apartment developers. Articles chronicled the heroic 'pioneering' struggles of the homeowner. The tears! The sandblasting! The builders! The apartment's exquisite design details would be described – alongside its seemingly infinite 'space and light' – with a vocabulary of familiar buzzwords: 'urban', 'cool', 'texture', 'arty, bohemian chic', 'hip and happening', 'funky', 'industrial', 'exposed', 'space', 'flexibility', 'blank canvas', 'raw', 'sandblasted', 'eclectic taste', 'mezzanine', 'zen', 'liberating'.

Apartments like Handelsman's were usually designed to minimise the struggle, but to leave enough in place so that they resembled, lightly, the pioneers from the 1960s and 1970s they emulated in their marketing. You had to work, at least a little, for your financial invest-ment. They were sold as shells, fully serviced with plumbing and electrics; the owner brought the interior decor. By the Noughties, though, you no longer had to bother with the decorating. Instead you could buy a 'boutique loft', ready-customised for your every aesthetic whim. At the Jam Factory in Borough, south London, you could pick from their brochure an interior designer to do it all for you. The building didn't even have to be old. At the Glass Building, north Lon-don, the entire building was new. Dressed top to bottom in glittering plate glass, it didn't even pretend to look like an industrial building, though it was still called a loft. Likewise loft livers were now not art-ists, or even ad-men, but investment bankers.

By the time Tony Blair entered 10 Downing Street in 1997 the warehouse loft – in fashion terms, at least – was dead. The media lam-ented the loss of the 'authentic' loft, now that its aesthetics had become mainstream. 'Aficionados of loft living must act, before it is too late,' worried *The Times* in 1997.[11] That year, Britart and design's glitterati held a show, called Aspirational Living, in London. One exhibit, by artist James Dean and mens' fashion designer Charlie Allen, created 'the world's smallest loft' – a garden shed from B&Q – satirising their ever-shrinking size, as developers sought to increase profits from their square footage.

Gentrification began in the 1950s and 1960s when a small sliver of the population in western countries changed where and how they were living. Today the domestic aesthetic this demographic sliver spawned has become mass-market. Furniture shops routinely sell low-slung, mid-century-style sofas from the era of Rauschenberg and Pollock for a couple of hundred pounds; laminate 'wood' floors are default, even if they contain no actual wood, just an image of wood in wafer-thin, artificial form. Homes, whether apartments or houses, urban or suburban, flaunt the same aesthestic, the same open-plan layouts, and are sold with the same language and associations. Homes must now not just shelter you – the laudable aim of the slum clearance, mass suburbanisation and social housing boom of the 1950s and 1960s. They must transform your individual identity. And they must make you money.

Thus the home – access to which not forty years ago was regarded as a 'right' not a privilege in a civilised society – has transformed into just another product to be bought, one brandscape among a legion of brandscapes, a method of fixing identity *and* wealth – especially newly acquired wealth – in an insecure world. Today we have a right to buy, but not a right to be housed. This is what happens when you leave the supply of shelter to the free market. It does what it always does: makes a profit in the most profitable form. The most profitable form in recent decades has been the gentrifier's home, the urban apartment, the loft. It is not, perhaps, the type of home western society most requires. But it is the the most profitable, the one that has seen its value most soar. That is why so many cities are suffering a so-called 'housing crisis': we are building and pouring money into homes designed to be bought and sold, not to be lived in. And too many millions of us have invested our own aspirations, dreams and financial plans for old age in them for this to change any time soon, no matter how many of our millennial sons and daughters these days are unable to afford the rent on a rabbit hutch, let alone a mortgage.

After the shocks of the 2008 financial crash – caused by extending credit too far in the property market – international investors from Russia to China to Abu Dhabi have been looking for safer returns, in the form of investment in prime residential property in settlements less at risk of political, economic or natural upheaval; and in physical forms that might guarantee long-term investment. It is telling that this investment has not generally been in the kind of suburban developments that were popular in the 1950s or 1960s, but, rather, in the dense inner core of cities; not in houses, but in flats – warehouse loft apartments by any other name. These developments might be luxuriously appointed, with marble and high-rise views, but they are essentially the same beast: mass-produced with a concrete or steel frame; free from heritage, of course, but wrapped instead in a cloud of marketing offering a more select form of individualism for a new class of super-nomads.

In January 2015, the housebuilder Redrow released a promotional film for one such development on the eastern fringes of London's financial heart: the London Collection Luxury Apartments, a high-rise residential tower in which penthouses were for sale at £4 million – a bargain compared with prime apartments in the more lucrative West End. The prospect of Britain's departure from the European Union may have caused palpitations in the hearts of flightier estate agents, but London remains a city in which apartments sell for £25 million, where, for the past twenty years, investors in property that is 'buy-to-let' have gleaned profits of up to 1,400 per cent, where inner-city social housing is demolished to make room for more apartment towers, its original inhabitants relocated in more distant climes, and where luxury apartment complexes are marketed not at Londoners or even Britons, but over the internet to those in Shanghai and Singapore after a 'buy-to-leave' home, one among many they own around the world, as their seasonal migrations dictate.

On its release, the London Collection's film caused a Twitter storm of ridicule and outrage, causing it to be withdrawn, though you can still find it digitally preserved in the nether regions of the internet. As the *Guardian*'s architecture critic, Oliver Wainwright, memorably put it, the video was 'beyond parody; as if J. G. Ballard had been put in charge of the opening titles to *The Apprentice*'[12]; some wondered whether it had been made as propaganda by the Socialist Workers' Party, so stereotypical was its depiction of the property development's target demographic: the international hotshot. 'They say nothing comes easy,' intones the narrator, as we see depictions of said hotshot's hard life – working hard, playing hard. The hotshot 'made the impossible possible' and has 'the world at [his] feet'. But he is 'more than an individual'. Where, oh where can this hard-living alpha male find shelter at the end of a long day?

The camera follows his gaze, as he returns, late at night, in his taxi. He spots a thin, bright blue line of light rising higher and higher: his high-rise home, marked out on the skyline by a neon outline built into its architecture. 'Rise and rise,' commands the narrator, as the hotshot leaves his taxi and walks, with a smile, into the comforting quiet and emptiness of the marble lobby of his luxury apartment complex. We follow the hotshot in his glass lift as it slides up the building's thin blue line, into his apartment, where a woman awaits in his rumpled bed. The apartment is immaculate, all sheen and sparkling light, with wine glasses lined up on the work surface, bottles in the cooler, shelves lined with designer knick-knacks and unopened graphic design books, and a cut-glass decanter on the marble-topped coffee table. He gazes out of the window at the glittering lights below. 'To look out at the city that could have swallowed you whole and say, "I did this,"' concludes the narrator. 'To stand with the world at your feet.'

CHAPTER SEVEN

THE CURIOUS HABITS OF THE STARCHITECT

'Gropius wrote a book on grain silos,
Le Corbusier one on aeroplanes,
And Charlotte Perriand brought a new
Object to the office every morning,
But today we collect ads.'

Alison and Peter Smithson[1]

The business of building

The entrepreneurial city requires entrepreneurial architects. And there's the rub. Architects, traditionally, do not always make the best business moguls. In 1962, for instance, alarmed by allegations about its members' old-fashioned practices, the Royal Institute of British Architects commissioned a study of their habits. 'The Architect and His Office' (first-wave feminism had quite a way to go in architecture) found that 70 per cent of its firms were small businesses with fewer than six staff, and achieved such small profits that their livelihoods, it concluded, must have been supported with a private income – inheritance, perhaps, or a trust fund. Architecture was still the profession for privileged gentlemen it had been in the eighteenth century. Lacking the drive for profit, these small firms, the report summised, were hardly thrusting entrepreneurs: ill-equipped to take on large projects, such as the skyscrapers then rising in Britain's property boom, their head for figures was perilously lacking, and their management skills, it concluded with a sniff, were 'incompetent and unrealistic'.[2]

This did not come as a surprise. Architects are constantly plagued with self-doubt over what exactly it is they do. Their occupation requires such a vast array of skills – spatial design, management, business, public relations, philosophy, drawing, politics, engineering, sociology, empathy, law, rhetoric, an eye for intense detail down to the smallest screw, an eye for vast strategic overview of an entire chunk of the planet – and their subject matter is so huge – from entire new cities to art galleries, science laboratories, houses, public squares, any and every kind of environment humankind in all its multiplicity might occupy – that it is rare to find all such skills and knowledge, or even some, in one human being. This predisposes architects to a lot of angonising introspection and dilemmas – who am I? What do I do? What am I good at? – as they defend their corner from more confident, easily defined competitors: engineers, perhaps, or surveyors. And the longest-running dilemma of all is whether architecture is a business or an art.

Until the Industrial Revolution, architecture was both, although the cause of art was invariably greater. The Platonic, Renaissance and eventually romantic ideal of the individual artist was, after all, deep-rooted in European culture. Mario Carpo, in his book *The Alphabet and the Algorithm* suggests that the idea of the architect *auteur*, a single creative, reached its apotheosis in the early Renaissance, in the careers of architects such as Leon Battista Alberti and Filippo Brunelleschi. At the time most building work was carried out 'by committee', by guilds of builders, for instance. Alberti, though, proposed that architects should be designers not makers, and created properly scaled drawings for the first time to communicate with his builders from the comfort of his drawing board, 'construction by remote control', as Carpo neatly puts it.[3] Brunelleschi, says Carpo, was equally determined that the end result should be 'seen as his own',[4] rather than that of his builders; so he devised working methods that separated him, as a designer, from those carrying out his wishes. He left models and instructions deliberately incomplete so that he had to be continually consulted. Accounts of Brunelleschi's life tell of more outlandish methods: personally inspecting each and every stone to ensure it was in the correct place, or – my favourite – carving models from turnips, so that in a few days the design would decay, and only Brunelleschi, the great artist, would be left with the Big Idea in his head.

Defined like this, architecture is an aesthetic cause, its lone geniuses creating buildings that embody their definition of an ideal, an attitude that only intensified for many during the Industrial Revolution. As the world changed violently, and cities ballooned with the poor, nineteenth-century architects and writers from A. W. N. Pugin to John Ruskin to Eugène Viollet-le-Duc penned various manifestos about how the world should be – not just aesthetically, but now morally and socially too. Nineteenth-century society was growing, in their eyes, uglier, more dissolute, and, in part, its architecture was to blame. Ever larger, ever more complex buildings were being built – railway stations, factories, skyscrapers – which demanded mass-produced materials, like iron and then steel, and mass-produced methods, such as prefabrication in factories. It was impossible to create such vast things as the artist-architect of old. Big firms with their eye on the bottom dollar and their boot on the neck of the builder were required.

Consequently, critics like Ruskin and his followers bemoaned the loss of compassion on the building site, and of the human touch in the buildings it produced. In 1892, one of Britain's most famous architects, Richard Norman Shaw, published *Architecture: A Profession or an Art?* By then architecture had been thoroughly 'professionalised' around the world to keep pace with the demands of industrial society, with bodies such as the Royal Institute of British Architects defining in law precisely what an architect was: a profession and a business. Shaw, though, disagreed: it was an art. Defining what architects did as an art, suggests historian Andrew Saint,[5] became a means of 'self-defence' as nineteenth-century architects discovered other professions invading their turf. Engineers might construct, surveyors might measure, but only architects, claimed architects, could create beauty. Trouble was, by 1892, how buildings were constructed had already become an immensely organised, technical and rationalised business, whether architects liked it or not. Shaw and his band of artist-architects, though, sat resolutely before the waves, commanding capitalism to stop.

American architects had few such misgivings. Perhaps it was their country's old frontier spirit, but since the foundation of the republic, America's cities and buildings had been constructed in a spirit of can-do pragmatism, not aesthetics. Beauty was a by-product of the bottom line, something to aim for once shelter and profit had been secured. American architects characteristically sold themselves not so much as creators of more *beautiful* buildings, but, thanks to their design skills, buildings more efficiently and economically produced. Many of their offices were indistinguishable from those of any large corporation. In the 1880s, one young architect visiting the illustrious Chicago firm of Daniel Burnham and John Root described it as 'like a large manufacturing plant', the huge office subdivided into its various tasks, and overseen by the twin figures of Burnham, salesman and schmoozer, and Root, the designer, with a 'charm and suavity coupled with a compelling idealism and enthusiasm'.[6]

It took half a century or more for the penny finally to drop for British architects. By then architects in continental Europe had developed their own response to the immensity, mechanisation and rationalisation of the modern construction industry by making an art out of them, but an art that was also an efficient business *and* a social agenda to curb the excesses of industrial society – killing all birds with one beautifully designed stone: modernist architecture. But when modernism finally arrived in Britain after the Second World War to clothe the buildings of the welfare state, it swiftly provoked a backlash among a new generation of architects and critics, such as Alison and Peter Smithson and Peter Reyner Banham. For them, like for many in Britain's avant-garde at the time, modernism had come too late to the party and dressed in the wrong clothes. America, not continental modernism, was the inspiration these days: in particular, America's commercial culture, the pop art, jazz, rock'n'roll, comic books, Hollywood films and advertising of its chrome-covered 'El Dorado'.[7]

Both the consumerist imagery of America *and* its can-do spirit and technological prowess were intoxicating for this young bunch. Some were ambivalent or ironic about it, that old anti-Yankee snobbery still lingering; others, like Reyner Banham, gushed about the anti-elitism and freedom that America offered to drab, parochial Britain. Others still were more inspired by the American way of *doing* things. Nineteen-fifties Britain wasn't building fast enough the homes, schools and hospitals promised by the young welfare state. In 1951, the Conservative government came to power promising to change this, to jump-start the economy by deregulating the development and building industry. Britain's architects could be gentlemen no more.

Across the Atlantic, the largest American architects had by then fully adopted the efficient, collaborative teamwork structures used by the latest US corporations. Since the late 1930s, many modernist architects fleeing the spread of Nazism in continental Europe, such as Mies van der Rohe and Walter Gropius, had settled in the USA. Their own collaborative ways of working, honed in art and design schools like the Bauhaus, and their interest in mass-production and prefabrication for efficiency and economy chimed with American firms looking to improve their bottom line. This unlikely love affair between America and Europe in the 1950s gave birth to an international style of corporate architecture that clothed the expansion of the US economy. As the critic Michael Sorkin put it, 'with a particular American genius, modernism was stripped of its naïve and hopeful ideological apparel and reattired in a business as usual suit'.[8]

Mammoth US architectural firms such as Skidmore, Owings & Merrill (SOM) fused modernist aesthetics with the latest American management techniques both in their own workplace and in those they created for the country's booming economy. As in the nineteenth century, the new building types required by this economy, like steel-framed skyscrapers, required not art and handicraft to design them but efficient organisation and teamwork. Such buildings tended to be constructed from a kit of parts, their air-conditioning systems or steel skeleton made in a factory, then assembled on site, requiring not artists to conduct their building sites but management consultants or specialists in technologies such as building services or structural engineering. SOM pioneered the kind of lightweight modernist architecture of factory-made steel frames and glass that characterised American architecture of the 1950s and 1960s – from aircraft hangars for the US military to glass-box skyscrapers such as Lever House (1951–2) in New York. Like the corporations and organisations it worked for, SOM was an efficient business. By the late 1960s it had more than a thousand staff in four bases across the continent.[9]

Alluring as this corporate, business-minded America was in the 1950s, though, few Britons, let alone British architects, had actually been there: America arrived in Britain instead through representations – music, TV, comic books and films. But this soon changed. The more forward-thinking architectural firms such as Yorke Rosenberg Mardall (YRM) and Gollins Melvin Ward (GMW) crossed the Atlantic to study the latest construction techniques and business models, copying them wholesale in mid-century mid-Atlantic buildings like London's Castrol House (1958–9), for the oil conglomerate, made with a cutting-edge US method of prefabricated mass-production[10] and complete with a car park in its basement – banal today, exotic then. Others, like Reyner Banham and the young Richard Rogers and Norman Foster, went to work in American firms or teach in its universities, on Fulbright scholarships or Harkness fellowships. The experience transformed them. Those who returned had seen a certain kind of future, one they were determined to import.

It would be a difficult task. After its damning 1962 report, 'The Architect and His Office', RIBA proposed liberalising the profession wholesale, cosying it up to construction firms, improving management techniques and technological knowhow and getting architects to think of themselves more like businesses. Fat chance. Instead, British architects found themselves increasingly employed by the state. By the late 1960s around half of them still worked for central or local government;[11] in 1971, 80 per cent of RIBA members had a salary based on public works. That didn't stop some, though, from adopting the more business-minded attitude they saw across the Atlantic. Richard Seifert, for instance, had a reputation for efficiency, sharp practice and a detailed knowledge of planning law that allowed him to extract the maximum commercial value from any plot for his developer clients. Another, John Poulson, transformed his small provincial office in Pontefract, Yorkshire, into a ruthless business, becoming a multimillionnaire in the process. 'I am in a position to assist you,' he would tell his clients, 'by being efficient and effective and not just a typical example of the English architect'.[12] When such business efficiency landed him in jail, though, exposing his methods of backroom deals with politicians and contractors, this morality tale only confirmed the suspicions of those architects opposed to commercialising – or, as many saw it, Americanising – the profession.

In America, meanwhile, the architecture industry was being revolutionised all over again. Its professional bodies in 1971 began relaxing their rules, allowing architects to become more entrepreneurial still and to work like property developers; by 1978, even 'dignified advertising' was allowed. I like that 'dignified'. Fast-track construction, similar to that revolutionising the car industry, was entering the mainstream, alongside 'design-and-build' methods, in which an architect designs a building's outline, but the contractor who builds it controls the overall project and finishes off the fine details, a method that today has become the norm. One American architect personified this newly liberated profession better than any: John Portman. The Atlanta-based developer-architect honed his entrepreneurial methods to perfect the latest building types being demanded by clients, such as massive corporate complexes for downtown urban renewal. His ambition, he said, was for his firm to become 'master coordinators for the physical development of entire cities'.[13] His techniques, like establishing multiple companies – some buying up land, others handling contracts, still more handling design or the building site[14] – were sharp; and his flamboyant developments, such as Los Angeles's downtown Peachtree

Plaza and Bonaventure Hotel, became *the* backdrop for a certain mirror-glassed, glamorous vision of the future in the 1970s.

Britain, however, was still some distance from a future of mirror glass and modern management. Reflecting the angst experienced by the entire nation in this most tumultuous of decades, the architectural profession entered yet another phase of self-doubt in the 1970s. In 1971, critic Martin Pawley was writing of a crisis for architects and their modernist dream; the 'architect is seen as a faceless government lackey who is somehow involved with the Ronan Point disaster [in which a block of prefabricated social housing collapsed after a gas explosion], and who is deeply implicated in all kinds of plans for the destruction of Old England'.[15] From the political left, Malcolm MacEwen argued after the 1973 oil crisis that architects had lost their moral compass, employed either by corrupt developers or a 'military-industrial complex',[16] with ideals far removed from those who inspired the social reform of early modernism. The John Poulson scandal was then tarring all architects as opportunists 'on the make'. This was indeed a crisis – a perfect storm. And it was just the start. Not only were British architects not trusted by the public; not only were many starting to scorn their modernist utopias; not only were they poor businessmen, ill-equipped for the free-market world of enterprise and entrepreneurialism that was about to be unleashed on western society; they were about to see their work dry up, too.

In 1968, a prescient policy document written in Britain by Lord Esher and Lord Llewellyn-Davies warned that if architects didn't modernise to become – like John Portman, perhaps – more in control of an increasingly commercial building process, 'they will find themselves sooner than they expected on the fringes of decision-making rather than at the centre, acting as stylists for other people's products'.[17] Architects across the world were already losing control of the building site, as more efficient construction conglomerates took over the work; the proportion of UK buildings wholly controlled by architects, for instance, fell from 40 per cent in 1964 to 26 per cent by 1974. In the wake of the massive public spending cuts after the oil crisis, both commercial and public work shrank for architects across the West. Developers and builders speculated less, and those architects working for the state slowly began to realise that their work designing social housing estates, say, hospitals or schools was disappearing.

Society was shifting from one in which the state set the rules, to one in which the free market was 'liberated'. As a result, the patrons and clients who paid for architecture to be built had fundamentally changed in nature. Architects had to transform themselves into entrepreneurs, or they would wither away. Those who had already done so were in pole position.

So-called 'hi-tech' architects, such as Richard Rogers and Norman Foster, had long idolised the efficiency and economy of lightweight, prefabricated American architecture. Their earliest clients were pioneers in Britain's emerging service economy in the late 1960s and 1970s, many of them American or connected to America, such as the Reliance Controls Factory for an electronics firm, or office complexes like that built for the Willis Faber Dumas insurance firm – Los Angeles imported to downtown Ipswich. However, by comparison with the pioneers they emulated – such as Charles and Ray Eames, whose Case Study house was made from cheap, off-the-shelf components – 'hi-tech' was a finely-wrought, bespoke version, every nut and bolt designed to the millimetre, created for display as much as for function, to show off just how modern architect and client were.

There was a market for such expensive flourishes, but as the British economy livened up in the 1980s it was the more commercially astute architects, those who had adapted to the realpolitik of the new entrepreneurial economy, who took the real work. Their clients were developers schooled in harder-nosed methods of construction. The sites were enterprise zones and American-style 'development corporations' – urban renewal with a new face. Architects, in response, employed the entrepreneurial techniques of even the sharpest of operators. As a study found in the early 1980s, 'despite his downfall, the type of architecture which [John Poulson] practised and of which he was something of an innovator, is becoming commoner, not rarer'.[18] Architects' professional

bodies slowly adapted too. RIBA began allowing architects to specu-
late, raise capital for expansion or to become public companies. They
could even advertise their services – a little.

Architects responded to their latest crisis as they always had done:
through self-defence. They reinvented themselves as business-minded,
in the business of aesthetics. The business of art. Only architects,
claimed architects, could create beauty. Despite calls by some, like
Malcolm MacEwen, for more ethics in architecture, and despite a
brief interest in the 1970s and early 1980s in, say, self-build architecture partly constructed by its users, more participation in planning (as
happened after the Covent Garden protests, for instance) or what was
called 'community architecture' – working with local communities to
plan neighbourhoods – that interest in progressive politics and utopian
change that had emerged in the mid nineteenth century and propelled
architecture until the late 1960s had by now dissipated. What replaced
it was an evangelical belief in that new concept, 'urban regeneration'.
Through the power of consumerism, cities could be born again. There
was no money in changing the world, only in adapting to it. Anti-
capitalist critiques were best left to continental philosophers.

In retrospect, in fact, the so-called 'style wars' between Prince
Charles and the modernists that dominated the architecture scene in
the 1980s were red herrings. Far more important was the revolution in
how buildings were made. While architects tore themselves apart,
and, wracked with the latest version of their interminable self-doubt,
indulged in tedious debates about whether the new breed of buildings
built for the rising service economy should be dressed in neoclassical
stone columns or modernist steel ones, they mostly ignored the more
harrowing social or political consequences of deindustrialisation and
the rise of the entrepreneurial city. The world had changed, once
again, around them. Efficient and economical fast-track methods of
construction had already entered the country courtesy of American
imports like McDonald's. The restaurant chain, which arrived in the
UK in 1974, was, write historians Murray Fraser and Joe Kerr, 'probably the first company in Britain to employ project managers . . .

whose job was to run the ultra-short building contracts involved, depleting further the power of the architects'.[19] Its restaurants were speedily prefabricated in factories to a standard model, then assembled on site with specialised project managers.

The architects best placed to grasp the nettle were those who had already adapted: American architects. After the Big Bang deregulated the Stock Exchange in October 1986, opening up Britain to foreign investment, American money flooded into the City. And bobbing along with the tide came its architects. A swathe of large American firms opened offices in Britain, such as SOM, HOK, Kohn Pedersen Fox (KPF), Swanke Hayden Connell and Gensler, firms that achieved economies of scale in the design and production of buildings by using new computer-aided design, or outsourcing the manufacture of build-ing components to the Far East. As one American journalist wrote about this US invasion: 'Unlike their British counterparts, US archi-tects are accustomed to fast-track scheduling and the organisational and management skills practised by their corporate clients.'[20] By 1992, there were so many American architects working in Britain, the Ameri-can Institute of Architects opened its first office outside the US, in London. 'What the Americans brought with them,' wrote office spe-cialist Frank Duffy at the time, 'was confidence in their own competence, contempt for the small-scale, confused and compromise-ridden habits of the less talented British commercial architects, and excellent under-standing of the American corporation.'[21]

Because they had been building them for decades, American archi-tects already knew how to build retail parks, shopping malls and office complexes – those new building types of the free-market economy that were transforming Britain's landscape in the 1980s and 1990s. They spoke the language. The most famous import was Canary Wharf, funded by the Canadian–American firm Olympia & York and designed in the main by American firms such as I. M. Pei, KPF and César Pelli. To show the Brits how it was done, a series of specialist engineers and subcontractors were flown over from the United States. Fraser and Kerr describe its innovative construction: 'A steel frame

was erected, then profiled steel sheets were laid onto the floor beams
and topped off with screed. A lightweight stone and glass cladding
system was clipped to the exterior . . . and then finally the internal
fixtures and services elements were installed . . . As a consequence, the
Canary Wharf towers rose at a much faster pace than anything seen
before in British office construction, aided by project managers
imported from the USA.'[22]

The architect had indeed been reduced to becoming, as that 1968
report had warned, 'stylists for other people's products'. Most no longer
controlled the whole process of building, and, as a result, had less and
less control over the final product, and less and less connection to you
and me, the end users. 'It led', concluded Fraser and Kerr, 'to the
spread of a new, leaner business model for British architecture . . . in
which fewer staff now work longer and harder on projects that have
been competitively tendered to cut professional fees. The consequence
is that architecture is being carried out, in architects' eyes, on the
cheap; or as clients would see things, consumers are getting a better
deal.'[23]

The more successful architects in this new free-market landscape
were not artists, or ideologues. They didn't write utopias on how
the world should be better, or look better. They were entrepreneurs,
pragmatists – just like the economy in which they worked. They were
flexible and adaptable, shapeshifting, easy to please, changing how
they worked and what architecture they produced according to which
way the political wind was blowing. Their architecture couldn't help
but follow suit. It was lightweight, efficiently manufactured, affordable, and, because the exterior walls were almost literally 'clipped-on',
could be adapted to the style of whatever context it found itself in, or
whatever its client demanded: traditional, iconic, modernist, post-
modernist. Chameleon architecture.

A day in the life of Daniel Libeskind

Daniel Libeskind gets into the office at 9 a.m. 'But sometimes it's 7 a.m.,' says his scheduling director, Thierry Debaille. Yes, scheduling director. This *is* Manhattan. This *is* one of the world's most famous architects. Libeskind's day is so skintight his spreadsheet schedule says things like 'Journey time: 2 hours 16 mins.' You hear Nina, his wife and partner (she's the dealmaker and ballbreaker), on the phone: 'A *whole day* with Daniel?! They kidding? Half an hour, we're talking.' So 9 a.m. is a lie-in. But it's the day after the Labor Day holidays, so cut him some slack.

Like a good New Yorker he's already hit the gym in his Hudson Street apartment. 'A good hour on the treadmill,' says Nina. 'If he didn't he'd never get through the day.' Striding away, he watches the History Channel, 'and memorises poetry,' she adds. 'Shakespearean sonnets. I'm not making that up.' (He did take Labor Day off, and went to the movies with his family. But we're talking Werner Herzog, not a romcom.)

Daniel, the world's favourite intellectual-architect-turned-celebrity, doesn't like life easy. 'I'm a marathon runner,' he chuckles. Designing Ground Zero's masterplan after 9/11 thrust this once-obtuse and most intellectual of academics into a limelight that will bathe him till the day he dies. Successful architects require showmanship in their blood, but it can be an awkward fit: Libeskind's infamous angular, challenging architecture, such as Berlin's Jewish Museum, sits uneasily with his appearance on *The Oprah Winfrey Show*, in a brief but vigorous post-9/11 PR offensive in which he appeared on TV in cowboy boots and a Stetson, keen to prove just how American this émigré was.

Few other architects in recent decades have so dramatically transformed themselves from intellectual to businessman. Few have been so relentless in their public relations. And, in doing so, few have chosen to so conflate the personal and the professional, to overlay their struggle with that of the world. Libeskind, the flayed architect, lays it all on

the table in an endless stream of interviews and photocalls, each touch-
ingly confessional, whether choosing fave cowboy boots for the *New
York Times* style section or remembering, on CNN, his misty-morning
first sight of the Statue of Liberty as a youngster arriving in God Bless
America with his Jewish immigrant parents. We know everything,
every last spat with developers and politicians, every last tale from his
heart-wrenching childhood – the Soviet labour camps, the relatives
lost to the Holocaust. Few other architects in history have said so
much to so many so charmingly, self-deprecatingly and in such an
over-excited, cuddly staccato. Libeskind now lives his own private
Truman Show.

Today, aside from me, he has TV cameras pirouetting round him
for a BBC2 documentary. Between lobby and limo, people stare. 'Hey
Danny,' shouts one. 'How's it going?' Daniel doesn't hear. 'Since we
arrived in New York, it's been relentless,' says Debaille. 'Like a pop star.
Girls ask Daniel to sign their chests. He gets letters from prisoners.
People are passionate, though it can get a little odd.' The death threats,
which Libeskind's received since Berlin's Jewish Museum, continue:
'I'm going to f-ing smash you, you f-ing . . . etc.'

First up on the schedule, round the corner to Ground Zero, is the
groundbreaking ceremony for Santiago Calatrava's Transportation
Hub. Mayor Bloomberg's there, Hillary Clinton, a gaggle of portly,
black-suited VIPs. But not me. 'No press,' says security. 'Security.'
Daniel's not speaking, but, of course, he has to be there. In the years
since 9/11, money has, with wearying inevitability, beaten architecture in the battle for Ground Zero and the scuffles between Libeskind
and its developer Larry Silverstein. The desire for memorialision,
emoting and symbolism was no match for the necessity for high-rent
office skyscrapers on a site where thousands once died. Years of intense
media training, though, means, somewhat implausibly, Libeskind
never once lets slip his disappointment. His Cheshire Cat smile is
always stretched across his face. 'Negotiation is the reality of architecture,' he grins, guardedly. Relatively powerless against cold, hard
money, he sees himself instead as watchdog of the site's integrity: 'You

write the score, you have to make sure it gets played right.' So far it's a bit of a cacophony.

Appointment number one completed, Daniel and Nina head back to the office. You can feel them arrive. They haven't walked in yet, but the air inside moves in anticipation. An advance guard of staff whisk back to their desks. 'Grab him, *grab* him,' Thierry tells one. 'He's got two hours.' The lift doors open. 'It was like an OVEN down there!' shrieks Nina, charging out. 'Eighty degrees. Water was pouring down your *back*, Daniel.' Daniel, always in black, disappears, mopping himself furiously. He's back in an instant. 'I showered in the sink,' he laughs. The man is like a spinning top. He even talks in a whirl, twirling between paragraphs. He tornadoes between staff, inspecting details. 'How are you? Anything to see?' A new balustrade for a 9/11 memorial in Padua, Italy – a salvaged World Trade Center fragment encased in a zig-zagged open book for a site mystically 'connected' to Manhattan's latitude, as if by ley lines – Danny's schtick to a T – 'How is it fixed?' 'Welded.' 'It would *have* to be welded. Can we do it in time?' It opens next week. Warsaw: he gets a scalpel and hacks away at a skyscraper model, 'I want a line here, whaddayouthink?' He likes models: 'I can barely use a computer.' Next, Denver, where he scribbles curves over the plan on kitchen greaseproof paper. Good absorbency, apparently. 'Curve it, at a very precise angle.' 'Something casual?' asks the architect. 'Casual, but elegant, you know? A knot! That's it. Or a loop.' 'No problem.' 'Now, Vegas?' He leaves the room. Those left behind scratch their heads.

Studio Libeskind takes up the nineteenth floor of one of those cute Gotham-era skyscrapers, where Downtown descends into its shabbier fringes. Inside it's like any other architectural firm: industrial style, glaringly white, zombie youngsters with eyes hypnotised by computer screens, vast menageries of angular models. 'Daniel keeps absolutely *every*thing,' says Debaille. 'We've a warehouse in Jersey.' Indeed, give or take the menagerie and the knowingly angular reception desk, it's the same as any office: interns, stationery cupboards, bored people photocopying.

Since Ground Zero, work has increased exponentially – skyscrapers, shopping centres, offices – and is designed in hyperactive swoops these days, not Libeskind's trademark angles – from Warsaw to that architects' gold mine, the Far East. In one room three dozen Koreans pore over crystal towers. His challenge, says Libeskind, is to maintain the intellectual rigour that's made his name as business booms. So he keeps his staff small, controllable. Which equals a tough schedule, says one of his architectural minions, Arnault Biou: 'Nine till eight, some weekends.' But this *is* Manhattan. 'I always have forty minutes for lunch. Of course! I'm French.' There was a time when that schedule kept the great man out of the office. 'That wasn't good,' says Libeskind. He likes face-to-face with everyone, even the interns, not just his lieutenants – rare for an architect of his stature. He likes back-slapping, shoulder-tapping and always, always, that Cheshire Cat smile. (He greets each of the Koreans individually in a series of beaming bows. 'Wonderful! Wonderful!')

'Architecture is about communication,' he says. 'The building has to communicate to an incredible range of people, and you have to communicate to an incredible range of people to get it built. That's why I'm a marathon runner. If people saw the unimaginable lengths you go to to get the simplest thing built, they'd be shocked. At Ground Zero we argue over inches. *Inches!*' Every job is just as fraught: endless choices and negotiation. 'It's all architecture. It's like cinema. If you slowed it down you'd see how it's made. But you don't. You watch the film. And, in the end you experience the building. All the arguments fade away.'

'Libeskind!' Nina beetles up to him. She plies him with San Pellegrino and aspirin. 'How're you feeling?' 'Not great.' 'You look wrecked. You got sunstroke.' It's already 4.30 p.m. I haven't seen him eat lunch. Thierry sweeps up. 'Jersey time!' 'What are you? Big Ben?' By the end of the day Thierry's brow is regularly furrowed. 'We're way behind schedule, way!' It's a two-and-a-half hour journey into New Jersey for a talk, a book signing, radio interviews, more smiles. 'A two-and-a-half-hour drive?' Nina cries. 'What are we going to do for two and a half hours?' He gets home at midnight. 'We managed to slip him a sandwich,' Nina says the next morning. 'You think we just got you in on the busiest day?' says Thierry. '*Every* day's like this.' 'I like the adrenalin,' says Daniel. 'This isn't a job. It's life. I could never do nine to five. Thierry sometimes puts in my schedule "2.15 p.m.–2.18 p.m: Relax." I say, "Thierry, it has never yet happened!"'

Fame and the architect

I know the exact moment I thought I wanted to be an architect (it was a phase; it passed). Aged thirteen, Sunday afternoon, on the sofa watching Gary Cooper playing Howard Roark – an unbending, unbreakable modernist architect – drilling, sweatily, into a quarry face in King Vidor's 1949 adaptation of Ayn Rand's novel *The Fountainhead*, smouldered over by Patricia Neal in skin-tight riding gear, whip in hand. Howard Roark, battling the world with minimalist aesthetics and an iron will! That world had insisted he compromise, slather his 'less is more' skyscraper with decoration. Roark never compromises. So, instead, he abandons architecture to slog in a quarry with the common man. Movie scenes don't get more thrilling to a late-starting, sexually confused adolescent with a prematurely middle-aged interest in Le Corbusier and black-and-white films.

Architects don't have the best of reputations. Just look at how Hollywood depicts them. If they're not egotistical autocrats like Roark, they're egotistical autocrats who fail. Architecture, a profession historically wracked with doubt over its identity – are we tradesmen or professionals, artists or businessmen, builders or thinkers, scientists or sociologists, or all of these in one god-like being? (the latter, many conclude) – provides the perfect vehicle for fables about ideals compromised. Told again and again are the age-old myths of Ozymandias, Icarus, or *The Master Builder*, Henrik Ibsen's tale of an architect who thought he was God then realising, in fact, he's just a human. Arrogant architects dare to be omniscient, building heavens on earth that turn into hells.

Some see their utopias belittled, like Charles Bronson in *Death Wish* (1974), an architect roaming with a gun the city he can no longer control with his pencil. Others are action men cursed by thought. Paul Newman in *The Towering Inferno* ('They say he wrestles grizzlies in Montana') represents the failure of brain against brawn, ideals against action. His skyscraper may reach for the heavens, but it's aflame, and it's fearless fire chief Steve McQueen who saves the day and gets the girl. Some compromise their masculinity (screen architects are almost always men; the only woman I can recall is Michelle Pfeiffer in *One Fine Day*, and she's practically a man, with all that power furniture in her office). In *Mr Blandings Builds His Dream House* (1948), the budget-blind architect designing Cary Grant and Myrna Loy's rural palace is not only bow-tied and affected, he's an Englishman, to boot – clearly dodgy. In *Get Carter* (1971), the architects momentarily caught up in all the rough, tough gangster action wear effete cravats.

In the early 1980s, when I was sprawled on my sofa watching *The Fountainhead*, the 'failed architect' archetype had reached its apotheosis in fact as well as fiction. Since the mid 1960s, the supposed shortcomings of modernist architecture had been a hackneyed storyline, confirming that centuries-old cultural stereotype of the autocratic architect controlling, but never understanding, our lives. This narrative had been disseminated endlessly in newspaper articles with black-and-white photographs of glowering housing estates, or gloomy TV diatribes such as Christopher Booker's 1979 BBC series *City of Towers*, and 'proven' by news events such as the collapse of London's Ronan Point tower block in 1968. It mattered less whether such depictions were correct or not, than that they comfortably confirmed what we had all suspected.

But there was still life in this story. On 17 May 1984, while celebrating the 150th anniversary of the Royal Institute of British Architects at London's Hampton Court Palace, Prince Charles made his now-infamous speech describing a proposed design for an extension to the city's National Gallery on Trafalgar Square as a 'monstrous carbuncle on the face of a much-loved and elegant friend'. Somewhat after the event – by comparison with the 1950s and 1960s, little was actually being built in Britain's early 1980s economic slump – the prince lambasted the imposition of buildings on communities, and the aesthetic failings of modernist architectures. The speech was the lead item that evening on TV news bulletins. Architecture never gets to be the lead item on TV news bulletins.

Whatever one thought about its content, the prince's speech electrified popular debate about architecture in Britain and around the world, a debate played out in the media for decades afterwards. In the years that followed, he continued his assault on architects, employing Fleet Street journalists as speechwriters, and tapping in to the cultural stereotype of failed architecture, unleashing similes crafted for newspaper headlines – buildings that resembled 'book incinerators', 'power stations' or 'concrete stumps', say – and nimble soundbites: 'You have . . . to give this much to the Luftwaffe. When it knocked down our buildings, it didn't replace them with anything more offensive than rubble. We did that.'

So unexpected was the prince's attack that it rather blindsided the architectural profession. Soon after the Hampton Court 'celebrations', for instance, the president of RIBA, Owen Luder, leapt to the defence of one of the entries in the National Gallery Extension design competition – by Richard Rogers – describing it as 'the work of a man who has said, "This is what I think the answer is and sod you."' Luder intended it as a compliment, which, perhaps, shows just how out of touch the architectural profession had become with the way in which it was being depicted. At a time when the public sector work on which architects had depended for decades was drying up, thanks to rapid cuts in public spending by Margaret Thatcher's government, the profession seemingly hadn't quite understood the newly important power of PR. 'Sod you architecture' would never be a positive headline, however you span it.

This was a problem of communication, of the inability of architects, either individually, as Luder had proved, or collectively, as, again, Luder had proved, to communicate or empathise with wider society.

Architects and their architecture had *been seen* to fail again, whether they had actually failed or not. Architects could not come up with a storyline for the media to compete with that of a celebrity, self-styled 'man of the people' (Prince Charles) fighting a rogue in a bow tie (the architect). The clash demonstrated, too, the profession's ignorance of how popular communication – the media – was then being revolutionised. The internet had not yet arrived, but moguls like Rupert Murdoch and Eddy Shah would soon use computing power to transform newspaper production in an effort to boost readership, with desktop publishing, and, crucially, the arrival of colour printing.

Crucially because this battle between Prince Charles and the architects focused on the *style* of architecture. The prince may have been equally interested in architecture's social aims, but his soundbites, written by those who clearly did understand the increased importance in the new media landscape of impact, brevity and visual image, were almost uniformly about the *look* of architecture. His 1988 BBC television programme was, pointedly, entitled *A Vision of Britain*. The accompanying book begins with a full-page reproduction of a Canaletto painting of London's skyline, across which the reader is invited to overlay a second image showing the same, supposedly degraded scene today.

Architects have long been ambivalent about selling themselves or defending their corner. 'Advertising', says a 1909 circular from the American Institute of Architects, 'tends to lower the standard of the profession, and is therefore condemned.'[24] Indeed, promoting or advertising your architectural firm was prohibited, or at least frowned upon, until the 1970s, revealing either a touching, if naive, faith in allowing your buildings to do all the talking; or, less charitably, a snobbery about 'grubby' commerce.

The canniest architects, though, have had no such prejudices, adeptly using whatever media their age provides for self promotion. The fifteenth-century arrival of the printing press, for instance, became the primary means by which Renaissance architecture was disseminated throughout Europe, through books such as Leon Battista

Alberti's *De re aedificatoria* (1485). The earliest surviving piece of writing about what an architect is and does, *De architectura*, written between 50 and 30 BC by an architect – Vitruvius – in retirement after a career advising the Roman army, contains his definition of the correct role of an architect, including the importance of charm, communication and the cultivation of fame to attract work.

Vitruvius tells the tale of Dinocrates, an ambitious fellow eager to work for Alexander the Great. Despite schmoozing and speaking to the right people, he just couldn't get an introduction. 'So Dinocrates', writes Vitruvius, ' . . . decided to help himself, for he was very tall, nice-looking and endowed with great physical presence and personal dignity.'[25] He took off his clothes, smeared his body in oil, covered his left shoulder in a lion skin, and went to the tribunal, where Alexander 'was dispensing justice'. The crowd, recounts Vitriuvius, took note of this 'remarkable vision'; so did Alexander. Beckoning him, Alexander was presented with one of Dinocrates's designs for Mount Athos, 'in the form of a male statue', said the architect, 'in whose left hand I have designed the walls of a vast city, and in his right, a bowl to collect the water of all the streams on the mountains'. Alexander was 'entranced by the idea . . . From then on Dinocrates never left the king.'

Three twentieth-century architects who received that accolade once proof of fame, appearing on the cover of *Time* magazine, were equally media-savvy. Frank Lloyd Wright, with his sharp wit and what he called 'honest arrogance', constantly played up to the image of the heroic, egocentric architect, and carefully constructed his media image (costume: cape and cane and floppy tie). Philip Johnson is less renowned for his buildings (he was a skilled copyist of greater architects' work) than for his appearance, his provocations and his skill as an 'operator' behind and in front of the scenes of the American architectural establishment. But it was Le Corbusier who was the most adept, crafting his media, such as the magazine *L'Esprit Nouveau*, or polemics like *Vers une architecture* (1923) with as much care as his buildings. He had a gift for the soundbite – 'the house is a machine for living' – and the visual image, innovatively photographing his buildings as 'photoshoots' with storylines, and including props, such as, in the 1920s, the new phenomenon of production-line cars, to accentuate their glamorous modernity.

Indeed, academic Beatriz Colomina, in her books *Architectureproduction* (1988) and *Privacy and Publicity: Modern Architecture as Mass Media* (1994) suggests that the modernist architecture of Wright, Johnson and Le Corbusier only became truly modern through its relationship with the new phenomenon of global mass media, 'making it circulate around the world', she wrote, 'as if it had suddenly lost mass and volume'.[26] Far, far more people now experienced a building through seeing it in a magazine or newspaper than visited it in reality. The irony, Colomina suggested, was that the posterity of architecture, its architects and their wealthy patrons was now assured not through building weighty monuments but via the ephemeral, ghostly media of mass reproduction.

This was a lesson architects en masse had yet to learn when Prince Charles hit the headlines in the 1980s. But they would. For the moment, a legion of British critics took up their cause, their newspapers and magazines eager for the headlines, and sales, that Prince Charles guaranteed. A PR drive began. Architects began learning again how to sell themselves. Exhibitions that treated them as more appealing heroes of a more appealing architecture proved popular: at London's Royal Academy, a show entitled New Architecture: Foster Rogers Stirling, in 1986, curated by two journalists, Simon Jenkins and Deyan Sudjic, marked 'a shift in what was deemed public opinion', wrote Kester Rattenbury (in one of the few studies of architecture in the mass media), establishing 'the new star system that continues to dominate the mainstream media's coverage'.[27]

RIBA itself went on a charm offensive, creating a new architecture gallery, and, eventually, a national award for contemporary architecture, the Stirling Prize, for some years transmitted on primetime television. It soon paid dividends, suggests Rattenbury. When the UK began its next binge of public building from the mid 1990s, she writes, first funded by the new National Lottery, and then the country's economic boom under New Labour, it was not in the traditional styles promoted by Prince Charles, but in a modern style, though one far more alluring than those black-and-white newspaper images of concrete buildings that had helped hasten modernism's fall from grace: full-colour architecture.

For a new generation of architects had taken note. From Zaha Hadid to Daniel Libeskind, Herzog & de Meuron to Rem Koolhaas, they would soon come to dominate skylines around the world. These rising stars were eager to create a new kind of architecture from the ashes of 'failed' modernism, one that was more appealing to mass society in the age of mass media, and, unlike their predecessors, these architects were far less sniffy about public relations. Indeed, they were astute at it.

This generation viewed their physical buildings as one form of media among many. They, in turn, had been taught by a generation soaked in the mostly French critical thinking on media and culture that had emerged while they were at university in the 1970s, by philosophers such as Roland Barthes and Jean Baudrillard. One of the fathers of this new generation, for instance, Bernard Tschumi, created a series of works from 1976 – *Advertisements for Architecture* – that employed the games with sexuality, surrealism and subconscious desire that had for decades been de rigueur among advertising executives on Madison Avenue. 'There is no way to "perform" real architecture in a magazine and through a drawing,' Tschumi proposed. 'The only way is to make believe. So, just as ads for architectural products (or cigarettes or whiskey) are made to triguer desire for something beyond the glossy illustration, these ads have the same purpose: to trigger desire for architecture.'

This new generation of architects recognised the importance of the image. They learned to flatter a media hungry for visual stimulation, a skill that became vital as the age of the internet dawned. They also understood the power of the brand. They understood that they, like their buildings, *were* brands. They monetised their artistry however they could, even creating diffusion lines. You might not be able to afford a whole building, but what about a designer toaster? The architect-designed *objet* was pushed in that most designer of decades, the 1980s, by firms like Alessi, who got hitherto-serious architects like Norman Foster and Aldo Rossi to turn out cups, kettles, corkscrews and cheese boards. Since then the licensing deals for 'signature' or 'celebrity' architects have proliferated.

ZHA, the firm established by the late Zaha Hadid, takes brand-building by means other than building perhaps most seriously of all. Using several companies registered with her name, Hadid created jewellery, footwear, handbags for Fendi, vases for Lalique, perfume bottles for Donna Karan, Adidas trainers with pop star Pharrell Williams. As Maha Kutay, director of the firm's design team, explained to the *Guardian*, 'Architecture takes years and years to produce, but with products you can get something to market within a year.'[28]

ZHA does top-drawer design: the 2005 Aqua table was auctioned in New York for $296,000, then a record for a living designer. It also does a few drawers down: its 'lifestyle collection' debuted at Harrods department store in 2014, though you'd still need quite the lifestyle to buy it. 'We're aiming for affordable pieces that can be bought on the high street,' her general manager Christian Gibbon told the *Guardian*, 'but which are also aspirational.'[29] The definition of affordable and aspiration, however, like so many things in life, is relative. Cups start at £38, serving platters are £9,999. There are scented candles, coasters, flasks and a chess set (on sale for £4,860). The objects are designed using the same computer software used to create the firm's buildings, so they share similar shapes, whether a perfume bottle or an office tower.

This generation also recognised the new-found importance of how they were represented in the media. In the age of the entrepreneurial city, there's no point retreating to the quarry, like Howard Roark. You have to be where the cameras are. I like to think a turning point came in 1996, when the BBC screened a documentary about the building of London's Tate Modern. Camera crews must have been following its famous architects Pierre de Meuron and Jacques Herzog for weeks. No doubt it was intrusive, though a necessary evil. But at one point in the documentary, Jacques Herzog, in his clipped Swiss accent, turned to the cameraman and director, and instructed them not to film his face from a certain angle. It was a moment of lucidity and honesty, as well as vanity and egotism, an architect at last recognising that he had a bad side, as well as a good.

Who's paying the bill?

The late American architect Philip Johnson was famous for many things – wit, Nazi-sympathising, designing Israel's first nuclear reactor – but morality was not one of them. 'I'm out to work for the Devil himself if he's building,' he quipped, though the closest he actually got to fashioning headquarters for Old Nick was designing a mirror-glass facsimile of the Houses of Parliament for Kuwaiti oil interests on London's South Bank in the 1980s (mercifully unbuilt). Asked a decade later whether he would have built buildings for Adolf Hitler, he replied, 'Who's to say? That would have tempted anyone.'

Architects have had a long and not-terribly-complex relationship with power. Basically, they like it. A little bit of dictatorship always helps smooth the path through planning permission. Put the patrons and designers of architecture over millennia in a corporate social responsibility committee and many, if not most, would fail: grotesque working conditions, questionable politics, blood money. Trace the money behind any building and at least a fraction is bound to be dirty. To take a few easy potshots, think of the beautiful monuments of ancient Rome, Greece and Egypt or the eighteenth-century buildings in British cities built with slave labour. Few architects in recent decades might have gone so far as to court Nazis – though Mies van der Rohe and Le Corbusier were tempted – but between the black pits of fiery hell and Mother Teresa there are infinite shades of shady clients tempting architects to accept a Faustian pact to realise their grand plans.

The more so today. As the political economy has shifted to the glo-balised free market, architects far more frequently find themselves working abroad as muddle-headed tourists in far-off lands about which they know little. It's become easier and easier to land in hot water. One of the professional hazards for western architects today is that much of the world's money, ergo much of the world's power, ergo much of the world's construction business, is in spots with a somewhat challenging relationship with polling booths and political transpar-ency, all after the kind of engineering and aesthetic expertise the West has accumulated since the Renaissance.

Kazakhstan, for instance, has had western architects flooding in to help it spend its oil cash. President Nursultan Nazarbayev was, after all, only doing what any self-respecting central Asian plutocrat who has ruled without genuinely democratic elections for decades, impris-ons critics, quashes public assembly and forcibly evicts residents in the way of his monuments *would* do. The biggest project of all is Astana, a new capital city masterplanned by the Japanese architect Kisho Kuro-kawa, dotted with self-aggrandising monuments apeing the Pharoahs. Examples include the Palace of Peace and Reconciliation, designed by Norman Foster, proof that if you have to call something a palace of peace and reconciliation, it probably isn't.

Yet there is no architectural equivalent of the Hippocratic Oath, few simple sets of principles laid down in law to follow in these easy-going days of the free market. Architects are not habitually taught ethics and politics when they train. Indeed, since the 1970s, the con-cern for ethics and politics that had dominated architecture since the Industrial Revolution has ebbed away. Architects have become less dis-posed towards criticising the social or political contexts in which they work. The entrepreneurial architect goes where the business is. Their greatest freedom, though, is their ability to choose where and where not to work. What counts in the entrepreneurial economy is the deal.

Trace the money behind any building and at least a fraction is bound to be dirty. The question is what kind of dirt are you comfortable with? Where do you draw the line? Daniel Libeskind drew *his* line in

2008. Speaking in Belfast, the Polish-born architect of Berlin's Jewish Museum attacked architects working in China: 'I won't work for totalitarian regimes,' he thundered. 'Architects should take a more ethical stance.'[30] But it depends where that stance is. Libeskind, for instance, has worked in Israel, anathema to some.

From another position, Patrik Schumacher, partner in, and now inheritor of Zaha Hadid's firm, has drawn his line – again and again. Schumacher, never afraid to use ten words when one might do, has become one of contemporary architecture's rare polemicists in the mode of Le Corbusier, publishing vast books of manifestos so inscrutable one critic, Jack Self, compared them to computer coding. Schumacher regularly and entertainingly takes to his Facebook page and the comments sections of prominent websites to launch his latest tablets of stone, attacking, say, the state funding of art schools, 'political correctness in architecture', and declaring: 'Architects are in charge of the FORM of the built environment, not its content. We need to grasp this and run with this despite all the (ultimately conservative) moralising political correctness that is trying to paralyse us with bad conscience and arrest our explorations if we cannot instantly demonstrate a manifest tangible benefit for the poor – as if the delivery of social justice is the architect's competency.' Precis: architecture and politics are not connected. Though by insisting this he automatically takes a political stance. Architecture cannot help but be political.

In the years before her death in 2016, his colleague Zaha Hadid, her opinions less strident than that of Schumacher, nevertheless became the focus for those attacking the blind eye architects often turn to the ways in which their architecture gets built. One of the prices of fame, particularly in today's communication culture, is that you can never control your public image, however hard you try. Your public image is exactly that, the public's.

Two projects have come to plague hers. The Heydar Aliyev Cultural Centre in Baku, Azerbaijan, is a memorial to Heydar Aliyev, Azerbaijan's late ruler, and its former KGB chief under the USSR – heavily criticised by Amnesty International for human rights abuses and electoral corruption. It was commissioned by the country's ruler, which, goodness, happens to be his son, Ilham, ushered into power after his father's death in 2003. Hadid even laid flowers at Aliyev's grave. Forced evictions were said to have taken place to make way for the cultural centre.

More controversial still was the firm's Al-Wakrah Stadium, for Qatar's 2022 football World Cup. The entire event has been dogged by controversy since Qatar won the bid, because of alleged corruption on the part of world football's organisation FIFA, and disbelief that the event was originally to take place at the height of summer, when temperatures can hit 50°C. But it was the conditions of the 1.6 million migrant workers – most from India, Pakistan and Nepal – building the event's venues, the infrastructure required for it and the accompanying hotels, offices and speculative apartment blocks, that hit the headlines too. In 2014, Hadid sued the *New York Review of Books* after it published a book review by architecture critic Martin Filler, which suggested that construction workers had died building her stadium. She donated the damages to a charity supporting labour rights. A year later, in September 2015, Hadid walked out of a live broadcast of one of the UK's biggest radio shows, BBC Radio 4's *Today*, with 7 million listeners, when the same accusation was made by one of its presenters, Sarah Montague. 'You should check your information before you say anything,' said an understandably tetchy Hadid.

Indeed. But once information and opinion is out there these days it is hard to control. The previous May, a blog by the *Washington Post* on migrant workers' deaths in Qatar caused a Twitter storm after suggesting there had been 1,200 deaths in the construction of World Cup facilities. In fact, the 1,200 figure, seemingly plucked from a 2013 report by the International Trade Union Confederation, was an estimate of all deaths, accidental or not, among Qatar's migrant workers, not specifically those working on World Cup facilities. Indeed, under worldwide pressure, the 2022 World Cup organising committee had insisted conditions be monitored on its stadium construction sites to a higher standard than was normal in Qatar. The *Washington Post* blog was hastily amended, following complaints from Qatar's government, but not before it had been shared millions of times and cited in the British Parliament.

Another report a year later, commisioned by the Qatari government, confirmed that 964 migrants from Bangladesh, Nepal and India had died while working there in 2012 and 2013 and recommended better monitoring of conditions on the part of its government. Similar reports by undercover investigators or independent organisations had pointed the finger at the appalling working conditions of those building Abu Dhabi's Saadiyat Island, much of Dubai's new construction, or of those transforming the raw materials behind building booms in newly emerged economies. In 2014, for instance, the UK-based NGO Union Solidarity International attacked what it called the 'blood bricks' being made by an estimated 10 million workers – including children as young as four – in India, under horrific conditions.

If such information about how architecture was created was more transparent, mistakes like those suffered by Hadid would be easier to correct. Little progress in Qatar, though, has been made to date. The suspicion therefore lingers that few in the construction industry or western national governments *want* such transparancy, for fear of losing lucrative contracts with or investment from countries such as Qatar. Hadid, in any case, had already made her stance clear when allegations first arose in 2014, in far fewer words than her partner, Patrik Schumacher, but with the same sentiments: 'It's not my duty as an architect to look at it.' See no evil, hear no evil, speak no evil.

Most architects, though, fall in the very muddy, smudgy ground between Hadid and Libeskind's stances. They find their own line to draw in it. Take Jacques Herzog and Pierre de Meuron, architects of the 'Bird's Nest' Stadium, centrepiece for the 2008 Olympic Games in Beijing. It is, of course, an astonishing building. As an image, it mesmerises – exactly what BOCOG, Beijing's Olympic committee, wanted beamed through TVs around the world as *the* image of New China, as instantly get-able as their cheesy sub-Coke slogan: 'One World, One Dream'. For a nation that deeply values formal architectural symbolism, creating a shape that simultaneously evokes heaven (a circle) and the auspicious bird's nest was a deft move.

There was little consternation in 2002, when Herzog & de Meuron won the commission. Six years later, though, the ground had shifted. The economy in the West was beginning the wobble that would soon lead to the worldwide economic downturn. And now that the world's media was focused on a patch of ground in Beijing, the politics underneath that ground seemed to have become much more noteworthy. Famous film director Steven Spielberg, for instance, pulled out of directing the illustrious opening ceremony of the Olympic Games, citing China's human rights record and involvement in Sudan's Darfur tragedy.

'It's very cheap and easy for architects and artists and filmmakers to pull out or to make this kind of criticism,' Herzog tells me, when I met the pair in their office in Basel, Switzerland. 'To criticise a country but also take advantage of it. Everybody knows what happens in China. All work conditions in China are not what you'd desire. But you wear a pullover made in China, or trousers or jeans. It's easy to criticise being far away. I'm tempted almost to say the opposite. How great it was to work in China and how much I believe that doing the stadium, the process of opening will change radically, transform the society. Engagement is the best way of moving in the right direction.'

'It would be arrogant not to engage,' adds de Meuron. 'Otherwise no politicians could go there, no athletes. You would just close the borders.'

'Literally everybody in the western world trades with China,' Herzog continues. 'This is a fact. So why should an architect . . . not?'

The biggest single symbol of the West's engagement in China – their stadium – they hope might be, if not a Trojan Horse, then a building which embodies and moves forward loose but, in China, radical ideas, such as freedom. Ai Weiwei, the famous dissident Chinese artist with whom Herzog & de Meuron worked on the stadium, said as much in a statement just before the Games, explaining why he, too, would not attend the opening ceremony: the stadium, he wrote, 'is designed to embody the Olympic spirit of "fair competition". It tells people that freedom is possible but needs fairness, courage and strength. Following the same principles, I will stay away from the opening ceremony, because I believe the freedom of choice is the basis of fair competition. It is the right I cherish most.' Ai has a rare talent for deftly combining politics, work and publicity, from which many architects might learn.

How the building embodies freedom, explains de Meuron, is in its very form – an open basket or 'bird's nest' of girders in which visitors can choose their own random paths, pointedly designed for its political symbolism as well as practical function. Up close, the exterior steel lattice, the 'architectural forest', looks impossibly complex. 'There is both order and disorder,' de Meuron adds. 'We wanted to do something not hierarchical, to make not a big gesture as you'd expect in a political system like that, but [something that for] 100,000 people [is still] on a human scale, without being oppressive. It's about disorder and order. It seems random, chaotic, but there's a very clear structural rationale.'

'The Chinese love to hang out in public spaces,' adds Herzog. 'This is something that surprised me coming from Switzerland, that they love to hang out and to play music and do t'ai chi, to dance. The main idea of the stadium was to offer them a playground, a bit like the Eiffel Tower is now an element of public life, and if we can achieve that we would have been stupid not to have done it.' In fact, it's hard to see anyone hanging out let alone doing t'ai chi in so frantic and vast a space – cosy it ain't – especially one suspended halfway up a stadium on the bleak edge of town in a barren monumental park. Nonetheless, Herzog and de Meuron make a distinction between creating a building that fosters a country's ideology – say Albert Speer's work for Hitler – and one which seeks to transform it through engagement. It is, Herzog acknowledges, 'a fine line'. But it is *their* – very nuanced – fine line.

If you can't beat 'em . . .

You can't escape it. Beijing is a flat city, vast too, but this building always seems to be there, peeping from behind another boring sky-scraper, its awkward angles elbowing past to grab the skyline. CCTV is extraordinary. The headquarters of China's state television organisa-tion is unlike any other building. It has a hole in it – nearly 200 metres wide – around which its gawky limbs contort in a huge angular loop. There are no easy-peasy right angles. Each titanic limb tilts away from or towards the next, like an Escher painting, culminating in a gravity-defying zenith in which two come together in a jaw-dropping, 'look, no hands' cantilevered corner, jutting out over the city and cut with three 4-metre-wide circular glass floors, so that white-knuckled visitors can stand, thrillingly, over 162 metres of air.

You may not like it. It looks terrifying, like some terrible omen from the future. Darth Vader could be holed up inside. Its dark, sombre, omnipresence, its Orwellian looks and, indeed, Orwellian function mean this is no easy building to love. But you can't deny its power. This is one of those moments when you know an entire culture – both architecture *and* China – is morphing into something else, something new, something you've never seen before, and there's nothing you can do about it.

Its architect is Rem Koolhaas. Or rather, the architectural firm behind it is the one co-founded in 1975 *by* Rem Koolhaas, with the pointedly bland name, Office for Metropolitan Architecture. Why so bland? Because Rem Koolhaas isn't a star. He doesn't sign toasters with his signature. He doesn't bring out diffusion lines of vases and coffee tables. He doesn't do politics. He doesn't do celebrity. Or, rather, he does – just on his terms. Confused? Good. That's just how he likes it.

When I first met him, in 2004, Koolhaas was in town to do four sell-out London gigs to launch his new book, *Content*, and grab the prestigious Royal Gold Medal for architecture, accompanied both by groupies in serious specs, angling for a photo with their hero, and by the great and good, here to pay respects and kiss ass. Frank Gehry might be more global, Daniel Libeskind more precocious, but Koolhaas has fame, brains and cognoscenti cool. Some idea of his cachet: the first time I (nearly) met him was three years earlier for an interview for *Wallpaper** magazine. But he was stolen – stolen! – by a rival fashion mag, who scooped him up in a taxi as he approached. I waited for him in the minimalist lobby of the Halkin Hotel for two hours. There's not a lot to stare at in a minimalist lobby.

The past twenty years have yanked Koolhaas from academic stardom to serious stardom, with cool/brainy bestselling books like *S, M, L, XL* and A-list work with Miuccia Prada. In person, the attraction's not obvious. Onstage at his gigs, Koolhaas looks every inch the nobody, dressed normcore in neutral slacks and a polo shirt of indeterminate colour, like your dad. He shuffles, fidgeting, itching his bony scalp with the awkwardness of a man fully aware he's a beanpole, all cheekbones, sinews and limbs. He's so folded up, his Nosferatu face so shadowy, he looks permanently on the verge of implosion. Star? He's a black hole. When – if – he speaks, it's in a low, muttering Dutch monotone delivering gnomic edicts of apparent contradictions, which the audience scribbles down as if he were Confucius: 'Did you understand that?' one whispers in the audience. 'No.' This week's pronouncements: architecture can be disfunctional and brilliant! Death to the skyscraper! And . . . pot calling the kettle black . . . Death to Star Architects!

That's Koolhaas, a slippery bunch of contradictions, wreathed in myth. The presence-less star, who squirms if he catches himself on magazine covers, yet consents to afternoons of photoshoots and throws a diva's hissy fit when he doesn't have the right pen to sign autographs. Who is (unsuccessfully) sued for stealing the work of an employee, yet allegedly copyrights certain words and, in *Content*, has a Patent Wall of inventions. Who hates branding, yet, in an exhibition, knowingly sells 'Rem' T-shirts. The thorn in the side of the establishment now winning the establishment's gongs, who moans to me, 'This permanent insistence that I declare myself!', yet, with a smirk, 'I think I declare myself all the time.' The half 'boring fascist' control freak, as he describes himself, half pinko Dutch hippie.

He likes, he says, 'floating in a kind of ambiguity', having his cake and eating it, he smiles at me, wickedly. This knowing slipperiness. This uncertainty. This feeling he's having a joke at your expense. 'I think it drives people crazy.' It does. It's too textbook postmodern, like a character in a William Gibson novel, the postmodern architect who lives neither/both here (London), nor/and there (Rotterdam, his 'refuge' from fame). Whose entire oeuvre is spent celebrating the very globalised modern condition he lives in, a mercurial life permanently on the run in airport lounges, hotels, shopping malls, corridors – what he calls 'junkspace' – resting only occasionally to swim (every day, wherever), and take the local temperature. All that smirking, knowing irony, this neither-one-thing-nor-another-ness: it's fishy. All these personas. 'The whole point of modernisation', he says, 'is that it is a plotless adventure, a movie, a huge cast, notable stories that collide, contradict, unravel but never integrate.' We all miss the point trying to tie everything down and define it.

It's this, the ruthlessly ambiguous but lateral way in which Koolhaas works and thinks, that's been so influential. It's why he's won, and deserves, the fame and the gongs. Real or fake, he's one of the few architects since the 1970s to actively address politics, and certainly the first to accept the neoliberal, free-market world as it has become, and rethink what an architect might be within it other than a brand-building starchitect. Architecture, as we have known it, is dead. Long live architecture. Out goes its perfection and utopias – which, with terrible irony, always needed totalitarianism to be built. Out go the stupid monuments and visually perfect icons that most, less enlightened, architects continue to build. In comes . . .

Possibility. 'Liberated from the obligation to construct,' he writes, '[architecture] can become a way of thinking about anything.'[31] If the world is indeterminate, multilayered, complex, constantly shifting, architecture must respond. Faced with this world, he doesn't design.

He edits. From eighteen to twenty-four he was a journalist on an Amsterdam weekly (his father was a left-leaning newspaper editor) and an LA film scriptwriter, jumping ship, he explains, in a 'thunderbolt' only because architecture seemed 'more critically interesting'. 'But I've never stopped doing journalism,' he says, watery smile washing over his face. 'Have I?'

True. He has a journalist's magpie mind for collecting and assimilating the ephemera and noise of society; details relevant to the intellectual task at hand get filleted out and processed through his design workplace, the Office for Metropolitan Architecture (OMA), and its inverse, AMO, the accompanying think tank, both 'catholic, shapeless educational establishments' through which most avant-garde Dutch architects, a fair few Britons, and intellectual luminaries like curator Hans-Ulrich Obrist have passed. It feels like a research lab – ruthlessly lateral – about anything that fascinates him. He has the luxury, or discipline, to choose work. He chose, for instance, not to tackle Ground Zero, preferring to court work in a 'more critically fertile' China. There have been plenty of lean years, and plenty of failed jobs (an extension to Manhattan's Whitney Museum, Ian Schrager hotels, a Universal Studios theme park). But that's fine, he says: the aim has never been money.

At the end, out pops the architecture. Though not always a building. The built form becomes just one, old-fashioned, medium amongst many Koolhaas might choose, to tackle the task or the question in hand. He might create an urban masterplan. Maybe a magazine: he advised Condé Naste to crossbreed titles, spawning hybrids like *Teen Vogue*. Maybe a strategy: he advised the European Union on how to sell the positives of European, as opposed to national, identity, producing a new European flag, a barcode of many colours. Maybe a book/magazine hybrid, like *Content*, complete with ads from Gucci to keep the price to an accessible £6.99. He's less interested in the internet, surprising, given his love of the in-between, unsurprising given his contrariness. Sometimes, he says, he prefers the old-fashioned tactility of books and buildings. 'Don't you?'

He's a deft writer. Architecture is chaotic, team-based. Writing –
'the most powerful medium . . . the one moment when there's no
ambiguity about authorship' – gives him more control. *Delirious New
York*, his 1978 celebration of modernity, remains one of the most
influential postwar texts on architecture. Twenty years later, the
doorstep-sized *S, M, L, XL*, with graphic designer Bruce Mau, altered
the way architecture was represented. Not pristine, uptight and 'archi-
tecty' but noisy and dirty, packed with verbal and visual games and
tricks, walls of statistics, nerdfacts, lists and pie charts, jump cuts and
collisions, stream-of-consciousness babbles from which you must tease
out an argument. It was, he says, his 'exit strategy' from architecture,
a calling card for the style gurus and politicians who then flocked to
his door.

From time to time, Koolhaas might build a building. Naturally, his
buildings are contrary, tellingly edited contradictions, all montage
and juxtapositions, which accept, rather than order mess. They don't
solve problems; they embrace them. His Student Centre addition to
Mies van der Rohe's Illinois Institute of Technology doesn't, like the
rival schemes of Zaha Hadid and Peter Eisenman, hide the commuter
railway that slices through, but hugs it, using its movement to disrupt
the formal perfection of Mies's plan. The buildings both solve and
confront their brief. Manhattan's Prada store is both a beautiful product of shopping as culture, and a shop whose claustrophobia, angles
and swinging display cages make you physically sick. All intentional,
I'm sure. When called upon to design an icon Koolhaas responds with
a style-less anti-icon, almost intentionally disappointing after their
hype: huge, boxy, bulky, all fidgety angles like the man himself, not
quite ugly, not quite beautiful, and wilfully badly detailed, luxurious
materials colliding with tat: Berlin's new Dutch Embassy uses fragile
aluminium as a surface, already scuffed, as if to stick two fingers up to
the PR photoshoots. He's an awkward bugger.

All this isn't just posturing (though, I suspect, it is a bit). In *S, M,
L, XL* he lambasts architects who design dreams, detached from reality, in cyberspace, 'where fascism may be pursued with impunity' (he

still smiles at that line: 'Sadly it's getting truer every day'). His aim always is to make forms, spaces, media which are connected to real life not as we think it is or should be, but as it actually is, all messy, ugly and dreary. He is, said one architect, a 'dirty realist', brutally honest, ruthlessly lateral. Why, he asks in his essay 'Junkspace', do architects continue, idealistically, to build icons and utopias? Are they living in an alternate world without McDonald's and Wal-Marts, the stupid big air-conditioned malls and 'endless buildings' of real/fake consumer society where we *really* spend our time? These days, he writes, 'civic society is one where shopping malls serve you cappuccino for twenty-four hours'. Capitalism, not the church or the state, is where the work is, where life is. 'You thought that you could ignore Junkspace,' he accuses architects, 'visit it surreptitiously, treat it with condescending contempt or enjoy it vicariously.' Now 'you've thrown away the keys . . . Junkspace will be our tomb.'[32]

His current glee for working in China is based on the same honesty. America, Europe? Dead. Can't you see Asia is where it's at? This is capitalism's front line, where instant cities sprawl and skyscrapers sit beside the medieval, where a new kind of city space and society is being formed, so different, he says, from the 'dead, stable cities, like Paris, New York'. Why would a curious architect work anywhere else? 'Go east' implores *Content*. (With typical contrariness, though, most of his work has been not junkspace in the east, but old-fashioned civic monuments in the west: libraries, embassies, concert halls, art galleries . . . Are his contradictions getting tiresome yet?)

CCTV is, though, his calling card in the wild East. When I visit, I'm met by Koolhaas's then co-architect from OMA, Ole Scheeren. 'We could have gone the easy route,' says Scheeren, nonchalantly, 'and built much taller like the others that bid for the job. But that's just not interesting, is it?' What *was* interesting, he says, was getting out of the 'my one's bigger than your one' race for the skies and 'creating a new type of skyscraper', one in which intelligence, not size, brain, or height, mattered. CCTV is the world's first anti-phallic skyscraper, a paltry 234 metres.

When Scheeren visited the site in 2000, 'Beijing city planners showed us an image of what would be the new central business district, with a forest of 300 skyscrapers to emerge in the next fifteen years.' They've arrived: dumb, phallic, boring. 'So faced with this, a question emerged. Asia now has more skyscrapers than the West. A typology invented in New York, Chicago, 100 years earlier has been adopted more successfully in Asia as a triumphant symbol of its own modernisation. So what could an Asian or a Chinese skyscraper become?'

Answer: an anti-icon, of course. Koolhaas, he says, despises the 'vulgar desire to impose flashy new form'. He prefers what he likes to call 'anti-icons', buildings like his Casa da Música in Porto, Portugal, whose odd, monolithic, awkward form both repels the tourist's camera and attracts it. The Casa's 'promenade' of 'intense space' is wrapped around the central auditorium, offering a succession of jump-cut, cinematic, often uncomfortable architectural experiences.

CCTV does the same. Its odd looks are pointedly chosen to stick out against its predictable neighbours – a 'building as logo'. 'But this is both an icon and a non-icon,' says Scheeren, as contradictorily as if Koolhaas himself were putting words in his mouth. 'Icons have a singular appearance. Look at them once and that's it. Traditional Chinese architecture, though, is something you cannot simply comprehend with a glimpse, you have to let the space unfold.' CCTV works similarly – like a giant piece of Chinese calligraphy, a single image made up of symbolically loaded parts. Move around the sculptural building 'and it unfolds, changes configuration. It has depth.' More importantly, he adds, its iconoclastic shape came not from wilfulness, but from the building's function – a public building on the world stage for an organisation renowned, rightly or wrongly, as chief propagandist for a one-party state.

Like most things in dizzying China, the media is changing at a frightening speed – in May 2008, just before I first visit the building, the government allowed CCTV and foreign journalists unprecedented access to the Sichuan earthquake disaster zone. CCTV itself is metamorphosing as an organisation. 'The group running this project is young,' says Scheeren, 'mid thirties to mid forties, incredibly well-educated, exposed to the West. It sees itself in a much more responsible, global context. The BBC is one of their role models. They talked about making part of CCTV an independent and more free enterprise. This seemed encouraging, and to try to support it worthwhile.' It goes for China as a whole, he says, an infathomably complex, contradictory country. 'Yes, it has many problems, but you either choose to change that, or you isolate yourself. Once you experience China, nothing's so black and white.'

So, like the Olympic Stadium's architects before him, Herzog & de Meuron, Scheeren excuses OMA's engagement with a country vilified for its human rights record by his faith in transforming it. CCTV, already deeply embedded in the city, and, of course, housing of all things the state's main tool of propaganda stands, I think, a greater chance of actually doing so than the isolated 'Bird's Nest'. Either way, Scheeren has been adamant about workers' conditions on site: 'We've had no casualties here. We were very explicit in all our intentions from the beginning,' says Scheeren. 'This was to be an exemplar. And we said let's create "public space" in the building, make it the most transparent TV station in the world.' Such words, innocent here in the West, are dynamite in China.

OMA hopes to achieve this transformation through how the building is organised. Scheeren pushed for 'collaboration and equality' in how CCTV, and its headquarters, was to be re-formed. Imagine the building's loop as a rope, made from several continuous strands, housing independent worlds, which twist around one another, and sometimes connect – a little like the independent upstairs-downstairs worlds of aristocrats and servants in a stately home. Chief among the loops is the 'TV-making loop' for the staff, and, wrapped around it, the 'public loop', a continuous promenade open to the public made up of theatrical staircases, processional ways and an unending 'museum of media', which throws you to windows one way looking onto the Beijing skyline, and the other revealing the smoke and mirrors of making TV, by glimpsing into studios, edit suites and green rooms. Underlying it is a philosophical play on the nature of 'real' and 'unreal' space, says Scheeren: 'you see how in real space TV is enacted, then see how it translates into virtual reality onscreen', and, through the muscular architecture how the unreal connects again to the 'real space of the city'. 'I hope all these different realities will collide and spark off one another so the building and its inhabitants take on their own life, become almost subversive.' We'll see.

Koolhaas gets away with building CCTV by calling it tactical and branding his critics from the left, like Mike Davis, western neo-colonialists. It's a neat trick. It's almost convincing. After all, just how many legions of other one-party command economies have been ma-gicked into multi-party democracies by one building? Exactly. His latest, rather less plausible, explanation: it was all One Big Architectural Metaphor! CCTV's 'unstable' design reflects, you see, the 'unstable' nature of China's political future as it opens up to capitalism. That's all right then.

Few other architects in the world have adapted to their changing habitat so cleverly as Koolhaas. Few have not only altered so well how they work in the entrepreneurial economy and the city of spectacle, but the tactics they use in it. Few, however, have followed in his path. His is a tough act to follow. It's hard work being so shapeshifting. But at least is shows that some response to free-market capitalism other than blind acceptance is possible.

However, Koolhaas's glee for shopping, consumerism, Far Eastern autocrats and big fat capitalists attracts accusations of irony, relativism, nihilism and cynicism. 'I'm not cynical about anything,' he says, amazed. 'I'm critical. A cynic could not be this industrious. A cynic is someone who doesn't believe in anything.' Koolhaas, as ever, is not all he seems. His approach to free-market capitalism and globalisation is not quite – but almost – 'if you can't beat 'em . . .' He's not Mother Teresa. He's shied away from obviously liberal projects like social housing. But he has ethics too. Architecture, he says, still needs 'generosity', 'altruism', 'some kind of commitment to the collective'. 'Every single project contains utopian notions.' He just thinks if you want to save the world, you can't do it the old way, with revolutions and charity, but stealthily and tactically, like a virus. 'There's no need to assume free market capitalism is the final condition. I've an underlying optimism that other conditions will prevail. You can be within one system in one part of the world, but you can engage with totally different systems elsewhere. That's the beauty of globalisation.' Slippery to the very end.

CHAPTER EIGHT

IF WALLS COULD TALK

'The eye . . . tends to relegate objects to the distance, to render them passive. That which is merely seen is reduced to an image – and to an icy coldness.'

Henri Lefebvre[1]

Searching for the right words

In the years after the Second World War, Nigel Henderson would wander the bombed-out, half-ruined streets of Bethnal Green in the East End of London with his scavenger's eye, looking for comfort in the continuity of everyday life. It did him good. Henderson had his war wounds like everyone else – not physical, but mental. Relentless flying duties in Coastal Command had left him with nervous exhaustion and, after a near-miss accident in 1943, he was put on limited duties. Henderson now attended a clinic at Guy's Hospital, after suffering a nervous breakdown at the end of the war.

The walks were therapy, a routine to help make sense of the mess inside him, and the ruins out on the streets. Henderson's other routine was making art. After two years of walking and staring, he was given a camera, and began photographing the fragments he saw around him as he wandered, fragments that, like him, had made it through the war. These tenacious leftovers seemed to comfort him. He'd notice the children playing beside bomb sites where their friends had died – girls skipping, boys on their bikes or shinning up lampposts. He scanned shop windows on Roman Road, their chirruping advertising slogans cheerful in the rain. He saw the war-wounded playing banjos for change, wives queuing up for rations, rag-and-bone men doing the rounds. The streets were bombed, the poverty aching, but the city still fizzed with life. Life goes on.

Few remember Nigel Henderson these days. Mention artists in postwar Britain and you think Francis Bacon and the Colony Room crowd. Henderson, though, was the quiet one in the background. That was how he wanted it. He was the antithesis of today's media-hungry creatives or contemporary operators like Bacon. He recoiled from fame, was hopelessly uncommercial; instead of selling or exhibiting his work, he stuffed it into cardboard boxes for the mice to nibble. Art was an amateur occupation, like collecting stamps, or, in Henderson's case, collecting his own private museum of pictures from the old city, to remind him who he was and where he came from. Art, he said, became his 'saving life-line' from boredom, depression and more mental breakdowns.

For all his reticence, though, Henderson was an unwitting catalyst behind a resurgence in British culture after 1945. He was, said art critic David Sylvester, a 'seminal figure' in postwar art, older brother to a more pushy, attention-seeking generation of British artists, architects and sculptors that also emerged, shellshocked, into the drab, shabby years of austerity, and tried, like him, to patch itself up. Henderson's street photography was so experimental that those who have traded off the genre ever since, such as Henri Cartier-Bresson and Roger Mayne, paid their dues. To some he is a father of pop art and postmodernism, an augur of a world soon to come.

Henderson must have seemed attractive to fellow students at the Slade School of Art in 1945. He was shy, with a clipped 'officer class' manner inherited from his upper-middle-class father, a former guardsman. He was also a quiet charmer; witty, even wild, thanks to his gregarious mother, Wyn, a former music-hall performer who'd made it big in the Bloomsbury Set a decade before. Through Wyn, Henderson got to know everyone who was anyone. He married Virginia Woolf's niece, exhibited with Marcel Duchamp and was good friends with pretty much the entire cultural elite of Europe, from Bertolt Brecht to Dylan Thomas. He knew more about modern art than his Slade tutors, who still regarded photography, said Henderson, as the 'devil's domain'.

'You have to remember how dreary postwar London was,' his friend, the architect Colin St John Wilson, once told me. 'And here was a man who could introduce you to Marcel Duchamp. So, we all saved up our seven shillings and sixpences to hop across to Paris with him as often as we could.' Sculptors William Turnbull and Eduardo Paolozzi came calling, then artists like Richard Hamilton, young hotshot architects Alison and Peter Smithson, and critics Lawrence Alloway and Peter Reyner Banham, who drummed the band together and gave it a name: the Independent Group. They were the 'youth wing', as they called it, of surrealist Roland Penrose and critic Herbert Read's Institute of Contemporary Arts, established to fulfill a long-held dream of creating a British modern art museum like New York's MoMA.

Compared with other artists of the early 1950s – the 'kitchen-sink' social realists, the Auerbachs and Kossoffs, with their gritty, but parochial, mud-coloured paintings – the Independent Group was impossibly glamorous. These tough-talking, arrogant British beatniks loved all at once the *art brut* of Jean Dubuffet, the existentialism of Jean-Paul Sartre and Samuel Beckett, but also the technology, space travel, jazz and consumerism of America. Contradictory? Definitely. 'We were more united by what we opposed than by what we supported,' said one of its members, Toni del Renzio. What they opposed, inevitably, was the establishment, whether the elitist Bloomsbury Set, or the old European avant-garde to whom Henderson introduced them. They both gorged themselves on Picasso, Giacometti and Le Corbusier, and railed against them as nostalgic, lacking relevance for the kind of postwar alienation *they* were feeling. Surrealism seemed feeble in war-torn London: 'Houses chopped by bombs while ladies were still on the lavatory,' wrote Henderson. 'Who can hold a candle to that kind of real-life Surrealism?'[2]

Even the 1951 Festival of Britain, that explosion of confident

modern British culture, felt old hat to this younger generation sav-
agely satirical about the failure to materialise of the glittering modern
country that had been promised in 1945. While Britain's socialist
government after the war had achieved astonishing things, such as a
National Health Service, there was disappointment among some
about how little had actually been built – housing, hospitals, schools –
thanks to rationing and shortages of building materials. However,
when this modern world finally did begin to materialise in Britain
and across Europe, in new towns and rebuilt cities, the Independent
Group's members thought it 'crushingly banal' and alienating. Rooted
in a prewar optimism irrelevant to a generation shattered by war, the
international modernism of Le Corbusier or Mies van der Rohe was,
they slammed, building 'yesterday's dreams, when the rest of us have
woken up today.'[3]

The Independent Group, though, were optimists as well as critics.
'Only through construction', wrote the Smithsons, 'can utopias of the
present be realised.' The Independent Group wanted to create some
sort of 'new attitude' to respond and provide answers to the psychological, social and physical upheaval their new, younger generation
were feeling. What the country needed, they felt, was an honest form
of cultural expression that spoke to the lives of ordinary people, rather
than dictating to them how an elite thought they should live. Of
course, they were not alone. All over the world figures from Jean-Paul
Sartre to Robert Rauschenberg were, in the 1950s, trying to make
sense of this new world after the war. In Britain, the plays of John
Osborne, or the films of Lindsay Anderson, were, like the Independent Group's work, 'real', angry, anti-intellectualising, about the
visceral experience of ordinary life, a new kind of culture plugged
more directly into the consciousness of its people. But what would this
culture actually *be*?

Henderson was an ambivalent figure in the group. A good fifteen
years older, he was their passport to a cosmopolitan prewar world, but
also part of the establishment they, mostly emigrés from the working-
class provinces, wanted to overthrow. At first, he became close to Paolozzi

and the Smithsons, forming an inner sanctum within the gang. 'We were like schoolboys,' Peter Smithson once told me. 'There was a lot of giggling and bad language.' To others in the group, they were 'as thick as thieves and wildly arrogant', said Colin St John Wilson. On their poster for the Independent Group's seminal 1956 exhibition, This Is Tomorrow, Henderson photographed the four of them sitting on ultra-modern Eames chairs in a grimy street of terraced houses, mean stares telling you they'd arrived.

Henderson was the 'image finder' for the gang. He'd take Paolozzi and the Smithsons on his walks round the working-class East End to spot things they thought worth salvaging from the old world to create whatever this new form of culture would be that the Independent Group hoped would rise, phoenix-like, from the bomb sites. They scrutinised this 'authentic' East End, recalled Smithson, as if it were 'another world which was slipping away. Because of the bombing and slum clearance, young families had moved out to the new towns. So you were left with this residual population, mostly old, left over from the 1930s.' Nigel and his wife, Judith, were at the time living in the East End, Judith one of the new postwar breed of positivist sociologists studying urban life. Her project, 'Discover Your Neighbour', was trying to winkle out exactly how the material and social culture of close-knit working-class areas had survived the war, and how their values might be replicated and improved upon in postwar rebuilding. It meant she had to live undercover as one of them, in 46 Chisenhale Road, while observing her neighbours, the Samuels family, at number 31.

This espionage on the working class made Henderson uncomfortable. Yet he was doing his own undercover research, spying with his camera. He used a Rolleicord, a hefty plate camera, which displaced him from direct contact with his subject. He called it his 'scrutiny box', perfect for a shy, upper-middle-class man to hide behind while watching noble savages in the streets of Bow. It was, he said, like 'watching live theatre . . . like an audience of one in a public theatre of All'.[4]

Across the Atlantic, of course, Jane Jacobs was soon to begin her own scientifically inspired study of the 'urban energy' she felt was inherent to dense old city neighbourhoods. In London's streets, though, Henderson, the Smithsons and Paolozzi hunted for 'the marvellous, the thing that you can never quite achieve except in dreams – the super-real', said Henderson. They looked for patterns, poetry or uncanny juxtapositions on the street, hidden behind the everyday routines of life. Henderson photographed the face of a real, distant-eyed lady caught for an instant between lookalike mannequin heads, graffiti, adverts, cracks in the walls whose pattern appealed. Back at his studio he'd experiment on what he called 'stressed' photographs, contorting images to represent the energy of the street by stretching printing paper as he developed it. He'd create photomontages or collages mixing photos with images and adverts. He and Paolozzi would stay up all night making camera-less 'Hendograms', placing objects scavenged from bomb sites – fabric, metal, wire mesh – into his enlarger, then projecting light through onto the paper. The objects became abstracted as patterns on the photograph, like cells or crystals.

They were looking for a new language, for new words, images and forms to express their new society. The camera was used not to reflect reality but, like those Victorian early photographers with their images of fairies, to expose a reality they felt existed beneath ordinary life. Henderson had become fascinated by the order of nature while studying biology before the war. To him the people he photographed on the street were little different to the cells he stared at down a microscope, or the landscapes he'd flown over as a pilot: anonymous, abstract. He, the scientist-artist was, like his wife, revealing a hidden order behind them all. It was a way of reassuring his post-breakdown self of an innate, natural structure behind life. But it was also, perhaps, an understandable response to the discontinuity of postwar society: how does culture carry on after concentration camps and Hiroshima? Or, as Theodor Adorno famously put it, could there be poetry after Auschwitz?

Henderson thought he found proof of his intuition in a book, *On Growth and Form*, by D'Arcy Wentworth Thompson, a Scottish embryologist, sent to him by Paolozzi in 1949. It was quickly passed around the Independent Group. 'We all became crazy about that book,' said Colin St John Wilson. Written in 1917, it discussed the proportion and geometry inherent in nature that could be revealed by scientific, rational study. It inspired one of the Independent Group's first shows, Growth and Form, in 1951, organised by Henderson and Richard Hamilton, to display the 'super-real' similarities behind their scrapbook of images, from electron microscope pictures and film stills to Henderson's photograms. It displayed the common language and shapes that they felt structured everyday life.

Critic David Sylvester called the effect the 'multi-evocative image': one image made from scraps that, through free association and suggestion, evoked a feeling or a concept in your mind. 'Multimedia' we'd perhaps call it today. 'The picturesque' they might have called it in the eighteenth century. Henderson, Paolozzi and the Smithsons created a more elaborate three-dimensional 'multi-evocative image' you could walk through for their 1953 exhibition, The Parallel of Art and Life, in which you were assaulted on all sides by a seemingly random assembly of images forcing you to make analogies between, say, a Dublin bus garage and Macchu Picchu, the tribal tattooing of an Eskimo bride and patterns in the mud on Grimsby's shoreline.

This was the closest the Independent Group ever got to forming their coherent new culture. The group's critic, Peter Reyner Banham, labelled it the 'new brutalism', a 'real' British reponse to the art brut of Dubuffet, although Paolozzi, Henderson and the Smithsons poohpoohed the name. Brutalism has since become a catch-all cliché for some to denounce all modernist architecture. But, translated from the French for 'raw', it was originally intended to describe the direct, truthful, raw language the Independent Group would use to speak to its generation.

This expression came in many forms, but perhaps the most famous was brutalist architecture. Architectural circles in America and continental Europe had also been intensely debating what kind of architecture should be built after the war, architecture that didn't just efficiently solve social problems like housing, or economic ones for corporations and property developers, but that actually *meant* something to people, that stirred them. Functionalism – that utilitarian strand of modernist architecture, its form slavishly following its function – gave way to arguments about how best to symbolise or embody society and the spirit of the age while still remaining resolutely modernist. In America, the 'New Monumentality' took hold, architects such as Louis Kahn offering alternatives to glassy commercial office towers with monumental concrete architecture shaped with 'timeless' and 'universal' geometric shapes.

In Britain, the brutalist architecture of the Smithsons and their followers also sought 'universal' and 'timeless' shapes, but ones gleaned from the shape of the city. The Smithsons hoped that their buildings would restore society's sense of self, by repairing Nigel Henderson's shattered East End streets subtly, like a surgeon with a scalpel, not a tyrant with a sledgehammer. They had, after all, studied the shape and feel of the inner city on their walks with Henderson. Instead of demolishing its landscape with urban renewal and comprehensive redevelopment, shipping whole neighbourhoods out to new towns or suburbs, disrupting people who had seen quite enough disturbance for one lifetime, the Smithsons proposed keeping the inner city as it was. Indeed, just as Jane Jacobs was to suggest, the Smithsons said we should learn from those qualities of urban life they, Paolozzi and Henderson had dug out from the old city and use them as DNA to create new buildings and neighbourhoods that would sprout out of the bomb sites.

Their new additions to it would be a gigantic version of the 'multi-evocative image' out on the streets, a more democratic language of architecture a far cry from classicism, gothic or even modernism, all created by elites of some sort or another, and imposed on the masses. This new architecture would speak to the masses in their own language, one somehow hardwired into our psyche. It would not drop out of the sky from the future, like the first-generation modernism of Le Corbusier; instead, it would connect to locality, landscape and history. It would speak to individual and mass society. It would be angry, populist, anti-intellectualising, democratic. It would wean the British off its habit of judging by the eye alone, and dismissing it with a sound-bite. The Smithsons wanted to create a raw, emotional architecture that grabbed you, and never let go. Their 'streets in the sky' would snake across the city, and somehow by their very form meld into the remaining fragments of the old city, to give the pockmarked land-scape that underlying cohesion to life sought by the Independent Group. The trick would be finding exactly the right architectural lan-guage, and the right shape, to speak to people.

They didn't. The reasons are long and complex. One, though, is very simple: the Smithsons never quite found a satisfying architectural form to communicate with mass society that could be mass-produced, without being as dully utilitarian as the classic modernist predecessors they attacked. What they did do, though, was equally important. They began a search – one which is still going on. They hit upon a fundamental problem in architecture: 'the problem of identity in a mobile society'.[5] How can an architect create a language of architec-ture that speaks to every member of society? How can a form of architecture mean something to you and me, en masse *and* individu-ally, with all our multifarious fractured identities in a constantly shifting, globalising world? It was the birth of postmodernism in architecture.

Or rather, it was a return to the same old story. Architects all over the world have been worrying about what kind of architecture to build appropriate to our ever-shrinking world ever since the Industrial Revolution and Enlightenment empire-building began churning up the planet with ever-increasing speed. When new building types, like factories, new phenomena, like industrial cities, and new building materials, like iron and steel, began appearing in the late eighteenth and early nineteenth centuries, they provoked intense debates over how best to weave them into society as it existed. The usual approach was to integrate these new arrivals into traditional architectural styles and landscapes, maintain the status quo, hence the blooming of histor-ical revivals in the nineteenth century, and the often-fierce arguments as to which particular style captured best the spirit of the age. Modernist architects tried the opposite tack, embracing new materials and techniques and creating a new kind of architectural expression that aimed to reflect immutable and universal values of humanity.

Both approaches were anathema to the Smithsons and their generation: one too old-fashioned, the other a cookie-cutter approach to architecture. Instead, they asked, in a society more democratic than ever before, how could architecture symbolise or engage with the masses? How could architecture, by nature and definition heavy and stationary and rooted to the ground, be appropriate for a world increasingly mobile and nomadic, constantly on the go?

As it turned out, that new culture the Independent Group sought *had* arrived by the mid 1950s, only not bottom up from the gritty streets of the East End, but via telecommunications from America. They saw it themselves. By the mid 1950s, the age of austerity was giving way to the far more tempting age of affluence, jazz, space travel and colour. People, it seemed, were more interested in leaving their postwar selves in the past, happily diverting themselves from existential angst with glamorous consumer materialism, not kitchen-sink reality. They'd had quite enough reality.

Eduardo Paolozzi, for instance, began rhapsodising about the aspirational freedom America offered. Richard Hamilton cast an ambivalent eye over America's new corporate culture. Peter Reyner Banham began a rather less ambivalent love affair with America's can-do consumerism. The Smithsons, too, shifted tack. They were now in thrall to a ruthless new kind of mass communication broadcast from Madison Avenue. 'Today,' they wrote, 'we [architects] are being edged out of our traditional role by the new phenomenon of the popular arts – advertising. We must somehow get the measure of this invention if we are to match its powerful and exciting impulses with our own.'[6] They began dreaming of hi-tech, *Jetson*-style houses, not concrete brutalism. In 1956, they were asked to design the House of the Future for the Ideal Home Show, Britain's biggest display of mass-market home consumerism. Their glamorous vision – showers that blow-dried you as well as your hair, a hexagonal coffee table that rose from the floor at the touch of a button – wowed the country. It was meant to. It was meant to goad the public into looking at the utilitarian reality of the drab welfare state being built around them and wonder what was going wrong. Sure, we can chuckle at the ludicrous Austin Powers fashions of its model residents: chunky-knit leggings with sewn-in shoes didn't quite catch on. But an open-plan pod of sensuous curves, prefabricated like a car, packed with consumer goods, all mod cons built in, lounged in by a leisured, childless couple in sportswear? Sounds prescient.

Nigel Henderson, though, was never really interested in this emerging pop art and architecture. He didn't want to make his name or change the world like his younger friends. His search for a new kind of culture was 'a small private vision', Henderson said, 'in praise of the world as far as I can sense it, and make some sense of it'. What is thought of as the pop-art high point of the Independent Group, their 1956 exhibition, *This Is Tomorrow*, was really their swan song, as their former catalyst, Henderson, slipped quietly away. The show displayed imaginings of the future. Most were hopeful, futuristic, celebratory: Richard Hamilton's *Fun House*, for instance, featured giant bottles of Guinness and blown up, pre-Warhol Marilyns. But the stand designed by Henderson, Paolozzi and the Smithsons was gloomy and nostalgic. Its collage of the kind of flotsam and jetsam Henderson once salvaged from bomb sites looked like the archaeological dig of an ancient, prewar world destroyed in a nuclear holocaust, said Reyner Banham. Dominating it was Nigel Henderson's sinister *Head of a Man*, an extraordinary photocollage of slivers of his landscapes, natural forms, fractured, shattered on the verge of decay. It was his warning to us about the persistence of alienation, as everyone else bounced into a consumerist future.

Henderson never worked on this scale again. From 1954 until he died in 1985, he and Judith lived in a small cottage up a potholed track on the Essex salt marshes at Thorpe-le-Soken. He still saw his friends; Paolozzi even moved in next door. He'd still, sporadically, make art, mostly collages that rearranged his personal scrapbook of images again and again, in ever-decreasing psychological circles. He never found a patron, but occasionally exhibited, when goaded by his friends. While they were carried away with pop culture, the latest in this and that, while the history books were written and reputations made, he was left behind, quite happily, to go fishing, shooting, or teach a few hours at Norwich School of Art. But what he'd enjoy most of all was quietly teaching art classes for fellow amateurs, in Clacton-on-Sea's putting green pavilion.

Can you feel it?

It is early in the morning. In a few hours the glamorous and the great of Rome, that most glamorous of great cities, will be here to celebrate the opening of Museo Nazionale Delle Arti del XXI Secolo (MAXXI). This gallery, though, has no art in it, from the twenty-first or any other century. The contents, we're assured, will arrive in a few months. This grand opening is for the spectacular building itself, containing just one exhibit – its designer, Zaha Hadid, who comes to the party resplendent in a fluffy Prada puffa jacket, flanked by sundry dark-suited Italian dignitaries in sunglasses, and legions of contemporary dance troupes. 'I do like a little drama,' Hadid tells me, drily. The building needs no art. The building itself is the art. And the architecture has to be pristine.

For now, though, I'm alone in this cavernous place, alone, that is, apart from a small army of cleaners. They are polishing the building – quite literally. I watch from one of the balconies as men dressed, like monks, in white hooded onesies sit oversized on little cleaning carts, knees poking left and right, and waltz and pirouette across the floor, energetically polishing its acres as if their lives depended on it. They get quite a sheen up. Some monks are air-brushing the building, too, delicately brandishing sprayguns that diffuse a mist of white paint across the large, swooshing reception desk that guards the museum's entrance. The building has an otherworldly glow. It has to look good for the cameras.

Rome's anticipation is palpable. MAXXI has been a long time coming. Zaha Hadid designed it in 1999. Ten years later it's still not quite finished. 'I want you to feel the excitement,' Hadid says to me, 'feel it through the space.' The string of spectacular, unique buildings Hadid created before her death in 2016 were all about such highly strung, melodramatic experiences. Walk into MAXXI and you enter a maelstrom, the concrete-walled entrance canyon striped with zooming perspectives and dizzying height, pumped up by go-faster striped fins on the ceiling, and labyrinthine black steel stairs and walkways which climb, meandering, up the canyon as if plucked from an Escher painting. To over-egg this pudding, the walkways have built-in light boxes; and, outside, streaks of scalding lights built into the building and the landscape scream into the twilight like car tail-lights caught on a long exposure photograph. It looks unreal.

There's almost no point in describing the shape – it's too complex. I'll try. There are no conventional floors and walls. Instead, imagine a long, curved, L-shaped tube of concrete, which splits at the corner into several branches that twist off, zooming up, and down, curling round and crashing into each other. The result, outside, is all thrusting concrete tubes careering round corners, shoving their elbows into the sky. Inside, it's a labyrinth: vast cavernous halls, long winding corridors; low ceilings; high ceilings; spaces that weigh down on you, others that open to distant views of the central canyon, or onto the city outside. There is no let-up. Every space is vertiginous. Even the quieter ones. You could get lost in here, stuck for ever inside that Escher painting, noisily going mad.

It is a strange building to open one year after an economic crisis has plunged the world into the deepest recession for decades. Rome, for one, will not see its like again for some time. This city's history lurches between torpid inertia and frantic progress, building frenzies remedying long spells of infrastructural chaos. In the seventeenth century Pope Urban VIII had Bernini modernise Rome with baroque churches and vistas. Mussolini embraced the motor car by careering roads round the Colosseum and delicate archaeological sites. MAXXI comes at the end of another, long building boom begun by mayor Francesco Rutelli, 'an architecture school dropout,' says Professor Francesco Garofalo, who wrote the plan for this art museum in the mid 1990s. 'He had big Mitterand dreams, or nightmares. He fell in love with regeneration in Barcelona and thought Rome needed big, big architecture.' A spate of big-big-budget buildings has now come to an end. MAXXI is the last icon. For now.

If Zaha Hadid is worried about world economic collapse putting the kibosh on her career, though, she's not showing it today at the building's opening. She slinks in all swagger and attitude – smaller than you'd expect, given her fiery reputation and publicity pics that show a hair-do engineered skywards into a 1980s power-bouffant. 'People say it's the end of the icon project,' she sneers. 'Psssht.' Nothing ever withered like a withering look from Hadid. 'It's too simplistic to say there'll be no more exuberance in architecture. Just look back. [Norman Foster's] Hong Kong and Shanghai Bank [skyscraper, Hong Kong] . . . when was that commissioned? During a recession. The Pompidou Centre? In a recession. It's too simplistic to say we're all afraid, we can't do icons, we have to restrain. What does that mean exactly?'

Back then, she had reason to be defensive. Architecture, a volatile business, was exceedingly hard hit by 2008's economic downturn, and Hadid, leading exponent of the kind of extravagant architecture some have equated to the excesses of the banking industry, had more to lose than most. Critics still say the 'iconic' architecture of starchitects like her is ill suited to leaner economic times. After 2008, Frank Gehry laid off half his office, Norman Foster a quarter. By comparison, Hadid and her team got off lightly. Some projects went on ice, and she made 'a small amount' of redundancies. But if the proverbial *did* hit the fan? 'I'd adapt. I have been there before,' she smiles, 'for decades'. Her firm, ZHA, had swollen in size through the Noughties, but even after her death still remains packed into the modest headquarters – a Victorian school building in Clerkenwell, central London – that's housed it for years. It feels like a monochrome student digs, as if nobody's had a millisecond to unpack a poster or a pot plant.

For decades Zaha Hadid was the architect who never got work, never got appreciated, who only designed impossible architecture that could never be built. Indeed, she arrived in London from Iraq in the early years of the 1970s to study architecture at a time when the world was once again tumbling into recession, and western cities were facing the full force of the urban crisis. 'It was worse for architects in the Seventies,' she told me once. 'There was political backlash to modernism. Nobody could get a job. The three-day week and blackouts and buying candles in the shops, having to rotate electricity with France whenever we wanted to watch *Top of the Pops* or take a shower. I remember drawing late into the night wearing blankets and gloves, with candles.' Little did she know at the time, she was drawing the future – the city of spectacle.

Hadid was then studying at London's prestigious private college of architecture, the Architectural Association (AA), housed in elegant Georgian townhouses just a few minutes' walk from those emptying warehouses and protestors in Covent Garden. She arrived there at a good moment. In 1971, having been threatened with closure, the AA welcomed its new head, the young, ambitious Canadian Alvin Boyarsky, who boldly reasserted the school's independence, and swiftly transformed it into the most influential architectural incubator in the world. His educational approach was prescient. He didn't dogmatically impose one style or approach on his students. Instead, he invited to teach there architects and educators of all persuasions, poached from institutions in America and continental Europe. Even Brian Anson, that firebrand Marxist, found a place here after the disappointments of Covent Garden, running his latest pitch for revolution: the Architects Revolutionary Council.

Boyarsky likened his approach to setting 'a well-laid table', which makes it sound more well-mannered that it was. For there was a fierce rivalry among his teachers. Every year, each competed with one another to sell their particular approach to architecture to incoming students. It was the free market in architecture, perfectly adapted for the realities of the entrepreneurial city, and the coming city of spectacle. That critique of the modernist architecture establishment begun by the Smithsons and the Independent Group had in the twenty years since spread to become the new normal; what had not yet been established was what kind of architecture would replace it. So the AA's eclectic mix of architects and educators laid out their stalls, each one offering a distinct new approach to how we build buildings, yet each essentially answering the same problem, the one set by the Smithsons: 'the problem of identity in a mobile society'. The Smithsons and Team X, that alliance of architects who first critiqued modernism, hadn't found an answer. Would this generation?

The way in which architecture communicated with us in an ever-changing society, or failed to do so, had become the biggest topic facing them. Indeed, how communication in general now functioned in a rapidly globalising world of mass media had become a topic of wider social concern for the past few years, as the popular culture that had fascinated pop artists in the 1950s swelled in importance a decade later. Debate in the West was dominated by Canadian theorist Marshall McLuhan, who proposed, grandly, that humankind had to adjust its world view to take account of mass media and computerisation turning the planet into a post-industrial 'global village', lorded over by media and multinationals. In the age of television, and the coming age of the computer, communication by language, sound or tactility, which had been so important to earlier civilisations, had given way almost entirely to communication via the eye. Visual sensation in and of itself was almost more important than the subject or substance being communicated. 'During the mechanical ages,' wrote McLuhan in *Understanding Media: The Extensions of Man* (1964), 'we had extended our bodies in space. Today, after more than a century of electronic technology, we have extended our central nervous system itself in a global embrace, abolishing both space and time.'[7]

When Zaha Hadid arrived to study at the Architectural Association, she said, 'there was talk of one man and one woman': Robert Venturi and Denise Scott Brown. Venturi had, in 1966, published a book that essentially addressed the questions that had puzzled the

Smithsons a decade before. *Complexity and Contradiction in Architecture* (1966) declared, controversially for the time, that it was OK to be a modernist *and* like history. Venturi wrote of his love for Renaissance architecture, for the baroque and mannerism, and called for a return to – well, complexity and contradiction in architecture, lost in the supposedly impoverished modernist landscape of the 1950s and 1960s. To Venturi the so-called failure of modernist architecture was that it hadn't invented the right way of communicating with us. It had been revolutionary in creating an architecture for mass society, rather than for different social or economic classes. But it lacked allusion, symbolism, richness, 'messy vitality'; qualities, he said, we all craved. To Mies van der Rohe's famous quote, 'Less is more,' Venturi infamously replied, 'Less is a bore.'

In many ways *Complexity and Contradiction* gave architectural form to the arguments of Jane Jacobs five years earlier, to those urban qualities she hankered after. However, his follow-up, *Learning from Las Vegas* (1972), written with his wife, Denise Scott Brown, and Steven Izenour proposed a more futuristic take on the past. Clearly suffused with the communication theories of Marshall McLuhan, the pop art of Andy Warhol, and an understanding of the new importance of mass media, it declared that it was now OK to be a modernist *and* love Vegas tack, that American commercial roadside vernacular of burger bars, neon signs and billboards. Thirty-five years before Rem Koolhaas wrote about learning from Junkspace, Venturi, Scott Brown and Izenour cast Caesar's Palace Casino as a modern-day Hadrian's Villa, and burger bars and neon as contemporary versions of ancient Greek temples or Christian churches with their narrative mosaics, murals and frescoes. 'Just signage,' they wrote, 'but we call it high art.'

Just as the Smithsons had declared in the mid 1950s, commercial pop culture from advertising to magazines to the movies was so much more efficient than architecture these days at communicating with the public. Venturi, Scott Brown and Izenour quoted with approval the mass-market architect-developer Morris Lapidus, anathema to the more 'artistic' architect: 'People are looking for illusions . . . Where do they go to find this world of the illusions? . . . Only one place – the movies. They go to the movies. The hell with everything else.'[8] It was Venturi's wife, Scott Brown, who nudged them to look at Las Vegas: a town planner and sociologist who in the late 1960s had studied, like so many at the time, the decaying inner city, she proposed, like Kevin Lynch before her, that the urban landscape was one gigantic communication system. Architects, they proposed, should learn from mass media and the tactics of Madison Avenue, to design buildings for this 'system' in the manner of the Independent Group's 'multi-evocative image' to better communicate with the public.

The problem with architecture, though, was that, by definition, it was all about space. Unlike the flickering, lightweight, ephemeral, two-dimensional media of billboards, television and movie screens, architecture was stationary, heavy, rather permanent and decidedly three-dimensional. Venturi, Scott Brown and Izenour decried what they called 'ducks': traditional, old-fashioned weighty buildings whose exterior shape might express what went on inside, but which would prove too inflexible to be changed when society changed. It would just sit there, a dead duck. Society needed something with the spirit of a TV screen: one kind of shape, capable of imparting infinite kinds of messages.

Venturi, Scott Brown and Izenour proposed instead the 'decorated shed' as their answer to the Smithsons' question. The main body of the building is housed in a kind of shed – a flexible, generic structure capable of being altered when the demands placed on it changed. At the front of the building, though, was a facade, almost like a TV screen, housing all the decoration, allusion, symbolism and communication systems you wanted. Their model was the Las Vegas casino, with a functional space out back efficiently designed to part customers from their money, and a flamboyant facade to attract them in. Function behind, form at the front. Implied throughout was a clear acceptance not only of the tactics of modern-day consumerism, but its ideology. The ambivalence of many pop artists towards pop culture had disappeared. Mass media and the free-market had come up with a way of not only communicating with people, but fulfilling their desires. 'Disney World', Venturi told the *New York Times* in 1972, 'is nearer to what people want than what architects have ever given them.'[9]

If architecture was to become a kind of mass media, what messages would it send to us? What shapes and colours and stories would be transmitted from its walls? Architects set to work, inventing countless new styles and languages. 'What if?' architecture bloomed, fantasies and possibilities of infinite variety, mostly on paper rather than on the streets: architecture as imagery. For a while, many – Venturi and Scott Brown included – took *Learning from Las Vegas* rather literally, designing buildings with often garish, self-consciously symbolic facades, an approach today nicknamed 'Po-Mo'. Those setting out their stalls at the Architectural Association, though, were selling a mostly higher-minded product. Many were inspired by an approach to mass communication that emerged at the same time as McLuhan's, and Venturi Scott Brown's, though from across the English Channel, not the Atlantic. French 'post-structuralist' cultural theorists like Jacques Derrida, Jean-François Lyotard, Jean Baudrillard and Roland Barthes had also begun taking popular culture seriously, analysing the hidden structures behind how it communicates. Baudrillard, for instance – suffused like much progressive French thought after the student riots of May 1968 with an acceptance of and curiosity about the 'American' consumer culture that had trumped 'European' idealism and utopia in the late 1960s – studied a society obsessed by visual images and what he called 'simulacra', a representation of something solid (a building, for instance) so convincing it almost replaces it. Architects such as Peter Eisenman attempted to translate such ideas into buildings, removing theories and ideologies from architecture and just designing shapes – pure architectural form without any ambition to 'change society', as modernism had once attempted. For a while it too dominated architectural debate.

Like the brutalism of the Smithsons, though, both Po-Mo and post-structuralism proved short-lived, though they were not without influence. The languages they chose seemed either too lowbrow or too highbrow, too easy or too difficult to understand. Ultimately more successful were the paths taken in the mid 1970s by others at the Architectural Association, who, while the western city was at its lowest ebb, began to look again at its qualities and its ability to communicate. They began to create architectural styles for a fractured, globalised, continually mobile world of instantaneous communication: a glittering, thrilling architecture of mass media unlike any before it. Out of the thousands of architectural languages that bloomed, Babel-like, after *Complexity and Contradiction*, it was *this* architecture, in decades to come, that would prove most successful. The gentrifiers of the city wanted an architecture of diversity, intensity, liveliness. Architecture was a free market now: the consumer was king. And the consumer wanted to be wowed.

In one classroom at the AA, for instance, Bernard Tschumi started critiquing the booming suburbs, revealing their darker side in the Los Angeles lauded by Reyner Banham and the Las Vegas praised by Robert Venturi and Denise Scott Brown: their social segregation and ghettoes. Tschumi instead suggested that in the future cities should be built that echoed the qualities of older cities, like Manhattan. A similar message to Jane Jacobs, but in a very different form. Tschumi wasn't interested like her in the old city's elegant 'urban ballet' and ability to unite myriad social groups in harmony, not segregation. He liked its mayhem. He proposed releasing its irrational, unpredictable and spontaneous qualities, perhaps inspired by the chaos then always threatening to rise to the surface during the urban crisis, and the cultural expressions, like punk, a product of it. He looked, for instance, at how mass advertising might be subverted not to manufacture desire in its audience, but to unleash desires hidden in all of us beneath the surface. He proposed what he would come to call 'event' architecture – not a fixed, heavy monument, but something with energy and motion, carnivalesque, that reflected and provoked change in its users, that could be read by different people in different ways at the same time.

The market stall that appealed to a young student Zaha Hadid, though, was Rem Koolhaas's. Koolhaas, in his thirties, was both teaching at the AA and, with a research fellowship at Cornell University, doing his own study of the old city. *Delirious New York: A Retroactive Manifesto for Manhattan* (1978) analysed what he called the city's 'culture of congestion'. He presented an alternative history of New York from the late nineteenth century, looking at not so much its lauded skyscrapers and avenues, but those byproducts of its capitalist culture, such as the Coney Island funfair and the landscapes of leisure built as 'pressure valves' for Manhattan citizens to let off steam. Drawing on Robert Venturi and Denise Scott Brown, Koolhaas proposed a kind of 'resort city' – a spectacular if disjointed place of pop culture, consumerism, leisure, and disconnected, almost random thrills, spills and dazzling experiences – as *the* shape of the future post-industrial city. Architects would not, like their modernist predecessors, design social housing, hospitals, schools, the architecture of need; they would design for consumerism, the architecture of want. Not Los Angeles, but old Manhattan – then crawling out of its bankrupt, crime-ridden past, but still energetic, surreal, thrilling and multi-layered – was the city of the future.

After Hadid graduated in 1977, Koolhaas gave her a job in his and Elia Zenghelis's new firm, the Office for Metropolitan Architecture. She didn't last long. (Koolhaas called her 'a planet in her own orbit'.) Hadid had her own ideas about 'what if?' architecture. Koolhaas might have come up with a blueprint for the entrepreneurial city, an idea about its nature, but she would be one of many architects who would create its *style,* what it looked and felt like, the kind of thrills, spills and dazzling experiences it would contain.

Where Koolhaas was foremost an editor, a writer, a theorist, Hadid was anything but. She was a precocious creator of images, not words. (The blurb, for instance, accompanying her winning entry for a 1982 competition to build a luxury club, the Peak, in Hong Kong is, characteristically, full of misspelling and jargon – 'following the demolishment of the existing apartments' – non sequiturs that at least *begin* with some logic – 'the architecture appears like a knife cutting through butter devastating all the traditional principles' – and complete what-*are*-you-on-about-Zaha?

sentences: 'the final criterion is a composite and total of all these pro-
grammatic beams looking over the mountainside, and these suspended
satalites [sic] constitute a Modern Geology.') But what images!

Her graduation project, a hotel perched over the River Thames on
London's Hungerford Bridge, was called Malevich's Tectonik, after
the suprematist artist Kasimir Malevich who in 1928 wrote: 'We can
only perceive space when we break free from the earth, when the
point of support disappears.' Well, what if it did? Hadid's language of
architecture followed suit, metaphorically seeming to break free from
the earth. In the late 1970s and early 1980s Hadid embarked on a
remarkable journey, what she called 'the discovery', manifest in a series
of abstract paintings depicting proposed buildings, such as the Peak, as
splintered forms eddying in a swirling landscape of impressionistic
shapes. The canvases were designed to get across the *feel* of her spaces:
conventional architectural drawings could never get quite manage it,
she said; paintings could communicate this experience better.

Her biggest influence, she once told me, 'really came out of the
European city. It came out of being in the UK. The biggest influence
on it is London,' that is the London of the 1970s, with its romantic
ruins and chaotic energy. Each painting and project was a search for a
new language of architecture exploding from the old city. Hadid
honed it and honed it and honed it. Her pictures, she said, created a
'geography of complex geometry', a landscape that 'intensified' space;
'and then the idea of distortion, of using many perspectival projec-
tions, and the interior urban space', bringing the city inside the
building, and building into the cityscape. As she explained it to me
she became, like her paintings, extremely animated: 'Fluid space . . .
to allow you to have a fluid interior, the idea of carving the ground,
layers, geology deeper down through all the layers, and the reverse,
building up layers.'

What she was after in the pictures was capturing the *experience* of
being within the architecture she wanted, one day, to build. 'I wanted
layering. Layering produces juxtapositions, or superimpositions, different situations. Which is more to do with archaeology or geology

than the obliteration of the landscape, or tabula rasa of the early modern era.' Something akin, perhaps, to the swirling sensory experience of being in the city in the 'culture of congestion'. Something akin, perhaps, to the 'multi-evocative image'. 'The same building appears in different ways [in the paintings]. With different distortions. I was always very interested in things like, if I took this glass and I shattered it, what are the repercussions? Or if I distorted or deformed it. The similarities and the differences.' Her buildings on the canvas did not, she explained, 'necessarily have a front and a back' but 'many fronts. Take [MAXXI in] Rome. Every twist of the building is responding to a twist on the site but a different kind of context, not to do with style, than the geography of the site, not throwing the baby out with the bathwater but reconfiguring it. It's like taking the Peak and melting it.'

Critics loved it, but many found her new shapes baffling. 'People criticised me years ago, "Oh, nobody understands your drawings," la, la, la, but every time we did plans too. They were always realisable.' It took some time for the building to come off the canvas and onto the street. Slowly but surely, though, curious clients emerged who were willing to spend money to realise Hadid's peculiar new architecture. It was a stuttering start. Her first big success, the Peak, was never built. Neither were buildings on Berlin's Kurfürstendamm, nor an art and media centre in Dusseldorf. Her first built project, the Fire Station at the Vitra factory, Switzerland, was a formal success but not a functional one: the fire engines moved out. The most notorious project, though, was her competition-winning design for the Cardiff Bay Opera House in 1994, abandoned by its funding body after noisy opposition from politicians wary of supposedly highbrow architecture. Popular taste was becoming more daring in the 1990s, but Hadid's ideas were as yet a step too far. It was a sobering experience, which set her office back for years, but one from which she learned. Hadid years later became philosophical about Cardiff, seeing it as a turning point in her career. Without dumbing down her work, she learned better the politics of how to get it built.

It worked. Slowly. A ski jump in Innsbruck, a tram station in Strasbourg. But it was Cincinnati's Rosenthal Center for Contemporary Art with its zigzagging walkways that gave Hadid her real break. The *New York Times* called it, without overstatement, 'the most important new building in America since the cold war'.[10]

Why so important? Hadid was the right architect at the right time. The experience of space, the feel of it, the immersive nature of architectural space – the fact that you can't escape it – helps it to bond and communicate with us, the people inside it. And Hadid had created an architecture so powerful in its effect on the visitor, you could not help but feel something, anything.

The CCA silenced all those who said her impossible architecture could never be built. Perhaps it wasn't as energetic as her paintings (what could be?), but this was just work in progress. And it was wildly popular. It brought in the punters. It gave Hadid the confidence to win a stream of commissions: designs for a ferry terminal in Salerno, Italy; a high-speed train station in Naples; a cinema and square in Barcelona; a housing project in Vienna; a public archive, library and sport centre in Montpellier, France; a bridge in Abu Dhabi; the Guangzhou Opera House and a masterplan for Beijing's Soho City, China; the Central Plant Building for BMW, Leipzig, Germany; the MAXXI Contemporary Arts Centre, Rome; the Ordrupgaard Museum extension, Copenhagen; and the Phaeno Science Centre, Wolfsburg, Germany, and on and on, even in that most conservative of countries, her adopted home, Britain. In all, the biggest challenge was that facing every architect of idealised spaces: getting what's in one's head out there, actually creating in three, real, dimensions the swirling forms of the imagination.

Her glass stations for the Nordpark railway in Austria, or her bridge in Zaragoza, Spain, with their sensuous Dali-esque curves, hint at her ambition – a building of impossible curves, designed in London by an Iraqi architect, whose components are manufactured in China, and assembled in Austria or Spain. An architecture of and about globalisation. But actually realising them in the real world is still work in progress. The engineering is there. But the details, the finesse, has not quite arrived yet. Get too close to Nordpark, or her bridge in Zaragoza, or the Guangzhou Opera House and the imperfections in them glower, like the first scratch on an iPod, a stain on an all-white carpet.

Hadid's work has been called 'cinematographic', and, yes, it is a little like being inside a film, shoved about by a director who explodes space into a series of tightly controlled vignettes. Walls, rarely at right angles, seem to slice and snap at you in all directions. Stair risers are set at an angle. It messes with your head. But never to make you queasy, only more aware of the space about you. Baroque architects like Francesco Borromini shattered Renaissance ideas of a single viewpoint perspective in favour of dizzying space designed to lift the eyes and heart to God. Hadid shatters both the classically formal, rule-bound modernism of Mies van der Rohe and Le Corbusier *and* the old rules of space – walls, ceilings, front and back, right angles – to reassemble them, she told me, as a 'a new fluid kind of spatiality' of multiple perspective points and fragmented geometry. Short of creating actual forms that morph and change shape as if they were the fluid, visual, ever-changing landscapes that lie behind the TV or computer screen (still the stuff of science fiction), Hadid creates the solid apparatus that makes us *perceive* space as seeming to morph and change shape around us as we pass through. Her buildings are rarely tactile; they don't invite touch. But they *look* incredible, literally so. They are visual fun-fairs, like being sucked past a computer screen into a CGI wonderland, looping the loop, tumbling through space, chased by a white rabbit. Baudrillard's simulacra, perhaps: a representation of something solid (a building, for instance) so convincing it almost replaces it.

What did Hadid want people to feel inside these dizzying spaces? She thinks long and hard. 'A sense of excitement. I was very touched a few years ago when I found out there were queues to go up and down my ski jump [in Innsbruck]. People had wedding anniversaries in the top. They were genuinely excited by it. I want them to feel . . .' Anything. That's it. An architecture of simple, bodily thrill: the perfect shape for the city of spectacle.

The decorated duck

In the 2009 film *Up in the Air*, George Clooney plays Ryan Bingham, a human resources consultant that firms employ to sack people. He travels on aeroplanes around the United States to land, momentarily, in an office somewhere, before destroying someone's life. 'How much does your life weigh?' he asks his audience at one of his motivational lectures; *he* travels light, without baggage, emotional or otherwise. The film is a pretty thinly disguised allegory for the kind of weightless consumer capitalist society that's sprung up in the past few decades, one constantly on the go to the next place, but which rarely touches the earth. 'Moving is living,' says Bingham. In the thoughtspeak of his age, being fired is not destruction but an opportunity, freedom to do all the things you always wanted, set loose from the ground.

The sociologist Zygmunt Bauman calls this condition 'liquid modernity', whose very speed and lightness are 'the paramount source of uncertainty for all'; change, fluidity and volatility are the norm, the new ordinary.[11] Political theorist Fredric Jameson ascribes this 'depthlessness' to 'postmodernism', or, as he corrects, 'the cultural logic of late capitalism',[12] where information and data rule, meaning is relativist and fractured, and certainty rests on shifting sands. For his part, Jeremy Rifkin calls it 'hypercapitalism': 'if the industrial era was characterised by the amassing of physical capital and property, the new era prizes intangible forms of power bound up in bundles of information and intellectual assets.'[13]

This presents architecture with a problem. Architecture is by its very nature physical, tangible and un-volatile. It has foundations in the earth. It does not flit about the globe as digital shadows. It shelters our lives. That is why the language of western culture equates architectural metaphors with trust and certainty: 'good foundations', say, or 'bricks and mortar'. Buildings, after all, are weighty. But they are getting lighter. In 1995, architectural theorist Kenneth Frampton wrote that the proportion of an average building's budget spent on its innards – the skeleton that holds it up, the guts, tubes, piping and nervous systems that make it function – had fallen from 80 per cent in the nineteenth century to around 20 per cent.[14] Look past the hoardings on most building sites today and you'll see a light steel frame going up, a skeleton, weighty concrete reserved for those parts, like foundations and the central core of a skyscraper, most rooted to the ground for ballast. This lightweight architecture has been invented for a good reason. It costs a lot of money and energy to defy gravity. The less you can spend on it the better.

Throughout the twentieth century, there has been a drive for many architects to create such lighter and lighter, less monumental buildings, a long-term trend academic Clare Melhuish describes as the 'dematerialisation of the physical environment'.[15] The heft of a building declined throughout the past 100 years under various strands of modernism, with concrete and then steel-framed buildings removing the need for walls internal or external to bear the building's weight. 'The concept of the building envelope [or facade] as a thin, insulated membrane,' she writes, 'held rigid by precisely manufactured, pared-down structural components began to take over from the idea of the building as a dense, solid mass.'[16]

Traditionally we have expected architecture to try to pin down meaning, to reassure us with its stability and sheer weight. No longer, says Melhuish: instead architecture has been on a crash diet, losing kilograms, countless tonnes, accompanied by a 'thoroughgoing de-stabilisation of physical form and structure' – an 'architecture of mutability'. Buildings today, she suggests, are designed to 'reflect, or make manifest, conditions of economic and cultural globalisation accelerated through the expansion of Western capital and the operation of information and media technology, particularly television and the internet, at a global scale'.[17]

They are fulfilling Venturi, Scott Brown and Izenour's prediction, though not quite in the form they predicted. They are no longer 'ducks' – sculptural, if static and unchanging lumps. They are not 'decorated sheds', simple forms wrapped in meaning. Better than that.

They are both. They are decorated ducks. Venturi, Scott Brown and Izenour did not predict how construction technology and computer design technology would so advance that today one can create light-weight, flexible, adaptable, buildings capable of changing as society changed, wrapped in a skin that communicates as adeptly as any form of mass media, but in any shape or sculptural form you want. Architecture is dematerialising. It is not quite as ethereal as the pixels on your computer screen, but give it time.

As a result, it is the decoration on the duck – the nature of its facade – that today has become of prime importance, and the way we used to experience architecture, three-dimensionally, in person, with all the senses, has given way to a new one: experiencing it from a distance, using the eye – often not even in person, but through photos, StreetView, Periscope, YouTube, CGI images. As the theorist Juhani Pallasmaa puts it: 'The architecture of our time is turning into the retinal art of the eye . . . Instead of experiencing our being in the world, we behold it from outside as spectators of images projected on the surface of the retina. As buildings lose their plasticity and their connection with the language and wisdom of the body, they become isolated in the cool and distant realm of vision.'[18] What a building *looks* like, its skin, its style, has become more important than ever.

'*Scheisse!*' My German's about as good as my brain surgery and my knowledge of football, but that's one word I recognise. Three pre-pubescent lads, head-to-foot in shiny Bayern Munich red, have just caught a distant glimpse of their team's new star from the U-Bahn and leapt – wide-eyed, drop-jawed – from their seats. But it's no footballer. It's a stadium.

Football's all in the emotion, and this stadium's architecture has been designed specifically to stimulate that passion, to bottle it up and then to shout it to the rooftops, as loudly as those three fans. True, architecture might not be at the front of most football fans' minds. All you really need for a game are jumpers for goalposts and twenty-two bodies. What it's housed in, though, can amplify the experience of watching and playing, and communicate it. Stadia can be like cathedrals – the same massive, sublime space, the same awe experienced when faced with something bigger than you, like a crowd in full chant. But mostly they're not. The excitement is there despite the architecture. The Premier League is rich; its architecture, though, is poor. Money might be lavished on players, but the spectators are housed in tin cans.

Today, of course, millions more people experience the experience of football through the media than through actually being there at the game in reality, in space. This, though, has not made the architecture in which it is housed redundant. It has given it new life. Academic Beatriz Colomina wrote that modernist architecture only became truly modern through its relationship with the new phenomenon of global mass media in the twentieth century, 'making it circulate around the world', she wrote, 'as if it had suddenly lost mass and volume'.[19] The more so today in a world of digital media. The trick to designing a successful football stadium these days is to design it in a way that allows it to communicate the emotion of the pitch to its audience, both those in the building and those thousands of miles away watching it on an iPad or Sky Sports. Besides heightening atmosphere and treating fans like more than animals, stadium design, like the kit on a player's back, can be all part of the (branded) experience designed to be beamed instantaneously around the world.

Bayern Munich used to play at Frei Otto and Gunther Behnisch's incredible stadium from the 1972 Olympics, capped with its doily of steel and glass: that's become heritage now, too precious to alter, but it gave fans quite a taste for architecture. Their replacement home has got mod cons and infrastructure in spades, a capacity of 66,000, acres of thrusting concrete columns and muscular terraces, a vast landscape of promenades from the U-Bahn station, coursing and controlling the crowd like a river, past ravines cut into the multi-tiered car parks below for light and air, and cliffs embedded with ticket booths. Inside it's like a sleek Munich BMW: roomy, efficiently planned, slightly bland but undeniably impressive, even tasteful in its silver-grey styling, buffed and moulded plastic terrace seats and sans-serif signage.

The Swiss architectural firm behind it, Herzog & de Meuron, hasn't reinvented the body of the stadium. It's a design recipe little changed since the Colosseum: the same of ring of terraces topped with retractable sun/rain shade awnings, here hung on projecting steel beams. But they have perfected it. Terraces are piled impossibly high in a tight, close ring – modelled on Shakespeare's Globe – to create a deep and intimate cauldron, bubbling with intensity. Even walking to your seat feels like walking onstage. But this building is all about the skin, not the bones and organs underneath.

Traditionally, stadia may be alive inside but their internalised, fortress-like exteriors are usually dead to the world outside. Stuck out, as so many, are at the edge of the city in no-man's-land, halfway to the airport, Allianz's only context is tin sheds and flyovers. Nevertheless, says its project architect at Herzog & de Meuron, Niko Happ, 'we wanted the building to communicate the emotions going on inside to everyone outside, so they can share in the feeling', whether you are travelling past it on the U-Bahn or the autobahn.

So Herzog & de Meuron has bound its fortress in bubble wrap. The tight, plump, diamond-shaped blisters of ETFE (basically two layers of plastic pumped with gas; very light) make it shine like it's box-fresh from the shop, and lend it that all-important nickname, the 'rubber dinghy'. The blisters are partly translucent – so the innards are barely visible – and embedded with light strips to make the entire facade glow like a low-resolution TV set, bearing the team colours. Bayern shares the stadium with local arch-rivals (though far from equals) TSV 1860: when one plays the stadium blushes red, when the other's inside it's blue; when it wants it, Mexican waves ripple in pulsing light; when a goal is scored the stadium flashes in celebration.

Freed from its duties holding up the architecture, since the invention of the steel frame in the late nineteenth century, a building's facade can be anything these days. The nineteenth-century German theorist Gottfried Semper predicted as much. Having lost its role as structural wall, he proposed, the facade of a building could now be something purely decorative, woven like a tapestry, painted like a picture, or it could fulfill other roles, such as creating a sense of enclosure or protection. You can keep it simple and cover it in glass walls, or you can run riot. Buildings are no longer like crabs, say, their rigid skins or armour providing the structure; they are like us, internal bones holding our bodies up, flesh and organs like plumbing, rooms and lifts, all wrapped in a skin that, like ours, performs many functions.

A century later, Jacques Herzog and Pierre de Meuron were, like Zaha Hadid and others of that post-Venturi generation emerging in the 1970s, acutely aware of this new-found importance of the skin of a building in an age of mass media. The facade has become architecture's most important element, its most lucrative asset. For the work that made them famous in the 1990s, a simple railway signal box in Basel, Switzerland, they tightly bound its concrete bones in ruddy copper strips, twisted up for light at the windows. It's austere, abstract, but oddly tactile and allusive, the copper pointedly chosen: it alludes to the copper wires carrying electricity within, and literally works as a Faraday cage, protecting the interior from external electrical interference. Its facade therefore communicates what it does, and helps do what it does: multifunctional, multisensory decoration.

This interest in the sensory, communicative nature of the skin of a building is deep-rooted in the pair. 'Decoration, the addition of layering, sensuous experience to architecture is vital,' Jacques Herzog tells me. 'To deny it is to deny human experience a certain richness'; a richness, indeed, that was and still is fast disappearing as globalisation relentlessly gobbles up local distinctiveness. But their decoration isn't overtly symbolic, let alone obvious, like so many of those early 'Po-Mo' buildings that came immediately after *Learning from Las Vegas* – say Portland, Oregon's city hall, the Portland Building, a 'gift to the city' designed by Michael Graves, well, like a boxed-up gift, wrapping paper, bows and all. Nor is it gnomic, overly intellectual and incomprehensible, like the work of those architects influenced by French post-structuralism.

Instead, Herzog and de Meuron are interested in something in between high- and lowbrow. Their pledge, says Pierre de Meuron, is 'to introduce all five senses to the icon', iconic architecture with depth and complexity of experience – tactile spectacle, perhaps – which offers more than just glib, throwaway intangible thrill. 'What is critical is not to build all over the world in the same way, that international architecture. That's very sad. We don't want to export or colonise, but to meet and engage.' Consequently, unlike many of their famous peers, they have no easily recognisible 'signature' style. Instead they have an attitude, a set of values.

Every building they make is unlike the last, united only by their odd looks, uncanny mood and evocative facades. Each is distinguished by celebrating the multisensory, multifunctional qualities of that metre or two of architecture on the outside of a building – concrete wilfully stained by the rain in their house at Leymen, Germany, glass or concrete printed with images, dissolved into ethereal gauziness at their library at Eberswalde, Germany, a thick fudge of pebbledash smeared over their Schaulager art gallery, Basel. Colourful polycarbonate turns the moving bodies of dancers inside the Laban Centre, London, into shadow puppets; the underbelly of polished metal foil at Barcelona's sea-front Forum is dented to recall glistening, foaming surf; Tokyo's Prada crystal ripples in glass lenses. Their extension to Minneapolis's Walker Art Gallery is covered in metal panels like silky, silvery crumpled paper flattened out, to catch the eye of passing motorists.

The concrete innards of their 2016 Switch House extension to London's Tate Modern is wrapped in a pixellated skin of brick and holes. Jacques Herzog likens it to knitwear. A woolly jumper, perhaps, stretched over a bony, angular body. Each 'pixel' is made of two bricks, surrounded on all sides by another 'pixel' of thin air, the bricks fixed at their edge to neighbouring bricks with concealed dowels. The entire skin is like a fabric. Air gusts through the holes into the building as it might between the threads of a jumper. As the building inside moves (all buildings move, by the way, albeit slightly) it flexes in response, like a piece of cloth on a moving body. It invites you to touch it.

These buildings are allusive; they remind you of something, but what is hard to fathom. It is not about the shape – a gherkin, a walkie-talkie, a shard. It's the material used in the facade that's doing the talking. What it is saying is not instantly comprehensible, either. You search your brain, your memory, trying to work out to what exactly the building is alluding. 'Every material is interesting,' Pierre de Meuron explains. 'There is not a bad material. Concrete is not a bad material. Wood is not only a warm material. I would like to go beyond those perceptions.' This interest in materials both functional and allusive, suggesting meaning without pinning it down, they owe to their education by conceptual artists, not architects – as common as trams in their home town, Basel. 'Almost all our friends we grew up with were artists,' says Herzog. They've collaborated with, designed spaces for and absorbed the methods of artists from Thomas Ruff and Rosemarie Trockel to Michael Craig-Martin at Tate Modern and Ai Weiwei in Beijing. 'Artists are clearly more interesting than most architects,' he says with a wintry smile. 'They are obliged to invent their own language. Nobody tells them anything.' Most influential of all on the pair was the German artist Joseph Beuys, whom they met early in their careers, and whose use of tactile, sensory materials in his work – most famously felt and fat – and their connection to the stories we tell about them, to responses to sensory experiences deep-seated in human beings, 'opened our eyes to an unknown world', said Herzog in an interview twenty years ago; 'made us aware of the invisible qualities of materials'.

The facades of Herzog & de Meuron's buildings offer not just a visual experience. Unlike Hadid's, they are multisensory – 'a sensory whirlwind,' says Herzog. 'In many other architectural cultures, say America, architecture is reduced to the visual. But we insist that we use all our [senses] otherwise we chop it off, we limit it, we mutilate it. But this has nothing to do with philosophy or over-intellectualising. It's just a fact. We're human beings. We can touch, we can smell things.' This creates a richer experience – an architecture of 'more' – 'architecture's only chance of survival,' they write, 'the only way [it] can compete with other media'.

Today, decoration is no longer applied to architecture like wallpaper, like a decorated shed, but is integral to it, part of the structure – just like a gothic cathedral, in which the engineering and the decoration are entwined, its soaring columns and vaults supporting the building but also providing its symbolism: raising your eyes to God. Indeed, says Pierre de Meuron, 'there is no longer this separation. The two-dimensional has become three-dimensional.' At Herzog & de Meuron's 'Bird's Nest' stadium in Beijing, for instance, 'the pattern, the decoration – the "bird's nest" – is the actual engineered structure,' says de Meuron.

The experience of architecture becomes another form of media, just like it was before the printing press was invented. The holy grail for some is the facade that comes alive with electronic screens and LED pixels, the building almost literally as a computer or TV screen like Piccadilly Circus or Times Square. Right now technology and cost limits architects to facades that perform at low resolution – like that at Bayern Munich's stadium – or which *seem* to perform, which trick the eye with surface materials and allusions. One day soon, a mere short technological hop away, all stadia (all buildings) may be like Bayern Munich's, though if the Premier League money men finally defeat the old-school Bundesliga fans, I bet there'll be more adverts than match highlights playing on their pay-per-view facades.

Communication breakdown

I hear Daniel Libeskind long before I see him, yap-yap-yapping to civic dignataries, his machine-gun Jewish New York voice rising excitedly above their soft Dublin accents. There he is, moving like a whirlwind in a cloud of groupies, TV crews, all bear hugs, that Cheshire Cat smile lit up again. Welcome to the Daniel Libeskind roadshow. He's in Dublin to promote his latest building – the Grand Canal Theatre, the city's first venue large enough to pack in punters for the crowdpleasers – *Swan Lake* tonight, then *Chitty Chitty Bang Bang*. The building is another Libeskind showstopper – Ireland's first and, with its national economy in tatters after the 2008 world financial crisis, *only* piece of 'starchitecture': self-consciously avant-garde, with Libeskind's trademark sharp, dynamic angles poking up over Dublin's low skyline, and a huge facade of splintered glass sheets, but – reined in and garnished with theatrical razzmatazz – not *so* weirdo as to frighten the civic dignatories.

Libeskind has honed an instantly recognisable design 'signature' – buildings that looked as if they'd survived an earthquake, with sharp angles plunging groundwards, in cold metal, slashed with lines and hieroglyphs. When it was first realised in Berlin's Jewish Museum in 2001, with its un-enterable voids, claustrophobic corridors, vertiginous walls and prison-like cells, this design was compelling: here, it seemed, was someone who could find genuine, gutsy architectural expression for deep-seated, often raw emotions. He became the go-to guy for architecture that memorialised with meaning, with sincerity. He was an architect who could combine the immediacy of Hadid with the subtlety of Herzog & de Meuron and add to them the layers and narratives of history: buildings that made you experience emotion with more depth and subtlety than a rollercoaster ride, full of illusion and allusion.

Libeskind likes getting his teeth into the Big Themes, like life, death, the Holocaust, global terrorism. He adapts a paraphrase from philosopher Henri-Louis Bergson: 'Architecture is . . . the machine that produces the universe which produces the gods.' His architecture, Libeskind once said, battles against 'the obsessive technologism, globalised marketing and withered modernism progressively eradicating spiritual life', no less. In creating our cultural landscapes, he suggests, architecture can help to weave the spirit back in, by being more than just functional or a pretty face, by being 'communicative' of collective themes and memories we hold dear. His buildings are emotionally manipulative contemporary versions of cathedrals, directing the soul, if not to God then . . . what?

To the Big Themes. Better bone up on your Heraclitus. Because for twenty years before Libeskind became a celebrity, he was a philosophy geek. The key is in a series of drawings, which, like Zaha Hadid's paintings, he made in the 1980s, his own 'what if?' architecture: 'Micromegas', energetic scribbles of complex, labyrinthine, abstract forms hung with references – Malevich here, Kafka there, a splash of Kandinsky – boiled down onto small sheets of paper. Like Hadid's canvases, they create an impression of the kind of metaphorical space Libeskind would later try to create in physical space – megamicros – eddying vortices of excitement, whose complexity, overlaid references and spatial meaning aim to approach the complex condition and nuanced complexity of literature or music. (Trained as a musician, Libeskind can't help but compare architecture to music, buildings to instruments tooting out a sense of place.) Three approaches are layered on top of one another. The first, abstraction – his musical heroes are Schoenberg and Messiaen – modernist, steel and glass and concrete, proportions disordered not harmonious. The second, illusion, manipulating space and our perception of it, as Hadid's buildings do, amplifying awareness so we become 'sensitised by the topos' (Libeskind really does speak like this). The third, allusion and symbolism: the literal 'voids' running through Berlin's Jewish Museum, for instance, represent the empty silence left by the Holocaust, while its overall shape has been formed at the intersection on the map of the addresses of murdered Jews. Libeskind doesn't care if you don't 'get' all the references, so long as you feel something pertinent.

Since Ground Zero, however, Libeskind's work has taken a turn for the showbiz. Having being skewered there by big money, Daniel Libeskind now embraces it. He appears to have capitulated in his battle against globalised marketing. High-class apartment buildings in Denver, even-higher-class apartments in Kentucky, designs for skyscrapers in Milan and Monte Carlo, a shopping mall in Switzerland, and a huge shopping and entertainment complex for MGM Mirage in, of all places, Las Vegas. Even Dublin's theatre is wedged between two office blocks and delivered by a docklands developer. This from a man who, until his late forties, was an intensely theoretical architect who'd built nothing and barely left the library. Has Libeskind sold out?

'No, no, ha, ha.' That smile again. 'The whole distinction between culture and commerce, this Marxist idea, is completely irrelevant in the twenty-first century. I tell you when I realised it. A developer came to me, Hyundai in South Korea, and they'd started a building and fired the architect. They said, "It's a very ugly building, can you do a facade?" And I said, "This is nonsense. I'm not going to do a facade. I'm an architect." And [my wife] Nina said, "Why not?" And everyone in the office was against it. "This is the most corrupt idea." But I did it. And I got another huge project from Hyundai. And I learned you have to be open-minded. But if it wasn't for Nina, who's the real socialist, saying, "Why not?" . . .'

And yet, as Libeskind's global brand has expanded from Holocaust to Las Vegas, its power seems to be diminishing. It's not the 'selling out' – architects have to work for someone. It's the quality. He says he enjoys jousting with developers. Yet since Ground Zero his projects have a 'churn 'em out' appearance, like he's running on empty. It's not just that 'they all look the same', that his trademark style has become just that – a trademark. As Libeskind says, in defence, 'You can't help it. You recognise Dostoyevsky novels from three sentences, you know Schubert the minute you hear it.' But his recent buildings aren't Dostoyevsky or Schubert, more pulp fiction, bubblegum pop. Instead of the subtlety and intense attention to site that marked the buildings that made his reputation, there is a tendency towards empty bombast, razzmatazz.

Like a true global brand, he doesn't mess with a formula – angles, slashed line, metal. But in Dublin, the new theatre's exterior has a distinctly spread-thin appearance: one shape, one big angle poked up on the skyline, three slashes, as if Libeskind designed it with the meter running. The architecture proper is crammed into the front 10 metres of foyer. It's not bad – inside is both intimate and showy; just not especially good.

The 'concept', too, these days, is taking on a decidedly hokey

quality. Libeskind has always prided himself on the theoretical symbolism and meaning behind his work. These days, though, he sounds
like he's selling real estate. Too often the same motifs are trotted out
to symbolise both Jewish dislocation and the frontier spirit –
whatever – rendering them essentially meaningless. The Imperial War
Museum North, in Manchester, he hopes, 'emotionally moved the
soul of the visitor', by emotionally moving their bodies, forming
spaces whose shape and our perception of it alters our mood; in that
particular case making us feel 'vulnerable' and aware of the dislocation
created by global conflict by literally dislocating walls and floors; its
overall shape was inspired, he says, earnestly, by intersecting fragments from a smashed globe. Dublin's theatre, meanwhile, is, according
to Libeskind's accompanying explanation, 'a transformation of the
energy of industry to the energy of the creative arts . . . a turbulent
curtain of glass . . . a prismatic curtain-like dramatic scenic form. But
from the inside you're in a ship . . .' It's 'vibrant', 'dynamic', a 'sheer
celebration' etc. etc. He doesn't quite say 'I believe that children are
our future . . .' but you fear it can't be long.

Libeskind's having none of it, though. He genuinely believes the
theatre is 'to do with the traditions of Dublin . . . It shows the complexity of the urban structure of Dublin, and the history. So I think it
is a very contextual building.' Though it's not obvious, and, when
explaining how, he starts talking about 'vectors', 'directionality' and
'prismatic philosophy'; whatever they are.

And then there's the Holloway Road. 'You've heard the jokes,
then?' says Brian Roper, then chief executive of London Metropolitan
University as it opened Libeskind's new graduate school on that
traffic-choked street. 'People thinking the building's already collapsed.' There was always cheap irony in awarding Ground Zero's
masterplan to Daniel Libeskind, an architect whose car-crash aesthetics recall chaos and collapse. The acid-tongued, arch-conservative
historian David Watkin likened one of Libeskind's buildings to 'a pile
of falling cardboard boxes'. The Graduate School's queer shapes loom-
ing over the Holloway Road in north London look more like a train

crash, to the untrained eye. Or, says its jolly head builder, Vic Stellyes, like 'a karate chop'. It's a modest building to ask one of the world's most famous architects to build. But Roper has chutzpah, inviting Libeskind to design humble seminar rooms, corridors, cupboards and cafés, and, while you're at it, something 'iconic', he says, to blow a raspberry, perhaps, at Oxbridge.

He tries, Libeskind says, to pack in as many experiences as he can into even small spaces like this, from the intimate to the 'phantasmagoric'. He nods, he adds, to the 'ingenious contrived world' of Nicholas Hawksmoor, or John Soane, experts in packing wee spaces like Hawksmoor's churches, or Soane's own house, with complexity. Outside, on the Holloway Road, the arrangement of the new building's three interlocking boxy volumes makes them seem in motion, frozen for an instant, maybe in mid karate chop. The ordered rhythm of the steel skin's triangular plates and neat rivets chimes against the crashing volumes: where they meet, the plates don't neatly align but rudely slice into one another.

Inside, successions of interconnecting and overlapping perspectival lines throw the eye this way and that, onto a neat balcony thrust over the Holloway Road – 'for meditation' (perhaps Libeskind hasn't noticed the road's endless roar of articulated lorries), through windows out onto the street. Like Zaha Hadid, Libeskind's architecture constantly challenges the eye and perception, distorting perspective through *trompes l'œil*, playing with your assumptions about what a building, what space, should be. But what does it all amount to?

This is where it gets sticky. I don't doubt that, being the kind of intellectual who's a virtuoso pianist on the side, Libeskind is thoroughly boned up on his metaphysics; and that yes, no doubt at some hidden, higher, intuitive level he sees profound themes in his buildings. It's just when he tries to explain them to mere mortals like me he comes over more Oprah Winfrey than Henri-Louis Bergson.

This bundle of seminar rooms comes, unfortunately, unequipped with its own Big Theme; though the Holloway Road does supply its own grungy brand of tragedy and misery, one of those noisy, brutish, unreconstructed rat runs out of London coursing 24/7 with traffic and detritus. 'It's a tough road, sure,' says Libeskind. 'I had this student come up to me. She said when she first arrived she came out of the Underground station and burst into tears. But there's got to be something enlivening here. So I looked up at the stars. I saw Orion in the sky and that became the key. The path of the constellation pretty much makes the points of the building.' Yes, Libeskind does astrology. Inside, says Vic Stellyes, even the ceiling lights are aligned with the motions of the spheres, though he's not exactly sure how.

Me neither. The theme at LMU is pretty baggy, Libeskind admits – 'I don't want to make too much of it'. But then the connection of Libeskind's themes to his architecture as he explains it often is: forced, arbitrary, post-rationalised. Maybe you can see the motion of the spheres on the Holloway Road, if you look hard enough. Or, most likely, you can't. 'At least it makes life more interesting,' says Brian Roper. 'Makes you think, while you're walking along to the shops, and there's nothing wrong with that.'

The Iconic Building: The Power of Enigma, by Charles Jencks, chronicles the rise, rise and rise of the architectural superstar from the Eiffel Tower through the Sydney Opera House and Gehry's Bilbao Guggenheim to Foster's Gherkin, appropriately montaged on the front cover, taking off for space. Jencks is architecture's Linnaeus. He 'discovered' and labelled postmodernism in the 1970s, and, ever since, he's been on the hunt for architecture's next big thing, ready to be stuffed and mounted in his latest tome. A few duff -isms later and he's found it. And, no, it's not iconism. Jencks considers so-called iconic architecture a mere side route – albeit a scenic one – off architecture's main drag, 'the move to a complexity paradigm, stemming from the new sciences of fractals, chaos and self-organising systems'[20] – frightening-sounding, but essentially that old chestnut, an architecture reflecting the zeitgeist – in today's case buildings which philosophically, formally and technologically represent the scientific, social, cultural revolutions mankind is currently experiencing, but whose full implications we probably won't grasp till Jencks and I are pushing up daisies. In the meantime, icons are essentially Mark I prototypes, buildings here to entertainingly fill the gap left by the death of God, and any unifying view of the world, and to stem off the alienation inherent in globalisation, by throwing us a few cultural symbols to worship, while regenerating the odd declining patch of the planet along the way.

While there have been icons before – the pyramids, the Colossus of Rhodes, Brunelleschi's dome for Florence Cathedral – never so many, or with such significance. Today they are *the* great building type of our media-saturated age, heralded, suggests Frank Gehry inside Jencks's book, by Philip Johnson's 1978 'Chippendale-topped' AT&T skyscraper in Manhattan, one of the few buildings to be slapped across the front covers of *Time* and the *New York Times*. Many may hate this world. But tough, says Jencks, we're stuck with it. If you can't beat icons, join them. Just join them with some aplomb, 'for the best work,' he writes, 'like all good architecture, shows the basic temper of the times and, as Ruskin said, judges its character.'[21] Like their human counterparts, celebrity buildings come in varying shades of bankability, A-list to D-list, depending on their charisma and talent. Only the great icons rise above kitsch, the bungled simile, the one liner, to become metaphors, 'enigmatic signifiers' of depth and resonance 'felt not named, suggested not explicit';[22] they 'intensify experience and make it more vivid so that it gnaws at the memory . . . The worth of an architect designing iconic buildings', Jencks concludes, 'can be seen in how well they handle the big issues . . . power, life, death, and our relationship to the cosmos.'[23] Icons only work, though, if people get the allusion, or the joke, and if, after all that, the whole experience is worth it. And in our complex society of splinters, of multifarious tribes, each with their own belief system and way of expressing it, how easy is it for *one architect* to find *one form*, however complex, nuanced and splintered that form, however 'multi-evocative' its image, that speaks to us all and has meaning to our lives?

More to the point, if Daniel Libeskind of all people – at the top of the architectural food chain, with his Bergson and Schopenhauer – is losing his battle with globalised marketing, what hope is there further down?

In Camden Town, north London, for instance, down the road from the Holloway Road, is 'Nexus One at Visage' (all cool apartment blocks now have names like newly privatised utility companies, early Eighties synth-pop bands or the latest Citroën). The show apartment is just lovely. A little cramped maybe, 'but this *is* London', says the nice lady from Barrett Homes showing me round. Perhaps the decor is a tad middle-aged, all that taupe and pussy willow. But feel the quality. Granite surfaces. Copy of *Hip Hotels* on the coffee table. Ripe for the airbrushed, chauffeur-driven, oyster-eating metrosexual high-fliers depicted in the marketing brochure.

Like the brochure says, 'prepare to be amazed'. Because only outside is the full eye-goggling hideousness of Nexus One at Visage revealed. What on earth *is* it? That, my friend, is trophy architecture.

Trophyism is what happens when a celebrity (A-, B- or Z-list) architect is chosen to design a 'signature building' – something with that wow factor, something to put Swiss Cottage on the map – gets planning permission, then is booted off. Or, rather, the architect resigns – the press release citing 'differences' – aghast at the cost cuts or, as the euphemism has it, 'value engineering' he or she is asked to perform. The actual architecture is carried out by someone else (generally cheaper and worse), which is like getting Marc Jacobs to design you a nice little dress, then getting Derek from the post room to wield the scissors.

Now, for a moment, pity if you will Camden Council, local planning authority and joint-client (no conflict of interest *there* then). Like so many in the entrepreneurial city, Camden Council has ambition but little money or power, so when it wants to do something big like regenerate Swiss Cottage, it has to go cap-in-hand to Mr Private Developer. Basil Spence's magnificent grade-II-listed 1960s library was beautifully restored. A nice new Hampstead Theatre by Bennetts Associates opened. A new crèche, a doctor's surgery. Good, saintly stuff. Only if you want Spence's equally magnificent swimming baths refurbished we'll have to to – oops! – knock them down, then rebuild them uglier, smaller, more cramped and, oh yes, privatised. And the other pound of flesh for this Faustian deal is we'll need to build fifteen storeys of luxury developers' apartments called Visage. But don't worry, we've got Terry Farrell to design them. Which indeed he did, until 2002, when they parted company after being asked to reduce his role from the original 'full architectural service'. S&P Architects, originally on board to do the internal fitouts, suddenly found themselves centre stage.

In vague squinty outline the building resembles Farrell's original (even *that* wasn't a looker). It's only when the eyes focus that it all goes wrong. The details. Now when architects whitter on about 'the details' mostly I just drift off and think about what I'm having for dinner tonight. But how right they are. God is in the details. But this, though, is Beelzebub's building. Farrell no doubt wanted its art-deco-ish juts to resemble a cruise ship. Prison ship is more accurate. Done by a talented architectural firm this jazzy stuff might have been passable. Done by Derek from the post room, the result is clumsy composition, and mind-numbingly boring, brutal, meanly detailed facades, with all the ambition to be 'signature' and none of the talent, like a tone-deaf wannabe on *The X Factor*. It gives nothing to the neighbourhood apart from fatcat residents, and yet it takes everything. The effect is worsened by being next to Basil Spence's restored library and the new leisure centre – actually built by Farrell, and not bad, though the kind of thing he could knock off with one eye on *Game of Thrones* – so that in 200 neat metres we can see exactly how far public architecture has slipped since the 1960s. Maybe soon we'll have 'architect-endorsed' buildings like those 'celebrity-chef-made' pasta sauces.

The misfiring icon, however, is now an all-too-common sight in our entrepreneurial towns and cities as they engage with 'globalised marketing' while watching the bottom line. The quality of their brandscapes is directly related to the quantity of income they are likely to achieve from them and their marketing's 'target demographic'. Take Portsmouth, on the south coast of the UK, whose Spinnaker Tower, at £30 million, was almost double its original budget, embroiled in squabbling politicians, and five years late for the Millennium party.

Despite its glorious heritage, Portsmouth's been on the slide for fifty years, so, like every other post-industrial city, it's set sail for a future serving a nation permanently on the piss and on the plastic. Its millennium project that actually opened on time was Gunwharf Quays, a big fat harbourside retail and leisure complex, whose bulk has been passably disguised with stick-on nautical detailing. What the city lacked, though, says Spinnaker Tower's blurb, was a 'beacon', to welcome sailors and tourists to twenty-first-century Portsmouth.

For many icons, showstopping looks are there to serve another function – housing art, say, or a corporate HQ. The Spinnaker Tower, though, is a pure icon, designed for no other purpose than to be looked at and looked from, a bimbo building to sell the city. At 170 metres high, the Spinnaker Tower is certainly big. From afar – far, far afar, like the Isle of Wight – it has a certain simple, simplistic attraction, its buffed-up form straight out of Dubai via Robert Venturi, its sheer size like a giant arrow pointing down at Portsmouth: 'Here we are, world.' It graces city marketing brochures – building as logo – perfectly.

Get close, though, and it all gets rather low-resolution. It's designed to resemble a spinnaker, a yacht's racing sail, to suggest with billowing sails a perfectly appropriate symbol for the future of this maritime city. Done well, by, say Santiago Calatrava or Wilkinson Eyre, you'd have had a tower with all the energy and elegance a sail suggests. But Portsmouth employed Scott Wilson instead. Who? Indeed.

Scott Wilson is a civil engineering firm based in Basingstoke. Their back catalogue includes the A46 Kenilworth bypass. When it comes to pavement engineering, doubtless nobody can touch them. When it comes to aesthetics though . . . ? The tower is as light and airy, and sadly as unmissable, as a binge drinker tottering out of a pub after closing time. Staggeringly inane and ugly, its billowing sails leaden, graceless and crude, its buffed-up engineering, like pectoral implants, more for show than structural function, it can't even get a simile right, let alone a metaphor. Asking it, in Charles Jencks's words, to 'handle the big issues . . . power, life, death, and our relationship to the cosmos' is a little unfair.

Being big and tall, the Spinnaker Tower has been a hit. And herein lies the problem with 'iconic buildings': like film stars, very, very few deserve the name, and the more there are, and the more exposed they become, what little enigma they have shrivels in the limelight. Still, Spinnaker Tower at least gives those in their luxury harbourside apartments something undemanding and impressive to gawp at from their balconies while they await 'the move to a complexity paradigm', as Jencks puts it. And when its fifteen minutes fade, Portsmouth can always impress guests with the vital statistics: 'The bows are formed from 1,200 tonnes of steel,' toots the spiel, 'the equivalent weight of twelve blue whales . . . This iconic structure, or sculpture, may well be as closely linked with Portsmouth as Big Ben with London, the Statue of Liberty with New York or the Eiffel Tower with Paris.' For Portsmouth's sake, I hope not.

Electric space, or a very brief history of architecture and computers

I watch Tom Wiscombe's hand as it dances over the desk. It flicks this way and that, and pauses; his fingers momentarily waft and grasp the air like the tendrils of a sea anemone. Then, half a second later, his hand darts off left, right, south-west, north-north-east. I see the skin of his hand pulse and pull, the small muscles beneath tensing and bulging, and the tendons behind his knuckles rising and falling like the strings of a puppet.

The palm of his hand grips a computer mouse and the pair swirl their *pas de deux* across a dancefloor in the shape of a mousemat. It's a rather more sophisticated mousemat than the one I have at home, a flat freebie from a trade fair. This one is contoured in soft, fleshy hills and hummocks. Hand and mouse rise, roll and waltz over its landscape, and as they do so, on the screen in front of him, a second dance mimics it, controlled from below, this time a figure alone, a single cursor darting around the pixels like a whirligig. Underneath the cursor, though, a shape moves in response, twirling and rotating, twisting and then suddenly racing towards us. It is a representation of a building. Though it's like no building I've ever seen. It looks more like a beetle or ectoplasm, a corpuscle or a protozoan cell, as fleshy and sinewy as the hand that is manipulating it.

Wiscombe is in the act of designing the building. These days, as he says, '*every* architect uses computers'. Even neoclassicists design columns and pediments on a screen, though I have met a few proud Luddites who can't give up the pencil, sticking to the tactile delights of past times like vinyl addicts. Walk into most architects' offices today, however, and you won't find the minions screened behind drawing boards with the pencils and set-squares of popular stereotype, but glued to computer screens, like any office. These are the coal-face workers behind every starchitect. CAD-jockeys, they're called, after the animal they ride and attempt to tame: computer-aided design.

It is a moot point when computers were first used to design a building. Most famously, the complex curves of Sydney's Opera House required a mainframe computer in the 1960s to number-crunch the complex equations behind its shape. But long before that, others were speculating about exactly how this new tool might change the buildings and cities in which we live. The impact of the vast strides made by computing technology during the Second World War by code-breakers such as Alan Turing at Bletchley Park reverberated across every part of culture in the years afterwards, architecture included. In 1954, for instance, cybernetics pioneer Norbert Wiener predicted that computers would enable a British or European architect to remotely design a building to be constructed in the USA by sending drawings and instructions across the Atlantic through new apparatus such as the teletypewriter or fax: 'The bodily transmission of the architect and his documents', he claimed, 'may be replaced very effectively by the message-transmission of communications which do not entail the moving of a particle of matter from one end of the line to the other.'[24] It has come to pass, and then some. Today, architects from London to Los Angeles routinely send data and drawings to be finessed in offices in Asia or Africa; components of a building – wall panels, windows, beams – are mass-produced in factories in China or Malaysia. The production process behind architecture has been broken up, separated and geographically dispersed.

At the time Wiener made his predictions, the conceit was emerging in much avant-garde engineering and architecture that the building, like a computer, was a system, and that it should be designed as such. Design should start with the services – plumbing and electrics and, in the years to come, increasingly complex IT systems – supporting whatever activity that took place inside, all wrapped in a skeleton and skin, like any machine; though not one of Le Corbusier's mechanical 'machines for living in', but a more futuristic version, electronic, cybernetic, a machine that, like a computer itself, might respond to how humans interact with it. Such ideas intoxicated many in the 1950s and 1960s, such as Buckminster Fuller, Archigram and Reyner Banham, who wrote enthusiastically of a future architecture like any consumer durable – 'the great gizmo' – designed and controlled by computer.

Where did the architect fit into this new world? At his keynote lecture to a seminal 1964 conference, Architecture and the Computer, the veteran modernist Serge Chermayeff proposed that the computer might, by taking on tasks once done by hand, free up the architect to busy themselves with speculation or better solutions to problems. Big mainframe systems such as Sketchpad could generate different ways to solve a problem, create complexity but make sense of it, too. However, the computer, he warned, 'cannot take the place of creative activity'; the computer would be the architect's tool not its master, the tail would not wag the dog. Perhaps. Others, though, wondered whether the computer might increase the gene pool of the architectural profession. A computer, after all, was not just a device for processing data; it communicated it, too. It could allow multiple people to work together on a solution.

Some in the 1960s, like the mathematics wunderkind Christopher Alexander, thought that computers might not only effortlessly number-crunch the complex equations behind harmonious proportion, they might in doing so allow some kind of universal architecture to emerge: a pattern language, he called it. This language would create a new architecture to answer that question posed by Alison and Peter Smithson: how could you create one architecture to speak to a mobile, multifarious society? Alexander's 'pattern language' was just that, almost a kit of parts that anyone who understood it could manipulate to create a building.

At the Massachusetts Institute of Technology (MIT), a young Nicholas Negroponte, the dyslexic son of a Greek shipping magnate who would go on to become an influential 'guru' in the digital and computer boom of the 1990s, took this intriguing idea one step further. Negroponte was training as an architect, obsessed by these early iterations of computer-aided design. He formed MIT's Architecture Machine Group in 1967 to study human–computer interaction, and the vast implications it held for the way we design buildings, what they look like, and how they function. Like many other tech pioneers emerging in the 1960s and 1970s, he was interested in the utopian, emancipatory possibilities the computer might bring to human society. He hoped that it might enable a new kind of democracy. His 1970 book, *The Architecture Machine: Towards a More Human Environment*, speculated that the computer would in time democratise design, every one of us influencing the shape and nature of the buildings we inhabit by collaborating at a distance with some virtual designer, leading eventually to an almost 'sentient' built environment responding to our every whim. The architect would wither away. We would all become architects of our own lives. Many of those who read Negroponte's book might have have witnessed such a sentient environment at the cinema two years earlier, in *2001: A Space Odyssey*. Negroponte, though, aspired towards a rather more optimistic outcome, a more benevolent HAL 9000.

It hasn't quite turned out like that, though it might. Back at Tom Wiscombe's Los Angeles office a few floors up the 'American Cement Building', a rather jazzy mid-century building on Wilshire Boulevard,

this architect is in no doubt about the emancipatory effect of computers, on the architect at least. Computer-aided design in the form of
software (most of it invented by American tech firms) like Autodesk's
AutoCAD 3D Studio Max, or Bentley Systems' Microstation, or rendering and modelling programmes like Rhino 3D, is so sophisticated
today the architect can design anything, any shape imaginable.

Architectural designs of lifelike perfection can exist for years before
an actual building is produced. Indeed, they can be used to generate
expectation and demand, a tactic much in use behind those seeking to
drum up support, say, for a controversial building. The Garden Bridge
proposed in 2012 by its trust to span the River Thames in London, for
instance, existed for years only as 'artist's impressions' of stunning
sophistication, created by engineers Arup and designer Thomas
Heatherwick, the better to be circulated around the media. At one
fundraising event hosted by the newspaper the *Evening Standard*, guests
were invited to don virtual reality headsets to experience visually
what they might soon experience with all the senses, should they
decide to contribute. Heatherwick hopes to repeat the trick in New
York City, unveiling in 2016 with mayor Bill de Blasio his 'Vessel'
structure for Hudson Yards, the largest single development in the city
since the 1930s. It looks incredible. It is designed to look incredible, its
154 staircases, in a honeycomb pattern, designed to be looked from
and looked at, online and, maybe one day, in reality. Until then, the
fabulous imagery of the structure whets the appetite.

Meanwhile, even more complex computer software systems like
BIM, or building information modelling, allow such dreams to be
built in reality, coordinating every player behind a building, from
architect to client to construction site manager to finance director,
and every last rivet. All take part in this multiplayer computer game.
Every last element of a building interconnects and becomes manipu-
lable by those taking part. If an architect changes a shape, every tiny
element changes shape too. If a bean counter removes a bean, the
entire building alters in response. A building can nimbly alter as the
free market demands.

'One way to use the computer,' says Wiscombe, 'maybe the earliest way, was to just sculpt on the computer. There was a lot of interest in digital form-making in the 1990s, when people realised they could do free-form sculpting that would allow them to quickly create more sophisticated forms.' The 'digital turn' this moment was called. In the early 1990s there was a rapid improvement in the processing speeds and memory capabilities of computers, but also the graphic capabilities of CAD software, much of it propelled by its use in Hollywood films. The successful Arnold Schwarzenegger sci-fi sequel *Terminator 2* (1991), for instance, became the standard-bearer of computer-created graphics, its depiction of an evil cyborg 'Terminator' able to morph from human shape into anything, via beads of shapeshifting mercury requiring vast technical and design ability. The Terminator looked like that because he *could* look like that. Computer-aided design meant that the kinds of complicated curves and shapes we saw all around us in nature – pebbles on a beach, for instance, each one unique – could be finally and convincingly copied in architecture, our artificial nature.

During the digital turn of the early 1990s, notes historian Mario Carpo in his book *The Alphabet and the Algorithm*, there was a sudden, seemingly random interest in the seventeenth-century philosopher and mathematician Gottfried Wilhelm Leibniz after avant-garde architects and their students read the 1993 translation of French philosopher Gilles Deleuze's 1988 book *The Fold: Leibniz and the Baroque*. All of a sudden folds and curves became all the rage on the computer screens of architecture schools, the kind of smooth, globular curves that shaped the Terminator. 'From car design to web design,' writes Carpo, 'from sex appeal to fashion magazines, curvaceousness was ubiquitous.' Behind such shapes lay an equation, an algorithm, what Deleuze called the 'objectile', which, applied to different contexts and parameters can produce similar but infinitely variable shapes.

This was the computer revolution that allowed those incredible visions on the canvases painted by Hadid, say, to be created on computer screen and, eventually, in reality. Any shape was now possible:

complex, irregular, warped, rippled, wavey, knotted, jagged; from gherkins to shards to spirals to pebbles to gigantic pairs of underpants to the beetle or ectoplasm on Wiscombe's screen. It is, in fact, a tae-kwondo arena and civic sports centre designed for a site in a Chinese city. Its client, 'of course', sighs Wiscombe, wanted an 'iconic build-ing; it has to stand out from the field'. His role as architect was to create an unobvious icon – 'something for people to identify with' – that's not too cheesy, that has depth of allusion and sophistication in performance even if it is not quite yet sentient.

Wiscombe begins with the basics, vaguely placing on his computer programme which rooms and functions go where, and then letting it help work out the optimum plan. Then the computer allows him to hone it and hone it, modelling endless iterations, as all the complex parameters behind it are fed in. He allows the computer to work out the answer to countless 'what ifs'. He can instantly alter the trans-lucency of the windows to respond to his whims or data about the levels of sun coming in at particular times of the day, or the quality of the views outside. In microseconds he can alter its structure as more accurate data about local seismic events comes in. He models the pos-sibility of getting rid of air conditioning, by running water through the bones of the building instead, letting it heat and cool in response to the climate. Reyner Banham's 'great gizmo', responding to our and Hal's whims, is nearer than we think.

Some architects are fascinated today about how computers can almost 'autogenerate' building designs. Create an aesthetic – globular curves, say, or DayGlo serrations – discover the algorithms behind it, feed in the complex specifics of a site or a building's function, and press Go (it is, of course, not *quite* as easy as I describe!). 'It's interest-ing, but I'm not personally interested in that approach,' says Wiscombe. 'I am still an artist and I'm not at all afraid to put my hands upon the work. It's not about autogenerating anything. I'm not sure about the ethics. Not sure about why it would be valuable for us to give more and more of the creative process away. Unless there was a big payoff.' For his part Wiscombe enjoys throwing creative spanners into the computer's works. He likes to play games with it, exercising his artistic skill. Before my eyes he does just that, transforming the 'optimum' shape of the building part-created by the software with his own what-ifs, aesthetic and functional. What if we expressed the tension felt by the structure on the skin of the building with different colours or contours, so you could see where the building was most straining to support itself? What if we made that particular window not translucent but transparent, because I like a particular view? Echoing the sentiment of Serge Chermayeff decades before him, Wiscombe says computers allow architects to 'see what's possible. A way of opening the mind'.

There are limits to the freedom though, he acknowledges. The tool inevitably creates a certain type of building. Just as designing with pencils creates buildings defined by the possibilities and limits of that technology, so certain computer design programmes produce certain looks. 'Certain softwares are designed for certain things,' Wiscombe explains. They were, after all, 'designed for Hollywood. And they have a certain aesthetic. You have to be careful.' The extremely geeky can tell if a building is produced by one kind of software or another. The really extremely geeky can hack this software, though, and play with it; another way to throw creative spanners in the works. It does open up an intriguing question: are buildings designed by coders or architects? Who has the ultimate power?

Wiscombe has made up his mind: the architect. The computer, he thinks, allows architects to resume their traditional role controlling the design of the building from imagination to realisation, a role lost to them during the emergence of the entrepreneurial city, if only the profession would realise it. Only the architect can synthesise and balance all the competing parameters behind a building. Only an architect can create beauty. Though I bet someone has invented a computer programme for that too.

Wiscombe has some sympathy for Nicholas Negroponte's suggestion in the 1970s that computers could open up the gene pool of architecture. But 'if we got 100,000 people on Facebook to interface and help design a building it would be disaster. There's some level of expertise to architecture. The architect is the only one who can synthesise all sorts of information from the construction industry, the people who are going to use the building, the client.' The architect should be in charge. But then he would say that.

Mario Carpo, though, envisages a different future. He suggests the arrival of the computer in architecture in the 1990s was as revolutionary as the arrival of the printing press during the Renaissance. Print enabled an architect to design, and to communicate his design, more speedily and faithfully. From ancient Rome to the fifteenth century, architecture had largely been created through words, the master builder talking to his team, the patron to the architect. It was collaborative, but much was lost in translation. Print, though, enabled the architect to better control what was built, enabling neoclassicism to become, says Carpo, 'the first international style in the history of world architecture',[25] reproduced around the world, and the architect to assume his now-stereotypical role of auteur, aesthetic dictator. The computer, though, allows teamwork to return to the production of architecture. We can all become architects.

Negroponte's almost anarchistic idea of participation, including us, the people that occupy buildings, in their design was in the air in the 1960s and 1970s, manifest in programmes such as the Whole Earth Catalogue, Belgian architect Lucien Kroll's 'improvised' buildings created with their occupants, or architect Walter Segal's 'self-build' system, a kit of building parts that could be assembled by a team of ordinary Joes. Like many emancipatory what-ifs, this particular dream was extinguished by the rise of the entrepreneurial city. In its competitive atmosphere, architects instead sought to protect their professional role, reverting as they usually did under threat, to self-defence. They adapted for survival. They became artists and auteurs. Only architects could create experiences for the experience economy; though the one experience they forgot about was including the people inside their buildings, the ones passively consuming the end product, within the production *of* the building. How could they speak to everyone without including us, somehow, in the conversation?

Now they can. The latest digital technology, writes Carpo, like the Web 2.0, and the kind of collaborative, democratic spirit behind Wikipedia, or open-source culture, is 'inherently and essentially averse to the authorial model that rose to power with mechanical reproduction, and is now declining with them'.[26] Such technology opens up the possibility of architecture created through the computer involving not just the architect, the finance guy and the client, but you and me. We can take part in the multiplayer game. The planning and landowning system behind the entrepreneurial city is stacked against us. Open-source design might level the playing field. Just as the computer has dramatically democratised participation in journalism and the media, music and culture, the tech industry and coding, it might do the same in architecture, to create towns and cities, buildings and styles of endless variability, customised, at no extra cost, to the whim of their inhabitants who have all had a hand in their creation. And by doing that we will not be just passive consumers of the towns and cities we live in, we will have a sense of ownership over it – in spirit, if not hard cash. Well, that's the grand plan.

Today, computer-aided design means that architecture can be 'sampled', cut, pasted and fiddled with, just like a bedroom musician samples music. Buildings exist, like so much today, as data, a digital file. The appearance of whole buildings – communicated through CGI, photos, the internet – can be copied and manipulated. In 2013, the appearance of a Zaha Hadid-designed building, Wangjing Soho, was mimicked – pirated, said some – in another building, Meiquan 22nd Century, in another city, Chongqing. In 2016, two artists walked into the Neues Museum, Berlin, with a 3D-digital scanner and scanned its famous bust of Queen Nefertiti, before uploading the data on the internet for all to copy, either as a digital ghost, or physically reproduced by a 3D printer. How long before we can do the same with buildings? Not long at all.

As the 'selfie' building created by architect Asif Khan for the 2014 Sochi Winter Olympics in Russia showed – its facade literally moving to create in architecture the faces of those passers-by uploading their self-portraits – this particular future is closer than we think. Imagine a city street whose buildings continually convulse in shape and appearance, pulsing with live streaming information and data, as people and their devices pass by. One answer to those questions posed by the Smithsons all those years ago: how can architecture talk to us, the nomadic masses, in all our diversity? An architecture of instantaneous communication. But two-way communication: communication *with*, not communication *at*. Architecture as true mass media.

CHAPTER NINE

MEET THE MOST FAMOUS ARCHITECT
IN THE WORLD

'A true artist should put a generous deceit on the spectators . . . No work of
art can be great, but as it deceives.'

Edmund Burke[1]

How not to meet the most famous architect in the world

'Who does *this guy* think he *is?*' Lesson one in how to interview Frank
Gehry: do not mention the word 'spectacle'. I did. And Frank does not
like it, not one little bit.

'This guy . . .' He jabs his finger in my direction, talking to nobody
in particular. 'This guy thinks I design *spectacles*.' He spits the word,
and begins pacing his studio – a vast, echoing hangar in Los Angeles –
like a boxer in the ring, dodging models, plinths and members of staff
without collision, quite a feat considering the clutter of the place. He's
not *quite* red in the face, but he's fairly fed up. You can see it in the
tightness of the mouth. For a chap in his eighties, he's quick on his feet.
'Is *that* a spectacle?' he points to a model of . . . I can't make out what
from the scrunched-up cardboard. 'Is *that* one?' He glares at me, accus-
ingly. There's one especially large model, though, that rises above the
rest: the Guggenheim gallery he's designed for Abu Dhabi. The model
alone is almost big enough for me to crawl into. It would make a splen-
did home for a colony of guinea pigs, a funhouse of plastic chutes,

cubes and not-quite-cones. It stands alone on a plinth amid the hullaballoo of his studio. It looks pretty spectacular to me.

'I don't know where you're going with this.' He comes, at last, to a stop. 'Are you trying to get me to admit that I'm an egomaniac who stamps myself on the city at the expense of all the poor citizens that live there? And I'm in your face? And I should stop?' All I'd asked him was what he thought of people who describe his work as 'empty spectacle'. But the 's' word, these days, is a red rag to a bull with Gehry. At a press conference in Spain in October 2014, a journalist asked the same question. Gehry showed him the finger. And if it's not the 's' word, it's the 'i' word'. In his dotage, Gehry has become pretty grumpy about being blamed for kickstarting the modern age of iconic architecture.

The Bilbao effect

Two decades on, the building that in 1997 made him the World's Most Famous Architect – the Guggenheim art gallery in Bilbao, Spain – has been photographed and reproduced ad nauseam in two dimensions. It appears on car ads and jewellery ads. It lures tourists to go on city breaks with low-cost airlines. It's appeared in the opening sequence of James Bond films. Rock bands have launched albums there. The building has become a celebrity; its architect has become one too, with famous friends like Laurence Fishburne and the late Dennis Hopper, and a superstar's swarming entourage of staff, PRs and hangers-on, such as Brad Pitt, who famously interned at Gehry's office.

Frank Lloyd Wright was famous. But that Frank never appeared on *The Simpsons*. That Frank never (quite) had a movie made about him by an Oscar-winning director (though, admits Gehry, he only did it because the director, his late friend Sydney Pollack, kept going on at him; it was the only way to shut him up). Almost twenty years after Bilbao opened, Gehry still hasn't quite recovered. Fame, 'you see, came late', he says, a little calmer now. 'I don't believe it. I try to ignore it.'

It's hard, though. These days everybody wants a piece of Frank and his sensational rock-baroque cathedrals of culture-consumerism. Everywhere wants the so-called 'Bilbao effect': bringing towns and cities in crisis back to life, Lazarus-style, through the glorious redemptive power of architecture.

Bilbao changed everything: for Gehry, for architecture, for cities. 'They asked me for the Sydney Opera House,' he smiles. Today, city mayors and property developers routinely ask for 'a Bilbao'. But in the mid 1990s, a couple of decades after it had opened, the Sydney Opera House still set the bar for fame in architecture. 'They were trying to resurrect the Basque Country as a viable place,' Gehry recalls. 'Their ship industry and steel industry was floundering.' Bilbao had lost 14 per cent of its population between 1981 and 1995.[2] This building, though, utterly transformed the city, as it would go on to transform architectural culture, and Gehry is extremely keen on quantifying that change: proof of transformation, proof of worth needs to be delivered by the business-minded architect to his business-minded clients.

At a 2001 exhibition showcasing Gehry's designs for a new Guggenheim in Lower Manhattan (one of his designs never realised) – held in Frank Lloyd Wright's own curvaceous Guggenheim in Manhattan's Upper West Side – there was a section called 'Measures of Success', which loudly trumpeted the statistics: the 1.2 million visitors to Bilbao's Guggenheim in year one; the $100 million cost, but the $400 million increase in tourist spending in the area; the 87 per cent of tourists now visiting from abroad. 'This last *year*,' Gehry tells me, with a salesman's zeal, Bilbao's Guggenheim 'brought in €310 million to the community. My building paid for itself in the first *eight months*, so the building was free. Economically it's revitalised the place. One bloody pishy building did it.' The magic continues, he says. Annual tourism to the city rose from 1.4 million in 1994 to 3.8 million in 2005, roughly a million of which visited the museum every year.

The 'Bilbao effect', though, was nothing new at all. By 1997, it had existed for decades. Sydney's Opera House, of course, and Paris's

Pompidou Centre, had since the 1970s been the most famous buildings in the world, lauded in particular for the regenerative effects their
pointedly spectacular looks were supposed to have had on their hosts.
Both looked like nothing built before on this planet. Both provoked
curiosity. And their curious, striking looks were circulated around the
world by the media, from stamps on letters to travel brochures. Spain,
too, had already dabbled in this curious new phenomenon. In 1992, the
Seville World Expo had dazzled with cutting-edge contemporary
architecture, and, on the other side of the country that year, Barcelona's
Olympics became the benchmark for a 'good' Olympics, combining
sporting spectacle with artistic spectacle, part of a thirty-year plan to
turn the city from grimy, unknown economic basket-case to one of the
most famously 'born-again' cities in the world.

The year before, in 1991, the Solomon R. Guggenheim Foundation
and the Basque authorities made contact. The Guggenheim Foundation, under its charismatic head Thomas Krens, had already begun to
change how it operated, functioning more like a corporation than a
traditional art institution. Krens planned to create a series of satellite
branches to position the Guggenheim as a global brand, circulating
the art that it owned around the world, and using it to conjure up
more corporate sponsorship, in a virtuous circle. The deal it made
with the city of Bilbao seemed like a win-win. Bilbao, like Barcelona,
had plans of its own – to transform its fortunes with construction: its
own thirty-year plan included a new metro system, designed by Norman Foster, and a new airport by Santiago Calatrava. For the new
gallery, the Guggenheim would lend its name and collection, while
the city and region, along with support from the European Union and
the Spanish government, would provide the money and land: a disused industrial site in the city centre, beside the river. Now it was up
to Frank Gehry to deliver the goods.

When the gallery was opened by King Juan Carlos in October 1997,
it was immediately used by the Spanish tourist board in their adverts,
alongside the slogan: 'Art outside. Art inside.' The intention was clear:
this was architecture beyond function. Like the work of his peers,

Zaha Hadid, say, or Daniel Libeskind, Gehry's architecture was inter-preted by others as being all about the experience, an aesthetic object in and of itself. It also looked unlike any building the planet had seen before. Indeed its very difference was the point. The Guggenheim looked different from its immediate environment. It signalled change. Bilbao is, for southern Europe, a dark city; the materials its streets are made from do not dazzle; its climate has a propensity for gunmetal grey skies as much as sparkling sunshine. Here, though, was a building that dazzled. The sheer, shimmering shininess of the building was unmissable, mesmerising. Its shape accentuated the shimmer, curling one way then another like a flickering flame. The titanium skin was layered in scales, each one etched, not mirrored; each scale, each scratch in turn catching the light. On Bilbao's slightly dour, rectilinear streets, your eye is uncontrollably drawn to its glittering curves, and their embodied metaphor of dirty, shipbuilding city transformed to sparkling post-industrial future is effortlessly delivered to your retina.

There's a very different kind of 'Bilbao effect' for some, though. One architecture critic, remembers Gehry, felt so aggrieved by the building, he trained his dog to leave a little gift on Gehry's lawn in Los Angeles whenever the pair passed on their daily walk. Gehry shows me in his conference room a plaster model of his head and torso dressed in a 'F**k Frank Gehry' T-shirt he picked up on his travels. 'A better accolade than the Pritzker [Prize], eh?' he smiles. At least his work provokes a reaction. The eminent art professor Hal Foster criticised his architecture as 'arbitrary and self-indulgent', divorced from con-text, with pretentions to art. In 2011, Germaine Greer wrote a savage attack in the *Guardian* on Gehry's proposed business school for the University of Technology, Sydney, immediately heralded by the press as the 'new Sydney Opera House', despite Gehry's protestations. 'Imagine five brown paper bags with fifteen windows cut in each side,' wrote Greer, 'scrunched up and then unscrunched and stacked together, and you've pretty much got it.'[3] Greer's article obviously still riles him; all day he keeps coming back to the subject: 'I just don't get it,' he mutters, grumpily.

More abrupt than most criticism, though, was a letter written to him by his rather earnest East Coast architectural colleagues and rivals, Peter Eisenman and Richard Meier: 'Dear Frank. You are a prick.' Gehry was notable by his absence in the vast outpouring of grief and *grands projets* following the 9/11 attacks at Ground Zero in Manhattan. Why hadn't the World's Most Famous Architect come up with a design to replace the World Trade Center, like the legions of less famous architects who did? Gehry poured oil on the flames by telling the *New York Times* exactly what he thought about the proposals submitted by colleagues to the design competition for the site, *and* the scale of fee being paid for the work. And so the kings of the East Coast architecture scene sent him a letter – short, but to the point. 'What can you do?' says Gehry. 'People have opinions. That's OK.' But us British critics are the worst. 'Why are you guys so sceptical? So crabby. Even if it's not true what you say. One guy when I was doing the Serpentine Pavilion [in London, 2008] said I was "a one-trick pony's one-trick pony". Whatever that means.'

And then there's the Bilbao effect on his own life. It took a while for Gehry to be convinced of the building's worth. 'When I went to Bilbao afterwards, when you drive into the city and I saw the building I said, "Holy shit, what have I done to these poor people?" It took me a couple of years to entertain it as a decent piece of work . . . I was embarrassed by it.' Before he won the small, invited competition, Gehry was not the man he is today. He thinks he won precisely because he was the outsider, the curveball coming from leftfield. There he was, just doing his thing, doing the same work he'd done for decades. Perhaps he was just the right man in the right place at the right time, in a kind of alignment of the stars.

Fame still sits uneasily with Gehry. Frank Lloyd Wright or Le Corbusier revelled in it, dressing to the nines with canes, capes and statement glasses, managing their public relations astutely. Gehry does the opposite, perhaps self-consciously so. You'd pass him on the street without a second glance. Short, tubby, unshaven today, and dressed in rumpled casual clothes he might have picked up at a thrift store, he looks like an uncelebrity. He arrived for this interview shuffling in sideways, eyes down, as if delivering pizza. There's something of his home city in all this. Los Angeles is, after all, famous for its carefully calculated casualness, *and* its own cultural insecurities faced with high-minded East Coast rivals. Perhaps this is just Gehry's schtick, his self-deprecation a way of charming you, charm being a vital, often rare skill in the successful architect. Spend any time with Gehry, and you start to think, 'Hell, there's a guy I could go bowling with, maybe sink a few beers with after.' You can hardly believe such vibrant, muscular, flashy architecture could come from one so diffident.

Gehry's a doer, a casual, hands-on kinda guy. He famously eschews computers for model making, and the loose 'LA school' of architecture he accidentally founded, with its ad-hoc collaging and theatrical curves, was always more about having a good time, 'riffing' with your buddies in the back-lot garage with a soldering iron and some scraps of metal, than intellectualising about French post-structuralism, like Peter Eisenman and the East Coast lot. 'There's a bit of the "aw, shucks" in me, yeah,' he admits. 'It's a defensive thing. I'm serious about what I do. I just don't take myself that seriously.' Maybe that's his secret weapon. Compared to other world-famous architects, he says, he doesn't court publicity. 'There are things I could do that would get me into the marketplace that I don't think I would do,' he says. 'To hire publicists, to go on the road.' Do the celebrity thing? 'Yeah, I try to avoid that.' And yet publicity continues to court him; a necessary evil.

Perhaps this explains his pathologically contradictory nature, at once self-deprecating and arrogant, sensitive and egocentric, grouchy and funny, optimistic and resigned. He disdains critics, but can't get them out of his mind. He dwells on setbacks *and* successes. Onstage, or talking to journalists, playing the part of the famous architect, he seems uncomfortable in his own skin, squirming in the limelight. It's no surprise that he's spent much of his life in therapy: 'half my life, in fact', he corrects me. His psychotherapist, Milton Wexler, has a prominent role in that film by Sydney Pollack, *Sketches of Frank Gehry*. Even – or perhaps especially – the World's Most Famous Architect gets insecure. 'I mean, I go *crazy*,' he cries. 'And I consider it healthy insecurity. It pushes me. I'm much more critical than any critic, even any British critic.' He nods, of course, to me. 'They haven't got a chance to be as critical of what I do as myself. They're not even in the ballpark.' When he visits his buildings, he obsesses over 'every connection, collision. I wish I'd done that better. I go through a holy hell. You don't want to be around me.' He laughs. 'The only building of mine I actually use is the Disney Concert Hall [in downtown Los Angeles]. And I sit next to the executive director and the first two years she said, "I'm moving seats." She didn't want to hear it. I think everybody has these . . . these self-doubts. It's human nature.'

The strangest thing of all, though, is that Gehry thinks he's unsuccessful. 'I don't think there's a demand for me . . . I get one [building] and that's it. Every time I go for an interview [Norman] Foster's there, and he gets most of them. And Renzo's done fifteen museums since I did Bilbao. So that's the marketplace telling you what it wants. I'm not being judgemental. It's the fact. And I have to live with that. Other architects maybe benefited from the Pandora's box I opened, but I didn't. I mean I had fame, which is nebulous. But work didn't come from it. Maybe after I die, somebody will look at my buildings and say, Maybe we should have . . .'" He trails off.

A different kind of architect

I have a sense that we've always got Gehry a little wrong, that we've put him into a box in which he sits rather uncomfortably. 'Everybody thinks they've been misunderstood,' he says. 'Don't we all?' We may think of him as *the* celebrity architect, but before he was famous he was a very different kind of architect.

He grew up, he explains, as Frank Owen Goldberg, born in 1929 to a hard-working, poor Jewish family in a working-class neighbourhood in Toronto. His father, Irving, sold slot and pinball machines to bars, before setting up a furniture business. Frank would make miniature buildings out of the junk from his grandfather's hardware store. 'I always tell this story,' he says, wearily, as if repeating his foundation myth for the umpteenth time. 'My grandmother used to get these funny shapes and wood cuttings from my grandfather's hardware store, and she'd take them home and open up her bag and *crash* they'd go on the floor, and then we'd sit, she and I, and we'd make buildings and cities.' And, although their family was poor, recalls Gehry, 'my mother did two things. She took me to art museums and she took me to concerts. They were accessible.' This love of openness, the freedom of the city, the value of civic democracy has remained with him ever since. In 1947, his father had a heart attack – during a furious row with the eighteen-year-old Frank – and soon after his business went bust. The family moved to Los Angeles to start again. Gehry got a place studying architecture at the University of Southern California, working as a truck driver to pay the bills.

To start with, at least, architecture was also something to pay the bills. He set up his own studio in the early 1960s, doing office buildings, shopping malls – standard commercial stuff. After hours, though, he'd hang out with – and be slightly envious of – the city's avant-garde. Though not LA's newly emerging pop artists. His inspiration, he explains, came from New York, 'from Bob Rauschenberg, my friend, because I was trained by a Viennese master to do impeccable details. And when I started my practice I didn't have clients that had the money to do that. Rauschenberg was making combines then, Jasper [Johns] was making paintings with beer cans and things and I loved what they were doing. I was deeply immersed in it. And I thought . . . "Take that into architecture." And it worked.'

It wasn't until 1978, though, that he honed a coherent approach. He was living in a pink Dutch Colonial-style suburban house in Santa Monica with his second wife, his vivacious Panamanian former secretary, Berta. He was, he says, always going on to her about his artist friends and how constraining designing for commercial clients was, especially in the cut-throat world of shopping malls. He'd even married Berta with the proviso that she would look after any future kids they had (they had two), so that he could concentrate on his creativity. 'So she turned around and said, "Go on then."' And it was she, he says, who really pushed him to begin by looking, really looking, at the architecture all around him – his home. Gehry stripped that suburban house back to its structural frame, and then reassembled it as a collage of angles, cubes and collisions, using lowly materials gleaned from the neighbourhood – corrugated metal, plywood, chainlink fence. He called it 'cheapskate architecture'.

The house still looks improvised, as if Gehry had made it up on the spot, directing the builders this way and that according to that morning's horoscopes, perhaps. Its neighbours are an eclectic bunch – *Flintstones* 1950s-style, more Dutch Colonial, stoops aplenty – but, decades later, Gehry's has spawned no imitators nearby. The suburb has absorbed it, as an eccentric old-timer: LA treats Gehry as a father of the city these days, so the house features on official tourist-board intineraries; tour guides stop outside; cameras point at it.

Like his public image, though, the house is studied in its casualness, an ad-hoc attack on the conformity of the suburbs, an expression of eccentric individualism. Like that casual public image, all of Gehry's buildings look thrown together, as if a kid has tipped out a box of building blocks; they are, of course, anything but. But this rough-and-ready DIY quality has stayed with him ever since. Even his glossiest-looking buildings, like Bilbao or Los Angeles's Disney Concert Hall, aren't that glossy in the flesh. When the Guggenheim's exterior started to rust, there was uproar. But that's the kind of building it is. 'It isn't a glossy icon,' Gehry explains. 'It's 300 bucks a square foot. It's not an expensive building. It's an industrial kind of building. It's in my DNA. I don't like spending a lot of money on marble. That's why I don't do rich guys' houses. Not even my own. It's not in my bones to do that.'

By the late 1970s, though, when Gehry belatedly found his mojo, architecture was full of younger guns doing exactly the same, trying to find the next big thing after modernism – postmodernism, a new language of architecture more attuned to an age of eccentric individualism, and hunting for a way out of the gruffer dog days of postwar

culture. A young Zaha Hadid was painting her first canvases of swirling, splintering forms. Rem Koolhaas had just published *Delirious New
York*, calling for a culture of 'congestion', spectacle and thrilling excess.
Gehry, then almost fifty, twenty years older than this new generation,
had his own take, to create a new urban vernacular from the culture
around him: licentious, chaotic, anything-goes, blowsy, artsy, gritty
and glossy suburban LA.

Santa Monica and Venice Beach are still studded with a series of
houses he built in the early 1980s for the artists and hippies he hung
out with, combining impeccably detailed rough-hewn DIY with
glossy pop — that Rauschenberg mixed-media combination of nails
and beer cans, art and sculpture and now architecture, all in one
object. The Chiat/Day/Mojo office (1985–91) in Venice he designed
with Claes Oldenburg and Coosje van Bruggen features a giant pair of
binoculars. The entrance to Aerospace Hall (1982–4) has a fighter jet
pinned to the facade.

'If you look at history,' Gehry tells me, 'the modern movement after
the war cleansed the Beaux-Arts, got rid of it, and developed a language
that was bastardised by the commercial sector, and created cities that
were lifeless and inhumane, boxes, mirrors, blah, blah, blah. Every
city in the world is now defined by that. There was a backlash to it.
The general public was looking for their nice little Victorian houses
and comfort.' He hugs himself. 'Norman Mailer hated modern architecture. So what do you do? He pulled himself into a cocoon of
historicism to make his modern statement. He was afraid of the real
world.' What did Gehry do? 'I'm trying to figure it out. How do you
replace nineteenth-century decoration, which *does* humanise environments, which *does* make for user-friendly places to be, which *does*
engage you, which *does* make you comfortable? We all have our houses
filled with stuff that we like, family pictures, candelabras from
Grandma, stuff like that. So I was looking for a way to make architecture talk to that.'

Moving pictures

His answer? Make buildings move. Or at least *seem* to move. It's not an original trick. Architects and master builders have been trying to make architecture deny its innate weightiness – shake off its heavy walls, uproot its leaden foundations, and get on the dancefloor – for centuries. In the seventeenth century baroque architects such as Borromini used *trompes l'œil* while constructing space to create buildings whose walls and pillars and domes seemed to writhe, alluringly, to an audience perhaps rather less used to immediate visual spectacle than our own. So how would Gehry grab the attention of a culture brought up on cable TV and Hollywood? With fish.

'I was searching for a sense of movement to replace decoration,' he explains. Everything about us moves.' Including fish. Well, everybody has their obsessions. Gehry unpacks his by remembering the live fish for Friday's gefilte his grandmother kept in the bathtub. Thinking back, he says, he was fascinated by how their shimmering scales hid their functional organs underneath, yet also how they could flex and curl. Even hemmed inside the bathtub, fish represented to him a kind of freedom and individualism, the liberating intuition of the natural world unencumbered by the self-doubts, ego and complexities of the human condition. 'It seems clearer and purer to work intuitively, because it's an immediate response to a place. And this intuition is well informed. What's in there', he taps his head, 'is a lot of stuff.'

If fish seem a little arbitrary, a little wacky as an architectural metaphor, they were no less arbitrary than the metaphors his fellow architects were coming up with at the same time in the great postmodern hunt for a new language of architecture to replace modernism . . . even the columns and pediments of revived classical architecture so adored by some in the 1980s. After all, why should a style of architecture born in the lands around the Aegean Sea in the fourth century BC have any more relevance in modern-day Los Angeles, Bilbao or Paris than Egyptian pyramids, Islamic mosques or, well, fish? 'We overcame postmodernism; but we learned a lot from postmodernism,' says Gehry. 'It brought humanity back to architecture, and I think it served a big purpose in doing that. But we've got to go on. And so I went on, for myself, anyway.'

What Gehry was hunting for was a language of architecture that went beyond relativism and anything goes, and beyond his own personal obsessions about fish in bathtubs. He needed to turn his own private language of architecture into one that communicated meaning to a wider public. He was after something universal, a kind of architecture that both a Saami herdsman in northern Finland and a hedgefunder in Manhattan could all relate to. 'I started with the sense of movement I experienced in Greek sculpture and Indian sculpture. It felt like it was moving. Well, if they were doing it, is there a way to do it architecturally? Because the world is full of movement, trains, boats, planes, all that crap, cars. Is there a language that would come from industrial methods, from making things that go fast, and could it be used in the building? Would it have the same effect? Would it make it possible to get rid of all that postmodern stuff?'

But why movement? 'A dance is an attractive thing,' he explains. It implies intimacy and connection. Gehry wanted his architecture to dance with you, to cavort, to draw you in and embrace you, to overcome the inevitable distance between us – the human being – and it – the building around or in front of us. And nothing draws you in better than the curves of the human body, the arch of an arm around the shoulder, the embrace of a hug. 'If you go back to antiquity people have been interested in the fold and the curve,' he points to the ones in the purple T-shirt hanging off his forearm. 'I think it's from when you're in your mother's arms as a baby. It's comforting. Bernini did it. Borromini did it. Michelangelo did it. Everybody did it. It's accessible. It's a primitive thing. But I don't know why.'

From chain-link cheapskate architecture, via the silvery skin of fish to the arms of an embrace. From his suburban home, via the Fish Lamps he designed in the early 1980s and the Fish Sculpture built on the waterfront for the 1992 Barcelona Olympics, to the

Guggenheim, Bilbao. 'I mean, Bilbao was contextual, even though people who see it in photographs don't realise it until they get there, and then they realise. That I was thinking about the river, the bridge, the nineteenth-century city behind, and I was organising a dance, if you will, with all that.'

And from movement and dancing, to courtship and ultimately sex. Gehry wants his buildings to court you, to seduce you. *That* is why he wants them to writhe, shimmer and cavort. They are *tableaux vivants*. 'Sex is a big deal [in my architecture]. I mean, it's obvious that high-rise buildings are phalluses and people want to make them higher and higher. It's just nice to admit that we're human and we have all these parts of our life that interfere and inspire and inform and they express themselves. You can see it in the buildings.' Take the building he designed for Prague, nicknamed Fred and Ginger, after Astaire and Rogers, for its paired shapes seeming to swoop on the dancefloor of the cityscape: 'Ginger has a skirt and you enter underneath it. So there is always that aspect. It's not conscious.'

Yet it is the visual allure of Gehry's buildings – or what he calls their 'painterliness' – that is their most striking characteristic. 'I think it's artist envy,' he suggests. 'I've always loved the immediacy [of artists]. If you look at Rembrandt's paintings they look like they were *just* made, even now, and I wanted to see if I could do that in a building.' Has he? 'I've no idea; they're trying to be, but I don't know.' In Sydney Pollack's *Sketches of Frank Gehry*, he describes the light and 'flutteringness' of the 'outside elements' that add to the buildings.

But what has made these buildings so successful is not just their visual allure, but their visual immediacy. They may be complex in shape, plan and metaphor, but their ability to be instantly understood – 'got' – even when reduced to (or reproduced as) a photograph or a logo has fuelled their fame. On the *Simpsons* episode featuring Frank Gehry, 'The Seven-Beer Snitch' (2005), Marge Simpson, aghast at the cultural desert in their hometown, Springfield, writes to Gehry, the 'bestest architect' in the world, inviting him to build a concert hall, a 'screw-you to Shelbyville', their more sophisticated neighbour. Cartoon Gehry picks up the letter from his mailbox (a miniature Guggenheim) out-side a faithful reproduction of his LA house and, in apparent disgust at yet another invitation to work, screws it up and throws it to the side-walk. One sight of the screwed-up paper, though, and inspiration strikes. 'Gehry!' he exclaims. 'You're a genius.'

As the academic Hal Foster put it, astutely, 'To make a big splash in the global pond of spectacle culture today, you have to have a big rock to drop, maybe as big as the Guggenheim Bilbao, and here an architect like Gehry, supported by clients like the Guggenheim and DG Bank, has an obvious advantage over artists in other media. Such clients are eager for brand equity in the global marketplace – in part, the Guggen-heim has become brand equity, which it sells in turn to corporations and governments – and these conditions favour the architect who can deliver a building that will also circulate as a logo in the media.'[4] Think of Bilbao today and it's impossible to detach it from Gehry's building. Obediently, the Guggenheim is reproduced as a logo on the city's road-signs, immediately recognisible 20 centimetres high, at 40 m.p.h.

A Frank Gehry building is a deeply visual experience, about what Foster calls 'stunned subjectivity'.[5] The allure is all in the anticipation, over once you get there. Indeed, seeing them in person after seeing them so often in two dimensions can be deflating. The look of his buildings implies that the sculptural shape of their skin is echoed on the inside. That is not the case. Behind the billowing facades are often fairly conventional buildings. Tap the columns holding up the main atrium at the Bilbao Guggenheim and they're hollow, hiding the steel beams within. It is about artifice, theatre. They have, I suggest, a lot in common with Robert Venturi and his decorated sheds. 'I always thought Bob was onto something. I didn't like where he went with it. And he doesn't like where I went with it. But we're really good friends. I would die for him, and he would stand in front of a bullet for me, too.

'I guess I am trying to lighten [architecture] and make it more accessible, less pontifical,' Gehry continues. 'I don't like the idea of lecturing to an audience about "You have to live this way because there's an intellectual construct that says that you have to live that way." It's in a democracy and they can do what they want and I don't give them a philosophy to live by. They concoct that themselves. It's their response to it that's important. I don't do what Mies or Frank Lloyd Wright did, putting the chairs in the same place.' With a scowl, he repositions the chair beneath him precisely, as if he had OCD. 'Like that, and you *have* to use their chairs. I don't do that at all. In fact, I back off. I want people to make the building theirs when they move into it. It's up to them if they want to buy a Louis XIV couch or something ... It's about pleasing people. It's about enriching people's lives. If you can't do that then why do it? And it's worked. And it's turned out to be financially rewarding to do that. It engages them emotionally, you know, like reading a book, you know you learn something. I mean, what do you feel when you go into Chartres Cathedral? I drop to my knees, emotionally stimulated. Like looking at a painting when it hits, when it gets you. They intended I be brought to my knees. And it works.

'I just want to bring feeling, and happiness and pride. Comfort. I'm saying, "I respect you. And I'm interested in making things better for you, nicer for you." It's overwhelming because in a second you can connect to so many people. It's scary. And you can get feedback.' In the end it's all about making buildings like humans. Gehry wants his buildings to talk to us. He, and his buildings, just want to be understood.

The entrepreneurial architect

Frank Gehry is at pains to maintain in the way he works something of the freedom he felt back in 1978, when he threw off both his professional shackles and the Dutch Colonial skin of his family home. Architecture, especially at the scale of an art gallery or concert hall, is complex, mind-numbingly so, so Gehry's search for a new language of architecture went hand-in-hand with finding a process with which to create it – not just the sophisticated engineering required to hold the building up, but a way of working that protected Gehry's creative freedom.

This working method has become the stuff of legend. 'This is what I do,' he begins. 'I study with the client. I study the programme, and I understand it. All at once I understand its scale, budget, site, client needs, blah. I understand it all. And there's a lot of drawings of it. I throw those away and I start over again. Because at that point – I call it the candy store – I'm now in the candy store. Now I can respond to everything because I know everything.' First he sketches. 'Sketching is hand–eye coordination, so there's more to it than you realise. I'm like a pussycat chasing some twine. Wherever it went I went. The first sketch I did for Bilbao – in the hotel, before I'd even got the job – if you look at the sketch and you look at the building you wonder why it took so bloody long to get there.' Next he and his team create countless models in cardboard, wood, glass, plastic, the clutter all around us in his studio. Only when he's close does he use a computer, and then only to digitally scan the physical model and replicate it onscreen.

More than two decades ago, Gehry took a computer programme created by French aeronautical design company Dassault to design the Mirage fighter jet and had it adapted to help design his buildings. CATIA, or the less-snappy Computer-Aided Three-dimensional Interactive Application, allows him to turn the three-dimensional models he makes by hand into two-dimensional images, complete with attendant data, by using a type of stylus that is drawn over the model's shape. This, though, is the part of the process Gehry likes least. The computer, he thinks, 'dries everything out. Takes the humanity out of a building.' But computers are excellent at sucking up data, nimbly tweaking his architectural shapes to improve their efficiency with materials, for instance, to answer those critics who accuse him of over-indulgence. You may not like the shape, but at least, he says, it's economical and functional.

'I'm not that prima donna about that kind of stuff. Architecture's a service business. I entered it as that. And I love that. And so I don't go into "It's art" and all that.' There's one of those contradictions again. Gehry wants to work like an artist, but be can't quite leave behind the business of architecture; business, after all, is what started him off back in the 1960s. Can he reconcile the two?

The modern architect, he says, has been 'infantilised' by the cartel of building contractors and developers that actually builds buildings, and whose tight grip on finances and scheduling reduces the role of the architect to a paid-by-the-hour artist brought in to add bells and whistles. 'We're not in control of the system that builds these things. The construction system puts architects into a corner and says, "OK, kid, you do your thing, but I know how to build everything." ' His solution is to play that part, the auteur, but the auteur businessman.

The computer enables him, he says, to wrestle back control over the entire building. His computer programmes not only allow him to innovate aesthetically; they allow him to cost the building down to the last rivet, and code them in a blueprint for the builders to use. 'I always wanted to be a master builder,' he half jokes. He shows me designs for Beekman Tower, a 76-storey residential skyscraper in Lower Manhattan, which has since been renamed 'New York by Gehry'. 'It's not in-your-face. It's pretty subtle. It's a New York building. It fits into the skyline. It doesn't compete with the Woolworth Building. I left the Woolworth Building intact as the icon of the place. I respected its iconicity. I didn't put a little hat on mine. And the ripples I made into bay windows'. His ornament, he says, has a function. 'And that building cost the same as the banal building next to it.' We're back to Gehry's obsession with quantifying his architecture, giving what seem like arbitrary aesthetic gestures not just a functional purpose, but a price tag. If anything, he says, this is what he's most proud of: not his aesthetics or his monuments, but the fact that they are, he says, functional and economic. Businessman to the end.

Whatever you want

Were it not for earthquakes, race riots and global recession, Los Angeles's Walt Disney Concert Hall, not Bilbao's Guggenheim, would have been the building that made Gehry famous. It was designed years before Bilbao. Goddammit, people should be talking about the 'LA effect', not Bilbao. For LA, too, wanted a new life courtesy of Frank. It's not industrially declined, like Bilbao. It's just been having a midlife crisis. For fifty years LA has been world's archetypical sprawling, privatised, centreless city of gated suburbs, fast food, fast, flashy architecture, malls and freeways – a city in which you need never sully your toes by touching a sidewalk. But now that Beijing, Shenzhen and Mumbai are out-LA-ing LA, LA has decided it should become Paris.

There is of course quite some irony in this: Los Angeles, the very archetype of suburbia, deciding in the mid Noughties that it wanted to be an old-fashioned city after all. It's been quietly turning its downtown – office towers, shabby heritage from the Twenties, eerily quiet bars, all filled with a curious mix of suits, Latinos and the homeless – into a proper city centre like the ones Jane Jacobs once lauded, like it used to be eighty years ago, before the car transformed it: with old-fashioned public space, lofts, pedestrian – gasp – boulevards, and properly public civic buildings like Rafael Moneo's masterly Catholic cathedral, and, the lynchpin, Gehry's Disney Concert Hall.

When the hall opened in 2003, Gehry's press blurb proposed its spaces would become the 'living room for the city'. In person he's more reticent. 'LA's civic life only exists in rhetoric. But maybe one building can contribute. I tried.' Downtown's revival is mostly about selling real estate rebranded for an era of gentrification, while keeping the natives happy. But there's genuine sincerity, too. After the Rodney King riots, says Esa-Pekka Salonen, the LA Philharmonic's musical director at the Disney Hall's opening, 'some people thought it was morally wrong to build an exclusive classical music concert hall in downtown LA when society was about to fall apart.' Now that it's built, he says, 'it will be a building that belongs to everybody. It's theirs. It's open. They can come in and discover it.' The hall would become, said Salonen, the city's symbolic 'unifying force', quite a job in a place where, until now, the only activity binding its disparate populations was cruising the freeways in your SUV.

In olden days, civic architecture was whatever the city told you it was, usually puffed-up columns and porticoes. That won't wash in multicultural, mosaic cities today. We need something baggier, more inclusive, whose symbolism won't offend any splinter in the new civic body. That's where laid-back Gehry's good-time architecture comes in. The Disney Hall, he says, is 'a child' of Berlin's Philharmonie concert hall, where Hans Scharoun built, he says, a 'magical' civic space where you can't help but hang out, meet people, be civilised. You can call Gehry's version flashy, empty gesturing, but, inside, even spoil-sports can't help but enjoy themselves. Gehry sweeps you straight off the sidewalk, revolutionary in LA, with a flash of silvery skin. There you lose yourself in a vortex – tighter, slicker, more controlled than Bilbao's looser version – with swirls, bulges and swoops in steel, white render, travertine marble, glass and Douglas fir (no expense spared for LA's new citizens), catching glimpses of sky through the chasms, and diving into impromptu pools of calm space, before escalators throw you into the eye of the storm, the calm, uncharacteristically symmetrical main auditorium, designed to build an 'intimate community between the orchestra and the people', says Gehry, in whose 'democratic' seats 'no one feels like a second-class citizen'.

Who could fail to have a good time? His work is an ambiguous form to be read however you like. To Frank, the hall writhes like a barrelful of carp, 'expressing movement with inert materials', rippling with aquatic light reflected from the Californian sun. Or maybe it's a giant bunch of steel flowers in a limestone vase, designed in honour of Lillian Disney, Walt's widow and the hall's founder. Lillian, LA and Frank love a bit of kitsch. For Salonen, it's 'that great cliché, Goethe's statement that architecture is frozen music. This building is the macro instrument.' And for LA's civic leaders, just like for Bilbao's, he's built a new civic logo, the perfect replacement for the Hollywood sign. You've gotta be bold to make it in LA, where every building comes wrapped in Versace. And the Disney Hall sure is bold. They double-take on the freeway. And its profile makes an ace badge for the tour guides.

Shorn of any collective intelligence to his allusions, his buildings become the objects of relativism. Like their architect, they are shapeshifters, chameleons. Unlike, say, Daniel Libeskind, Gehry offers no explanations, no theoretical positions. Like all his work, the Disney Hall, he says, 'is whatever you want it to be. I agree with anything. When I talk to my ice hockey friends I say the curves come out of carving the ice. Musician friends say the shapes are musical, and I say, "Yes, I guess they are." If you think they are, they are.'

It's the perfect civic building to relaunch the ultimate city of spectacle in its midlife crisis: the building as party. Be whatever you want to be. Everyone's invited: Latino, Korean, Buddhist, Jew or the homeless on Spring Street.

The backlash

When Gehry visits Bilbao these days, he isn't entirely happy. The Guggenheim today is surrounded by a menagerie of modern buildings, built after Gehry's, and not entirely certain if they should beat their chests in rivalry, or bow their heads in reverence. 'The buildings around my building *are* a mishmash,' he confesses. 'They don't really hold their own. They're not beautiful things in themselves yet. A lot of those people were worried about their relationship to it. I think they think they're deferring to it. [Álvaro] Siza just went blank [designing his building nearby]. He must have thought, "I'm not going to mess with Frank's thing." And [Rafael] Moneo did similarly. The original sin with that is the city planner. I talked to him when we were doing Bilbao, and I said, "You got two ways to go here: one way is the way you're going, which I think is wrong, which is to prettify this. You have an industrial site, wonderful, tough . . . Most artists I know love this gutsy place. And if you start planting it up with cherry blossoms à la Washington, DC you're going to screw it up." And I talked myself blue in the face. But that's what they did. Once they go that way, it's lost. It's funny to me. It could have been so much better. I spent all this time making it relate to the city and so on, and now that's lost because they've made it pretty.'

This is the *other* Bilbao effect: what Gehry calls 'the culture of pretti-fication' – and what others call spectacle – that has come to dominate architecture since 1997. Of course, one can't blame Gehry for how his buildings have been interpreted, or reproduced. 'One could make a value judgement that [Bilbao] inspired other people to go wild, and that's my fault. But the people that went wild, I don't like most of what they did.' We're back to that 's' word. Gehry is off again. 'I think society is a runaway train, and value systems are kind of wacky, and they're still spending 30 to 40 per cent of the world's money and resources on arms; that's the context we're in. And [there's an] impli-cation that one pishy little building in Bilbao, which you want to call spectacle, is gonna upset the world, and the implication of that is people should go back to doing dumb neutral boxes, and there's a whole group of people who want to do that and it doesn't lead to an architectural profession of much substance because it doesn't float your boat, it doesn't excite you, it doesn't make things you're proud of. I mean, go to China and see the cities sprouting up instantly; 10, 15 mil-lion people and they're just repeating these banal environments.'

He draws breath, momentarily. 'If I did in my lifetime thirty Bil-baos, which I'm not going to do, so you don't have to worry, it ain't gonna derail the world. It might help eliminate a few guys pushing baskets in the street because the economy of the town has benefited. So I don't see I should change what I'm doing. Compared to the hun-dreds and hundreds of buildings of banality that *do* demoralise, that *do* make us feel like we're robots . . . If my building is spectacle, who gives a fuck? Why worry about it? Spectacle is what our world is all about lately. I'm happy to go back to sleepytime, the past, so long as people aren't starving in the streets. I could move to a little village in Ireland. The world is about spectacle. But what do you do about it? I can't change it. I'd like to be able to change it, but I can't. So you pick your fights. I'm an architect. I do buildings. In one lifetime if I'm lucky I'll do two or three hundred buildings. A hundred years from then somebody will say, "That one's worth saving." The marketplace tells you what it wants. It is what it is. When you talk about a cacophonic environment, you're talking about democracy. And it allows for individual freedom and expression. We developed it, the US. LA especially. And it's confrontational. But that model, if you go to Seoul, if you go to Beijing, it's there. That's what we got. We don't have the pure thing: you're asking for too much. A lot of it's corruption, obviously. Read the newspapers. It's filled with corruption, financial manipulation, politicians. How do you find your way through it? The world is like a truck coming down a hill at 90 miles per hour. And you stand in front and get run over, or you can jump in the cab and grab the steering wheel. That's what I thought we should do.'

He's off again. 'There's always a negative backlash to it. But it's human nature to do that. I'm probably the backlash to somebody else.' In fact he's started his own backlash to himself. He no longer designs shimmering titanium titans. 'People employ me cause they want a Frank Gehry. And then I don't give them it.' That's partly why he's surprised at the backlash to his building in Sydney that caused Germaine Greer such grief. It's built with a facade of bricks, in homage, he says, to the everyday brick architecture that British and Irish builders brought with them when they colonised Australia. Some even called the building 'dowdy'. His recent work has ramped up the rough-hewn quality, as if trying to escape the stereotype that haunts him. The Maggie's Centre cancer care facility in Dundee, Scotland, is like a cosy, wooden bothy. His 2008 Serpentine Pavilion in Kensington Gardens, London was like a storm in a timber yard, great chunks of wood and rivets swirling in the trees.

Another recent building – the 2011 New World Center concert hall and academy in Miami – doesn't look like a Frank Gehry building at all. At least, not the Frank Gehry we've come to expect. It's not covered in glittering titanium. It's in plain white and glass. It's not even a funny shape. It's a box, a plain white box. Great facades of glass are held up with industrial metal I-beams, fittings are finished in rough-to-the-touch plywood, and titanium is banished to a canopy above the bar. 'It doesn't have to be perfect,' he says. 'Why does everything have to be *designed*?' There's the odd Frank-ism peeking out: a wibbly porch, a swooping sheet of white over a window. But this is Frank Gehry going back to his DIY roots.

When I meet him at the building, Gehry shuffles up to me in a better mood. 'Gimme another shot of coffee,' he reaches over to his assistant, before breaking out into poetry. 'Know what that is?' I don't. 'You *don't*? Shame on you. It's Walter Scott. We used to read it as a kid. Growing up in Canada we got all the British culture.' Then he starts crooning 'God Save the King'. ' "Send us victorious, happy and glorious" . . . I sing it the old way. When I was a kid it *was* a king.' Yep, Frank's in a better mood.

So, what's with the building? Is this 'Frank does age of austerity'? 'I play to context. I made a building for Miami Beach.' It's true that once you look past the art deco, Miami is a city of generic parking-lot architecture, the kind of glossy, slick pap garnished in palm trees you'd see on *Miami Vice*. '[New World] looks like an office building that comes from downtown,' Gehry explains. And it's not as if there's no excitement: inside, the atrium bulges with pavilions for the rehearsing musicians, shaped like bed linen on the washing line caught in the wind – or sails, as Frank likes to imagine them – stacked high to form a landscape of bleached white canyons. But it's not 'slick'. And it is definitely not an 'icon'.

At the New World Center his client is conductor Michael Tilson Thomas, its founder, whom Gehry babysat in the San Fernando Valley fifty years ago. It is, therefore, a very personal project. The programme – a building to de-stuff the often highfalutin world of classical music – is very Gehry. The building is 'not precious', he says. 'This interior we're in, which looks fixed and permanent. It's not. So in the next few years if someone wanted to clear this place out, make it a whatever, they could. It's essentially an industrial building with a stage set inside.'

Maybe that's why he's in such a good mood. He's doing what he wants for once: that creative freedom he yearned for in the 1970s. He's ignoring what he has become. He's ignoring the public relations, the celebrity, the image, the expectations. That way lies misinterpretation, therapy. He's just being Frank, take it or leave it. And so is the building. New World – its atrium open for Miami citizens to wander through and spy on the musicians – is Gehry at his best: open, unpretentious, his wilfulness restrained. He enters the auditorium to hear some Thomas Adès. 'It's so great. It envelops you. The music almost makes me cry. It's so beautiful. Just a few notes.' He beams. Job done.

Have you seen the future?

As we get up to leave, Gehry asks his secretary to get me copies of two articles. The first is about when and how he said something before Rem Koolhaas did. The other is from the *New York Times*: 'If you still don't get it,' he says, as he shuffles off, 'read this.'

And so I do.

Gehry's success, the success of any architect, is in part down to how the architecture is interpreted, how its 'effect' is understood and disseminated. The architect might intend this or that, might wish for their building to be thought of in a certain way, but once they have left the building site, the building is no longer theirs. It is ours. The building then takes on a new life as it is reflected in infinite interpretations by all who visit it, in their sketches and photographs, in what they say to their companions about it. Or, today, in our age of instantaneous global communication, in the millions of Tweets or tourists' Instagrammed images that accumulate. Indeed, you no longer have to visit a building to experience it. The academic Beatriz Colomina once wrote that modernist architecture, in the first half of the twentieth century, was the first in humankind to be experienced more by people who had not visited it than by those who had.

The article Gehry gave me was written in 1997 – the year the Bilbao Guggenheim opened – by the then architecture critic of the *New York Times*, Herbert Muschamp. Muschamp was renowned not just for his sharp critical incisiveness, but for the floridness of his prose, rising and falling in vertiginous similes and metaphors, rather like the architecture of Frank Gehry. Both he and Gehry shared the same psychotherapist. So here at last was the official line, the correct prism through which to view Gehry's work. This was what he wanted his architecture to sound like in words.

I hadn't read it before, but I knew it. It's one of the most famous, infamous pieces of writing about architecture in the past two decades. This was the newspaper article which, when it was published, anointed Frank Gehry and his very famous building, in the very public arena of the *New York Times Magazine*. This is the building as interpreted for the intellectual masses. In an era before the internet was really the internet, let's just say it went viral.

Muschamp begins by describing Bilbao, 'a small, rusty city in the northeast corner of Spain'. It is, he says, 'an unremarkable place'. What it requires is clearly the converse, the remarkable. It has got it. Gehry's building, declares Muschamp, is 'wondrous', 'miraculous'. Muschamp was not afraid of breathless hyperbole and his article delivers it, describing the experience of the building as akin to religious conversion. The building is 'Lourdes for a crippled culture'. Being in it will transform you. It will bring people together; a shattered world with all its social fragmentation can be united by Gehry's language of architecture, through the shared act of experiencing its 'beauty' and 'optimism', 'truth' and 'meaning'. He takes a while to settle on one metaphor: he describes the building's 'surprise', the 'shining', its 'play'; it 'flashes' like a 'crystal', he writes, is 'sensuous', puts on a 'spectacular . . . show', 'seems to billow'. The building is 'a sanctuary of free association'. It looks like anything you want it to be, and, because of its ability to be individually interpreted, unites people collectively. 'It's a bird, it's a plane, it's Superman. It's a ship, an artichoke, the miracle of the rose.' Gehry 'wrap[s] his arms around a city'. Then he finds it. The building is a woman, one with 'voluptuous curves'. It is, writes Muschamp, 'the reincarnation of Marilyn Monroe'. The building is a celebrity, a seducer. And, tellingly, as such it is the embodiment of 'an American style of freedom'. 'Architecture has stepped off her pedestal. She's waiting for her date outside a bar on a rainy early evening in Bilbao, Spain.'

The Bilbao effect was not just about the invention of a new kind of architectural language, but a new verbal and visual language with which to interpret it. Muschamp's article created a template for how buildings subsequently should be measured and judged. It established an expectation about what successful architecture should achieve. It should transform us. It should seduce us. For what? The oldest games in the book. Not religion, after all, but money and sex.

It's not often a building makes the front cover of the *New York Times Magazine*, but the Guggenheim managed it. On the cover, the building, lit up at night in an otherworldly glow, was accompanied by the headline: 'The Word Is Out That Miracles Still Occur'. The words continue: 'A major one is happening here. Frank Gehry's new Guggenheim Museum won't open until next month, but people have been flocking to Bilbao, Spain, to watch the building take shape. "Have you been to Bilbao?" In architectural circles, the question has acquired the status of a shibboleth. Have you seen the light? Have you seen the future?' Twenty years later, the future had arrived.

CONCLUSION

THE NEW BABYLON

'Everything that was directly lived has moved away
into a representation.'

Guy Debord[1]

The architect and artist Constant Nieuwenhuys unveiled his life's work,
New Babylon,[2] to a packed audience in the Stedelijk Museum, Amsterdam one December evening in 1960.[3] He switched on his slide projector
and began his presentation. Modern architects, he told the rapt crowd,
were ignoring massive changes in modern life, turning their back on a
generation born after the war. Cities all over the world were growing
outwards into the suburbs; indeed the world would soon become one
vast urban sprawl. But life in these cities had become a utilitarian drudge,
a highly efficient process for squeezing work and money out of their
inhabitants. Architecture, Constant explained from the stage, affects the
psychology, emotions and mood of all of us living inside it. So instead
of beating us down, why couldn't architecture stimulate us, invigorate
us? What would happen if we could create the kind of buildings that
would tap into our innermost desires, that would liberate us all?

Technology, he suggested, would be the key. It alone could equip
inhabitants with the freedom to shape their own places and their own
lives. As automation made work wither away, so a life of pleasure and
leisure would replace it. Architects, planners and politicians would all
wither away too. We would all become architects of our lives in '*Le
grand jeu à venir*', the great game to come.

Constant's slide projector whirred on, revealing an architectural model of a most peculiar landscape, an almost never-ending structure with long, thin rectangular buildings zigzagging in columns across an orange ground, with red and green splodges suspended high above, and, beneath, a web of lines speeding this way and that, with cars discarded below on a pockmarked moonscape that hinted at some future apocalypse. This was Constant's new city: the New Babylon. Within it, huge multi-level buildings extended in a chain, an endless expanse of air-conditioned space. The next slide was a bird's-eye photograph of a model made from transparent plexiglass, with dense, overlapping surfaces. More slides in the projector moved the audience ever downwards through the giant, endless 'building', each layer feeding into the next, while Constant played sounds on a tape recorder next to him on the stage of aeroplanes landing on the roof deck of New Babylon, of disconnected city noises – traffic, animals, people, music.

'New Babylonians', Constant told the audience, 'play a game of their own designing, against a backdrop they have designed themselves.' This is a city made up of buildings that people have freely created themselves, by manipulating a lightweight structure like those proposed by the famous engineer Buckminster Fuller – or Konrad Wachsmann's 'space frames', only ones that can mould and morph around you with moveable floors, ramps, walls, bridges, ladders. The city would become an ever-changing organism full of intense experiences, like an enormous playground, or 'an atmospheric jukebox', Constant explained, that can only be played by a completely revolutionised society'.[4]

In this society, freed from the compulsion to own property, nomadism would become the norm. Upon this vast swirling infrastructure, an open fretwork of moveable partitions and deep, seemingly endless vistas, are hung 'opportunities' for people to make their own architecture (architects, thought Constant, 'will disappear'), an architecture less about style than ambience. Cybernetics, electronics and computers would control everything. The city would be plugged directly into the desires of its citizens. Character, atmosphere, passion were what was absent from the modern city, so its replacement, New Babylon, is entirely composed of them. 'Cool and dark spaces,' wrote Constant, later, 'hot, noisy, chequered, wet', would be hung on slim columns 16 metres above a ground freed for fun. Grottoes, the ruins of the old city and nature, would all be viewed from promenades above: 'everything is discovery', he continued, 'everything changes'. This was the shape of the world once capitalism had died.

Constant died in 2005, aged eighty-five. There were few obituaries beyond his home country, the Netherlands. True, the man hadn't exactly been front-page news for a decade or three. Yet this was the intellectual leader behind the Provos, those pot-smoking anarchists whose artsy pranks in the 1960s ushered in the modern-day stereotype of liberal, libertarian Netherlands. Constant (he soon ditched that unsnappy surname) co-founded the Situationiste Internationale, too, Jean-Luc Godard's 'children of Marx and Coca Cola', Gauloise-puffing inspiration for every sulky counter-cultural movement from beatniks through May 1968, from punk to Occupy Wall Street. The man – did he collect postwar, left-wing art groups? – was also a leading light of CoBrA, whose paintings – great childlike scrawls designed to unsettle bourgeois society – are today the kind more admired by art theoreticians than genuinely loved. And he also happened to be the most influential architect since the war.

Few of you will have heard of him. The man didn't lay a brick his entire life. But his one great conceptual work, New Babylon, was so powerful a vision of the future, the true heir to great architectural fantasists on paper from Piranesi to Sant'Elia, that there are few architects since who don't owe him an intellectual debt. New Babylon begat the swirling forms of Frank Gehry and Zaha Hadid, even the pragmatic hi-tech of Richard Rogers and Norman Foster, and certainly the provocations of Rem Koolhaas. You name them, they'll namecheck him.

In 1956, Constant met Guy Debord, soon to become leader of the Situationists. Debord was a tricksy old so-and-so – a drinker, continually excommunicating his friends – but the two hit it off. Their ideas chimed, giving direction to Constant, who'd been adrift since CoBrA fell apart in 1951. Constant and Debord were far from alone in being unhappy with the cities that had been built since the Second World War. They knew well the work of the Independent Group, Team X, and the Smithsons, but proposed something more radical still: revolution. This was the era of Castro and McCarthy. Genuine communist revolution was palpable in cities across the world, and Paris, rocked by the Algerian War and awash with left-wing splinter groups, was as good a place as any, the pair thought, for it to begin.

Both had a vision of what urbanism and society *should* be. But, before that, both also had a vision of what urbanism and society *should not* be: neither the bourgeois, class-riven city of old, nor the corrupted modernist utopias rising in the *banlieues*, nor the new consumerist cities of America that would come to dominate the West, what Debord later called the 'society of the spectacle', a 'city of things' whose inhabitants, drugged-up on shopping malls, had become 'spectres', shadows of their former selves. There was in the world, wrote Debord, a 'culture of separation',[5] separation from one another and from ourselves. The nature of capitalist society was to rationalise things, break them up into parts, divide them. Creativity had been stripped from work and, instead, become another product to be sold, one of many promising fulfilment to the alienated masses: spectacle. The society of the spectacle created addictive and dependent behaviour in its citizens. We are constantly hunting for the next hit to make us whole again.

By subverting society with 'guerrilla' acts, though, ones both violent – insurrection – and benign, like the 'derive' (random rambling wherever your soul took you through the modern city, a snub to the over-ordered, over-planned landscape that Jane Jacobs also decried, from a rather less revolutionary position), Constant and Debord believed that a more authentic, alive city, long-since buried by capitalism, might be unearthed that would unshackle individuals, and society as a whole. 'Beneath the pavement, the beach,' went their slogan. 'The sole end of architecture', wrote Debord, 'is to serve the passions of men.'[6]

If Debord gave Situationism a language, Constant, its artist and architect, gave it form. New Babylon, a name pointedly chosen by Debord, was a city not of sin, but of pleasure. It became Constant's obsession for almost twenty years, rendered in paintings, lithographs, models, writings, collages and sketches. Constant imagined a future where humans, freed into permanent leisure by technology, would drift in endless fulfillment. Unlike the dystopian futurist visions of *Metropolis* or *Things to Come*, this freedom and leisure was communist, shared by all, not just an elite. Constant designed it in furious labyrinthine swirls, like the ones he once put on canvas for CoBrA, curls which thumbed their noses at the grids of the modernists. The Situationists loved instead the organic bulges of Frank Lloyd Wright, the heart-pumping curls of the baroque.

Debord, at first, loved the work, seeing in Constant what people so often see in architects, someone who can realise their thoughts in three dimensions. Soon after, though, in a charactistic fit of pique, he excommunicated Constant from the Situationists, in part because of the very act of making concrete, even in impressionistic swirls, a post-revolutionary world that Debord believed should remain blank until revolution itself had occurred. Constant, though, never believed New Babylon was anything other than his personal interpretation of the 'feeling' of utopia. But he did hope architects and artists could create physical manifestations of this utopia that might hasten its arrival. Architecture could be one of the Situationists' 'situations', 'a creative game with an imaginary environment', a starting gun to provoke change, to change society, to jolt people out of their daze.[7] Constant refused to use the word 'utopia'. But he refused, too, to give up hope that it could be achieved right here right now, growing, virus-like, from within the old city, fed with the creative energy of its more bohemian residents.

Ten years later such hope was as dated as rock'n'roll. The failure of Paris's unrest in May 1968, directly stirred by Situationism, fired instead a very different starting pistol. This was not Debord and Constant's revolutionary moment. Instead the entrepreneurial city was born, the true city of spectacle. Capitalist society did what it has always done: it assimilated its critics, neutered them, and sold to us their more easily appealing aspects. A version of New Babylon came true, in aesthetic – if not political or utopian – spirit. A very different revolution had taken place, and they knew it. Constant returned to painting in 1974. Twenty years later Guy Debord put a gun to his head and pulled the trigger.

It became quite fashionable a few years back to quote the Situationists. Few, though, have bettered their critique of contemporary society. We all live in Babylon today, though it's a moot point just how new it is. It *looks* new. The old city has been reborn. People have returned to it. Money has returned to it. It has changed its face. Constant's everchanging organism of intense experiences, his gigantic playground, his 'atmospheric jukebox', has been built by those architects who came after him, who have given literal, though not spiritual or political, shape to Constant's vortices in multisensory blobs, shards and splinters. They share the aesthetic aims of much modernist architecture – mass architecture for mass society – in postmodern form, splintered and heterogeneous for a splintered and heterogeneous society. You can have any architecture you want, within limits. For today's architects have abandoned the political aims of much modernist architecture. Freed from an obligation to better the entrepreneurial city of spectacle, its architects have become witting or unwitting apologists for it. With few exceptions, their response to the rise of the entrepreneurial city was not to challenge it, but, when their traditional role and position in society came under threat, to accept it on its own terms, and to adapt to it. Only architects could create beauty. Only architects could create the city of spectacle. As Frank Gehry told me in frustration, 'The world is like a truck coming down a hill at 90 miles per hour. And you stand in front and get run over, or you can jump in the cab and grab the steering wheel.' It's the direction they turned the steering wheel, though, that's the problem.

Since 2008's economic downturn, it has become common to say that this so-called iconic architecture is dead. Who has the money,

these days, to build spectacles? I have lost count of the number of articles I have read claiming that the future is lo-fi, hand-crafted,
un-iconic. Indeed, a whole breed of architects have gathered strength
offering an alternative to the spectacular. The Swiss architect Peter
Zumthor, perhaps, whose work is crafted and unflamboyant, about
weight and tactility, not image and lightness, as rooted to place and as
nutritious, he once told me, as 'slow food. Slow architecture, ha, I
think so.'

Such architects, though, only really critique the aesthetics of spectacle, not the political economy behind it. They simply create their
own versions of the aesthetic utopias created by their more showy rivals.
They offer not a challenge to the world but an intoxicating retreat from
it. Slow architecture, like slow or organic food, or the single-estate coffee sold in an artisan coffee shop, takes time and money to produce. But
it is no response to a planet of 7.4 billion people and rising, not without
a serious adjustment to society.

The age of spectacle – and the free market that drives it – is still
with us today. Though the free market in the gentrified city is hardly
free, just open to the highest bidder. What power do any of us have to
say yes or no to this building or that? The right to the city has been
replaced by the right to buy it.

Instead, we nomadic citizens of today's city of spectacle dutifully
circle it as passive tourists, hungry for fulfillment through experience.
The free market anticipates, stimulates, manipulates and delivers the
desires of its citizens, for a price. It just lacks the freedom bit. We are
not architects of our lives, as Constant had hoped. Life in the modern
city remains a utilitarian drudge, a highly efficient machine for
squeezing work and money out of their inhabitants. And we are the
lucky ones. The city of spectacle is a prettier city, to some, but as anyone living in its overpriced, cramped housing or evicted from its
newly privatised land might tell you, it is not a *better* one. It is a city
which most of us visit, but do not inhabit, let alone own. We rent it,
and its architecture, by the hour.

Today, as a result, architecture has become a luxury product. At its worst it is a thing to be observed, rather than inhabited, designed for the camera, visual titillation that attempts to make a connection with us by looking like giant underpants or cavorting fishes. Its spectacle hides the structures of power behind it, and blinds us to the alternative stories that could be told about it. At *best* it is a visceral experience for all five senses, if you have the money to pay for it. Either way it is a thing to be consumed, a product, a brandscape, something delivered *to* us as passive recipients, but over which we have no control. Either way, it can never hope to reflect or fulfill society in all its multiplicity.

All architects needed to do, though, was to include us – the ones who live in their buildings, who sleep in them, play Lego with the kids in them, argue in them, sit bored at computers in them, doze off in front of the TV in them – somehow, in the conversation. Instead of trying to second guess us, or, worse, stimulate and manipulate our desires, they could have just asked us. By and large, they chose not to. Architecture, historically hardly the most inclusive or diverse of professions, closed in on itself for protection.

Maybe it will open itself up. Maybe. It may be that a generational shift will occur in architecture – is occurring in architecture – as it is occurring right now in politics, economics and other forms of culture; that millennials and post-millennials, tired of the establishment, will tear down its spectacular monuments and build a kinder, more inclusive landscape through as-yet-untold revolutions in how architecture and our cities get built, by drones, perhaps, robots, or the simple sweat and tears of those who will inhabit it.

The Situationists hoped that the power of critique and subversion would unleash other tales of the city buried under its spectacle, enough tales to bring about democratic social change, to transform life. The point to this new life was that it should be participatory, cooperative and communal. We should not be passive spectators. We should take part, and be transformed through the experience. We should be given the power to make our own places, our own towns and cities, our architecture. That is the only way we will truly feel attachment to and ownership of the land beneath our feet – by weaving the richness of ordinary human experience back into the production and experience of the landscapes we live in, creating little utopias in the city from which change might spread. And perhaps, in the burgeoning movements against gentrification in towns and cities across the world, or campaigns for affordable housing, a tax on increasing land values or the 'right to the city', something of the communal, subversive spirit we saw in Covent Garden and countless other cities in the 1960s and 1970s is returning. The question, today, as well as back then, though, is how to ensure these unstable coalitions of such different peoples stick together; and even, once that fragile unity is achieved, what to campaign FOR, as well as against. Opposition is the easy bit. Coming up with an alternative to the entrepreneurial city, that's the rub.

Remember, Constant said, technology would be the key. It alone could equip inhabitants with the freedom to shape their own places and their own lives. Architects, planners and politicians would all wither away. We would all become architects of our lives in '*Le grand jeu à venir*', the great game to come. His idea of a city plugged directly into the desires of its citizens foreshadows the rise of the internet. Perhaps, as Mario Carpo suggests, the more collaborative culture of open-source computing, the more collaborative nature of digital natives, will simply replace free-market competition with cooperation, a kind of anarchism, its architecture somehow 'self-organised' like the towers produced by termites, or the hidden structures of coding created by Linex junkies, democratising by stealth at last those least democratic of industries, architecture and property. In his recent book, *Together: The Rituals, Pleasures and Politics of Cooperation*, sociologist Richard Sennett proposes just such a communal, cooperative alternative to a contemporary society in which competition has, for too long, been valued over consensus. Distanced 'spectating', rather than what Sennett calls 'mutual ritual', emerged during the Reformation, but centuries on, has become a pathology in western society, the more so in one made more hyperactive by social media. We are, Sennett suggests, more physically alienated from one another than we have been for centuries, as we tap away on computers, tending to our virtual identities online. A more communal city must be built. Perhaps the great game to come has yet to be truly played. Perhaps. That city has yet to be built. It is too soon to tell. I have a sneaking suspicion, though, that after the divisive election of Donald Trump as US president, in this era of rising nationalism, when walls and barriers physical and social are being built once again between nations and peoples even within cities, this is just wishful thinking on the part of those at the wrong end of the telescope.

Until then, the city of spectacle will continue to be built. One visit to Hong Kong, to Caracas, to Rio, to Bangalore, to Beijing or Shanghai or any of the myriad new Chinese megalopolises tells you so. Architectural spectacle and flamboyance are far from dead. In fact, rather the opposite – they are growing and growing, becoming ever wilder. No sooner is the Burj Khalifa in Dubai the tallest building in the world than does a new plan pop up for a building twice as high. The spectacular building has not died, because the conditions that created it – global capitalism, revolutions in mass media – have not died either. They have just shifted focus, shape and position. Architecture is simply migrating, as it always does, to where the money and power are. The city of spectacle is the West's parting gift to the new world.

ACKNOWLEDGEMENTS

This book could not have been written without those who have taught me, and who continue to do so. I owe the biggest debt of all to David Harvey, Professor of Geography at Oxford University during my time there. I started out at Oxford studying English Literature for sixteen months before succumbing to the temptations of geography. My English tutors thought I was insane. How could soil erosion, cartography and terminal moraines compete with Charles Dickens and Shakespeare? Well, in my crazy mind they could.

By chance, swapping an English degree for Geography, I stumbled into a faculty run by one of the twentieth century's most original thinkers on how spaces and places help make society. David Harvey won't remember me from Dick or Harry, but I shall never forget him, his thundering lectures about the politics of space and the doors he opened to a world of incisive, inspirational thinkers, such as Marshall Berman, Mike Davis and Ed Soja. Harvey pulled the scales from my eyes.

Thanks, too, to my tutors at Oxford, Judith Pallot and David Matless, who taught me how to look at a landscape. And, while at the Bartlett School of Architecture, University College London, to Adrian Forty, Iain Borden, Murray Fraser, Joe Kerr and Jane Rendell, who taught me how to look at the things we build on top of it.

This book could not have been written, too, without all those who have either taught me to write, or given me the opportunity to do so. I thank the late architectural historian Giles Worsley for his generosity and open-mindedness, and his precision in thinking and writing;

Giles gave me my first job after leaving university, and, despite being an expert on classical architecture, allowed me to write about Daniel Libeskind and deconstructivism at a place – the Prince of Wales's Institute of Architecture – not renowned for its broadmindedness. I thank, too, Caroline Roux and Kath Viner at the *Guardian*, and, while I was architecture critic at *The Times*, Sarah Vine, Alex O'Connell, Tim Teeman and Nancy Durrant; all of you, in the most troubling of times for journalism, were kind enough to prise away some column inches to allow me to write about buildings. Much of what I have written for all of you has formed the skeleton of this book.

At the BBC, Channel 4 and many, many television and radio production companies, I must thank magnificent editors, directors and commissioners such as Alan Hall, Tabitha Jackson, Mike Christie, Eddie Morgan, Janet Lee, Basil Comely, Tom Garland and countless other directors, researchers, cameramen, sound recordists and interviewees. Being a writer, historian and critic can be a peculiarly isolating affair, tucked away tapping on keyboards stuck with your own thoughts. You've all made bouncing ideas and realising radio and TV programmes enjoyable. Much of what we have all worked on has also formed the skeleton of this book.

Thanks to all my interviewees in this book, from property developers to architects to inspirational renegades like Brian Anson and John Toomey. You were generous with your time, your opinions and your passions. Meeting many of you has truly changed my life. And hearty thanks to my agents at Janklow & Nesbit, Tim Glister and Will Francis for asking me to write this book in the first place; to my editors at Penguin Random House, Nigel Wilcockson and Nick Humphrey; and to copyeditor Lindsay Davies, proofreader Alice Brett, and indexer Marian Aird for their patience and precision.

I thank my family, who have had to put up with me wittering on about town planning and architecture since I was a child. My parents never lived to read this book, but – of course – I owe them everything. It was their love of learning, and their family day trips to obscure places, that switched me on to landscapes and architecture. Armed with a guide book, I would, precociously, commandeer these day trips on 'Tom Tours', so I could surreptitiously visit a medieval tithe barn or an astonishing bollard. I hope my sisters can forgive such behaviour. There was nobody else in our extended family who shared my peculiar obsessions. Thanks to you for indulging them.

And finally I thank my wife, who continues to indulge and support me; and our children, who were born while I wrote this book, and whom I look forward to dragging round towns on future Tom Tours, surreptitiously showing them medieval tithe barns and astonishing bollards.

P.S. And thank you, Royal Festival Hall – one of the last patches of London where you can do almost anything (like write this book) without buying a coffee or bribing a security guard.

PICTURE ACKNOWLEDGEMENTS

Picture credits for the black and white photographs are as follows:

The Shard, London (p. 26): Colin/WikiCommons. Licensed under CC BY-SA 4.0: https://creativecommons.org/licenses/by-sa/4.0/legalcode
Covent Garden, London in 1974 (p. 50): London Metropolitan Archives
Faneuil Hall, Boston (p. 94): nobleIMAGES/Alamy Stock Photo
One New Change, London (p. 118): PSL Images/Alamy Stock Photo
ArcelorMittal Orbit, London (p. 146): you_only_live_twice/Flickr. Licensed under CC BY-SA 2.0: https://creativecommons.org/licenses/by-sa/2.0/legalcode
Westfield Shepherd's Bush, London (p. 182): Jon Arnold Images Ltd/Alamy Stock Photo
World Trade Center, New York (p. 218): Joe Mabel/Flickr. Licensed under CC BY-SA 2.0: https://creativecommons.org/licenses/by-sa/2.0/legalcode
Heydar Aliyev Cultural Center, Baku (p. 260): mauritius images GmbH/Alamy Stock Photo
Guggenheim Museum, Bilbao (p. 316): Ardfem/WikiCommons. Licensed under CC BY-SA 3.0: https://creativecommons.org/licenses/by-sa/3.0/legalcode

Colour photographs are courtesy of the author, unless otherwise stated:

City of London skyline: Dun.can/Flickr. Licensed under CC BY 2.0: https://creativecommons.org/licenses/by/2.0/legalcode
The Shard inauguration: Yola Watrucka/Alamy Stock Photo
Covent Garden market: Henry Kellner/WikiCommons. Licensed under CC BY-SA 3.0: https://creativecommons.org/licenses/by-sa/3.0/legalcode
'The Flying Tabletop': Taxiarchos228/WikiCommons. Licensed under CC BY 3.0: https://creativecommons.org/licenses/by/3.0/legalcode
Westfield Stratford City: Berit Watkin/Flickr. Licensed under CC BY 2.0: https://creativecommons.org/licenses/by/2.0/legalcode
Guggenheim Museum: Phillip Maiwald/WikiCommons. Licensed under CC CC BY-SA 3.0: https://creativecommons.org/licenses/by-sa/3.0/legalcode
'Bird's Nest' Stadium: Jorge Láscar/Flickr. Licensed under CC BY 2.0: https://creativecommons.org/licenses/by/2.0/legalcode
Nordpark Railway Station: Arcaid Images/Alamy Stock Photo

NOTES

1 Henri Lefebvre, *The Production of Space* (Wiley-Blackwell, 1991), p. 92
2 Lord Henry Wotton's speech to Dorian Gray, Oscar Wilde, *The Picture of Dorian Gray*, in *Complete Works*, general editor J. B. Foreman (Collins, 1948), p. 32

PROLOGUE: THE BUILDING THAT LOOKS LIKE A PAIR OF UNDERPANTS

1 'British-Designed Skyscraper Resembles Big Pants, Say Angry Chinese', *Daily Telegraph* (4 September 2012)

INTRODUCTION

1 Jane Rendell, '"Bazaar Beauties" or "Pleasure Is Our Pursuit": A Spatial Story of Exchange', in Iain Borden, Joe Kerr, Jane Rendell, with Alicia Pivaro (eds), *The Unknown City: Contesting Architecture and Social Space* (MIT Press, 2001), p. 106
2 Junichiro Tanazaki, *In Praise of Shadows* (Jonathan Cape, 1999), p. 48
3 Quoted in Geoffrey Broadbent, 'Architects and their Symbols', *Built Environment*, vol. 6, no. 1 (1980)
4 *Sunday Times* (15 December 2002)
5 Roland Barthes, in Beatriz Colomina, *Privacy and Publicity: Modern Architecture as Mass Media* (MIT Press, 1994), p. 100
6 G. W. F. Hegel, T. M. Knox (transl.), *Hegel's Aesthetics: Lectures on Fine Art, Vol. II* (Oxford, 1975), pp. 82–5
7 Beatriz Colomina, *Privacy and Publicity*, p. 13
8 Henri Lefebvre, *The Production of Space*, pp. 93–94
9 Adrian Forty, in Iain Borden, Joe Kerr, Alicia Pivaro and Jane Rendell (eds), *Strangely Familiar: Narratives of Architecture in the City* (Routledge, 1996), p. 5
10 John Berger, *A Fortunate Man: The Story of a Country Doctor* (Granta Books, 1967), p. 1

CHAPTER ONE: THE VIEW FROM HERE

1 *Evening Standard* (3 March 2006)
2 *Guardian* (13 September 2013)
3 http://www.cam.ac.uk/research/news/who-owns-the-city
4 *Evening Standard* (4 July 2012)
5 *Guardian* (25 June 2012)
6 *Evening Standard* (9 October 2014)

CHAPTER TWO: CITY OF THE DEAD

1 Margaret Drabble, *The Ice Age* (Weidenfeld & Nicolson, 1977), p. 62
2 Bill Risebero, *Fantastic Form: Architecture and Planning Today* (The Herbert Press, 1992), p. 73
3 Terry Christensen, *Neighbourhood Survival: The Struggle for Covent Garden's Future* (Prism Press, 1979), p. 124
4 Edward Glaeser, *Triumph of the City: How Urban Spaces Make Us Human* (Pan Books, 2012), p. 8
5 Ibid., p. 42
6 Andy Beckett, *When the Lights Went Out: Britain in the Seventies* (Faber & Faber, 2010), p. 241
7 David Harvey, *The Condition of Postmodernity: An Enquiry into the Origins of Cultural Change* (Wiley-Blackwell, 1991), p. 143
8 Peter Reyner Banham, *Los Angeles: The Architecture of Four Ecologies* (Pelican Books, 1987), p. 238
9 Murray Fraser and Joe Kerr, *Architecture and the 'Special Relationship': The American Influence on Post-War British Architecture* (Routledge, 2007), p. 127
10 Peter L. Laurence, 'The Death and Life of Urban Design: Jane Jacobs, The Rockefeller Foundation and the New Research in Urbanism, 1955–1965' in *Journal of Urban Design*, vol. 11, no. 2 (June 2006), pp. 145–72
11 Edward Glaeser, *Triumph of the City*, p. 54
12 F. H. W. Sheppard (ed.), *The Survey of London XXXVI: The Parish of St Paul* (Athlone Press, 1970), p. 5
13 Terry Christensen, *Neighbourhood Survival*, p. 20
14 Murray Fraser and Joe Kerr, *Architecture and the 'Special Relationship'* , p. 149
15 Terry Christensen, *Neighbourhood Survival*, p. 20
16 Covent Garden Planning Team, *Covent Garden's Moving* (Greater London Council, 1968), p. 22
17 Brian Anson, *I'll Fight You For It! Behind the Struggle for Covent Garden* (Jonathan Cape, 1981), p. 20
18 Ibid., p. 102
19 Terry Christensen, *Neighbourhood Survival*, p. 23
20 Oliver Marriott, *The Property Boom* (Pan, 1967), p. 15

21 Simon Jenkins, *Landlords to London: The Story of a Capital and its Growth* (Constable, 1975), p. 215

22 Ibid., p. 221

23 Ruth Glass (ed.), *London: Aspects of Change*, Centre for Urban Studies (Mac-Gibbon & Kee, 1964)

24 Ibid., p. xiv

25 Ibid., p. xviii

26 Ibid., pp. xviii–xix

27 Murray Fraser and Joe Kerr, *Architecture and the 'Special Relationship'*, p. 156

28 Ibid., p. 215

29 Raphael Samuel, *Theatres of Memory: Past and Present in Contemporary Culture* (Verso, 2012), p. 92

30 Geoffrey Fletcher, *The London Nobody Knows* (Penguin, 1965), p. 132

31 Raphael Samuel, *Theatres of Memory*, p. 92

32 Ruth Glass (ed.), *London: Aspects of Change*, p. 153

33 Richard Yates, *Revolutionary Road* (Methuen, 2001), p. 24

34 Richard Sennett, *The Uses of Disorder: Personal Identity and City Life*, (Faber & Faber, 1996), p. 72

35 Ibid., p. 84

36 Ibid., p. 107

37 Ibid., p. 185

38 Alice Sparberg Alexiou, *Jane Jacobs: Urban Visionary* (Rutgers University Press, 2006), p. 39

39 Peter L. Laurence, 'The Death and Life of Urban Design', pp. 145–172, p. 156

40 Ibid., p. 163

41 Ibid., p. 159

42 Kevin Lynch, *The Image of the City* (MIT Press, 1960), p. 2

43 Ibid., p. 1

44 Alice Sparberg Alexiou, *Jane Jacobs*, pp. 29–30

45 Simon Jenkins, *Landlords to London*, p. 239

46 Brian Anson, *I'll Fight You For It!*, p. 55

47 Ibid., p. xii

48 Ibid., p. 82

49 Terry Christensen, *Neighbourhood Survival*, p. 43

50 Ibid., p. 41

51 Brian Anson, *I'll Fight You For It!*, p. 107

52 Ibid., p. 73

53 Ibid., p. 134

54 Ibid., p. 173

55 Terry Christensen, *Neighbourhood Survival*, p. 47

56 Brian Anson, *I'll Fight You For It!*, p. 179

57 Ibid., p. 181

58 Ibid., p. 190
59 Terry Christensen, *Neighbourhood Survival*, p. 84

CHAPTER THREE: PEOPLE POWER

1 Edward Glaeser, *Triumph of the City*, p. 11
2 Andy Beckett, *When the Lights Went Out*, p. 345.
3 Ibid., p. 346
4 William Menking, 'From Tribeca to Triburbia: A New Concept of the City', in Iain Borden, Joe Kerr and Jane Rendell, with Alicia Pivaro (eds), *The Unknown City*, pp. 90–103
5 Ibid., p. 94
6 David Harvey, *The Condition of Postmodernity*, p. 92
7 Ibid., p. 298
8 Ibid., p. 91
9 Berton Roueche, 'A New Kind of City', *New Yorker* (October 21 1985), pp. 42-53
10 'Portland: How its Downtown Became the Lazarus of American Cities', *Architecture: The Journal of the American Institute of Architects* (July 1986)
11 Carl Abbott, *Portland: Planning, Politics, and Growth in a Twentieth-Century City* (University of Nebraska Press, 1983), p. 2
12 *Architectural Record* 145 (April 1969), pp. 161–4
13 Ibid., p. 161
14 Ibid., p. 162
15 Ibid., p. 163
16 Ibid., p. 164
17 Janet M. Levy, *Design Research: Marketing 'Good Design' in the 50s, 60s, and 70s*, Masters thesis MA program in the History of the Decorative Arts and Design, in partnership with Cooper-Hewitt, the National Design Museum, the Smithsonian Institution and Parsons The New School for Design (2004)
18 Ibid., p. 8
19 Mildred F. Schmertz, 'Boston's Historic Faneuil Hall Marketplace: Restored and Transformed by Architect Benjamin Thompson and Developer James Rouse into a Triumphantly Successful Downtown Center', *Architectural Record*, vol. 162, no. 8 (12), (December 1977), pp. 116-127, p. 122
20 Ibid., p. 126
21 David Ley, 'Gentrification and the Politics of the New Middle Class', *Environment and Planning D: Society and Space*, vol. 12 (1994)
22 René König, *A la Mode: On the Social Psychology of Fashion* (Seabury Press, 1973), p. 148
23 Jon Caulfield, '"Gentrification" and Desire', *Canadian Review of Sociology and Anthropology*, vol. 26, no. 4 (1989), reprinted in Loretta Lees, Tom Slater and Elvin Wyly (eds), *The Gentrification Reader* (Routledge, 2010)

24 Brian J. L. Berry, 'Islands of Renewal in Seas of Decay', in Paul E. Peterson, *The New Urban Reality* (Brookings Institution Press, 1985), reprinted in Loretta Lees, Tom Slater and Elvin Wyly (eds), *The Gentrification Reader*, p. 42

25 Mildred F. Schmertz, 'Boston's Historic Faneuil Hall Marketplace: Restored and Transformed by Architect Benjamin Thompson and Developer James Rouse into a Triumphantly Successful Downtown Center', pp. 116–127, p. 127

26 Ibid., p.127

27 'The Case for Design Quality in Today's Marketplace: Four Studies of Collaboration Between Architects and Developers that Explore the Arithmetic of Excellence', *Architectural Record* (December 1977), pp. 81–128

28 Robert Thorne, *Covent Garden Market: Its History and Restoration* (Architectural Press, 1980), p. 90

29 *Independent* (4 March 1997)

30 Ruth Glass (ed.), *London: Aspects of Change*, pp. xviii–xix

31 *Guardian* obituary (19 September 2007)

32 Robert Thorne, *Covent Garden Market*, p. 80

33 Ibid., p. 82

34 Richard MacCormac, 'Appraisal', *The Architect's Journal* (27 May 1981), pp. 1003–1008

35 Geoff Hollan, 'Same Strategy – Contrasting Tactics', *The Architect's Journal* (27 May 1981), pp. 1011–1012

CHAPTER FOUR: SELLING THE CITY

1 *Building Design* (3 October 1975), p. 1

2 Tom Phillips, ' "This Is Just the Start": China's Passion for Foreign Property', *Guardian* (29 September 2016)

3 Murray Fraser and Joe Kerr, *Architecture and the 'Special Relationship'*, p. 199

4 Ibid., p. 462

5 Ibid., p. 455

6 Ibid., p. 453

7 Ibid., p. 456

8 Anna Minton, *Ground Control: Fear and Happiness in the Twenty-First-Century City* (Penguin, 2009), p. 41

9 *Building Design* (8 February 2012)

CHAPTER FIVE: BRANDSCAPES

1 Rem Koolhaas, 'Junkspace', in Chuihua Judy Chung, Jeffrey Inaba, Rem Koolhaas, Sze Tsung Leong (eds), *Project on the City 2: Harvard Design School Guide to Shopping* (Taschen, 2001), pp. 408–421, p. 409

2 *The Age* (7 August 2006)

3 Helen Carter, 'Liverpool "Is the New Barcelona"', *Guardian* (15 July 2004)

4 *Helsingin Sanomat* (4 August 2006)

5 Richard Florida, *The Rise of the Creative Class: And How It's Transforming Work, Leisure, Community and Everyday Life* (Basic Books, 2002)

6 Brandon Taylor, *Modernism, Post-Modernism, Realism: A Critical Perspective for Art* (Winchester School of Art Press, 1987), p. 77

7 Lucy Tobin, 'The Grape Escape for Oxford Circus', *Evening Standard* (24 June 2011)

8 Mike Davis, 'Fear and Money in Dubai', *New Left Review* 41, (September–October 2006)

9 David Ward, ' Liverpool Woos Guggenheim', *Guardian* (9 July 1999)

10 Nicholas Serota, *Experience or Interpretation: The Dilemma of Museums of Modern Art* (Thames & Hudson, 1996), p. 5

11 Ibid., p. 55

12 Marshall McLuhan in Sean Perkins (ed.) *Experience: Challenging Visual Indifference Through New Sensory Experience* (Booth–Clibborn Editions, 1995), p. 13

13 Anna Klingmann, *Brandscapes: Architecture in the Experience Economy* (MIT Press, 2010) p. 76

14 Naomi Klein, *No Logo: Taking Aim at the Brand Bullies* (Picador, 1999), p. 155

15 B. Joseph Pine II and James H. Gilmore, *The Experience Economy* (Harvard Business School Press, 1999), pp. 1–17

16 Sharin Zukin, *Landscapes of Power: From Detroit to Disney World* (University of California Press, 1991), p. 42

CHAPTER SIX: THE RIGHT TO BUY

1 Émile Zola, *The Ladies' Paradise,* trans. Brian Nelson (OUP, 1998), p. 28

2 Murray Fraser and Joe Kerr, *Architecture and the 'Special Relationship'*, p. 99

3 Jonathan Prynn, 'Westfield Goes East in Search of Inspiration for Vast New Mall', *Evening Standard* (11 March 2010)

4 Richard Florida, 'The Death and Life of Downtown Shopping Districts', *The Atlantic Cities* (4 June 2012)

5 Bruce Weber, 'Jon Jerde, Architect of Merging Visions, Dies at 75', *New York Times* (18 February 2015)

6 Leon Whiteson, '"This Is Our Time": Jon Jerde Is Trying to Write "a Different Urban Script" for LA', *LA Times* (20 January 1988)

7 Frances Anderton (ed.), *You Are Here: The Jerde Partnership International* (Phaidon Press, 1999), p. 128

8 Ray Bradbury, 'Free Pass at Heaven's Gate', in Frances Anderton (ed.), *You Are Here*, pp. 6-7

9 Caroline Roux, 'A Return to the Lofty Idea', *Independent* (3 November 1996)

10 Peter York, 'Room for Inner Improvements', *Guardian* (9 February 1998)

11 Amanda Loose, 'A Campaign for Genuine Lofts', *The Times* (5 February 1997)
12 Oliver Wainwright, '"American Psycho" Property Promo Pulled after Twitterstorm', *Guardian* (5 January 2015)

CHAPTER SEVEN: THE CURIOUS HABITS
OF THE STARCHITECT

1 Alison and Peter Smithson, 'But Today We Collect Ads', *Ark* (18 November 1956) p. 50
2 Royal Institute of British Architects, 'The Architect and His Office' (1962), p. 142
3 Mario Carpo, *The Alphabet and the Algorithm* (MIT Press, 2011), p. 17
4 Ibid., p. 74
5 Andrew Saint, *The Image of the Architect* (Yale University Press, 1983), p. 61
6 Ibid., p. 87
7 Mark Girouard, *Big Jim: The Life and Work of James Stirling* (Chatto and Windus, 1998), p. 57
8 Michael Sorkin, *Exquisite Corpse: Writings on Buildings* (Verso, 1991), p. 45
9 Murray Fraser and Joe Kerr, *Architecture and the 'Special Relationship'*, p. 187
10 Ibid., p. 209
11 Ibid., p. 29
12 Andrew Saint, *The Image of the Architect*, p. 140
13 John Portman and Jonathan Barnett, *The Architect as Developer* (McGraw-Hill, 1976), p. 135
14 Andrew Saint, *The Image of the Architect*, p. 153
15 Martin Pawley, 'Architecture and the Philosopher's Stone', *New Society*, vol. XVII, no. 448 (29 April 1971), pp. 718-720
16 Malcolm MacEwen, *Crisis in Architecture* (RIBA Publications, 1974)
17 *RIBA Journal*, 75, October 1968, p. 450
18 Andrew Saint, *The Image of the Architect*, p. 139
19 Murray Fraser and Joe Kerr, *Architecture and the 'Special Relationship'*, p. 427
20 D. K. Dietsch, 'Americans in London', *Architecture*, vol. 79, no. 9 (September 1990), p. 65, quoted in Ibid., p. 420
21 Francis Duffy, P. Hannay (ed.), *The Changing Workplace* (Phaidon, 1992), p. 204
22 Murray Fraser and Joe Kerr, *Architecture and the 'Special Relationship'*, p. 463
23 Ibid., p. 423
24 Crystal Bennes, 'Where Does Architecture End and Marketing Begin?', *Architectural Review* (May 2015), pp. 28-29
25 Vitruvius, *On Architecture*, trans. Richard Schofield (Penguin, 2009), p. 35-36
26 Beatriz Colomina, *Privacy and Publicity: Modern Architecture as Mass Media* (MIT Press, 1994), p. 43

27 Kester Rattenbury, 'Naturally Biased: Architecture in the UK National Press', in Kester Rattenbury (ed.), *This Is Not Architecture: Media Constructions* (Routledge, 2002), pp. 136-56, p. 141

28 Oliver Wainwright, 'Harrods Launches Zaha Hadid's Luxury Homeware Line', *Guardian* (18 September 2014)

29 Ibid.

30 Austin Williams, 'The Ethics of Being Ethical Come into Question as our Urban Fabric Crumbles', *Architectural Review* (18 August 2011)

31 Rem Koolhaas, AMO-OMA et al., *Content: Triumph of Realization* (Taschen, 2004), p.20

32 Rem Koolhaas, 'Junkspace', in Chuihua Judy Chung, Jeffrey Inaba, Rem Koolhaas, Sze Tsung Leong (eds), *Project on the City 2*, pp. 408-421

CHAPTER EIGHT: IF WALLS COULD TALK

1 Henri Lefebvre, *The Production of Space*, p. 286

2 Victoria Walsh, *Nigel Henderson: Parallel of Life and Art*, (Thames & Hudson, 2001), p. 50

3 Alison and Peter Smithson, 'The Built World: Urban Re-identification', *Architectural Design* (June 1955), p. 185

4 Victoria Walsh, *Nigel Henderson*, p. 49

5 Alison and Peter Smithson, John Lewis (ed.), *Urban Structuring: Studies of Alison and Peter Smithson* (Studio Vista, 1967), p. 21

6 Alison and Peter Smithson, 'But Today We Collect Ads', p. 50

7 Marshall McLuhan, *Understanding Media: The Extensions of Man* (McGraw-Hill, 1964), p, 5

8 Quoted in Robert Venturi, Denise Scott Brown and Steven Izenour, *Learning from Las Vegas* (MIT Press, 1977) p. 80

9 'Mickey Mouse Teaches the Architects', *New York Times* (22 October 1972)

10 Herbert Muschamp, 'Zaha Hadid's Urban Mothership', *New York Times* (8 June 2003)

11 Zygmunt Bauman, *Liquid Modernity* (Polity Press, 2000), p. 121

12 Fredric Jameson, *Postmodernism, or the Cultural Logic of Late Capitalism* (Verso, 1991)

13 Jeremy Rifkin, *The Age of Access: The New Culture of Hypercapitalism, Where All of Life is a Paid-for Experience* (J. P. Tarcher/Putnam, 2000), p. 30

14 Kenneth Frampton, *Studies in Tectonic Culture: The Poetics of Construction in Nineteenth and Twentieth Century Architecture* (MIT Press, 1995), p. 381

15 Clare Melhuish, 'From Dematerialization to Depoliticisation in Architecture', in Kester Rattenbury (ed.) *This Is Not Architecture: Media Constructions* (Routledge, 2002), pp. 222-30

16 Ibid., p. 223

17 Ibid., p. 224
18 Juhani Pallasmaa, 'An Architecture of the Seven Senses', in A&U Special Issue *Questions of Perception: Phenomenology of Architecture* (July 1994), p. 27
19 Beatriz Colomina, *Privacy and Publicity*, p. 43
20 Charles Jencks, *The Iconic Building: The Power of Enigma*, (Frances Lincoln, 2005), p. 196
21 Ibid., p. 7
22 Ibid., p. 111
23 Ibid., p. 99
24 Norbert Weiner, *The Human Use of Human Beings: Cybernetics and Society*, (Da Capo, 1988), p. 98
25 Mario Carpo, *The Alphabet and the Algorithm*, p. 14
26 Ibid., p. 44

CHAPTER NINE: MEET THE MOST FAMOUS ARCHITECT IN THE WORLD

1 Edmund Burke, *A Philosophical Enquiry into the Origin of our Ideas of the Sublime and the Beautiful* (George Dearborn, 1834), p. 62
2 Edward Glaeser, *Triumph of the City*, p. 52
3 Germaine Greer, 'Frank Gehry's New Building Looks Like Five Scrunched-Up Brown Bags', *Guardian* (9 January 2011)
4 Hal Foster, *Design and Crime (and Other Diatribes)* (Verso, 2002), pp. 27–8
5 Hal Foster, *The Art–Architecture Complex* (Verso, 2011), p. xii

CONCLUSION: THE NEW BABYLON

1 Guy Debord, Donald Nicholson-Smith (transl.), *Society of the Spectacle* (Zone Books, 1994), p. 12
2 You'll find a fine account Constant's work in Mark Wigley, *Constant's New Babylon: The Hyper-Architecture of Desire* (Witte de With Center for Contemporary Art/010 Publishers, 1998). His description of the Stedelijk lecture, from which the following quotes are taken, begins on p. 9
3 Unpublished manuscript of lecture 'Unitair Urbanisme'
4 Mark Wigley, *Constant's New Babylon: The Hyper-Architecture of Desire*, p. 11
5 Guy Debord, *Society of the Spectacle*, pp. 11–24
6 Guy Debord, 'Intervention lettriste', *Potlatch* 23 (October 1955), p. 34
7 Constant, 'New Babylon' (1960) in *Constant: Amsterdam*, catalogue of the Städtische Kunstgalerie, Bochum (1961)

INDEX